A WAR FOR THE SOUL OF AMERICA

A War for the Soul of America

A History of the Culture Wars

ANDREW HARTMAN

The University of Chicago Press CHICAGO AND LONDON

The University of Chicago Press, Chicago 60637
The University of Chicago Press, Ltd., London
© 2015 by The University of Chicago
All rights reserved. Published 2015.
Paperback edition 2016
Printed in the United States of America

22 21 20 19 18 17 16   3 4 5 6 7

ISBN-13: 978-0-226-25450-0 (cloth)
ISBN-13: 978-0-226-37923-4 (paper)
ISBN-13: 978-0-226-25464-7 (e-book)
DOI: 10.7208/chicago/9780226254647.0001

Library of Congress Cataloging-in-Publication Data

Hartman, Andrew, author.
A war for the soul of America : a history of the culture wars / Andrew
Hartman.
pages ; cm
Includes bibliographical references and index.
ISBN 978-0-226-25450-0 (cloth : alk. paper) — ISBN 978-0-226-25464-7
(ebook) 1. Culture conflict—United States—History—20th century.
2. Social change—United States—History—20th century. 3. Social
problems—United States—History—20th century. I. Title.
HN90.S62H37 2015
306.0973—dc23
2014048487

♾ This paper meets the requirements of ANSI/NISO Z39.48-1992
(Permanence of Paper).

I dedicate this book to Asa and Eli.

Contents

Introduction

When Patrick Buchanan declared "a war for the soul of America" during his raucous primetime speech before the 1992 Republican National Convention in Houston, he reiterated a theme that had animated his underdog campaign against President George H. W. Bush in that year's primaries. This theme was the "culture wars," a struggle, in Buchanan's words, "as critical to the kind of nation we will one day be as was the Cold War itself." With such urgent rhetoric, the right-wing former adviser to presidents Richard Nixon, Gerald Ford, and Ronald Reagan aimed to elevate the stakes of that year's presidential election. The nation was confronted with more than a choice between Bush and the Democratic challenger Bill Clinton: it was a decision "about who we are," "about what we believe," about whether "the Judeo-Christian values and beliefs upon which this nation was built" would survive.[1]

Buchanan's notorious speech punctuated a series of angry quarrels that dominated national headlines during the 1980s and 1990s. Whether over abortion, affirmative action, art, censorship, evolution, family values, feminism, homosexuality, intelligence testing, media, multiculturalism, national history standards, pornography, school prayer, sex education, the Western canon—the list of such divisive issues goes on and on—the United States was beset by "culture wars." Buchanan's "war for the soul of America" was on.[2]

The issues at stake in the culture wars were real and compelling. Such a seemingly straightforward notion defies a well-worn argument, forwarded by Thomas Frank in his 2005 jeremiad *What's the Matter with Kansas*, that the culture wars were superficial and helped engender an irrational political landscape. In pithy fashion, Frank relates the hullabaloo over the artist Andres Serrano's blasphemous *Piss Christ*, a photo of a crucifix submerged in a jar of the artist's urine, to his thesis that "culture wars get the goods." "Because some artist decides to shock the hicks by dunking Jesus in urine," Frank writes, "the entire planet must remake itself along the lines preferred by the Republican Party, U.S.A." Frank's argument goes as follows: religious conservatives often voted against their own economic interests due to their illogical obsession with the culture wars, to which Republican politicians cynically lent rhetorical support as they attended to more important matters, such as rewriting the tax codes in favor of the rich. Frank's fellow Kansans defy his populist expectations that they direct their anger at the wealthy—at those responsible for making their economic lives so precarious. In this schema, debates about the idea of America are sideshows.[3]

But the history of America, for better and worse, is largely a history of debates about the idea of America. Ever since the nation's founding, Americans have wrestled with Hector St. John de Crevecoeur's famous 1782 riddle: "What then is the American, this new man?" Disputes over this knotty question have marked out the battleground of American cultural conflict. And such disputes intensify during tumultuous times of rapid change. The unique period in American history known as "the sixties" and the turbulent decades that followed were just such times.[4]

The sixties gave birth to a new America, a nation more open to new peoples, new ideas, new norms, and new, if conflicting, articulations of America itself. This fact, more than anything else, helps explain why in the wake of the sixties the national culture grew more divided than it had been in any period since the Civil War. Americans split over how to think about this new America. The gulf that separated those who embraced the new America from those who viewed it ominously—those who looked to nurture it versus those who sought to roll it back—drew the boundaries of the culture wars. Sociologist James Davison Hunter put it like this in his important 1991 book *Culture Wars*: "Our most fundamental ideas about who we are as Americans are now at odds."[5]

The history of the culture wars, often misremembered as merely one angry shouting match after another, offers insight into the genuine transformation to American political culture that happened during the sixties.

This is not to say that these transformations emerged from the sixties whole cloth. The sixties counterculture—the ethics of "sex, drugs, and rock 'n' roll"—flowered from the earlier cultural sensibilities of Beats like Allen Ginsberg and Jack Kerouac, who brought bohemia to the masses with their unconventional poems and books. New Left organizations such as Students for a Democratic Society were sustained by the earlier political sensibilities of leftist intellectuals like C. Wright Mills and Paul Goodman, whose radical visions for America transcended Cold War conformism.[6]

Likewise, those sixties conservatives who supported violent police crackdowns on student protestors at the University of California at Berkeley, which Governor Ronald Reagan called a "haven for sex deviants," emerged from the earlier cultural sensibilities of those angered by Elvis Presley's pelvic gyrations on the *Ed Sullivan Show*. New Right organizations like Young Americans for Freedom were nourished by the earlier political sensibilities of intellectuals like William Buckley Jr., whose withering critique of "secularist and collectivist" professors gave life to a powerful conservative imagination that had supposedly been rendered obsolete.[7]

Similarly, the demise of intellectual authority and traditions, another upheaval in American life that helped spark the culture wars, was not necessarily new to the sixties. This so-called postmodern condition, or the realization that "all that is solid melts into air"—liberating to some, frightening to others—had long ago shaken the foundations of American thought. The French philosopher Michel Foucault, the most widely read theorist in the American humanities since the sixties, was thought to have revolutionized American intellectual life with relativistic statements of the sort that "knowledge is not made for understanding, it is made for cutting." In fact, Lynne Cheney, who chaired the National Endowment for the Humanities from 1986 to 1993, argued that Foucault's "ideas were nothing less than an assault on Western civilization."[8] But by the time Cheney had written those words, it had been nearly a century since the American philosopher William James made the antifoundationalist claim that "'the truth' is only the expedient in the way of our thinking, just as 'the right' is only the expedient in the way of our behaving." Germane to this point, in the 1940s university students across the country, particularly at elite schools like Harvard University, were assigned to read the American anthropologist Margaret Mead, who, according to the historian David

Hollinger, "explicitly and relentlessly questioned the certainties of the home culture by juxtaposing them with often romanticized images of distant communities of humans." That many Americans gained familiarity with Mead's cultural relativism—which promoted the idea that much of what was called "natural" was, rather, "cultural"—was an indication that perhaps part of American political culture had fractured well before the sixties.[9]

But the sixties universalized fracture. Many Americans prior to the sixties, particularly middle-class white Americans, were largely sheltered from the "acids of modernity," those modern ways of thinking that subjected seemingly timeless truths, including truths about America, to a lens of suspicion. Put another way, prior to the sixties many Americans did not yet recognize the hazards of a world freed from tradition. They did not yet realize that their sacred cows were being butchered. Many Americans felt their world coming apart only once they experienced such chaos as a political force, as a movement of peoples previously excluded from the American mainstream. They grew wary of "an assault on Western civilization" only after the barbarians had crashed the gates. The radical political mobilizations of the sixties—civil rights, Black and Chicano Power, feminism, gay liberation, the antiwar movement, the legal push for secularization—destabilized the America that millions knew. It was only after the sixties that many, particularly conservatives, recognize the threat to their once great nation.[10]

After the sixties—and during the culture wars—whether one thought the nation was in moral decline was often a correlative of whether one was liberal or conservative. Joseph Epstein called the sixties "something of a political Rorschach test. Tell me what you think of that period," he wrote, "and I shall tell you what your politics are." Those who argued that the sixties had shepherded in ethical anarchy, and that such confusion threatened the very fabric of the nation, tended to be conservative. For instance, conservative historian Gertrude Himmelfarb wrote: "The beasts of modernism have mutated into the beasts of postmodernism, relativism into nihilism, amorality into immorality, irrationality into insanity, sexual deviancy into polymorphous perversity." Conservative jurist Robert Bork echoed these sentiments: "The rough beast of decadence, a long time in gestation, having reached its maturity in the last three decades, now sends us slouching towards our new home, not Bethlehem but Gomorrah."

Himmelfarb and Bork's right-wing declension narratives advanced a theory of historical change that, no matter how hyperbolic in tone, was more or less accurate. An older America had been lost.[11]

In the postwar years—the nearly two decades between the end of World War II and the assassination of John F. Kennedy—a cluster of powerful conservative norms set the parameters of American culture. These cultural standards are best described by the phrase "normative America," an analytical category I use to refer to an inchoate group of assumptions and aspirations shared by millions of Americans during the postwar years. Normative Americans prized hard work, personal responsibility, individual merit, delayed gratification, social mobility, and other values that middle-class whites recognized as their own. Normative Americans lived according to stringent sexual expectations: sex, whether for procreation or recreation, was contained within the parameters of heterosexual marriage. Normative Americans behaved in ways consistent with strict gender roles: within the confines of marriage, men worked outside the home and women cared for children inside it. Normative Americans believed their nation was the best in human history: those aspects of American history that shined an unfavorable light on the nation, such as slavery, were ignored or explained away as aberrations. Normative Americans often assumed that the nation's Christian heritage illuminated its unique character: the United States of America really was a "city on a hill."[12]

The normative America of the postwar years—the normative America of the 1950s—was more omnipresent, and more coercive, than it had been before or has been since. During the 1950s, an unprecedented number of Americans got in line—or aspired to get in line—particularly white, heterosexual, Christian Americans. Even those Americans barred from normative America by virtue of their race, sexuality, or religion often felt compelled to demonstrate compliance. In part, such an extraordinary degree of conformity had to do with Cold War imperatives: a global struggle against an alien system required cultural and ideological stability. But even more, the cohesiveness of postwar normative America was a byproduct of the internal threats to it—threats made manifest during the sixties. It was as if dark clouds of dissent were visible on the not-too-distant horizon. It was as if Americans embraced cultural conformity in order to suspend disbelief about what lurked beneath such a facade.[13]

The new America given life by the sixties—a more pluralistic, more secular, more feminist America—was built on the ruins of normative America.

This basic historical fact explains the flood of laments about a once great America that emerged by the 1970s. President Nixon expressed such an idea in his second inaugural address of January 20, 1973: "Above all else, the time has come for us to renew our faith in ourselves and in America. In recent years, that faith has been challenged. Our children have been taught to be ashamed of their country, ashamed of their parents, ashamed of America's record at home and its role in the world. At every turn we have been beset by those who find everything wrong with America and little that is right." For Nixon, American renewal meant forgetting the sixties, when too many Americans quit loving their country unconditionally.[14]

Newt Gingrich, Republican Speaker of the House from 1994 until 1998, wrote an entire book, appropriately titled *To Renew America*, on a similar proposition. "From the arrival of English-speaking colonists in 1607 until 1965," Gingrich wrote, "from the Jamestown colony and the Pilgrims, through de Tocqueville's *Democracy in America,* up to Norman Rockwell's paintings of the 1940s and 1950s, there was one continuous civilization built around commonly accepted legal and cultural principles." For conservatives like Nixon and Gingrich, the America they loved was in distress. Returning to the values that animated the nation in the 1950s was the only way to save it.[15]

Those on the left, by contrast, tended to view American life through the eyes of the sixties—through the eyes of the women, racial minorities, gays and lesbians, secularists, and other Americans whose existence symbolized a challenge to normative America. For them, American culture was always fractured. Conservatives viewed American culture as something that, once whole, had been lost; they felt challenges to normative America to be the shattering of worlds. Whereas the Left considered post-sixties American culture a closer approximation of its ideal form, the Right considered it an abomination. None of which is to say that the American Left was entirely victorious—far from it! In the realms of economic policy and electoral power, conservatives did very well—a historical development that has been amply documented. But in the sphere of culture, the Left had its share of victories. The culture wars were fought on this terrain where the Left was successful.[16]

The culture wars were battles over what constituted art, and over whether the federal government should subsidize art that insulted the most cherished beliefs of millions of Americans. The culture wars were debates over transgressive films and television shows, and over whether insensitive cultural programming should be censored. They were brawls over the public schools, and over whether American children should learn divisive subjects like evolutionary biology. They involved struggles over the university curriculum, and over whether American college students should read a traditional Western canon or texts that represented a more diverse range of perspectives. The culture wars were fights over how the nation's history was narrated in museums, and over whether the purpose of American history was to make Americans proud of the nation's glorious past or to encourage citizens to reflect on its moral failings. In sum, where the Left enjoyed success—in the nation's cultural institutions—conservatives fought back with a ferocity that matched their belief, as Patrick Buchanan put it, that "culture is the Ho Chi Minh Trail to power."[17]

This dramatic struggle, which pitted liberal, progressive, and secular Americans against their conservative, traditional, and religious counterparts, captured the attention of the nation during the 1980s and 1990s. For a period of about two decades, the culture wars, like a vortex, swallowed up much of American political and intellectual life. The culture wars were the defining metaphor for the late-twentieth-century United States. This book tries to make sense of the war.

1

The Sixties as Liberation

In the grand arc of American history, the sixties were unusual. Erratic behavior became common across the political spectrum. In response to a violent police crackdown on antiwar protestors at the 1968 Democratic National Convention in Chicago, a splinter faction of Students for a Democratic Society (SDS) formed the infamous Weathermen, a small underground cell of aspirant revolutionaries named after Bob Dylan's line "You don't need a weatherman to know which way the wind blows." The Weathermen—ultimately responsible for exploding several small bombs, including one at the Pentagon—had given up not only on American democracy but also on the utopian principles of "participatory democracy" upon which SDS was founded, a vision of a citizenry empowered from the grassroots up.[1]

At the other end of the power continuum, Richard Nixon's White House, equally disdainful of democracy, countered high-profile leaks of classified information by setting up a clandestine special investigation unit, the notorious "plumbers" who, among other illegal activities, broke into and wiretapped the Democratic National Headquarters at the Watergate Hotel. Although many Americans recoiled at the exploits of both the Weathermen and the Nixon administration, and although few had any clue which way the wind was blowing, they could not help but notice that, as the rock band Buffalo Springfield heralded in 1967, "there's something happening here."[2]

That "something" was the revolution otherwise remembered as "the sixties."

Liberating to some, frightening to others, the sixties brought the disruptive forces of modernity to the surface of American culture with a vengeance. A set of youth-driven movements shattered the fragile consensus that had settled over American political culture during the 1950s. Long-downplayed divisions in American society—between white and black and between men and women, to name but two of the most obvious—were made subjects of national debate. Consensus gave way to conflict.

On one side were those who defied normative conceptions of Americanism. As Malcolm X declared in 1964: "I don't see any American dream; I see an American nightmare." On the other side were those who opposed such challenges. Ronald Reagan gave voice to this America in 1966 when he described the conduct of student radicals as "contrary to our standards of human behavior." In short, the sixties ushered in an intense new form of polarization that hinged on the very question of America and its meaning. What was America? Was it fundamentally racist and sexist and thus in need of a revolution? Or was it inherently decent and thus worth protecting? Such stark questions informed an increasingly contentious political landscape. There seemed to be no middle ground.[3]

Because "sixties radicals" commonly play the role of villains in right-wing elegies to a once great nation, historians often assume conservatives overstate the role that leftists played in recasting American culture during the sixties. Indeed, the other side of the sixties—the side represented by Reagan and a powerful conservative movement that was just coming into its own—often serves as evidence that the sixties were not so revolutionary after all. But conservative hyperbole includes more than a few grains of truth. The sixties were a watershed decade due in large part to the role played by the New Left, a loose configuration of movements that included the antiwar, Black Power, feminist, and gay liberation movements, among others. In the ways in which its desires were incorporated into mainstream America, and in the conservative reaction against the threats to a seemingly traditional America that it represented, the New Left was immeasurably influential. Even though its utopian political dreams never approached fruition, the New Left reshaped some of the most important institutions of liberal America, such as Hollywood, the universities, and even, to some extent, the Democratic Party.[4]

The reappearance of the Left during the sixties is a curious episode in American history. Prior to then, the success of American radicalism tended to inversely reflect the economic health of the nation, or more precisely, the material prospects of activists. Prairie radicals organized under the banner of Populism in the late nineteenth century to challenge the corporate monopolies that gravely threatened their livelihood. Hundreds of thousands of workers joined the mass labor unions of the Congress of Industrial Organizations (CIO) in response to the Great Depression. Even the Communist Party, always suspect in American political life, enjoyed a surge in its American ranks during the 1930s, thanks to the relatively common view that the Great Depression had sounded the death knell of capitalism.[5]

But the New Left that came of age in the sixties was different. "We are people of this generation, bred in at least modest comfort, housed now in universities, looking uncomfortably to the world we inherit." This, the first sentence of the Port Huron Statement, a 1962 manifesto authored by twenty-two-year-old Tom Hayden that announced the birth of SDS, illuminates the distinctiveness of sixties radicalism.[6]

The New Left was younger and more affluent than any American left before or since. This was particularly true of the hundreds of thousands of young white Americans who, inspired by the civil rights movement and radicalized by the Vietnam War, committed themselves to leftist activism of one sort or another. The nucleus of the New Left, particularly the white New Left, was found on the nation's college campuses. This was no surprise given that the university system, or what University of California President Clark Kerr poignantly termed "the multiversity" in 1963, was growing in size and significance as millions of baby boomers came of age. In 1960, 3,789,000 students enrolled in American colleges; by 1970, that figure had more than doubled to 7,852,000. Students were a new demographic force to be reckoned with. When graduate student Mario Savio stood on a police car on December 2, 1964, and loudly proclaimed his own existence and that of his fellow Berkeley protestors — "We're human beings!" — he did more than give voice to the Free Speech Movement that bedeviled Kerr's flagship campus and angered Reagan's conservative constituents.[7]

Savio's protest also sought to embody the alienation of an entire generation. Despite having grown up in the richest nation in the world — at a time when the gross domestic product grew on average more than 4 percent annually, and when unemployment levels were unprecedentedly low — millions of young Americans expressed dissatisfaction with the promise of American life. That Hayden and Savio, products of capitalism's "golden age"—not to mention the offspring of conservative Catholic parents—would become leaders of a large radical movement speaks to the New Left as a novelty and to the sixties as a sui generis decade.[8]

The young white radicals who joined the New Left, affluent or not, grew up in solidarity with the civil rights movement that ended the brutal Jim Crow caste system in the states of the former Confederacy. Many of the young northerners who headed south in 1964 to participate in Freedom Summer, inspired by what the Port Huron Statement singled out as "the most heartening and exemplary struggle," returned home to organize against racism in their own cities. This fact helps explain the idealism of white radicals. But many young Americans, even affluent white college students, committed themselves to the New Left for idealistic *and* self-interested reasons: in addition to ending racism, they wanted to stop a war that might mean their own death or dismemberment. The sixties antiwar movement, the largest in American history, reverberated from Lyndon Johnson's 1965 escalation of a war in Southeast Asia that resulted in the death of fifty-seven thousand Americans, most of whom had been conscripted, and an estimated three million Vietnamese. As unparalleled numbers of young Americans hit the streets to register their dissent from Johnson's war, SDS grew into a vehicle for a nationwide movement, with chapters springing to life on college campuses across the country.[9]

The transformative effects of this movement were to be found in shifting cultural sensibilities. Rock music, the idiom of sixties-style liberation, offered a cacophony of lyrical testimonials to the changes set off during the decade. In his "San Francisco (Be Sure to Wear Flowers in Your Hair)," a 1967 paean to a rising youth rebellion, Scott McKenzie sang: "There's a whole generation, with a new explanation." A few years later, Marvin Gaye crooned "What's Going On," not as a question but as a statement of fact that, indeed, something was going on. To put it less lyrically: the disruptions of the sixties did not present themselves in a vacuum. Whereas New Leftists might have failed in their efforts to revolutionize the American political system, they succeeded in reorienting American culture. The New Left blew a deep crater into the surface of traditional American culture. Normative America, though still large, still powerful, was nonetheless disfigured beyond repair. Despite the fact that its political goals never really got off the ground, the New Left, in the words of historian Michael

Kazin, "nudged Americans to change some deep-seated ideas about themselves and their society." In other words, even if they failed to end racism and war, they made the nation less hospitable to racists and warmongers.[10]

New Leftists had no shortage of intellectuals to help them explain their estrangement from America. Two of the most influential such thinkers, C. Wright Mills and Paul Goodman, offered young radicals a vision of an America that transcended the rigid conformity of the postwar consensus. New Leftists liked Mills because he projected the image of a renegade: the Texas-born sociologist rode a motorcycle and donned a leather jacket. More to the point, his ideas enunciated the type of antiauthoritarianism that excited New Leftists such as Hayden, who wrote his master's thesis on Mills and modeled the Port Huron Statement on Mills's thought. In his popular 1951 book *White Collar*, Mills depicted America as a dystopian, bureaucratic "iron cage." In his equally influential *The Power Elite*, published in 1956, Mills similarly applied Max Weber's lens to the institutional structures of the American rich, "those political, economic, and military circles which as an intricate set of overlapping cliques share decisions having at least national consequences." This intensely hierarchical theory of American power challenged the consensus view, held by most political theorists, that the political system was composed of counterbalancing forces and was thus inherently democratic. The college students who voraciously consumed Mills contended that America was quietly approaching totalitarianism. For them, reading Mills provoked individualistic urges to rebel against the repressiveness of cultural conformity.[11]

Paul Goodman's popularity with the New Left owed to his uniqueness among the renowned New York intellectuals, a singularity highlighted by his anarchist intuitions and his open bisexuality. Like the other New York intellectuals, Goodman was a secular Jewish leftist, he attended the City College of New York, he wrote for all the same little magazines, and he flocked to the same parties, where booze and ideas flowed in equally copious amounts. Yet unlike the others, Goodman never joined the Communist Party or any of its Trotskyist offshoots. His anarchism precluded his joining political groups committed to discipline and doctrine. Instead, Goodman believed social change required that individuals simply live differently. Such an approach resonated with New Leftists, who sought alternative ways of living that bypassed corrupted institutions. "Goodman's fusion of the utopian and the practical," writes Dick Flacks, an original SDS member, "provided substance for the impulses of resistance and the visions of a decentralization and community that defined the youth counterculture and the early New Left."[12]

Goodman's anarchist skepticism informed his eclectic intellectual interests, including Gestalt psychology, a theory he helped innovate about how people needed to reject the social structures that impeded self-actualization in order to overcome alienation. Antiauthoritarianism also shaped Goodman's educational thought, where he contended that socialization was the problem, not the solution. He despised both the practice of adjusting children to society and the social regime to which children were being adjusted. The book that unexpectedly made Goodman famous, *Growing Up Absurd: The Problems of Youth in the Organized Society*, published in 1960 and eagerly read by youthful multitudes over the following decade, carried forward the analysis of the bureaucratic straitjacket that had been the fodder of Mills and many other critics during the 1950s. Unlike most of those commentators, however, Goodman focused his anger on how the "iron cage" made life most miserable for young Americans. In this, *Growing Up Absurd* dealt with two of the most analyzed issues of the time, the "disgrace of the Organized System" and juvenile delinquency, arguing that the former caused the latter. It is easy to understand why reading Goodman came to be a cathartic experience for so many young people, even young women who overlooked Goodman's glaring misogyny while embracing his antiauthoritarianism.[13]

The ways in which Goodman blurred the boundaries between political and cultural radicalism portended the affinity between the New Left and what became known as "the counterculture." The antinomian shibboleth ubiquitous at New Left rallies—"It is forbidden to forbid!"—illustrated how countercultural expressions flowed from counterestablishment protests. In 1968, New Leftist Theodore Roszak explained how this worked: "The counter culture is the embryonic cultural base of New Left politics, the effort to discover new types of community, new family patterns, new sexual mores, new kinds of livelihood, new aesthetic forms, new personal identities on the far side of power politics, the bourgeois home, and the Protestant work ethic." Abbie Hoffman and Jerry Rubin founded the Youth International Party—the Yippies—in order to make explicit the alliance between the politically serious New Left and the libertine counterculture. In

1968 they playfully advanced a pig for president, "Pigasus the Immortal," and advocated group joint-rolling and nude "grope-ins" for peace. Of course, this coalition never materialized to the degree that the Yippies had hoped. Pete Townsend, the lead singer of The Who, symbolically severed such an alliance at the 1969 Woodstock Music Festival. When Hoffman, high on LSD, grabbed the microphone to make a speech about a political prisoner, Townsend swatted him away with his guitar, screaming at him to "get the fuck off my fucking stage!"[14]

Allied with the New Left or not, the counterculture represented a real threat to traditional America. By its rejection of authority, its transgression of rules and standards, and its antipathy to anything mainstream, the counterculture pushed the envelope of American norms. True, many of those dubbed "hippies"—typically middle-class whites who repudiated normal America, grew their hair long, smoked marijuana, dropped acid, listened to psychedelic music, and enjoyed frequent recreational sex—merely acted out a mostly harmless generational drama before returning to the fold of capitalist America. But there was no going back to "square" America. In this the counterculture was living out the utopian dreams of the Beats, those unconventional poets like Allen Ginsberg who kept the flames of romanticism burning in bohemian quarters like Greenwich Village until such alienation went national in the sixties.[15]

In addition to rejecting traditional pieties, the counterculture revolted against rationalistic explanations of human experience. Columbia University psychologist and countercultural theorist Abraham Maslow grounded his notion of self-actualization in a "hierarchy of needs" that deemphasized intellect as against emotion. Maslow's 1964 book *Religions, Values, and Peak-Experiences*, lionized by the countercultural movement, sought to explode the arbitrary demarcations between mind and spirit, the natural and the transcendental. Maslow argued that humans are biologically programmed to have "peak experiences," or hallucinatory emotional releases, and that such events occur most often in the course of religious worship. Rationalistic individuals who relegated peak experiences to the realm of the psychotic denied themselves the full range of human consciousness. Maslow's theory had serious implications for those who wanted to achieve self-actualization but were disenchanted with the monotheistic religious traditions of their parents. In what should be understood as the religious side of the counterculture, the sixties saw the advent of New

Age syncretic religions. A growing number of Americans selectively mixed Eastern religious traditions drawn from Buddhism and Confucianism with a variety of Native American, pagan, and mystical practices. These were disturbing developments to millions of Americans who conflated America and Christianity.[16]

For those who desired peak experience minus the religious baggage, even of the New Age variety, mind-altering chemicals were the preferred alternative. Maslow indicated that peak experiences could be manufactured by ingesting LSD. More notoriously, psychologist Timothy Leary, who lost his job at Harvard University in 1963 for running controlled experiments with hallucinogenic drugs, became the nation's premier evangelist for the salubrious effects of LSD. Leary even coined the countercultural motto "Turn on, tune in, drop out," conveying his desire to become more "sensitive to the many and various levels of consciousness and the specific triggers that engage them," drugs being one such particularly effective trigger. Rock music, the perfect counterpart to drug culture, was another means to accomplish a peak experience because it evoked movement, feeling, and experience rather than thought or form. Some of the most popular rock stars of the sixties—Jim Morrison, Janis Joplin, Jimi Hendrix—doubled as some of the most expressive, antirationalist, and, coincidentally or not, self-destructive. "If 6 turned out to be 9, I don't mind," Hendrix sang, "'cuz I got my own world to look through, and I ain't gonna copy you." Musicians like Hendrix put to lyrics Charles Reich's philosophical celebration of the counterculture, which he sketched out in his 1970 bestseller *The Greening of America*. Reich theorized that human consciousness had evolved to fit historical circumstances and that the countercultural youth represented the highest state, "Consciousness III." With "less guilt, less anxiety, less self-hatred," Consciousness III individuals proudly proclaimed, "I'm glad I'm me."[17]

Although most American youth abstained from dropping acid, cultural change proved difficult to contain. This was made evident by the incorporation of countercultural expressions into powerful mainstream institutions. On television, the most powerful cultural medium in postwar America, the "hip" and the "mod" became fodder for competition between network executives seeking to make inroads into the enormous baby-boomer market. In 1966 NBC began broadcasting *The Monkees*, the first show to make explicit countercultural appeals. Based loosely on *A Hard Day's Night*, a film about The Beatles, *The Monkees* portrayed the wacky exploits of four young musicians composing a rock band tailored for the program. The show routinely scoffed at the symbols of the establishment, such as in one telling episode that featured the boys toying with a hapless authoritarian ex-marine general, a slick caricature of "the man." Many of NBC's rural affiliates refused to air *The Monkees*, but the show achieved the network's objective by attracting a huge youth audience in the nation's growing metropolises.[18]

CBS also sought to lure young viewers by adding *The Smothers Brothers Comedy Hour* to its primetime lineup in 1967. Network executives believed that Tom and Dick Smothers, hosts of the whimsical comedy-variety show, were just edgy enough to attract countercultural attention but not too subversive for those viewers with more traditional tastes. This formula worked well at first. The coveted baby boomers watched the show religiously, and so did plenty of others. But after the first season, the Smotherses attracted the kind of attention the network wished to avoid as they increasingly used the show as a platform for radical political positions. The first whiff of controversy arrived with the second season premier, when the Smothers invited radical folk singer Pete Seeger onto the show to sing his antiwar song "Waist Deep in the Big Muddy." Beyond the song, Seeger's very presence was a bone of contention, since he had been on the Hollywood blacklist since the early 1950s red scare. CBS executives cut the song from the episode. Outraged fans convinced the network to soften its stance, and Seeger was invited back to perform "Waist Deep" for a later episode. Explaining this decision, a CBS executive reflected: "It is almost impossible to present contemporary popular songs which do not contain some comment directly or indirectly on issues of public importance: war, peace, civil rights, patriotism, conformity, and the like."[19]

Such benevolence quickly dissipated during the show's shortened third season. CBS removed *The Smothers Brothers Comedy Hour* from the airwaves in April 1969, due, ultimately, to its radical politics. In retrospect, it should have been obvious that the show was doomed after the first episode of that season, which aired on September 29, 1968, one month after the Democratic National Convention in Chicago. The network censored musical guest Harry Belafonte's "Don't Stop the Carnival," about a police riot, which he performed against a backdrop of film footage of the Chicago mayhem.[20]

The rise and fall of *The Smothers Brothers Comedy Hour* revealed that in their efforts to captivate the coveted youth demographic, television networks would take risks with countercultural programming. But they drew the line at broadcasting politically radical messages. From then on, television mostly rendered hippies in ways that domesticated them. For example, the NBC western *Bonanza*, a favorite of traditional Americans, ran an episode in 1970 that sympathetically depicted hippielike characters. Although Ben Cartwright, the show's patriarch, didactically warned against dropping out, he and his morally upright sons tolerated the strange ways adopted by the countercultural "Weary Willies" who had set up a commune on their land. Similarly, Aaron Spelling's *Mod Squad*, first aired in 1968, portrayed three modish misfits who, in order to redeem themselves with a society ready to cast them out, helped the police solve crimes in the countercultural underworld. Such were means of making countercultural styles more acceptable to more people. Although countercultural expressions never entirely replaced traditional American forms, the two came to rest uncomfortably alongside one another, helping to set the parameters of an increasingly divisive cultural politics.[21]

Historian David Farber argues that hippies were the "shock troops" of the culture wars because the sons and daughters of respectable America were expected to toe the line. Their intransigence proved traumatic to many Americans, such as those Californians who voted Ronald Reagan into the governor's mansion in 1966 in part due to his rhetorical attack on Berkeley countercultural protestors. "I'd like to harness their youthful energy," Reagan quipped, "with a strap." But such compelling evidence notwithstanding, the identity-based movements of the New Left—Black and Chicano Power, women's and gay liberation—were ultimately more threatening to the guardians of traditional America than was the counterculture.[22]

For New Leftists struggling for full recognition of their identities, contravening normative America, more than a game of Oedipal rebellion played out by white college students, was serious business. For Black Power spokespersons Stokely Carmichael and Charles Hamilton, normal America equated to the "white power structure" that had bottled up black freedom for centuries. For radical feminist Robin

Morgan, breaking rules meant fighting patriarchy in the name of a future "genderless society." And for gay liberationist Martha Shelley, subverting tradition entailed informing "the man" that homosexuals "will never go straight until you go gay." It is because of the identity-based movements of the New Left that the sixties were an unusually liberating era for a great number of Americans. It was this element of the sixties, even more than the antiwar and countercultural movements, that shook up normative America.[23]

The identity-based movements of the sixties offered the promise of cultural liberation to those on the outside of traditional America looking in. Black Power, for instance, was a cultural response to a politically perplexing racial landscape. As President Lyndon Johnson proclaimed in a famous speech at Howard University on June 4, 1965, "equality as a right and a theory" was not the same thing as "equality as a fact and as a result." This chasm was made horrifyingly apparent by the numerous riots that plagued American cities in the sixties, beginning with one that exploded in the predominantly black Watts neighborhood of Los Angeles in August 1965, resulting in thirty-four deaths, thousands of injuries, and untold millions in property damage. That the Watts riot erupted only a few days after the Voting Rights Act outlawed discriminatory voting practices highlighted the vast discrepancy between equality as a right and equality as a fact. The Black Power movement took up the cause of trying to bridge this gap.[24]

Black Power activists believed the best path to equality was to forge their own. As poet LeRoi Jones put it: "The struggle is for independence." For many African Americans, independence meant piecing together an entirely new cultural identity, one ostensibly tied to the African continent from which their ancestors were captured and taken into slavery. In Los Angeles, Ronald McKinley Everett changed his name to Maulana Ron Karenga and created the cultural nationalist US Organization in 1965. Members of US learned to speak Swahili, dressed in African robes, and invented the Kwanzaa celebration as a substitute for Christmas and Hanukkah. Black nationalists contrasted halcyon days of African empires past with the wretched state of contemporary black America and logically concluded that a crime of epic proportions had been committed against African Americans in the interim. Glorifying African history and culture, they believed, would facilitate in young African Americans a positive image of themselves. "We must recapture our heritage and our identity if we are ever to liberate ourselves from the bonds of white supremacy," asserted Malcolm X, the personification of Black Power. "We must launch a cultural revolution to unbrainwash an entire people."[25]

Although the cultural nationalism of US would have long-lasting influence, the Black Panther Party for Self Defense, which represented a more militant, more political side of Black Power, inspired a wider audience during the sixties. The Black Panthers, founded in 1966 by Oakland radicals Huey Newton and Bobby Seale, brought "Marxist-Leninist" rhetoric into the Black Power movement. Eldridge Cleaver, author of the electrifying 1968 book *Soul on Ice*, which he wrote while an inmate at Folsom State Prison, articulated the Black Panther ideology in his capacity as the party's minister of information. Arguing that economic exploitation was the primary cause of black second-class citizenship, Cleaver contended that the Black Panthers were to be the vanguard in the movement to liberate the "black urban lumpen-proletariat." But the appeal of the Black Panthers had less to do with such Marxist-inspired vocabulary and more to do with their innovative and infectious aesthetics of confrontation. Black Panthers donned black leather jackets, dark sunglasses, and black berets atop large if neat Afros. Their omnipresent logo of a sleek, powerful black panther springing into action signified the angry spirit of Malcolm X's ghost. And most extraordinarily, the Black Panthers openly exercised their Second Amendment rights by carrying guns in public. White New Leftists mimicked the Black Panther aesthetics of confrontation by adopting the Black Panther term *pigs* as a catchall moniker for cops and other authority figures, including university administrators. But despite the white New Left's flattery by imitation, the Black Panthers, like the larger Black Power movement, emphasized that their goal was not racial integration but rather black self-determination. In this way they agreed with other cultural nationalists about the importance of learning a specifically black history, or, in the words of the Black Panther Party's "Ten-Point Program," "our true history."[26]

The Black Panthers struck a chord. "By the late 1960's," historian Manning Marable writes, "the Black Panthers had become the most influential revolutionary nationalist organization in the U.S." Even more telling was the response by J. Edgar Hoover, the longtime director of the Federal Bureau of Investigation (FBI) who epitomized the repressive side of normative America. In a 1970 report written for President Nixon, Hoover labeled the Black Panther Party "the most active and dangerous black extremist group in the United States." Such threatening rhetoric was anything but idle. The Black Panthers were the targets of 233 out of a total 295 counterintelligence operations directed at black political groups during that era. FBI infiltrators even helped sow discord between the Black Panthers and US, which led to a deadly 1969 shootout between the two groups on the University of California–Los Angeles campus. The Black Panther Party's confrontational approach proved a self-fulfilling prophecy, resulting in a demise accurately reflected in the title of Huey Newton's 1973 memoir, *Revolutionary Suicide*. And yet the legacy of the Black Panthers cannot be reduced to such failure. They contributed to the irrepressible spirit of rebellion that transformed how millions of people viewed normative America and their place within it.[27]

Black Power and the other identity-based movements of the sixties underscored new forms of knowledge, a new intellectual agency in relation to oppression that might be termed an epistemology of liberation. In doing so these movements created new ideas about identity. Identity was something to be stressed; it was something to grow into or become. Only by becoming black, or Chicano, or a liberated woman, or an out-of-the-closet homosexual—and only by showing solidarity with those similarly identified—could one hope to overcome the psychological barriers to liberation imposed by discriminatory cultural norms. Becoming an identity—identifying as an oppressed minority—meant refusing to conform to mainstream standards of American identity.

As opposed to normative America, black nationalists found solidarity in international anticolonial movements. If they saw the American nation as good for anything, it was as a launching pad for their diasporic struggles. The "third world" shaped the worldviews of Black Power leaders like Malcolm X, Cleaver, Stokely Carmichael, and Robert F. Williams. For the latter two, such moral geographical commitments became physical: Carmichael relocated to Guinea and changed his name to Kwame Turé; Williams fled federal agents to a life of exile in Cuba and China. In this spirit, Black Power advocates viewed identity politics as nothing less than revolutionary. Some of the more revolutionary anticolonial thinkers likewise had displayed elements of identity in their politics. These included the renowned Argentinian doctor and Cuban revolutionary Ernesto "Che" Guevara, who became a global icon of rebellion. In his classic 1953 memoir of his prerevolutionary travels across South America, *The Motorcycle Diaries*, Guevara displayed attentiveness to identity as a liberating force. Critical of education "according to the white man's criteria," he believed that only by virtue of Indian or mestizo identity could one grasp "the moral distance separating" Western civilization from a once proud indigenous civilization. Although the young Guevara of *The Motorcycle Diaries* accentuated political economy, anticipating his later turn to communism, he also emphasized "spreading a real knowledge of the Quechua nation so that the people of that race could feel proud of their past rather than ... ashamed of being Indian or Mestizo."[28]

Even more than Che, Frantz Fanon was arguably the most important thinker to the "third world" revolutionaries in the United States. Cleaver, for instance, claimed it was Fanon who showed him that American blacks were part of the vast colonized peoples of the world. At first glance, it would seem that Fanon eschewed identity politics. He concluded his 1952 book *Black Skin, White Masks* on a universal note that rejected racial identity: "The Negro is not. Any more than a white man." In his seminal 1963 book *The Wretched of the Earth*, an anticolonial text par excellence, he criticized black nationalist celebrations of ancient African civilization. But Fanon also recognized such racialized expressions of history and culture as necessary first steps in severing ties with colonial power, especially since the representatives of Western civilization "have never ceased to set up white culture to fill the gap left by the absence of other cultures." In short, cultural identity was integral to Fanon's existentialist musings on "the experience of a black man thrown into a white world." In this his position resembled Richard Wright's well-known response to Bandung, where Wright called for a "reluctant nationalism" that "need not remain valid for decades to come." Both Fanon and Wright joined the Second Congress of the Negro Writers and Artists in Rome in 1959, dedicated to the "peoples without a culture," a mission aligned with one of Fanon's more famous dictums: "The plunge into the chasm of the past is the condition and the course of freedom." No wonder Black Power activists were known to carry tattered copies of Fanon's books around with them.[29]

Harold Cruse, another intellectual who helped shape Black Power, argued in his 1967 tour de force *The Crisis of the Negro Intellectual* that the role of black intellectuals was to reconceptualize black identity as independent of white society. The objective of black thinkers was

to gain control of those "cultural institutions" responsible for representing black history and culture. Fashioning identity politics as real-
ism, Cruse wrote: "The individual Negro has, proportionately, very
few rights indeed because his ethnic group (whether or not he actually identifies with it) has very little political, economic or social
power (beyond moral grounds) to wield." Carmichael and Hamilton
made a similarly nationalistic argument in their book *Black Power:
The Politics of Liberation*, also published in 1967: "Group solidarity is
necessary before a group can effectively form a bargaining position
of strength in a pluralistic society." Such thinking highlights a crucial
difference between the white and black New Lefts. Against the antinomianism of the white New Left, especially in its countercultural expressions, which made individual expression sacrosanct, Black Power
thinkers saw the need to conform to a collective black identity.[30]

   That Black Power theorists understood black identity as crucial
to their struggle does not entail that identity was simply something
to celebrate. Rather, accurate conceptions of blackness in relation to
whiteness helped them make better sense of racial inequality and,
more generally, the American political economy. In *Black Power*, Carmichael and Hamilton upended decades of social science by drawing
a critical distinction between personal and "institutional racism." As
opposed to personal racism, bigotry easily condemned by enlightened
whites, institutional racism, the insidious ways in which the American
social structure favored whites over blacks, "originates in the operation of established and respected forces in the society, and thus re-
ceives far less public condemnation." The most glaring case of institutional racism was the American system of property appraisal, in which
houses in white neighborhoods received higher value ratings. Given
the cultural significance attached to home ownership in the United
States, not to mention the long-term economic advantages, it was no
wonder Black Power activists lamented living "in a society in which
to be unconditionally 'American' is to be white, and to be black is a
misfortune." By coining the analytical category "institutional racism,"
Carmichael and Hamilton showed that the Black Power turn to cultural analysis was not necessarily a reductionist rejection of economic
thought. Rather, the attention to racial identity ushered in an innovative hybrid approach—bringing together cultural and economic
analysis—that became the bedrock of leftist and academic thought.[31]

   Less prominently than the Black Power movement, but just as

effectively, the Chicano movement trumpeted a similar brand of collective identity politics. Rodolfo "Corky" Gonzales was one of the more eloquent spokespersons for "Chicanos," a label embraced by those Mexican Americans who practiced identity politics. Gonzales directed the Crusade for Justice, a Chicano activist group based in Denver with a mission to foster "a sense of identity and self-worth" among Mexican Americans. Both in his speeches and in his poetry Gonzales persistently emphasized that improvements to the Mexican American condition would require group solidarity and cultural awareness. Speaking to a group of college students in 1969, Gonzales complained that so many Mexican Americans identified with "the Anglo image" instead of with Aztlán, his term for the Mexican Diaspora. It was imperative, he pleaded, to "admit that we have a different set of values." Chicanos needed to be more aware of "their cultural attributes, their historical contributions, their self-identity and most importantly their self-worth."[32]

Gonzales's epic 1967 poem *I Am Joaquín* mixed hyperattention to Chicano identity with countercultural tropes about alienation. Joaquín, representative of Aztlán, existed "in the grasp of American social neurosis." "Unwillingly dragged by that monstrous, technical industrial giant called Progress," Joaquín recalled venerable rebel leaders of the Mexican past—Benito Juárez, Pancho Villa, Emiliano Zapata—in order to symbolically resist "a country that has wiped out all my history, stifled all my pride." Identity was Joaquín's battleground. "I am the masses of my people, and I refuse to be absorbed." *I Am Joaquín* "was a journey back through history," according to Gonzales, "a painful self-evaluation, a wandering search for my peoples, and, most of all, for my own identity." In the words of Carlos Muñoz, founding chair of the nation's first Chicano studies program at California State University–Los Angeles, "the most significant aspect of *I Am Joaquín* was that it captured both the agony and the jubilation permeating the identity crisis faced by Mexican American youth in the process of assimilation." In other words, the constraints and prejudices of a normative American identity pushed Chicanos to theorize alternative identity formations.[33]

Like the intellectual advocates of Black Power, Gonzales did not view Chicano nationalism as narrow or inhibiting. "Nationalism is a tool for organization not a weapon for hatred," he wrote. Gonzales saw Chicano nationalism as a stepping-stone to an international movement of oppressed peoples, in turn a springboard to universal human liberation. However, there was a proper order of struggle, and the particular preceded the universal. "Dealing only within our own sphere of involvement," Gonzales argued, "we must teach on a grassroots level and identify with our own self worth and historic ties." "El Plan Espiritual de Aztlán," created by Gonzales and the other participants in the National Chicano Youth Liberation Conference, hosted by the Crusade for Justice in 1969, expressed how sixties identity politics mixed cultural nationalism with more universal, even anticapitalist desires: "Our cultural values of life, family, and home will serve as a powerful weapon to defeat the Gringo dollar value system and encourage the process of love and brotherhood."[34]

Because Gonzales believed that his fellow Mexican Americans needed a shift in consciousness, he prioritized education in his activism. He led a walkout of Mexican American students at Denver West High School in March 1969 to pressure the Denver school board to "enforce the inclusion in all schools of this city the history of our people, our culture, language, and our contributions to this country." The students also demanded "that payment for the psychological destruction of our people, i.e., inferiority complexes, anglo superiority myth, rejection of our own identity and self worth, . . . be settled by a free education for all Mexican American youth from Headstart through college." In a letter to Crusade for Justice members in 1973, Gonzales praised Chicano movement advocates as "the forerunners in the battle for positive and relevant education for Chicanos." He was especially proud of the "Chicano Studies Programs sprouting in the universities that provide income for Chicano Study experts." In sum, theories about Chicano identity and nationalism, as propounded by Gonzales and others, were crucial to the formation of Chicano studies in universities. The same was true of black studies.[35]

The first department of black studies was formed at San Francisco State College in 1969 in response to a large student protest known as the Third World Strike. Most of the earliest black studies programs were established in reaction to black student protests. At San Francisco State College and elsewhere, student protestors were almost always Black Power activists, whose strong presence on campuses across the United States in the late sixties ensured the birth of black studies. Shortly after founding the Black Panther Party, Bobby Seale and Huey Newton worked to establish black studies at Merritt College in Oakland in 1967 on Fanon's premise that a genuine national culture was necessary to break the chains of colonialism. They believed African Americans constituted an internal colony and that independence demanded cultivating black nationalist institutions such as black studies programs. Black Panther Jimmy Garrett, who helped lead the Third World Strike in San Francisco, hosted Black Power reading groups at his house, where "we would talk about ourselves, seeking identity." "A lot of folks," a bewildered Garrett reflected, "didn't even know they were black. A lot of people thought they were Americans."[36]

The vigilantes of Americanism reacted to black student protest with hostility. Reagan routinely condemned Third World Strikers. San Francisco State College president S. I. Hayakawa, heeding Reagan's calls to quit coddling militant college students, disrupted a Third World Strike rally by pulling the wires out from a student loudspeaker. Elsewhere, authorities quashed student protests with increasingly draconian force. This was particularly true where black students were historically few in number, such as at the University of Illinois in downstate Urbana-Champaign, where the student body was over 98 percent white as late as 1966. When Illinois administrators took steps to admit more black students, due to federal laws that required affirmative action at public institutions, tensions erupted. In September 1968, 250 black students, mostly from Chicago, where black nationalism had deep roots, were arrested for a sit-in at the student center. Many of those arrested were expelled from the university. Yet the protests were not a total failure. In order to defuse such unrest, administrators approved the creation of a black studies program. Much to their chagrin, the program remained firmly committed to the Black Power tradition even after the larger movement died out, as a 1981 overview of the program's mission made clear: "The study of the Black Experience is to develop means for achieving liberation—freedom from oppression—and self-determination for Black people."[37]

Chicano studies developed along a similar trajectory. As with black studies, the key early moments in establishing Chicano studies revolved around student protest, especially the East Los Angeles walkout by high school students in March 1968 led by Sol Castro. According to Carlos Muñoz, who helped Castro organize that protest and later led the push for Chicano studies on campuses, "The major purpose of the Los Angeles walkouts was to protest racist teachers and school policies, the lack of freedom of speech, the lack of teachers of Mexican descent, the absence of classes on Mexican and Mexican American culture and history, and the inferior education provided to Mexican American students." Muñoz remembers the movement as "a quest for identity, an effort to recapture what had been lost through the socialization process imposed by U.S. schools and other institutions." For this reason Muñoz and other Chicano movement leaders, understanding "the need to take on that socialization process," prioritized Chicano studies as one institutional response to what he terms the "identity problematic."[38]

The passions and methodologies of the Black and Chicano Power movements informed the activism of other minority groups, especially in California, where peoples of "black, brown, yellow, and red" backgrounds endowed the New Left with a remarkable diversity. The Japanese American poet Amy Uyematsu wrote a formidable 1969 essay, "The Emergence of Yellow Power," about an emerging movement for Asian American liberation that she claimed had been set into motion by the Black Power movement. Uyematsu argued that Asian Americans, like blacks, were victims of "white institutionalized racism" and thus had to free themselves from the ideological shackles of normative white America. Asian Americans, she said, were "beginning to realize that this nation is a 'White democracy' and the yellow people have a mistaken identity."[39]

The American Indian Movement (AIM) was founded in 1968 with a similar mission, made weightier by the fact that it sought liberation for the only ethnic group indigenous to the North American continent. Such a thirst for long-denied freedom informed the Native American activists who occupied Alcatraz Island in San Francisco Bay on November 20, 1969. The goal of the nearly two-year occupation was to compel the federal government to give American Indians control of the island and allow them to convert the former location of an infamous prison into a center for Native American Studies. "Red Power" activists, those whom *The Nation* magazine called "Our Most Silent Majority"—a riff on Nixon's label for the presumably white, middle-class majority of Americans who supported his presidency—thought it was a small price for white America to pay in return for centuries of broken treaties.[40]

The combined forces of these movements for ethnic liberation congealed into another massive student strike in 1969, this time at the University of California's Berkeley campus. Although the official response to this second Third World Strike was draconian—Governor Reagan sent in the National Guard to break it up—the protestors won the sympathy of many of their fellow students. And Berkeley faculty even voted to join the strike unless the university created an ethnic studies department. The university gave in to the pressure. In 1969 Berkeley became home to the nation's first department of ethnic studies, and San Francisco State College became home to the nation's first and only College of Ethnic Studies. University chancellor Roger Heyns wrote a statement admitting that the state's system of higher education had failed to incorporate the experiences of racial minorities into the curriculum. The upshot of all this activism: radical identity movements had planted permanent institutional beachheads on the enemy territory otherwise known as white normative America. Those were heady times.[41]

Radical identity politics also animated the young activists of the women's liberation movement. Like ethnic identity activists, feminists pioneered academic programs—women's studies—that rejected traditional forms of American socialization. To get to that point, feminists had come a long way in a short time. A few years prior, feminists took their cues from less militant liberals like Betty Friedan, author of the 1963 instant classic *The Feminine Mystique*. After surveying her fellow Smith College alumni, Friedan argued that despite the material comforts of suburbia, middle-class women tended to suffer from symptoms of depression, what she famously named "the problem that has no name." Reflecting the cultural turn taken by social critics in an age of affluence, Friedan, formerly a labor reporter who called herself a socialist, made clear that economic security alone did not satisfy human wants, especially those of highly educated women barred from elite professions. From 1966 until 1970, Friedan served as the founding president of the National Organization of Women (NOW), which eventually blossomed into the largest feminist organization in the United States. NOW attracted tens of thousands of members thanks to its successful record of lobbying to "bring women into full participation in the mainstream of American society now." But for radical feminists who rejected mainstream America, such liberal reformism was too tepid. In contrast, radical feminists—in contemporary nomenclature, the women's liberation movement—sought to subvert American institutions, such as the traditional family, on the grounds that they were hopelessly patriarchal.[42]

In spite of the women's liberation movement's efforts to distance itself from liberal feminism, its principles pivoted from similar cultural tendencies. Just as Friedan made the psychology of housewives a political issue, radical feminists theorized that relations between the sexes, no matter how intimate, needed to be reformulated in political terms. Feminists of all varieties staked a claim to the enduring slogan "The personal is political," the title of Carol Hanisch's 1969 essay that first appeared in a pamphlet distributed by Redstockings, a radical feminist group founded by Shulamith Firestone and Ellen Willis. Despite such similarities, radicals went much further than liberals in politicizing the personal. By undertaking what they called "consciousness-raising," a popular tactic of the women's liberation movement, radical feminists brought awareness to how the seemingly mundane stuff of everyday life could repress women. As Hanisch wrote, consciousness-raising "forced [her] to take off her rose colored glasses and face the awful truth about how grim my life really is as a woman." Radical feminists formed consciousness-raising groups, where activists helped their sisters relate their individual difficulties to the larger problem of being a woman in a patriarchal society. Their concrete personal narratives served to illustrate the abstract political concepts of feminist theory. "We regard our personal experience, and our feelings about that experience," according to the Redstockings manifesto, "as the basis for an analysis of our common situation."[43]

Although radical feminists are remembered for inventing "The personal is political," the idea behind the phrase grounded the political philosophy of the New Left from its outset. In 1959 C. Wright Mills had argued that people could connect their "personal troubles to public issues" by learning how to think about a subject from multiple perspectives—an analytical style that owed to what he called "the sociological imagination." Tom Hayden, putting his own sociological imagination to work in writing the Port Huron Statement, contended that alienation resulted from a politics that denied individuals the freedom to find "meaning in life that is personally authentic." Many radical feminists learned how to think about personal politics as members of various New Left organizations, especially SDS and the Student Non-Violent Coordinating Committee (SNCC). This was ironic, of course, since politicizing the personal, taken to its logical conclusion, led many women to believe that the New Left organizations to which they belonged were chauvinistic. Stokely Carmichael's notoriously misogynistic quip that "the position of women in SNCC is prone" symbolized the need for women to prioritize their own liberation.[44]

Robin Morgan's political transformation was indicative of the trajectory that brought women of the New Left to radical feminism. Morgan began writing for New Left publications in 1962. Throughout the decade, she was dedicated to ending the Vietnam War and even briefly joined forces with the Yippies. But beginning in 1967, she expanded her activism to include women's liberation, helping to found New York Radical Women, which protested the Miss America Pageant in 1968. Soon after committing to women's issues, Morgan's notions about radical politics metamorphosed. "No matter how empathetic you are to another's oppression," she wrote, "you become truly committed to radical change only when you realize your own oppression." In 1970 Morgan joined a group of women who took control of *Rat*, a New Left newspaper known for its sexism, by staging a coup. In a 1970 essay, "Goodbye to All That," she publicly severed ties with the New Left in poetic fashion: "We have met the enemy and he's our friend." Morgan had grown incredulous that so many of her comrades persisted in avoiding women's issues, such as rape and child care, which they denounced as too "bourgeois." In contrast, Morgan contended that patriarchy was the world's "primary oppression," a common theoretical move made by women weary of being relegated to secretarial duties in a movement supposedly seeking universal human freedom.[45]

Naming patriarchy as the most pervasive hierarchy in world history was central to the epistemology of women's liberation. Nobody was more explicit about this than Kate Millett, author of the groundbreaking 1970 book *Sexual Politics*. Millett theorized that "unless we eliminate the most pernicious of our systems of oppression"—patriarchy, with its "sick delirium of power and violence"—"all our efforts at liberation will only land us again in the same primordial stew." Taking her cues from Simone de Beauvoir, Millett contended that whereas male identity was understood to be normal, "woman" was reified as a sexual object. "Nearly all that can be described as distinctly human rather than animal activity," as Millett pointed out, "is largely reserved for the male." Millett posited that if women consented to patriarchal constraints it was because they had been conditioned to assume that certain gender norms were natural. The revelation that gender was malleable had a liberating effect on feminists. If gender could be made, then it could also be unmade.[46]

Unmasking patriarchal gender norms was common practice in the women's studies programs that burst onto college campuses in 1970, when the first program was created at San Diego State College. From there the number of women's studies programs quickly mushroomed: by 1976 there were 270, and by 1981 there were a whopping 350 programs nationwide. Along with black, Chicano, and ethnic studies, women's studies grew as an offshoot of the sixties identity movements. Feminist activists undertook to implement women's studies programs in order to institutionalize women's liberation. In 1969 Cornell University organizers invited Millett, then an unknown doctoral student, to campus to read from her unfinished manuscript *Sexual Politics*. Listening to Millet's jarring analysis of patriarchy evoked new political desires among many of the women in attendance, catalyzing their struggle to create a women's studies program at Cornell. Armed with a newfound political consciousness, women's studies aimed, as the Hunter College Women's Studies Collective put it, to "examine the world and the human beings who inhabit it with questions, analyses, and theories built directly on women's experiences." In other words, campus feminists integrated consciousness-raising into the academic curriculum, consistent with the epistemology of liberation that animated the identity movements of the New Left. Beyond liberating, women's studies scholars also deemed consciousness-raising pedagogically necessary since until then women had largely been erased from the university curriculum. Women's experiences were one of the only sources of knowledge with which to build a new curriculum.[47]

Consciousness-raising was not the sole preserve of women's liberation. It was also a formative tactic of the gay liberation movement that exploded after the Stonewall Riot. On the night of June 27, 1969, eight policemen emerged from the Stonewall Inn, a popular Manhattan gay bar, with several prisoners in tow, whom they sought to load into a paddy wagon. What seemed like a routine police raid on a technically illegal gay bar was transformed into an event of lasting significance when a crowd of angry onlookers ignored orders to disperse and loudly encouraged those held captive to resist arrest. Badly outnumbered, the police took shelter back inside the bar, ceding the street to the indignant mob. The confrontation calmed down later that

night, but as word of the astonishing event spread the next day, thanks
to abundant press coverage, which included a front-page story in the
New York Times, gays began to gather again outside the Stonewall Inn.
By early the next evening, a huge crowd had amassed, tinged, as gay
rights activist Craig Rodwell described it, with a "real anger by gay
people that was just electric."[48]

Stonewall was a watershed moment in the history of gay rights.
When Allen Ginsberg saw "Gay Power!" scrawled on the Stonewall
Inn two nights after the initial riot, he told a reporter: "We're one of
the largest minorities in the country—10 percent, you know. It's about
time we did something to assert ourselves." Inside the bar that night,
which had been cleaned up and reopened, Ginsberg noticed that the
patrons had "lost that wounded look that fags all had 10 years ago."
A New York City police officer in charge of "public morals" echoed
Ginsberg when he claimed that gays suddenly were "not submissive
anymore." The dominant tone of gay activism had shifted from de-
murring to confrontational. The Mattachine Society, the nation's most
prominent homophile organization prior to 1969, relied upon liberal
heterosexual allies to speak on behalf of gay rights, since most of its
members were hesitant to publicly pronounce themselves gay. Such
reticence was logical, of course, given the cultural stigma attached
to homosexuality—a stigma reflected by the American Psychological Association (APA)'s designation of homosexuality as pathological.
Exemplifying the new militancy, post-Stonewall activists disrupted
APA meetings, nudging it to remove homosexuality from its list of
disorders in 1973.[49]

The Gay Liberation Front (GLF) best represented the "gay liberation movement," the new name for post-Stonewall gay rights activism. In contrast to earlier activists, the founding members of GLF,
mostly veterans of the New Left, were cultural radicals by disposition. In this the gay liberation movement was emphatically within the
New Left milieu. But more than that, gay liberation represented the
full flowering of New Left sensibilities. Against the bedrock traditions
of heterosexual America, openly declaring oneself gay was an act of
considerable transgression, a politicization of the personal to a radical
new degree. That some of the most renowned New Left intellectuals
were homosexuals, such as Ginsberg, James Baldwin, and Paul Goodman, was emblematic of a gay inclination to chip away at repressive
American norms that inhibited individual freedom. Being publicly

gay "branded one's consciousness with a marker of difference," in the words of historian John D'Emilio. "It necessarily made one perpetually aware of separation, of division in the body of humanity, of marginalization and ostracism." In this way, the history of gay liberation is essential to understanding how the New Left transformed American culture.[50]

Just as Robin Morgan's biography illuminates how many New Left women found their way to radical feminism, a biographical sketch of Karla Jay, a founding GLF member who later became a professor of women's studies, demonstrates how gay liberation both emerged from the New Left and was its culmination. Jay grew up in a conservative Jewish household where, because heterosexuality was assumed, sexuality in general was never spoken about, leaving her incapable of making sense of her sexual inclinations. Jay belatedly learned that homosexuality was taboo during her freshman year at Barnard College in 1964, when two of her classmates at that female-only school were expelled for having sex in their dorm room. Not surprisingly, she hid her sexual identity until years later. As the sixties wore on, Jay's politics grew increasingly radical. In 1968 she participated in rowdy Columbia University protests against the institution's expansion into nearby black neighborhoods and in opposition to its military-sponsored research. But like so many other women, Jay grew convinced that sexism plagued the New Left, so she joined Redstockings. In a Redstockings consciousness-raising group, she finally came out of the closet as a lesbian. "Coming out" as a political tactic elevated consciousness-raising to a new level of importance for gay liberation. "Speaking freely and honestly to other gays in the protected atmosphere of a consciousness-raising session," Jay explained, would, in theory, "ramify outward" to obliterate the heteronormativity at the core of traditional American identity. "We want to reach the homosexual entombed in you," as Martha Shelley told Americans in her canonical essay "Gay Is Good."[51]

If gay liberation represented the apex of sixties-era liberation for some, for others it signaled the decline of Western civilization. D'Emilio draws upon a pithy analogy to explain this declension narrative: "We might as well be reading Edward Gibbon's *The History of the Decline and Fall of the Roman Empire*, the classic eighteenth-century work that tied Rome's collapse to sexual immorality." Conservatives were those most likely to take a dim view of gay liberation. But they were not alone. Many on the Left implicitly connected the decline of organized labor to the rise of gay liberation and the other identity movements of the New Left. This was most evident in responses to George McGovern's 1972 campaign for presidency, which ended in a landslide loss to Nixon. Even though McGovern had a near perfect voting record on labor issues while a senator, and even though he had long been genuinely interested in labor concerns, having written a doctoral dissertation on the infamous Colorado Coal Strike of 1913 and 1914—the strike that resulted in the tragic Ludlow Massacre—the most powerful unions never rallied to his support. This included the massive American Federation of Labor and Congress of Industrial Organizations (AFL-CIO), led by cigar-chomping George Meany. Meany not only abstained from supporting the McGovern campaign but also implicitly aided Nixon's reelection efforts by tarring McGovern as a lackey of the identity movements that many white male unionists believed had captured the Democratic Party.[52]

Labor's disenchantment with McGovern grew out of its anger at him for heading the reform commission that overhauled the demographic composition of the Democratic Party delegation. When youthful party insurgents failed to stamp their imprint on the party platform in 1968—a failure that was due, they determined, to the corrupt delegate system, with its "secret caucuses, closed slate-making, widespread proxy voting, and a host of other procedural irregularities"—these so-called "New Politics" Democrats had struck back by forming the Commission on Party Structure and Delegate Selection. The net effect was to open up the party delegation to young people, minorities, women, and gays, while dislodging many of the old guard, mostly the white men of organized labor. Whereas 2 percent of the delegates to the Chicago convention in 1968 were younger than thirty, 23 percent of the delegates were that young at the Miami convention in 1972. Similarly, black representation increased from 5 percent to 14 percent. And both the women's and gay liberation movements "found expression in the campaign," in the words of McGovern aide Bob Schrum. As opposed to 1968, when 14 percent of the delegates were women, 36 percent of the Miami delegates were women, most of them active in the feminist movement. Similarly, gays gained a foothold in the party for the first time, particularly in New York, as that state's delegation included eight gay rights activists, as compared, astonishingly, to only three delegates from the ranks of organized labor. The McGovern campaign, much like some Hollywood programming, and much like black, ethnic, and women's studies programs, exemplified how sixties liberation movements gained an institutional foothold in liberal America.[53]

The sexual revolution also signaled that the sixties liberation movements had ushered in new cultural sensibilities. From its outset, of course, the sexual revolution meant different things to different people. To radical feminists, it signified their refusal to be "exploited as sex objects," as proclaimed by a 1969 Redstockings manifesto. But to many other young Americans, the sexual revolution was less about equality and more about liberty—more about ending the constraints that rendered sex taboo. This libertarian side of the sexual revolution was indeed revolutionary. Public morality came out of the sixties much less prudish. Universities abandoned *in loco parentis* duties, including imposing curfews and separating the sexes. Public censors lost their firm grip on popular culture, owing in part to an increasingly permissive Supreme Court, which ruled in its 1966 "Fanny Hill" decision that a cultural product could be branded obscene only if it was thought to be "utterly without redeeming value." Such a precedent, which set the bar for censorship high, enabled the popularization of hypersexual films theretofore confined to the underground. *The Chelsea Girls*, Andy Warhol's otherwise banal 1966 film, packed theaters across New York City due to its graphic depictions of sex, "as if," one critic imagined, "there had been cameras concealed in the fleshpots of Caligula's Rome." By the late sixties, Americans increasingly expected controversy, even obscenity, when they frequented movie theaters. In 1972 the pornographic film *Deep Throat* stormed the country, briefly inspiring a highbrow fascination with pornography remembered as "porno chic."[54]

The fruits of the libertarian sexual revolution could be felt nearly everywhere. The Sexual Freedom League, which grew in numbers and notoriety after *Time* magazine featured it in a 1966 article, hosted thinly disguised orgies it dubbed "nude parties." Philip Roth became a literary celebrity on the heels of *Portnoy's Complaint*, his 1969 novel about Jewish American identity that doubled as an ode to adolescent masturbation. *Joy of Sex*, a 1972 sex advice book that included graphic illustrations, sold millions of copies and spent over fifty weeks near the top of the *New York Times* best-seller list. Norman O. Brown gained acclaim by endowing the sexual revolution with a patina of

philosophical rigor: by repressing our common desire for "polymorphous perversity," Brown theorized, humans had unwisely chosen to
side with the languid trappings of "civilization" over the deliverance
promised by "eroticism." The libertine side of the sexual revolution
seemed complete, evident in *New York Times* editor Anthony Lewis's
cocksure assertion that "the Philistines are on the run."[55]

Television, if not quite "wallowing in sex," the lament of one industry executive, incorporated the new sexual morality. By the 1970s,
popular shows like the situation comedy *Three's Company* and the light
drama *Love Boat* seemed indicative to Americans raised on *Leave It to
Beaver* that primetime television was a veritable fleshpot. But perhaps
more troubling, television programming also, in more limited fashion,
absorbed themes drawn from the feminist side of the sexual revolution. Norman Lear's situation comedy *Maude*, which aired on CBS
from 1972 to 1978, starred Beatrice Arthur as Maude Findlay, a thrice-
divorced, outspokenly liberal forty-seven-year-old woman. *Maude*
spun off from another Lear production, *All in the Family*, a wildly popular show about the family of working-class rube Archie Bunker, played
by Carroll O'Connor. The Maude character had first appeared on *All
in the Family* as Archie's hapless wife Edith's opinionated cousin, described by Lear as "the flip side of Archie." "Maude breaks every rule
of television from the start," said CBS president Robert Wood. "It's
not so long ago that you couldn't show a woman divorced from one
husband, let alone three." Divorce was not the only hot-button issue
Maude tackled. In November 1972, just months before *Roe v. Wade*,
Lear dedicated two episodes—"Maude's Dilemma"—to the topic of
abortion. After discovering, incredibly, that she is pregnant, Maude
agonizes about whether to abort her unplanned pregnancy. In the
end, she heeds her feminist daughter Carol's advice and goes through
with the abortion, thereupon convincing her fourth husband to ac-
quire a vasectomy. Immediately following the broadcast of "Maude's
Dilemma," Lear and CBS were besieged with angry phone calls and
letters. Catholic organizations called *Maude* "open propaganda for
abortion and vasectomy." Several local affiliates chose not to broadcast
reruns of "Maude's Dilemma," including in Boston, where the station
manager proclaimed, "[T]here is nothing particularly funny about a
47-year-old woman getting an abortion."[56]

Beyond Catholic fears about the liberalization of abortion, the fuss
over "Maude's Dilemma" reflected more generic anxieties about the

empirical decline of the traditional family, as measured by rising rates of divorce, out-of-wedlock pregnancy, premarital sex, and nonmarital cohabitation. The angry reaction to *Maude* was also symptomatic of concerns about female empowerment. Of course, these two sets of fears—about family declension and female liberation—were not mutually exclusive. Divorce became more frequent partly as a consequence, at least initially, of no-fault divorce laws that feminists had long supported as a tool for women to escape abusive marriages. The conservative political movement for "family values" that came to life in the 1970s thus should be seen as a reaction to one of the many ways in which the New Left had recast American political culture. Conservatives fought for their definition of the good society, for their traditional, normative America, by resisting New Left sensibilities. In fact, the reactionary forces that aligned against the New Left, forces that included a diverse range of people, suggest that the sixties were indeed liberating. Or at the very least, it shows that the sixties liberation movements—the New Left, broadly construed—lobbed the first shots in the culture wars that would come to define late-twentieth-century American political culture.[57]

2

The Neoconservative Kulturkämpfe

If New Leftists gave shape to one side of the culture wars, those who came to be called neoconservatives were hugely influential in shaping the other. *Neoconservatism*, a label applied to a group of prominent liberal intellectuals who moved right on the American political spectrum during the sixties, took form precisely in opposition to the New Left. In their reaction to the New Left, in their spirited defense of traditional American institutions, and in their full-throated attack on those intellectuals who composed, in Lionel Trilling's words, an "adversary culture," neoconservatives helped draw up the very terms of the culture wars.[1]

When we think about the neoconservative persuasion as the flip side of the New Left, it should be historically situated relative to what Corey Robin labels "the reactionary mind." Robin considers conservatism "a meditation on—and theoretical rendition of—the felt experience of having power, seeing it threatened, and trying to win it back." In somewhat similar fashion, George H. Nash defines conservatism as "resistance to certain forces perceived to be leftist, revolutionary, and profoundly subversive." Plenty of Americans experienced the various New Left movements of the sixties as "profoundly subversive" of the status quo. Neoconservatives articulated this reaction best. In a national culture transformed by sixties liberation movements, neoconservatives became famous for their efforts to "win it back."[2]

One of the primary assumptions that made someone a conservative partisan in the culture wars was the idea that American culture was in decline. Throughout the twentieth century, most American conservatives, especially those with a Christian fundamentalist theological bent, located the origins of American cultural decay in Darwinism, biblical criticism, and other nineteenth-century harbingers of secularism. Neoconservatives, in contrast, believed the decline resulted from much more recent phenomena. For instance, Gertrude Himmelfarb, the eminent historian of Victorian Britain, fashioned a convincing declension narrative that, although eclectic, nicely demonstrated how neoconservatives set their moral vision apart from all that the sixties had come to signify. Himmelfarb argued that sheathed in Victorian virtues, Western culture had weathered the storms of modernity— that is, until the sixties. It was only during and after that landmark decade that the moral certainties of the Victorian mind were destroyed by a countercultural ethos that had gone mainstream.[3]

Himmelfarb's declension narrative was one example of the many ways in which neoconservatives endowed the conservative movement with a more contemporary framework with which to engage the culture wars. Himmelfarb's husband, Irving Kristol—"the godfather of neoconservatism," and one of the few who actually embraced the label for himself—argued that neoconservatism was tasked with converting "the Republican party, and American conservatism in general, against their respective wills, into a new kind of conservative politics suitable to governing a modern democracy." Although Kristol overstated the larger significance of the movement he helped found, his assessment was precise with regard to the particular role neoconservatism played in setting the terms of the culture wars.[4]

Neoconservatism was the New Left's chief ideological opponent. In assuming such a duty, neoconservatives set themselves up for a hostile response. Fortunately for them, their prior experiences had prepared them well for the task. Many of the early neoconservatives were members of "the family," Murray Kempton's apt designation for that disputatious tribe otherwise known as the New York intellectuals. They had come of age in the 1930s at the City College of New York (CCNY), a common destination for smart working-class Jews who otherwise might have attended Ivy League schools, where quotas prohibited much Jewish enrollment until after World War II. Himmelfarb, Kristol, and their milieu learned the art of polemics during years spent in the CCNY cafeteria's celebrated Alcove No. 1, where young Trotskyists waged ideological warfare against the communist students who occupied Alcove No. 2. During their flirtations with Trotskyism in the 1930s, when tussles with other radical students seemed like a

matter of life and death, future neoconservatives developed habits of
mind that never atrophied. They held on to their combative spirits,
their fondness for sweeping declarations, and their suspicion of leftist dogma. Moreover, long after they had eschewed political Marxism, they maintained the analytical Marxist tendency for diagnosing
problems in relation to root causes, internal logics, and overarching
structures. New York intellectuals espoused a universal understanding
of the world and believed that any problem, no matter how provincial, should be related to larger forces. Such an epistemological background endowed neoconservatives with what seemed like an intuitive
capacity for critiquing New Left arguments. They were uniquely qualified for the job of translating New Left discourses for a conservative
movement fervent in its desire to know its enemy.[5]

Whereas for many neoconservatives confronting the New Left was
a chore that often resulted in broken friendships, for Irving Kristol
such activity seemed more pleasurable than burdensome. Kristol had
expunged any residual affection he had for radical politics long before revolution came back into fashion in the sixties. In 1947 he joined
the staff at *Commentary*, a little magazine published by the American
Jewish Committee that professed a sophisticated brand of anticommunism. As a quintessential Cold War liberal from the moment when
Winston Churchill announced that an "iron curtain" had descended
upon Europe, Kristol fit in well writing for *Commentary*. In 1953 he
moved to London, where he helped Stephen Spender found *Encounter*, the literary organ of the Congress for Cultural Freedom. The congress was charged with showing how capitalist nations were more
hospitable to cultural innovation than communist societies. Beyond
aiding in that mission, *Encounter* also sought to extinguish the inclination to remain neutral in the Cold War—an inclination that lingered in
the minds of many Western European intellectuals.[6]

In 1966 both the New Left magazine *Ramparts* and the *New York
Times* reported that the Central Intelligence Agency (CIA) had subsidized *Encounter* for many years, including during the entirety of Kristol's tenure, which lasted until 1958. In response to these revelations,
historian Christopher Lasch, at that time a favorite of the New Left,
famously assailed Kristol and his fellow Cold War liberals for demonstrating "an unshakable faith in the good intentions of the American
government." In Lasch's view, since intellectuals had a responsibility
to remain independent, those who took bribes from the government

lost credibility. Diana Trilling, a literary critic for *Encounter*, admitted that she and her colleagues had suspected that the CIA funded their endeavors. Kristol never conceded as much. But whether or not he was aware of CIA largesse, it is doubtful that such sponsorship shaped his editorial guidance. Even prior to editing *Encounter*, Kristol was a stringent anticommunist. The Cold War revealed that anti-Stalinist leftists like Kristol were typically more anti-Stalinist than leftist. Kristol's anticommunism ran so deep that he publicly defended the pugnacious Joe McCarthy—a breach of Cold War liberalism's avowedly moderate style. "There is one thing the American people know about Senator McCarthy," Kristol wrote. "He, like them, is unequivocally anti-Communist. About the spokesmen for American liberalism, they feel they know no such thing."[7]

In 1965 Kristol started a new journal along with his fellow New York intellectual and former Alcove No. 1 comrade the sociologist Daniel Bell. Originally Kristol and Bell sought to position their journal above the ideological fray. This was made clear by its title, *The Public Interest*, which derived from a telling Walter Lippmann passage: "The public interest may be presumed to be what men would choose if they saw clearly, thought rationally, acted disinterestedly and benevolently." Such intentions were consistent with Cold War liberalism's obsession with consensus, pluralism, and technical expertise, a zeitgeist that found its apotheosis in Bell's 1960 book *The End of Ideology: On the Exhaustion of Political Ideas in the Fifties*. According to these so-called pluralist thinkers who dominated American social thought during the 1950s, the era of encrusted ideologies, whether expressed from the Left or from the Right, had been rendered outmoded by the age of affluence. Government by scientific experimentation was the new order. President John F. Kennedy certified this technocratic ethos in a 1962 speech in which he declared that the nation's problems were merely "technical and administrative" and, as such, "do not lend themselves to the great sort of passionate movements which have stirred this country so often in the past."[8]

Although *The Public Interest* started in the technocratic mode, the journal quickly became more renowned for its profound skepticism regarding the merits of liberal reform. In fact, *The Public Interest* was instrumental in undermining the liberal idea that government policy could solve problems related to racism and poverty. It consistently featured influential scholars who considered such notions naive and ultimately dangerous in their proclivity to make things worse. Kristol, who had showed early signs of pessimism about liberal reform, led the magazine's charge in this direction. Although throughout most of the sixties he claimed to support a generous welfare system for poor Americans, the title of a *Harper's* piece he wrote in 1963 — "Is the Welfare State Obsolete?"—testified to his latent suspicions. In 1971 Kristol conveyed his misgivings more explicitly in an unfavorable *Atlantic* review of Frances Fox Piven and Richard Cloward's "crude" and "quasi-Marxist" book *Regulating the Poor: The Function of Public Welfare.* Whereas Piven and Cloward contended that poor people deserved welfare benefits that were more generous and came with fewer strings attached, Kristol believed that welfare had become "a vicious circle in which the best of intentions merge into the worst of results." Anticipating a slew of later conservative welfare critics, Kristol argued that a more generous welfare system would create more dependency. Such logic had prevailed in *The Public Interest* as early as 1966, when frequent contributor Earl Raab wrote an article critical of President Lyndon Johnson's "war on poverty," a key piece in Johnson's larger efforts to create a Great Society. Raab contended that government efforts to supplement the incomes of people capable of working would "pin a badge of inferior social status upon them"— one example of the many ways in which the nascent neoconservative journal highlighted the unintended consequences of liberal reform.[9]

Even though Kristol acknowledged in 1963 that he considered some aspects of the Democratic Party's efforts to expand the welfare state dubious, his allegiance to the party of Cold War liberalism persisted through 1968, when he voted for Democratic presidential nominee Hubert Humphrey. But a mere two years later Kristol was dining at the White House with Nixon, the two men brought together by their shared hatred of the New Left. According to the *New York Times*, which reported on the Nixon-Kristol dinner as part of a story on the administration's intensification of surveillance measures in the wake of New Left bombings, Kristol agreed with Nixon's crackdown, comparing "young, middle-class, white Americans who are resorting to violence" to the privileged Russian Narodniki who murdered Czar Alexander.[10]

In 1972 Kristol joined forty-five intellectuals, including Himmelfarb and several other incipient neoconservatives, in signing a full-page advertisement that ran in the *New York Times* just prior to Nixon's landslide defeat of George McGovern. "Of the two major candidates for the Presidency of the United States," the signatories declared, "we believe that Richard Nixon has demonstrated superior capacity for prudent and responsible leadership." Kristol and his colleagues might have remained Democrats in 1972 had their only major point of contention been with the party's well-intended if ineffective welfare policies. They pulled the lever for Nixon rather because they believed the New Left, in the form of the "New Politics" movement that enabled the McGovern nomination, had captured the Democratic Party. Diana Trilling, who refused to sign the declaration, claimed the pro-Nixon advertisement marked the advent of the neoconservative movement. It was certainly no coincidence that 1972 was the year Kristol became both a fellow at the American Enterprise Institute and a columnist for the *Wall Street Journal*—the year Kristol, in sum, became a full-fledged member of the conservative movement.[11]

Although the McGovern nomination represented a breaking point for Kristol and many other Cold War liberals, their frustration with the increasing influence of the New Left had been bubbling toward the surface for years. The earliest flashpoint was the controversy that engulfed what became forever known as "the Moynihan Report." Daniel Patrick Moynihan, an urban sociologist who regularly contributed to *The Public Interest* and who went on to a long career in politics that culminated in a twenty-four-year tenure in the US Senate, wrote a polarizing paper in 1965 while serving as assistant secretary of labor in the Johnson administration. In his controversial report, officially titled *The Negro Family: The Case for National Action*, Moynihan argued that the equal rights won by blacks in the legal realm—fruits born of the civil rights movement—brought newfound expectations of equal results. But achieving equal results would prove more difficult because blacks lacked the cultural conditioning necessary to compete with whites, an analytical framework Moynihan gleaned from the Chicago school of sociology that had dominated the discipline since the Progressive Era. University of Chicago sociologists explained urban black poverty as the result of "social disorganization" produced by the cultural lag that black migrants from the rural South suffered upon moving to northern cities. Since poverty stemmed from culturally conditioned behavior, their solution was to acclimatize black migrants to modern industrial habits. For hard-boiled skeptics like Moynihan, the idea that culture impeded liberal reform efforts was an illuminating lens through which to view black poverty.[12]

The most contentious aspect of the Moynihan Report was its focus on how differences in family structure isolated African Americans from the rest of the nation. "The fundamental problem," Moynihan argued, "is that the Negro family in the urban ghettos is crumbling." Moynihan was cagey on what came first: family disintegration or poverty. In the first place, he thought family instability "the fundamental source of the weakness of the Negro community at the present time" and considered ghetto culture a "tangle of pathology," dysfunctional in ways unique to black culture. The cause of such dysfunction, Moynihan argued, was that the black family tended to be matriarchal, a pattern that dated back to slavery. This, he believed, put blacks in a distinct disadvantage because male breadwinners were the source of American family stability. But despite this accentuation of the culture of poverty, Moynihan concluded his report with a call to expand jobs programs, since the black family could be made solvent only if black men had decently paying jobs. This "case for national action" made its way into Lyndon Johnson's signature speech at Howard University on June 4, 1965—cowritten by Moynihan—in which the president proclaimed that he sought "not just equality as a right and a theory but equality as a fact and as a result."[13]

The Moynihan Report quickly became a national sensation. In part this was due to the violent race riot that exploded in Watts that summer: Moynihan's theory was the conventional explanation for why blacks revolted so angrily even after passage of the Civil Rights and Voting Rights Acts. The *Wall Street Journal* spelled out Watts in an article inspired by the Moynihan Report, titled "Family Life Breakdown in Negro Slums Sows Seeds of Race Violence—Husbandless Homes Spawn Young Hoodlums, Impede Reforms, Sociologists Say." Beyond this mindless echo, though, reactions to the Moynihan Report were diverse. A self-described "disgusted taxpayer" from Louisiana sent a caustic letter to Moynihan that encapsulated the racist response: "People like you make me sick. You go to school most of your life and have a lot of book learning but you know as much about the Negro as I know about Eskimos. There has never been a Negro family to deteriorate, that is, not a family as white people know a family." Moynihan expected such bitterness from Jim Crow apologists. But he was

caught him off guard when a host of civil rights leaders and intellectuals denounced the report's gratuitous emphasis on black pathology,
worrying that it would be used as justification for limiting the scope
of reform. Writing in the *New York Review of Books*, Christopher
Jencks critiqued Moynihan's "guiding assumption that social pathology is caused less by basic defects in the social system than by defects
in particular individuals and groups which prevent their adjusting to
the system. The prescription is therefore to change the deviance, not
the system."[14]

Thanks to this public squabble, the Moynihan Report instigated a
national conversation about whether expanding the welfare state was
the solution to the problems of poverty and race—the same conversation being conducted in the more exclusive pages of *The Public Interest*. As with most burgeoning neoconservatives, Moynihan's position
on this issue was in rapid flux. When he wrote his report in 1965, he
argued that rates of illegitimacy among blacks, one of several pathologies that concerned him, paralleled levels of black unemployment.
That was why Moynihan concluded the report with an argument for
a jobs program. But a few years after Moynihan wrote his report, an
even greater number of black families were receiving welfare, and to
make matters worse, black illegitimacy continued to spike in spite of
the fact that black unemployment rates had improved significantly.
These counterintuitive factors helped convince Moynihan that government action alone could not improve the lives of poor blacks.[15]

Owing in part to the ideological success of the sixties liberation
movements, especially Black Power, a large number of critics sharply
rejected the logic that undergirded much of the Moynihan Report. In
particular, Moynihan's left-leaning detractors dismissed the conceit
that African American culture was a distorted version of white American culture. They also repudiated the corollary assumption that assimilation to prescribed norms—to normative America—was the only
path to equality. In his bitter takedown of the Moynihan Report, William Ryan, a psychologist and civil rights activist, coined the phrase
"blaming the victim" for what he described as Moynihan's act of "jus-
tifying inequality by finding defects in the victims of inequality." Just
as Black Power theorists Stokely Carmichael and Charles Hamilton
explained racial inequality in institutional terms, Ryan emphasized
how the American social structure favored whites over blacks. The
behavior of poor blacks, whether actually dysfunctional or not—and

Ryan raised concerns about the validity of this claim—was nothing more than a red herring.[16]

Moynihan's shift from liberalism to neoconservatism, perhaps more than that of anyone else who traveled these grounds, was partially due to the personal anguish he suffered when his left-leaning critics accused him of "blaming the victim," a polite way of calling him a racist. "I had spent much of my adult life working for racial equality," Moynihan later reflected, "had helped put together the antipoverty program, had set the theme and written the first draft of President Johnson's address at Howard University, which he was to describe as the finest civil rights speech he ever gave, only to find myself suddenly a symbol of reaction." In his 1967 article describing the fallout, Moynihan concluded that honest debate about race and poverty was no longer possible. "The time when white men, whatever their motives, could tell Negroes what was or was not good for them, is now definitely and decidedly over. An era of bad manners is certainly begun."[17]

From Moynihan's perspective, the failure of the Left to address the causes of urban disorder meant that it had become "necessary," as he told an audience of stalwart Cold War liberals in 1967, "to seek out and make much more effective alliances with political conservatives." Heeding his own advice, Moynihan accepted Nixon's invitation to join his cabinet in 1969 as the counselor to the president on urban affairs. During his time working for Nixon, Moynihan wrote several unusually candid memorandums to the president. One such 1970 memo, "A General Assessment of the Position of the Negroes," made Moynihan the subject of yet another racial controversy after it was leaked to the press. In the memo Moynihan conveyed his long-standing concern that blacks were behaving in increasingly antisocial ways. "Apart from white racial attitudes," he argued, the biggest problem afflicting black Americans was that they "injure one another." "The time may have come when the issue of race could benefit from a period of benign neglect." Critics hammered Moynihan for this "benign neglect" phrase—an epithet used thereafter to tar Moynihan as a racist—while ignoring the larger context of the argument. Even though he had grown skeptical of government reform, Moynihan did not oppose all measures to improve black urban living conditions. Rather, he merely wanted to scale back racial rhetoric, whether it came from Black Power leaders like Carmichael or from inflammatory conservatives like Vice President Spiro Agnew. "The forum has been too much

taken over by hysterics, paranoids and boodlers on all sides," Moynihan declared.[18]

The response to Moynihan's analysis of race convinced neoconservatives that most American liberals were unwilling to fight the battles
that would ensure the survival of an orderly society. Later in 1970, in
another memorandum written for Nixon's benefit, Moynihan warned
about the grave threat posed by the "collapse of traditional values."
He implied that the moral anarchy besetting the nation encouraged
the chaos plaguing its cities. He advised Nixon that beyond expecting
support from the "silent majority" responsive to his calls for "law and
order," the president should foster an alliance with the group of not-
so-silent formerly liberal intellectuals who wrote for *The Public Interest*. These thinkers, Moynihan contended, supported Nixon's efforts
to crack down on the "avowed revolutionaries" who sowed disorder in
the land. Among such intellectuals "there is an increased perception
of how fragile and vulnerable a free society is, and how much care is
needed to preserve it."[19]

Included among the prominent intellectuals whom Moynihan
counted as Nixon's allies was Norman Podhoretz, the longtime editor of *Commentary*, another magazine crucial to the formation of the
neoconservative persuasion. Like Kristol and the other New York intellectuals, Podhoretz grew up in Brooklyn, raised by working-class
Jewish immigrants. In contrast, however, Podhoretz had attended
Columbia University. Ten years Kristol's junior, he was among the first
generation of working-class Jews admitted to Ivy League schools in
the years immediately following World War II. After being mentored
at Columbia by Lionel Trilling, Podhoretz took a graduate degree in
literary criticism at Oxford. But he spent most of the 1950s, aside from
a brief stint in the Army, rapidly ascending the ranks of the New York
intellectual hierarchy. A prodigy of sorts, in 1960 he was named chief
editor at *Commentary*, a position he held until 1995. Under Podhoretz's editorial prowess, the little Jewish publication quickly became
one of the most exciting and, eventually, influential magazines in the
United States.

In the 1970s Podhoretz joined Kristol as a leading light of the conservative intellectual movement. But to reach this final destination
the two traveled somewhat different roads. Unlike the Alcove No. 1
generation, Podhoretz was never a Trotskyist. He positioned himself
as a Cold War liberal throughout most of the 1950s, but in contrast

with the focus of the former Trotskyists, anticommunism was not yet his chief concern at that time. Perhaps for this reason, Podhoretz was more open to the New Left ideas that cropped up in the early sixties. After he took over the editor position at *Commentary*, Podhoretz's first move was to publish Paul Goodman's *Growing Up Absurd* in three parts. Signaling the direction the magazine would take during the sixties, Podhoretz also showcased prototypical New Left writers such as Norman Brown and Norman Mailer, the latter of whom Podhoretz considered a close friend, at least for a short time. Podhoretz claimed he was never a New Leftist. But at the very least he was a fellow traveler, made evident not only by those whom he consorted with and published but also by his *Commentary* editorials. In one such essay he charged Lyndon Johnson with manufacturing the Gulf of Tonkin crisis.[20]

Like Moynihan's, Podhoretz's break with the Left was motivated in part by personal factors. And like Kristol, Podhoretz gave off early signals that such a break was coming. In 1963 he wrote an essay for *Commentary*, "My Negro Problem—and Ours," that generated buzz among the literati for its honest admission that most whites, even liberals, were "twisted and sick in their feelings about Negroes." In a conversation with James Baldwin, who convinced Podhoretz to write "My Negro Problem," Podhoretz said he had grown weary of black arguments for special treatment, given that Jews never received such treatment and yet had managed to overcome past discrimination. He pointed to his childhood memories of the black children in his Brooklyn neighborhood: rather than focus on their studies as he and his Jewish friends did, they roamed the streets terrorizing Podhoretz and the other white children. In writing this piece, Podhoretz claimed his intention was merely to demonstrate the difficulties presented by racial integration. But plenty of readers interpreted it differently. Stokely Carmichael, never one to mince words, proclaimed Podhoretz, simply, a "racist."[21]

A few years later, Podhoretz was once again embroiled in a literary dustup with the publication of *Making It*, his 1967 confessional memoir that arguably stands as his most lasting literary accomplishment. In that book Podhoretz argued "that it is impossible to grow up in America without believing that the goal of life is to be a Success." More contentiously, he wrote that "it's also impossible to grow up in America without believing that Success requires, and bespeaks, a radical corruption of the spirit." *Making It*, in short, shined a light on the dirty little secret of the New York intellectuals: ambition, more than attention to higher aesthetic principles, is what gained them their prominence. Although Podhoretz's depiction of striving intellectuals was mostly autobiographical, and although he had come to believe that ambition was necessary, perhaps even good, those New York intellectuals whom he implicated, whether by name or by insinuation, reacted angrily. Mailer's biting review of *Making It*, for instance, felt to Podhoretz like "an act of fratricide." In a 1969 interview, Podhoretz attributed this hostile response to the book's argument that "it is possible to live a reasonably decent life and maintain one's moral, intellectual and spiritual integrity within American society without becoming a revolutionary." Such an idea, at that time, was "a kind of blasphemy."[22]

In the aftermath of *Making It*, Podhoretz distanced himself from New York intellectual life, where he had become persona non grata. He even took a hiatus from *Commentary*. During this interlude, he had what he later described in religious terms as a conversion experience. By the time he returned to his editorial desk in 1970, Podhoretz was an unapologetic neoconservative. He earnestly commenced an ideological offensive against the New Left, the counterculture, and all that he deemed subversive about the sixties. In one of his first postconversion editorials, Podhoretz argued that the lesson to learn from the sixties was that heady political optimism was more damaging than the pessimism that had pervaded the 1950s. He also rationalized his own political peregrinations by claiming that he and the New York intellectuals arrived at their various positions, including radicalism, "via the route of ideas," as opposed to most New Leftists, who followed "the route of personal grievance." Podhoretz and the neoconservatives assumed that their political cues were abstract, impersonal, and objective. In contrast, New Leftists — student radicals, feminists, and black militants — responded to a set of particular, personal, and subjective signals.[23]

Podhoretz thought that nothing less than the soul of America was at stake in his campaign to stamp out the New Left's undue influence. Kristol similarly believed that he was living in a dangerous moment: every question, no matter how small, demanded large answers; every debate, no matter how provincial, appealed to fundamental beliefs. Kristol used the occasion of a 1970 *Commentary* piece, "Urban

Civilization and Its Discontents," nominally about the unrest spreading like wildfire across America's cities, to score a much larger point.
He reasoned that if the American citizenry "behaved like a bourgeois
urban mob" it was because the countercultural belief system lacked
the qualities of republican self-rule: "steadiness of character, delib-
erativeness of mind, and a mild predisposition to subordinate one's
own special interests to the public interest." Kristol's elegy for small-*r*
republican virtues, in other words, doubled as a brief against the countercultural mores that had prevailed in much of the culture. The counterculture, he believed, was doing what it could to destroy the Protestant work ethic that buttressed the democratic social order. Charles
Reich's "Consciousness III," alive and well, threatened the nation that
neoconservatives had come to love.[24]

"If there is any one thing that neoconservatives are unanimous
about," Kristol wrote, "it is their dislike of the 'counterculture' that
has played so remarkable a role in American life over these past fifteen years." This was certainly true for Podhoretz, whose break with
the New Left liberated him to explore his long-standing yet latent distaste for countercultural values, first revealed in 1958, when he wrote
a scathing *Partisan Review* essay on the Beats titled "The Know-
Nothing Bohemians." The young Podhoretz thought "the Beat generation's worship of primitivism and spontaneity" bespoke a dangerous
irrationalism; the Beats' tortured grammar implied a secret desire to
"kill those incomprehensible characters who are capable of getting seriously involved with a woman, a job, a cause." Even as early as 1958,
Podhoretz worried about the pernicious effects of an antinomianism
that scorned traditional American commitments. Such concerns grew
by leaps and bounds after he moved to the political Right.[25]

By the early 1970s, Podhoretz had declared ideological war against
those who had taken up the cause of the Beats, those New Leftists and
counterculture enthusiasts who cast middle-class American values "in
terms that are drenched in an arrogant contempt for the lives of millions and millions of people." "Are they not expressing," Podhoretz
asked, "the yearning *not* to be Americans?" He and his fellow neoconservatives were unable to sympathize with people who hated a country that had given them so much opportunity. Where else could Jews
from working-class backgrounds achieve so much, they wondered. In
seeking to explain an attitude that seemed to them almost inexplica-
ble, the neoconservatives developed a persuasive theory about a "new

class" of powerful people whose collective interests were inimical to traditional America. They innovated this theory by reworking an older Soviet dissident discourse founded by nineteenth-century anarchist Mikhail Bakunin, whom the anti-Stalinist Left deemed a prophet for anticipating that Marx's "dictatorship of the proletariat" would devolve into "the most distressing, offensive, and despicable type of government in the world." "New class" thought gained a larger audience in the United States after the publication of Yugoslav dissenter Milovan Djilas's 1957 book *The New Class*, which postulated that the communist elite gained power through the acquisition of knowledge as opposed to the acquisition of property.[26]

Neoconservatives, many of them former anti-Stalinist leftists, found the "new class" thought that migrated from the communist world compelling. However, more central to their analysis of an American "new class" was Lionel Trilling's famous examination of the avant-garde revolt against bourgeois society, what Trilling termed the "adversary culture." Modernist artists had long challenged conventional bourgeois norms. Such an adversarial attitude, Trilling noted, was the very premise upon which modernism was founded. But for most of its history, modernism found refuge from philistinism in the protective enclaves of bohemia. Modernists did not originally attempt to convert bourgeois society; rather, they walled themselves off from it. By the sixties, however, bohemia had come to the masses; the adversary culture had slipped into the mainstream of traditional American culture. Trilling's theory about the popularization of "the adversary culture"—an appellation that came to be used interchangeably with "the new class"—was a powerful tool for understanding the anti-American turn taken by those in academia, media, fine arts, foundations, and even some realms of government, such as the social welfare and regulatory agencies. It also came to be the default neoconservative explanation for the culture wars that grew out of that polarizing decade. A 1970 Moynihan memo to Nixon exemplified this framework: "No doubt there is a struggle going on in this country of the kind the Germans used to call a *Kulturkampf*. The adversary culture which dominates almost all channels of information transfer and opinion formation has never been stronger, and as best I can tell it has come near silencing the representatives of traditional America."[27]

Neoconservatives, of course, were not the first Americans to verbally assault intellectuals. As Richard Hofstadter's Pulitzer Prize–

winning 1964 book *Anti-intellectualism in American Life* made abundantly clear, animosity directed at intellectuals was not new. Indeed, the ambiguous "new class" bore some resemblance to the equally amorphous "liberal establishment" scorned by the likes of Joe McCarthy. By the postwar period, a growing number of conservative intellectuals, led by William Buckley Jr., founding editor of *National Review*, coalesced to form what Sidney Blumenthal called a "counter-establishment." Buckley and his fellow counterintellectuals had made a career of lambasting intellectuals well before Kristol and Podhoretz took their fateful turns to the Right. Buckley's 1950 treatise against Yale professors, *God and Man at Yale*, was a lamentation over professors who subverted the curriculum to their "secularist and collectivist" ends. Buckley, ever the humorist, peppered his essays with delightful anti-intellectual ripostes. "I'd rather entrust the government of the United States," he famously quipped, "to the first 400 people listed in the Boston telephone directory than to the faculty of Harvard University."[28]

Where "new class" thought differed from previous strains of conservative anti-intellectualism was in how neoconservatives formulated it specifically to the task of understanding the New Left. Intellectuals of the older Right, in contrast, never worked to get inside the mind of the New Left. More commonly they understood the New Left simply as liberalism followed to its logical conclusion. Russell Kirk, the regular education columnist for *National Review* and founder of the traditionalist journal *Modern Age*, even admitted to feelings of schadenfreude when New Leftists angrily confronted the liberals who oversaw "what is foolishly called the higher learning in America." Kirk understood the New Left's attempt to seize control of the university as behavior consistent with the reigning liberal philosophy of John Dewey—a philosophy Kirk had spent the better part of his life criticizing. As he wrote in 1955: "The pursuit of power and the gratification of concupiscence are the logical occupations of rational man in a world that is merely human and merely natural." Kirk did not seek to separate New Left thought from the relativistic liberalism that preceded it because, shorn of God, neither was redeemable; neither liberals nor their close cousins on the New Left could abstain from the pursuit of human power without the traditional constraints imposed by religiously ordered hierarchy.[29]

Unlike traditionalist conservative thinkers who conflated liberal-

ism with the New Left, neoconservatives believed the New Left had
infected the liberal intellectual culture they loved. That they detected
such a change was one of the central reasons for their political conversion; it was one of the primary reasons neoconservatives proved
so useful to the modern American conservative movement. Thus the
texture of post-sixties anti-intellectualism was best revealed in neoconservative writings, even in fiction. In the 1969 novel *Mr. Sammler's
Planet*—the neoconservative novel par excellence—Saul Bellow drew
a picture of the "new class" type distinct from older anti-intellectual
caricatures. In the opening scene, Artur Sammler complains that "intellectual man has become an explaining creature. Fathers to children,
wives to husbands, lecturers to listeners, experts to laymen, colleagues
to colleagues, doctors to patients, man to his own soul explained."
Despite being an explainer himself, Sammler is alienated because he
believes that most explanation contradicts the "natural knowledge"
innate to the human soul. Having fun with Hegel's "Owl of Minerva,"
which takes flight only at dusk—a reference to Hegel's allegory about
philosophy being revealed only after phenomena—Sammler says that
the soul rests "unhappily on superstructures of explanation, poor bird,
not knowing which way to fly." Bemoaning that intellectuals increasingly dedicated their work to rationalizing bad behavior, Sammler offers a thinly veiled critique of the sixties liberation ethos: "The labor of
Puritanism was now ending, the dark satanic mills changing into light
satanic mills. The reprobates converted into children of joy, the sexual
ways of the seraglio and of the Congo bush adopted by the emanci-
pated masses of New York, Amsterdam, London."[30]

By siding against contemporary intellectual mores, Bellow and the
neoconservatives aligned with the more authentic sensibilities of average Americans. In other words, the neoconservative mind was the
intellectualization of the white working-class ethos. As a *Commentary* writer put it: "Three workingmen discoursing of public affairs
in a bar may perhaps display more clarity, shrewdness, and common
sense" than a representative of the "new class" with his "heavy disqui-
sitions." In this way neoconservatives elaborated on the crude conservative populism of George Wallace's presidential campaigns. They
gave theoretical expression to Spiro Agnew's colloquial eviscerations
of the "nattering nabobs of negativity." Most important, they helped
make sense of the seemingly incongruous fact that some of nation's
most privileged citizens doubled as its most adversarial. These were

the people the Catholic intellectual and budding neoconservative Michael Novak labeled the "Know-Everythings": "affluent professionals, secular in their values and tastes and initiatives, indifferent to or hostile to the family, equipped with postgraduate degrees and economic security and cultural power."[31]

It should be noted that "new class" thought was often a tool better suited to neoconservative polemics than to accurate analysis. In a series of "portraits of familiar character-types" that she wrote for *Commentary* in the early 1970s, Dorothy Rabinowitz constructed caricatures of the "new class" built on a flimsy edifice of psychological reductionism. For example, Rabinowitz's "radicalized professor" got that way because he felt the sting of status anxiety: his chosen profession did not accrue the social rewards he believed himself entitled to. Such resentment was then transferred into sympathy for "black and Third World people" and others with better cause to be resentful. Rabinowitz mocked the radical professor's inability to distinguish right from wrong in even the most basic duties required of his job. "Asked to select the most exciting literature he knows for introductory college courses," she decried, "he selects black literature. (He is excited that black people can actually write books.) The anonymous backwash of a vast Western literature never excited him as much." Rabinowitz lampooned "new class" professors for replacing the timeless classics of Western civilization with au courant literature—works she deemed noteworthy not for their excellence but only as proof of the radicalized professor's irreverence.[32]

Polemics against the "new class" reached even greater levels of hyperbole when the subject was the left turn taken in the sixties by the *New York Review of Books*. That particular magazine annoyed neoconservatives not only because it had become a vehicle of "anti-Americanism"—making it all the more necessary for *Commentary* to become an instrument, in Podhoretz's words, of "anti-anti-Americanism"—but also because it was read much more widely than their magazines. The *New York Review*'s stable of writers indeed included some of the most scathing critics of the United States, such as Noam Chomsky, Christopher Lasch, Mary McCarthy, and I. F. Stone. The cover of the August 1967 issue, published in the wake of the massive riots that brought death and destruction to the streets of Detroit and Newark, featured an infamous diagram of how to manufacture a Molotov cocktail. In that issue, Andrew Kopkind compared Martin Luther King Jr.'s nonviolent philosophy unfavorably to Malcolm X's and Frantz Fanon's more violent theories of revolution, writing: "Morality, like politics, starts at the barrel of a gun." A *Commentary* reviewer described that line as "perhaps the most offensive and offending sentence ever to have appear in *The New York Review*."[33]

Beyond its polemical uses, "new class" theorizing was believable because it was grounded in plausible sociology. Take academics as a case study. By the sixties, the university credential system had become the principal gateway to the professional world, a sorting mechanism for white-collar hierarchy. In this sense, class resentment aimed at academics made sense, in a misplaced sort of way, since they indeed held the levers to any given individual's future economic success. The number of faculty members in the United States increased from 48,000 in 1920 to over 600,000 in 1972. As this growing legion of academics tended to lean left in their politics, particularly in the humanities and the social sciences, where debates about the promise of America framed the curriculum, Podhoretz's claim that "millions upon millions of young people began to be exposed to—one might even say indoctrinated in—the adversary culture of the intellectuals" did not seem so exaggerated.[34]

The intellectual who best elaborated neoconservative anxieties about the trajectory of higher education was Nathan Glazer, another product of CCNY's Alcove No. 1. In 1964 Glazer took a position in the University of California sociology department. Teaching on the Berkeley campus perfectly positioned him to observe the radicalization of the student movement, from the 1964 Free Speech Movement to the antiwar movement of the later sixties. In 1969 Glazer argued that student protests menaced the freedoms that had historically thrived at universities. "The threat to free speech, free teaching, free research," Glazer warned, "comes from radical white students, from militant black students, and from their faculty defenders." Glazer was sympathetic to some of the causes championed by the students. He was critical of the Vietnam War from its outset. But Glazer believed the university should be spared their destructive wrath because it "embodies values that transcend the given characteristics of a society or the specific disasters of an administration." Glazer never became a full-blown neoconservative: unlike Kristol and Podhoretz, he continued voting Democratic. But the actions of campus radicals dissolved his reluctance to admit he had become more conservative. As Glazer wrote in a 1970 *Commentary* piece that explained his "deradicalization": "I argued from the start that the new tactics, the new violence of language, and the new joy in confrontation and political combat contained more of a threat to what remained valuable within the universities than a hope either of changing them or of changing public policy."[35]

For Glazer and the neoconservatives, the American university stood for all that they valued about American society: beyond being a forum for free inquiry, it was a meritocratic melting pot where smart people, even working-class Jews, could thrive. An attack on the university was an attack on them. For this reason, student uprisings arguably did more than any other issue to galvanize formerly liberal intellectuals against the New Left. A host of neoconservatives, including Glazer, Kristol, Bell, philosopher Sidney Hook, and sociologist Seymour Martin Lipset, wrote or edited books about "academic anarchy" and the "rebellion in the university." In his 1968 Columbia University commencement speech, given minutes after several hundred radical students staged a walkout, Richard Hofstadter preached that "to imagine that the best way to change a social order is to start by assaulting its most accessible centers of thought and study and criticism is not only to show a complete disregard for the intrinsic character of the university but also to develop a curiously self-destructive strategy for social change." Political scientist James Q. Wilson took this argument a theoretical step further in a 1972 *Commentary* piece where he contended that higher education was digging liberalism's grave by being far too open to the adversary culture that had taken root in its hallowed halls. "Freedom cannot exist outside some system of order, yet no system of order is immune from intellectual assault." In issuing an ominous warning that "the bonds of civility upon which the maintenance of society depends are more fragile than we often admit," Wilson hinted that the United States manifested conditions precariously similar to those of Weimar Germany, a specious comparison that nonetheless became a neoconservative mantra.[36]

In his *Commentary* article Wilson listed a number of changes to higher education that he disliked, including the controversial "adoption of quota systems either to reduce the admissions of certain kinds of students or enhance the admissions of other kinds." Neoconservatives were the first and most vociferous critics of racial quotas, embraced by many universities in the sixties as a way to comply with President

Johnson's Executive Order 11246, which mandated that "equality as a fact" necessitated affirmative action. In 1968 political scientist John Bunzel authored a critical article for *The Public Interest* about the newly formed black studies program at San Francisco State College, where he taught. Bunzel worried that black studies would intensify the groupthink tendencies he believed were inherent to Black Power and other identity-based movements and that it would "would substitute propaganda for omission," "new myths for old lies." But to Bunzel, the worst idea put forward by black studies was that high standards codified racial discrimination and would therefore need to be revised or dumped altogether. This premise worked at two levels. First, black studies scholars believed that their knowledge must be created from scratch in order to undo the scholarly reproduction of racist norms. Thus they eschewed footnotes, peer review, and other traditional practices that, for Bunzel, ensured standards of scholarly excellence. Second, black studies advocates desired admission quotas in order to ensure that the majority of the students who majored in black studies were in fact black. Nathan Hare, the first director of the San Francisco State College program, even argued that college applicants should provide photos. "How else," he asked, "are we going to identify the blacks?" In response to this reasoning, Bunzel asked a question of his own, exemplary of the "colorblind" rhetoric that shaped the conservative critique of affirmative action: "Is color the test of competence?"[37]

Quotas were formative to neoconservative thought because they drove a wedge between Jews and blacks, an interethnic alliance that had helped cement the powerful New Deal coalition that had dominated Democratic and national politics since the 1930s. Of course neoconservatives typically made their case against quotas in nonethnic and nonracial terms. Podhoretz, speaking as an abstract American, contended that quotas fundamentally upended the "basic principle of the American system," that the individual is the primary "subject and object of all law, policy, and thought." Podhoretz's point willfully ignored that Jews merely ten years his senior, including Kristol, had been unable to attend Ivy League universities due to anti-Jewish quotas. Earl Raab offered a less timeless and more accurate defense of individual merit when he wrote that quotas reversed the American "ascendance of achieved status over ascribed status." But beyond appeals to broadly applicable concepts like individual merit, whether historically accurate or not, neoconservatives also made their case against quotas based on the particular interests of American Jews. In his 1968 article "The New Racialism," Moynihan, as a Catholic, addressed this issue in ways that his likeminded Jewish intellectual friends could not. "Let me be blunt," Moynihan stated. "If ethnic quotas are to be imposed on American universities and similarly quasipublic institutions, it is Jews who will be almost driven out. They are not three percent of the population." In other words, since the end of the older quota system that protected WASP privilege, Jews had made remarkable advances, especially in higher education and in the professions that required advanced degrees—advances disproportionate to their overall numbers. As a result, Moynihan and other neoconservatives reasoned that race- and ethnic-based policies, particularly proportional quotas, would only hurt Jews.[38]

Beyond fretting that quotas would limit the ability of Jews to improve their status, neoconservatives also worried that the very debate was raising the specter of anti-Semitism. As *Commentary* contributing editor Milton Himmelfarb worded it in 1969, "To hear some people talk these days, one would think that the merit principle is a Jewish conspiracy." Given that Jews were climbing the postwar American social ladder with remarkable speed, and given that such opportunities were supposedly granted to those who merited them—to those who mastered a set of seemingly objective standards—when Black Power theorists reduced such standards to expressions of institutional racism, people on both sides of the quotas debate drew sinister conclusions. "Jews have gotten to be identified as the quintessential Americans," Podhoretz noted. "The Jews have gotten to be thought of as the 'echt' (pure) bourgeoisie, the most American of the Americans, the most middle class of the middle class, the most suburban of the suburbans, the ones who've made it. If you hate the American middle class and you believe this is what Jews are, obviously you are going to think Jews stink." As was his style, Podhoretz overstated the case. Most Americans did not conflate American Jews with anything so specific as the middle class. Even in the sixties, when American political rhetoric was hotter than usual, anti-Semitism functioned much as it always had, consistent with historian Stephen Whitfield's befitting metaphor, "the dog that did not bark." However, given the polarizing teacher strikes that dominated New York City headlines at the end of the sixties—the Ocean Hill–Brownsville crisis that brought black-Jewish tensions to the surface with a vengeance—Podhoretz and the neoconservatives can be somewhat forgiven their embellishments about anti-Semitism.[39]

At the center of the Ocean Hill–Brownsville crisis was Albert Shanker, the longtime head of the New York City United Federation of Teachers (UFT) and the American Federation of Teachers (AFT), who would come to be considered a neoconservative despite being a lifelong unionist and social democrat. Shanker was arguably the most polarizing educational leader in US history, a fractious legacy evident in that he was both lampooned in Woody Allen's 1973 film *Sleeper*, as the man who blew up the world no less, and posthumously awarded the Medal of Freedom by President Bill Clinton. When Shanker infamously led the UFT out on three separate teachers' strikes in the fall of 1968, he was defending not only his union members but also a system of standards that he believed to be meritocratic. In this his actions were consistent with neoconservative arguments against quotas, at least those of the abstract kind. But the racial dynamics of the Ocean Hill–Brownsville crisis muddied the waters of Shanker's universalistic rationale. Shanker and many of the unionized teachers he worked for were Jewish; those who opposed them were either black or allies of the Black Power movement.[40]

In 1967 black citizens in the Ocean Hill–Brownsville neighborhood of Brooklyn, with political and financial support from a host of white liberals and New Leftists—including Mayor John Lindsay, Ford Foundation president McGeorge Bundy, Paul Goodman, and the editorial boards at the *New York Times* and the *New York Review of Books*— undertook a controversial experiment in community control of their schools. Ocean Hill–Brownsville activists, influenced by the Black Power theories of Malcolm X, Stokely Carmichael, Charles Hamilton, and Harold Cruse, believed their schools were failing largely because of the racism built into the city's educational institutions. Such institutional racism was evident not only in resource disparities, which had in fact been leveling as a result of increased federal support under the aegis of Johnson's Great Society. Ocean Hill–Brownsville organizers also pointed to the racism of the teaching force. In this they were not alone. Respected liberal psychologist Kenneth Clark, whose famous "doll study" influenced the Supreme Court's 1954 *Brown v. Board of Education* decision by demonstrating the damaging effects segregation had on the psyches of black children, wrote in his 1965 book *Dark Ghetto* that black children "are not being taught because those who are charged with the responsibility of teaching them do not believe that they can learn, do not expect that they can learn, and do not act towards them in ways which help them to learn." Even Shanker admitted that the UFT rank and file was racist to varying degrees. Given this, community controllers hired black teachers to replace predominantly white teachers on the grounds that unlike their white counterparts, they would not presume black students incapable of academic achievement.[41]

To Shanker and the union, whether or not black teachers would better serve black students was less important than the fact that community control infringed upon a collectively bargained contract whereby teachers were hired and promoted in accordance with a set of standardized tests they took at several points along their career. The better educators scored on these exams, the more job security they obtained and the quicker their careers advanced. The New York City teacher merit system, which Shanker and UFT members believed was objective and thus meritocratic, generally served whites well, especially Jews, who composed a majority of the union. But it often left black teachers behind. Thus as part of their community control prerogatives, Ocean Hill–Brownsville activists violated the terms of the UFT contract and fired several white teachers, replacing them with black teachers and nonunionized whites who were committed to the principles of community control. This move, predictably, brought down the wrath of the powerful and savvy Shanker, who, thanks to union solidarity, decisively defeated the Ocean Hill–Brownsville community controllers. When fifty-four thousand of the fifty-seven thousand teachers in New York City's public schools went on strike as a response to the Ocean Hill–Brownsville community board's decision to terminate unionized teachers, not once, not twice, but three times, Shanker and the UFT brought Mayor Lindsay to his knees. By 1970 black community control was dead in New York City.[42]

The Ocean Hill–Brownsville crisis shattered an affinity between Jews and blacks that had formed the bedrock of New York City's twentieth-century cosmopolitanism. Prior to the battle over community control, the official pedagogical approach of the UFT reflected the moderate cultural pluralism of Cold War liberalism best expressed by Glazer and Moynihan's celebrated 1963 book about ethnicity, *Beyond the Melting Pot: The Negroes, Puerto Ricans, Jews, Italians, and*

Irish of New York City. As opposed to the more coercive assimilationist strategies of earlier educators, pluralist teachers took their cues from Glazer and Moynihan, who theorized that ethnic consciousness was an enduring social form. The UFT gently nudged teachers to recognize ethnicity in their curricula, so long as they also taught students to value individual achievement and national cohesion. This Cold War liberal version of pluralism was softer than that promoted by Progressive Era pluralist thinkers like Herbert Croly, Randolph Bourne, Horace Kallen, and Alain Locke, who had militantly embraced ethnic diversity in the face of a repressive Americanism that Croly described as an "instinctive homogeneity." These earlier pluralists expected that the interests of various ethnic groups, even when incompatible, would, contrary to conventional wisdom about national unity, help preserve a durable national fabric insofar as there was strength in diversity. Cold War liberal pluralists like Glazer and Moynihan reversed this formula. They postulated that recognition of ethnic difference, no matter how enduring, was politically possible only under the umbrella of a muscular national identity.[43]

Ocean Hill–Brownsville community control activists failed to find value in pluralist pedagogies that conformed to a normative American identity. Reproducing good Americans was not their priority. During the short era of community control, one white social studies teacher was censured by the Ocean Hill–Brownsville board for instructing his students that moderation was the superior approach to race relations, a philosophy he transported into his classroom with leading discussion questions such as "Why is the key to peace and happiness found in observing moderation in things?" The biggest complaint Black Power activists leveled against the moderate pluralist curriculum was that it treated African American history similarly to the history of European ethnic groups, the implication being that if Irish, Italian, and Jewish Americans could thrive by overcoming discrimination, then so too could black Americans. Such dissonant racial interpretations left the two sides at an impasse. This, in turn, led to an uptick in incendiary rhetoric, some of which traded in ugly anti-Semitic stereotypes. One black teacher allegedly wrote a vile poem about Shanker: "Hey, Jew boy, with that yarmulke on your head, you pale-faced Jew boy, I wish you were dead." A letter addressed to the UFT "money changers" indicted them "for the serious educational retardation of our black

children." Though the letter went unsigned, Shanker distributed half
a million copies of it to help discredit the community control project,
a tactic that proved highly successful.[44]

Neoconservatives assumed the worst about the Black Power movement. When black militants began regularly citing Israel among the
colonial aggressor nations they opposed, neoconservatives believed
anti-Semitism was the motivating factor, seemingly confirmed by
Stokely Carmichael when he proclaimed, "The only good Zionist is
a dead Zionist." More confounding to neoconservatives was that so
many intellectuals abetted such prejudice. Glazer explained the apparent rise of anti-Semitism "as an element of the enraged nihilism
that so many white and Jewish intellectuals have encouraged and supported among blacks." Podhoretz maintained that intellectuals largely
supported community control, in spite of its unseemly elements, simply because they believed it was the morally superior position to take
on race relations. UFT officer Patrick Harnett, writing in *the Village
Voice*, argued that intellectuals of the "upper middle-class milieu" supported community control because race was an abstract issue to those
who lived "on Park Avenue" or in "Connecticut Shangri-La." "Everyone knows," Harnett wrote, with more than a touch of clever sarcasm,
"that the slave-owning Southern gentleman was less bigoted than the
non-slaveowning white." Whitney Young, president of the National
Urban League, reinforced the notion that pro–community control
intellectuals were class bigots when he argued that racism was more
common among the "affluent peasants" who made up the UFT, the
"lower- and middle-class whites who've just made it—who are a generation away from the WPA and welfare—people with middle-class
incomes but not undergirded by civilized views, by aesthetic, cultural
and educational experiences." Of course, class bias notwithstanding,
the debates over busing and crime that riddled national politics in the
early 1970s illustrated that Young's analysis included a few grains of
truth—or at least that the politics of race and class on display in the
Ocean Hill–Brownsville crisis were more perplexing than most contemporary observers realized.[45]

In 1972 another controversy involving public schooling in another
Brooklyn neighborhood made clear the shifting racial and ethnic parameters of post-sixties America. This time around, the section of
Brooklyn in question was Canarsie, a largely Jewish and Italian neighborhood just south of the majority black Ocean Hill–Brownsville. Ca-

narsie residents boycotted their public schools to protest desegregation. In an act of what historian Jonathan Rieder calls "deferred white vengeance for the New York school crisis of 1968," the UFT supported the actions of Canarsie residents, conveniently reversing the union's stance on community control. One Canarsie resident seethed at "the God-damned liberals" who "screamed along with the blacks in 1968 for community control. Now whites want what the blacks have," he continued, "and you say we can't have it." Where Ocean Hill–Brownsville organizers failed, Canarsie protestors succeeded. The city board of education caved to their demands and scrapped its plans to desegregate Canarsie schools. The drama of white Americans resisting desegregation was played out again and again in the 1970s in struggles over busing across the nation.[46]

Busing black students into white schools, and vice versa, had become the primary mechanism to desegregate schools by the late sixties. In 1971 the Supreme Court codified this tool with its *Swann v. Charlotte-Mecklenburg Board of Education* decision, ruling that federal courts were within their legal bounds to mandate busing. But whereas judges deemed busing a logical solution to an unconstitutional situation, the majority of the nation's white citizens, particularly those affected, considered it an unreasonable imposition. By the 1972 presidential election, *busing* had emerged as a catchword of American political rhetoric. Nixon in particular gained political advantage by staking an antibusing position, which, combined with the anticrime stance that had worked to his benefit since the 1968 campaign, allowed him to leverage new fissures in the Democratic Party. As Thomas and Mary Edsall argue, busing "fell like an axe through the Democratic Party, severing long-standing connections and creating a new set of troubled alliances: white, blue-collar northerners with southerners against blacks and upper-middle-class liberals." Antibusing in this way played an important role in forming the Silent Majority that handed Nixon such an enormous electoral majority over McGovern.[47]

Unsurprisingly, neoconservatives, who aligned with Nixon on most domestic issues, had a lot to say about busing. In a 1972 *Commentary* piece — "Is Busing Necessary?" — Glazer argued that integrated schools were a bad idea when race was the only consideration. "Integrating the hapless and generally lower-income whites of the central city with lower-income blacks, particularly under conditions of resentment and conflict," Glazer argued, "is likely to achieve nothing, in educational terms." Neoconservatives like Glazer added social scientific heft to the popular view that busing was just not worth the cost. They offered academic cover to politicians such as Nixon and his successor Gerald Ford, both of whom, unlike the more demagogic George Wallace, did not necessarily want to be lumped with any race-based backlashes taking place in places such as Canarsie and south Boston. The latter city experienced its own battle over busing in 1974 when white Catholics violently revolted against plans for their schools to be integrated with students from the nearby black neighborhood of Roxbury. Evidence-based arguments against busing afforded Nixon and Ford room to side with the reported 80 percent of Bostonians opposed to busing without having to seem aligned with those who hung inflammatory signs outside South Boston High School such as "Bus Them Back to Africa!" On this issue as with so many others, neoconservatives presented intellectual rationalizations for a white working class less and less sympathetic to liberal reforms, particularly those that seemed to benefit blacks at its expense.[48]

Crime was another issue that aligned the neoconservative imagination with white working-class sensibilities. Irving Kristol famously quipped that a neoconservative is "a liberal who has been mugged by reality." Given their tough-on-crime ethos, the quote would also have made sense in slightly abbreviated form: a neoconservative "is a liberal who has been mugged." James Q. Wilson did more than any other neoconservative—more than any other thinker—to translate anxieties about growing levels of crime into draconian policies adopted by both Republicans and Democrats. Just as Wilson argued that the openness of a liberal education would survive only if order was maintained on the nation's college campuses, he made the case that democracy would endure only in an orderly urban environment. And for that to happen, the liberals who dominated official thinking about the justice system needed to get honest about race and crime. "The fact that blacks commit a disproportionate share of certain crimes," he wrote, "led those who spoke for or about blacks in the 1960s either to deny the fact, to explain it as the result of a discriminatory police system, or to argue that blacks are driven to it by poverty and segregation."[49]

Wilson was correct that by the end of the sixties many liberals, and most New Leftists, believed that crime resulted from social factors inextricably linked to institutional racism. Thus the left-liberal solution to crime was to create a forgiving judicial system focused more on ameliorative forms of prevention than on punishment. Wilson pointed out that the left-liberal tendency to view crime as a consequence of a racist society was hugely unpopular with voters, who increasingly voted for politicians less hospitable to criminals. But Wilson also argued that the left-liberal approach was simply wrong, citing studies showing that beefed-up police forces and stricter sentencing were the only proven methods for successfully reducing crime. "Though continued improvements in prosperity and in ending discrimination may ultimately be the best remedies for crime," he conceded, "in the short term society's efforts must be aimed at improving the criminal justice system as a mechanism for just and effective social control." In other words, the grandiose abstractions of left-liberal criminology served to distract from implementing effective ways to fight crime, another of the many unintended consequences of leftism that neoconservatives like Wilson sought to highlight.[50]

That Wilson's policy prescriptions were relatively unsympathetic to the plight of black Americans—and that such recipes, when put into action by politicians bent on waging a "war on crime," predictably led to the mass incarceration of young black males—revealed a great deal about neoconservative racial attitudes. Yet far from being ugly racists on the order of Bull Connor, the Birmingham commissioner of public safety whose name became synonymous with the southern white defense of Jim Crow when he unleashed attack dogs and water cannons on nonviolent civil rights activists in 1963, urbane New York intellectuals frowned upon provincial bigotry. And yet the neoconservative belief that black Americans could overcome racism if only they would work hard—if only, in other words, they would heed the example of Jewish Americans—belied their cosmopolitan pretensions. Neoconservatives were blind to the enormously significant fact that black Americans, as historian David Hollinger writes, "are the only ethno-racial group to inherit a multicentury legacy of group-specific enslavement and extensive, institutionalized debasement under the ordinance of federal constitutional authority." Neoconservatives' obvious misreading of history quite possibly stemmed from the fact that they understood their own peculiar circumstances to be more universal than they in fact were. In this, neoconservatives viewed America through the lens of the typical assimilated immigrant, more learned, for sure, but still typical. As Jacob Heilbrunn argues more broadly about the neoconservative shift from Left to Right, the way to appreciate it "may be to focus on neoconservatism as an uneasy, controversial, and tempestuous drama of Jewish immigrant assimilation—a very American story."[51]

By moving discourse away from overt racism and toward a "color-blind" defense of individual merit—"Is color the test of competence?"—neoconservatives also pivoted away from Black Power–inflected discussions of institutional racism. In this neoconservative racial thought melded with microeconomic forms of social analysis that were gaining a foothold in academic and policy circles. Neoconservatives, in other words, turned the cultural radicalism of the New Left on its head by arguing that adversarial ideologies made for both bad culture and bad economics. They interpreted New Left movements as both hostile to traditional American values and dangerously anticapitalist. Neoconservatives tapped into a powerful American political language that separated those who earn their way from those who do not. During the Populist uprisings of the late nineteenth century, or during the great union drives of the 1930s, a rapacious corporate elite was assigned the role of leeches. Neoconservatives, in reverse, argued that the New Left—especially the Black Power movement—enabled a parasitic culture.

The idea that New Left sensibilities were dangerously anticapitalist also informed the neoconservative critique of women's and gay liberation. That neoconservatives leaned to the right on gender issues is hardly surprising given the highly charged masculine sphere inhabited by the New York intellectuals. But it is also paradoxical given that the neoconservative intellectual who wrote the most about gender issues, Podhoretz's wife Midge Decter, rejected notions that hers was a sexist world. Decter, born in 1927 and employed by various little magazines that dotted the New York intellectual landscape during the postwar years, claimed to have always been somewhat traditional on matters related to sex and family, despite divorcing her first husband relatively young. Her second husband Podhoretz's biographer writes: "Both Midge and Norman understood their 'gender' roles in what academics call 'essentialist' terms." Decter unleashed her "essentialist" or conservative gender politics in response to "women's liberation." She forcefully articulated her antifeminist views in two books, *The Liberated Woman and Other Americans*, published in 1971, and *The New Chastity and Other Arguments against Women's Liberation*, published the very next year. By doing so, Decter served notice that rather than enlisting in the war between the sexes, she was volunteering her services for the culture wars.[52]

Decter's overarching contention was that American women had it better than ever. For example, women had newfound abilities to secure gainful employment and control pregnancy through birth control. And yet, as she sought to show, even with such advances, or perhaps because of them, feminists blindly lurched against patriarchal strictures. Decter argued that women joined the women's liberation movement not out of a desire for new freedoms but rather out of fear that with brand-new freedoms came brand-new responsibilities. "Women's Liberation does not embody a new wave of demand for equal rights. Nor does its preoccupation with oppression signal a yearning for freedom," she complained. Rather, it emerged from "the difficulties women are experiencing with the rights and freedoms they already enjoy." For instance, if women were going to enter the workplace like men, Decter reasoned, they had to be prepared to compete in the cutthroat capitalist labor market that men had long grown accustomed to. In short, Decter believed that feminists were adversarial to the discipline enshrined in American traditions, such as the Protestant work ethic that the mostly Jewish neoconservatives came to adore.[53]

Decter's antifeminist analysis was a paradigmatic expression of neoconservative "new class" thought. She fretted that the feminist intellectual propensity to overtheorize "everyday life" experiences, such as "marriage, divorce, raising children, working for a living, getting old, and, lately above all, sex," created problems where none previously existed. As opposed to the feminists of the adversary culture, Decter believed it her mission to close the gap between the common, "natural" ways in which people experienced life and the contrived ways in which feminists overintellectualized experience. For Decter, as for all neoconservatives, the sixties warped the worldviews of the supposedly overindulged young women who hoisted the flags of women's liberation. "Above all, being a creature of the sixties rather than the fifties, [the young feminist] need not know that freedom is an end in itself, a value whose strongest connections are thus not with happiness but with responsibility." Decter continued: "[T]he freedom she truly seeks is of a rather different kind. It is a freedom demanded by children and enjoyed by no one: the freedom from all difficulty." Responsibility became a sacrosanct American tradition for Decter and her fellow neoconservatives. Their disdain for the "new class" grew from their belief that its members shirked responsibility and, worse yet, convinced a new generation of Americans to do the same. American decline, cultural and economic, owed to the influence of the adversary culture. Only a conservative cultural and economic reawakening might renew America.[54]

Of course, neoconservative gender analysis often translated into what could only be described as prudery and, in its more prejudiced forms, homophobia. Daniel Bell, who called himself a "socialist in economics, a liberal in politics, and a conservative in culture," lamented the transgressive ethos of the sixties—for which he used Andy Warhol's *Chelsea Girls* as a reference point—with its "obsessive preoccupation with homosexuality, transvestism, buggery, and, most pervasive of all, publicly displayed oral-genital intercourse." Decter's homophobia was on even fuller display in her infamous 1980 *Commentary* article "Boys on the Beach," a vicious anecdotal attack on the gay liberation movement. In that article Decter framed her general opposition to gay rights by way of her observations of the gay men who populated Fire Island, a Long Island beach resort where she and her family spent their summers in the early sixties. Among other slanders, Decter interpreted Fire Island homosexuality as a "new class" flight from the responsibilities imposed upon men by women and children. She accused Fire Island gays of flaunting their narcissistic behavior in the face of the straight men who duly went about their unexciting but meaningful lives. The straight men Decter defended felt "mocked most of all for having become, in style as well as in substance, family men, caught up in getting and begetting, thinking of mortgages, schools, and the affordable, marking the passage of years in obedience to all the grubby imperatives that heterosexual manhood seems to impose."[55]

Decter's article caused a literary scandal, brought to life when master polemicist Gore Vidal reviewed it in *The Nation*. Vidal's essay, "Pink Triangle and Yellow Star," critiqued Decter for style—she wrote, he sneered, "with the authority and easy confidence of someone who knows that she is very well known to those few who know her"—and, more important, for substance. On the latter, Vidal took offense at Decter's assumption that the ostentatious Fire Island gays represented all gays. Plenty more gays, Vidal argued, hid in plain sight due to widespread homophobia. Vidal also mocked Decter's notion that gays lived to torment straight men. "Although Decter's blood was always at the boil when contemplating these unnatural and immature half-men, they were," he suspected, "serenely unaware of her and her new-class cronies, solemnly worshiping at the shrine of The Family." By titling his article "Pink Triangle and Yellow Star," Vidal called attention to Decter as a Jew and to *Commentary* as a Jewish publication. "In the German concentration camps," he wrote, "Jews wore yellow stars while homosexualists wore pink triangles." In the context of Ronald Reagan's election to the presidency in 1980, and with the newfound political visibility of evangelicals, who openly touted antigay messages, Vidal reasoned that Jews and homosexuals once again had common enemies and should unite. And yet instead "Mrs. Norman Podhoretz," he seethed, "has managed not only to come up with every known prejudice and superstition about same-sexers but also to make up some brand-new ones. For sheer vim and vigor, 'The Boys on the Beach' outdoes its implicit model, *The Protocol of the Elders of Zion.*"[56]

For Vidal to call attention to Decter as a Jew in this way was inflammatory. It was also wrong in terms of judging the Jewish position in the United States. That some Jews, particularly those of the neoconservative persuasion, had found common cause with evangelicals did not constrain their freedom as Jews in the United States. Quite to the contrary, as George H. Nash convincingly argues, the conservative turn taken by the Jews at *Commentary* demonstrated that Jews were more of the mainstream than ever before. "In 1945, *Commentary* had been born into a marginal, impoverished, immigrant-based subculture and an intellectual milieu that touted 'alienation' and 'critical nonconformity' as the true marks of the intellectual vis-à-vis his own culture," Nash writes. "Two generations later, *Commentary* stood in the mainstream of American culture, and even of American conservatism, as a celebrant of the fundamental goodness of the American regime, and Norman Podhoretz, an immigrant milkman's son, was its advocate." In celebrating the "fundamental goodness" of America and its institutions, neoconservatives believed they were providing an important service to the regime they loved: they were protecting it from the New Left that they thought was out to destroy it. This shouting match between the New Left and the neoconservatives—this dialectic of the cultural revolution known as the sixties—helped bestow upon America a divide that would become known as the culture wars.[57]

3

Taking God's Country Back

In an influential 1976 essay, "What Is a Neoconservative?," Irving Kristol wrote that he and his fellow neoconservatives tended "to be respectful of traditional values and institutions," religion being perhaps the most important such traditional institution. Yet Kristol was not very religious himself. As it was for other New York intellectuals, even most neoconservatives, Judaism was more about his cultural identity than about his religious affiliation. Nevertheless, he valued religion as foundational to representative democracy, believing it helped curb the unmoored urges of people left to their own devices. "The individual who is abruptly 'liberated' from the sovereignty of traditional values will soon find himself experiencing the vertigo and despair of nihilism." These feelings, Kristol warned, were what tempted people to submit to authoritarian rule.[1]

In this elocution, neoconservatives helped articulate yet another conservative paradigm for understanding the dangers presented by cultural radicalism, endowing conservative America with a powerful rhetorical weapon to fight the culture wars. And yet it is doubtful that neoconservatives entirely grasped the full extent of "the vertigo and despair" that millions of Christian Americans felt living in post-sixties America. This was particularly true of white evangelicals, whose interpretations of the sixties cultural revolutions grafted onto older understandings about the grave dangers posed by modernity.

Thanks to several Great Awakenings since the colonial era, the United States has long been home to the world's largest population of evangelical Christians, Protestants who pay less attention to liturgy than to personal conversion and piety and who believe entry to God's kingdom requires that they spread his word on earth. That evangelicals have tended to mix their religious and national identities has long tinged the rhetoric of American cultural politics with an eschatological hue. This became increasingly so in the twentieth century as more and more religious Americans felt scarred by the acids of modernity, which burned gaping, irreparable holes in the fabric of Christian America. For them the culture wars, more than a battle over national identity, have served as a struggle for the *soul* of America, a clash over what it means to live in a world in which all foundations had been pulled out from under, a world in which, at its starkest, "God is dead."[2]

Even devout evangelicals—devout evangelicals especially—had to act upon the implications of modernity. In pushing back against modernist forms of knowledge that fanned the flames of religious skepticism, such as biblical criticism and Darwinism, early-twentieth-century conservative evangelicals—many of whom, by the 1920s, accentuated biblical inerrancy and began referring to themselves as "fundamentalists"—successfully enacted laws that mandated reading the King James Bible in schools and outlawed the teaching of evolution. Such activism sprang from a desire to reassert religious control over a society that was becoming increasingly modern and secular.[3]

By the 1970s, conservative white evangelicals were confronted with a perfect storm of secular power that they deemed a threat to their way of life and to the Christian nation they believed the United States once was and ought to be again. This realization, more than anything else, led religious conservatives to take up arms in the culture wars. Worldly activism became more imperative, so much so that conservative evangelicals formed an uneasy political alliance with conservative Americans from different theological backgrounds. Even fundamentalists, whose insistence upon correct doctrine meant that minor differences in biblical interpretation often led to major schisms, reluctantly joined forces with conservative Catholics, Jews, and Mormons. This was all the more remarkable given that many fundamentalists viewed the 1960 election of John F. Kennedy, a Catholic, as a sign that the end times were fast approaching.[4]

The overarching issue for religious conservatives, and what brought them together with their former adversaries, was the threat posed by an increasingly secular state. School prayer, long practiced in most American public schools, had been rendered unconstitutional by the landmark 1962 *Engel v. Vitale* Supreme Court decision. In 1978, in another example of how the secular state encroached upon Christian America, the Internal Revenue Service (IRS) implemented a federal mandate requiring that Christian private schools comply with deseg-regation practices or risk having their tax-exempt status revoked. The Christian Right—as it came to be known by 1980, the year it helped elect Ronald Reagan president, signaling its arrival as a powerful po-litical alliance—worked from the assumption that an increasingly sec-ular government represented the gravest threat to Christian values. Part of this had to do with the conservative religious impression that the government conspired against the traditional family unit. In an earlier era, when William Jennings Bryan's biblically inspired popu-lism appealed to millions of Americans, evangelicals had often mar-ried their anxieties about the family to progressive economic concerns about the destructive force of unregulated monopoly capitalism. But by the 1970s, the traditionalist worldview of conservative Christians and the antistatist premises that inspired more and more Americans were no longer mutually exclusive ideological trajectories. As an in-structive example, conservatives posited that government's meddling in the form of welfare policies weakened the traditional family struc-ture. "Families are strong when they have a function to perform," con-servative activist Connie Marshner contended. "And the more gov-ernment, combined with the helping professions establishment, take away the functions families need to perform—to provide their health care, their child care, their housing—the less purpose there is for a family, *per se*, to exist."[5]

By the same logic, the Christian Right focused on the role of public education. State-run schools were thought to be the primary secular institution geared to disrupt the inculcation of religious values that had traditionally transpired in the family.

As long as there has been American public education, there has been resistance to elements of it, hailing from a variety of different forces all along the political and religious spectrums. Such resistance took on mostly conservative overtones in the twentieth century, when the national curriculum slowly but surely merged with the progres-sive curriculum innovated by John Dewey and a cohort of prom-inent pedagogues at Columbia University's Teacher's College. Pro-gressive education was a secular movement that sought to distance the national curriculum from the ecumenical Protestantism that had

been its organizing force since Horace Mann's common school movement in the early nineteenth century. Not surprisingly, progressives
clashed with fundamentalists over an assortment of curricular items,
particularly over mandatory Bible reading and over whether to teach
Darwin's evolutionary science or creationism. This collision famously
sparked the 1925 Scopes Monkey Trial in Dayton, Tennessee, which
put fundamentalists on the map, often as a source of derision for more
cosmopolitan-minded Americans. H. L. Mencken's acerbic commentary on the trial painted a harsh picture of fundamentalists as rubes
who promoted the story of Genesis because it was "so simple that
even a yokel can grasp it."[6]

By the end of the 1930s, to the dismay of conservatives, the progressive curriculum had become even more prevalent in many schools
across the country. Teacher's College professor Harold Rugg's popular textbooks *Man and His Changing Society*, which incorporated the
scholarship of progressive historian Charles Beard, who subjected
the American past to the paradigm of class conflict, were assigned to
more than five million students in five thousand school districts. But
conservative resistance to progressivism grew as well, made evident
by the successful movement in the early 1940s to remove Rugg's textbooks from schools. By the early Cold War, conservative educational
vigilantism, abetted by McCarthyism, had turned back the tides of
the progressive curriculum across the nation. In the 1950s, as thousands of progressive educators learned the hard way, mere mention
of Dewey was likened to summoning the ghost of Karl Marx. But despite its reach, Cold War conservatism kept a lid on liberalizing curricular trends for only a short time. The cultural earthquakes of the
sixties shattered the short-lived antiprogressive consensus formed in
the early Cold War. By the 1970s, the Christian Right had valid reason
to believe that the nation's public schools no longer represented their
moral vision.[7]

The Supreme Court enshrined secularism in the schools with a series of landmark cases, most famously the 1962 *Engel v. Vitale* ruling
that New York's twenty-two-word school prayer violated the First
Amendment's Establishment Clause. In 1963 the court built an even
higher wall of separation between church and state with its *School
District of Abington Township v. Schempp* decision in favor of Ellory
Schempp, a Unitarian freethinker who challenged the constitutional-

ity of mandatory Bible reading in his high school. In polls taken since the sixties, the school prayer and Bible-reading rulings have routinely ranked as the most unpopular Supreme Court decisions, particularly among conservative Christians, many of whom considered *Engel* and *Abington* the beginning of American civilization's downfall. Some members of Congress received more letters about school prayer and Bible reading than any other issues. Millions of Americans showed their displeasure with the new law of the land by disobeying it, as students in schools across the country, particularly in the South and Midwest, persisted in their age-old practice of praying and reading the Bible together. Those who disagreed with *Engel* and *Abington* contended that it was undemocratic for the "philosopher-kings" on the Supreme Court to overrule the majority of Americans who wanted children to pray in school. William Buckley Jr. gave voice to a growing conservative displeasure with the Supreme Court, which, due to its "ideological fanaticism," he argued, "is making it increasingly difficult for our society to breathe normally: to govern itself through established tradition and authority; to rule by the local consensus; to deal effectively with its domestic enemies; to carry forward its implicit commitment to the faith of its fathers."[8]

Post-sixties curriculum trends also distressed conservative Christians. In social studies classes, students were increasingly challenged to clarify their own values, independent of those instilled by parents and churches. In science, teachers slowly overcame the perpetual taboo against teaching evolution. And in health classes, honest discussion of sex came to replace moral exhortation. A popular anthropology curriculum created for elementary students by psychologist Jerome Bruner in the early 1970s—MACOS, or Man: A Course of Study— exemplified the secularization of the curriculum. During a MACOS unit students examined the Netsilik Eskimo culture, including their practice of killing the elderly, in order to understand and not judge cultural differences. Such relativistic lesson plans became the norm. In 1969 the National Education Association (NEA) advocated what it called the "inquiry method" of instruction, a Socratic discussion technique that would allow students "to view knowledge as tentative rather than absolute" and thus "to see that value judgments cannot be accepted solely on faith." Opposing MACOS-style learning became a rallying cry for Christian culture warriors. "Your tax dollars are being used," Jesse Helms cautioned recipients of a 1976 fundraising letter, "to pay for grade school courses that teach our children that cannibalism, wife swapping, and the murder of infants and the elderly are acceptable behavior."[9]

Religious conservatives organized against these curriculum reform efforts from the outset, particularly against sex education, which was becoming an increasingly common feature of the national curriculum. In 1963 Dr. Mary Calderone founded the Sex Information and Education Council of the United States (SIECUS) on the premise that objective sex education was a more realistic means to suppress the sexual revolution than chastisement. Many educators agreed with her, including Sally Williams, a school nurse in Anaheim, California, who created a popular sex education curriculum. Williams sought to direct students away from premarital sex, but her curriculum described sexual intercourse in relatively graphic fashion for students as young as twelve and provided information to older students about birth control, in recognition that premarital sex was likely. Religious conservatives, predictably moralist, opposed such an approach and in 1969, after gaining a majority on the Anaheim school board, promptly ended the sex education program.[10]

Conservatives elsewhere replicated the efforts of Anaheim activists. Fundamentalist preacher Billy James Hargis's Christian Crusade helped launch a national movement against sex education. Hargis's lieutenant Gordon Drake authored a pamphlet—"Is the Schoolhouse the Proper Place to Teach Raw Sex?"—that purportedly sold ninety thousand copies in three months. Hargis and Drake forever engraved SIECUS, "the pornographic arm of liberal education," as a subversive group in the conservative lexicon, "all a part of a giant communist conspiracy." In his stock speech, Hargis claimed that sex education was part of a larger plan hatched by progressive educators to "destroy the traditional moral fiber of America and replace it with a pervasive sickly humanism." In a letter to Christian Crusaders, Hargis complained about a sex education program in Jefferson County, Colorado, where the principal "said that the concept of morality being taught in his school to elementary grade children was quite different from that of their parents and pastors, and the kids would have to decide which was right."[11]

In Kanawha County, West Virginia, violent protests erupted when the school board sought to align with a 1970 state regulation mandating that all West Virginia students read texts reflecting the nation's multiethnic composition. The Kanawha textbook fight, described in hyperbolic fashion as "the shot heard around the world," influenced the Christian Right's approach to later curriculum battles. Alice Moore, the wife of a local evangelical minister who was elected to the Kanawha board in 1970 on a conservative platform that included an anti–sex education plank, was the first to object to the proposed reading list. Due to her tireless campaigning during the summer of 1974, when the Kanawha schools opened that September at least 20 percent of the student population stayed home. In sympathy, county coal miners organized a wildcat strike. Violence marred the campaign: buses were shot at, teachers were harassed, and a school district building was firebombed. National right-wing groups descended upon West Virginia to join the cause, including the John Birch Society and the Ku Klux Klan, the latter of which held a notorious rally at the state capitol. Behind the scenes, the newly formed Heritage Foundation, still a relatively unknown right-wing think tank, offered free legal support to protestors and organized a conference on the rights of parents. Connie Marshner, the Heritage Foundation's first director of education, later maintained that the West Virginia story called attention to "the textbook problem across the country" and helped inform the Christian Right during its later culture war struggles.[12]

Not surprisingly, racial anxieties factored into the Kanawha textbook battle. Local conservatives seemed horrified that Eldridge Cleaver's *Soul on Ice*, depicted as "anti–white racism," appeared on the reading list. However, such racial concerns often mixed with religious and moral panic. The inclusion of *The Autobiography of Malcolm X* on the approved list seemingly offended Alice Moore not because of its frank discussion of white supremacy but rather due to Malcolm's giving "all praise to Allah" that he was no longer a "brainwashed Christian." Jack Maurice, editor of the local newspaper, attributed the controversy to the "renewal of the theological dispute ... pitting the Fundamentalists against the Modernists ... the Literalists in their interpretation of scripture, against the Symbolists." As opposed to traditionalism, the modernist educators glorified, in Moore's words, "self-actualization," "clarification of their own values," and the dangerous idea that "truth is whatever is truth to that individual." For the Kanawha conservatives, such relativism was a slippery slope to a host of dangerous anti-

Christian ideologies. As one parent remembered: "They were teaching my kids socialism, homosexuality, and situational ethics."[13]

The NEA sent a panel of educators to Kanawha County in December 1974 to hold hearings on the nature and scope of the protests. The panel issued a final report recognizing that religious differences moved the protestors to action. "For generations, a fundamentalist religious belief has given meaning to the mountain way of life and has given the mountain people the strength to withstand its hardships." This echoed how a national correspondent described the protests: as "a full-scale eruption of frustrations against a worldly culture imposed on an area literally a world apart from the rest of the country." Though correct about opposition to cosmopolitan ideas, the condescending notion that such anger was isolated to a rural backwater failed to capture the growing national dissatisfaction with the increasingly secular features of public education in the United States.[14]

The movement against the secular curriculum was part and parcel of the rising Christian Right, in part because it blended so easily with the politics of "family values," a new umbrella referent for concerns about feminism, abortion, divorce, premarital sex, and gay rights. Mel and Norma Gabler, devout Southern Baptists who converted their small-town Texas home into a national center for exposing liberal bias in the nation's textbooks, said that their main concern was that textbooks were "destroying the family" by means of so-called values clarification. Interviewed about the West Virginia textbook brouhaha, Mel Gabler said: "What really bugged me was that textbooks seem to divide the children from their parents, especially the social studies which appear to teach the child a philosophy alien to the parents." Such pedagogy violated the biblical mandate that parents raise their children to be Christians. "Considering Ephesians 6:4, which tells us to bring up our children 'in the nurture and admonition of the Lord,'" they asked, "can we as Christian parents entrust the education of our children to current textbooks?" The Gablers became enormously influential. This owed in part to the fact that they lived in Texas, where citizens were automatically granted a hearing before the state board of education. As the Gablers became trusted fixtures at board meetings, publishers were forced to tailor books to pass muster with them. And since Texas was one of the nation's largest textbook purchasers, giving it the power to dictate to the national textbook market, the Gablers' ideological inspections had far-reaching implications. Yet their influence resulted from more than mere coincidence of geography. Their message was convincing. And they were far from alone in their holy war against secular schools.[15]

Some of the most influential evangelical writers of the 1970s, including Francis Schaeffer and Tim LaHaye, placed education at the center of their plans to redeem American culture. They contended that the schools had been taken over by an elite who sought to spread an anti-Christian ideology they termed "secular humanism." In the religious conservative imagination, secular humanism replaced communism as the alien ideology most threatening to Christian America. Rousas John Rushdoony, an evangelical intellectual who founded the somewhat theocratic Christian Reconstructionist movement, taught conservatives that secular humanism rationalized a blasphemous culture because it was a hubristic philosophy of "man striving to be God." In this way, the critique of secular humanism allowed conservatives to make sense of previously unimaginable cultural trends, such as the teaching of sex in the public schools. Such manifestations of cultural decadence were the logical consequences of a society's abandonment of long-standing traditions rooted in biblical tenets.[16]

Although Christian Right rhetoric about the dangers posed by secular humanism was overstated, the United States had indeed become a more secular nation. Proof of this was not necessarily found in the growing number of Americans who adhered to the creed set forth in the 1933 *Humanist Manifesto*: "that the nature of the universe depicted by modern science makes unacceptable any supernatural or cosmic guarantees of human values." Yes, the number of secularists, naturalists, humanists, freethinkers, and atheists increased throughout the twentieth century, owing much to the fact that universities, secularizing institutions par excellence, bulked so large in the culture. But the United States remained an extremely religious nation, particularly relative to nations of comparable wealth. Gallup polls from the 1950s through the end of the century showed that upwards of 90 percent of Americans claimed to believe in God.[17]

Twentieth-century America became more secular due not to a lapse in the number of religious people but rather to a waning in the scope of religious authority. The most obvious engine of this decline was the Supreme Court's revolution in constitutional interpretation, which radically redrew the boundaries between church and state. In its 1947 case *Everson v. Board of Education of Ewing Township*, the court applied the First Amendment's establishment clause to the states. This reinterpretation of incorporation then led to a series of cases that strengthened individual rights relative to religious or moral authority. All of a sudden, viewing obscene material in private was legal, but organized prayer and Bible reading in school were not.[18]

The paradox of American secularization—the perplexing fact that religious authority dwindled even as the vast majority of Americans doggedly persisted in religious belief—helps explain the culture wars. White Protestant moral authority, which extended beyond the religious sphere for most of American history, had been put on the defensive. Conservative Christians, formerly part of the establishment, had come to see themselves as cultural counterrevolutionaries. Foregrounding such a counterrevolution was the fact that for many conservatives, particularly white evangelicals, religion expressed a larger national identity. Christianity was crucial to a normative framework of Americanism. One of the primary aspirations of the Christian Right was to reestablish, in the words of philosopher Charles Taylor, an "understanding that used to define the nation, where being American would once more have a connection with theism, with being 'one nation under God,' or at least with the ethic which was interwoven with this." But as Taylor also posits, "the very embattled nature of these attempts shows how we have slid out of the old dispensation." In other words, the Christian Right's emergence was predicated on a secular shift. Its efforts to return the sacred to the realm of national politics were in symbiosis with secularization.[19]

Despite the interdependent relationship between secularization and the growth of the Religious Right, the culture wars were not only a battle between religious and secular Americans; they were also an internal feature of American Protestantism. Some Protestant thinkers, especially mainline Protestants, who tended to be more liberal than their evangelical counterparts in both theology and politics, sought to radically adjust their doctrines to the earth-shattering epistemological implications of modernity. Conservative evangelicals, in contrast, responded to the challenges of modernity with doctrinal and political reaction. This intra-Protestant struggle played out at the 1979 Southern Baptist Convention (SBC), where conservatives who felt threatened by modern sexual mores—feminism, abortion, and gay rights—took control of the SBC, to the dismay of their more moderate coreligionists. Conservatives elected as their new president Adrian Rogers, a

Memphis pastor whose platform urged that the SBC return to the principles of "conservative, Bible-believing congregations ... that believe in the inerrant, infallible word of God." Given that the SBC was the nation's largest Protestant denomination, the Christian Right's political fortunes grew rosier after the SBC's 1979 political jump to the right.[20]

That evangelicals resisted some of the implications of modernity is not to say that they did not find ways to accommodate modernity, with the qualification that accommodation did not entail agreement or, much less, wholesale adoption. The influence of evangelical thinker Francis Schaeffer demonstrated that conservative Protestantism found ways to adjust to secular modernity and that the Christian Right was both reactionary and often innovative. Schaeffer furnished evangelical Christianity—despite the notorious fundamentalist insistence upon doctrinal purity—with an ecumenical spirit, at least in its willingness to form political alliances with nonevangelical conservatives. Such an ecumenical disposition was crucial to the Christian Right culture wars. "It is little exaggeration," James Sire writes, with just a touch of exaggeration, "to say that if Schaeffer had not lived, historians of the future looking back on these decades would have to invent him in order to explain what happened."[21]

Schaeffer, the hippielike evangelical sage of L'Abri, a Swiss mountain retreat for Christian and non-Christian wanderers alike, became famous in the 1970s, late in his life, when his books and documentary films touched millions of American evangelicals. Growing up in working-class Pennsylvania, Schaeffer had been "saved" at a tent revival in 1929. His theology was shaped by the great debates of the 1920s, when his mentor J. Graham Machen was fired from Princeton Theological Seminary for maintaining fundamentalist beliefs at a time when liberal theologians—those who more actively reconciled their faiths to modernist thought, including Darwinism—were on the rise. Schaeffer attended Westminster Theological Seminary in Philadelphia, which Machen founded as a conservative alternative to the more liberal divinity schools. He pastored a number of churches in the United States before moving to Switzerland as a missionary in 1947. After fundamentalist firebrand Carl McIntire astonishingly accused him of being a communist and fired him from the mission, Schaeffer and his wife Edith founded L'Abri in 1955. Although charging Schaeffer with communism was outrageous even by the standards of McIntire, living in Europe had indeed led Schaeffer to reject the pietism of American evangelicalism and to embrace a more modern spiritualism, part and parcel of his newfound interest in art, music, and philosophy.[22]

Edith Schaeffer, the child of Christian fundamentalist missionaries, was also a persuasively modernist force in her husband's life. The product of a privileged upbringing in a mission in China, Edith passionately loved high culture. But she was not always happy about the tension inherent to being both a cultural highbrow and a Christian fundamentalist. Her son Franky remembers his mother's defensive objections to H. L. Mencken's antifundamentalist caricatures: "We're not like that! He would never have written those horrible things if he had ever met me!" Franky, who ultimately rejected his parents' theology, puts a somewhat different spin on their seemingly oxymoronic combination of fundamentalism and high culture. "I think my father lived with a tremendous tension," he writes, "that pitted his growing interest in art, culture, music, and history against a stunted theology frozen in the modernist-fundamentalist battles of his youthful Christian experience." Rather than stunting, however, this modernist-fundamentalist tension lent great significance to Schaeffer's role: he helped American evangelicals reconcile their fundamentalist readings of scripture to modernity, or at least modernity shorn of modernist epistemologies. In order to do battle with modernity, Schaeffer's theology incorporated all that he had learned from modernist forms. "Dad spent his life trying to somehow reconcile the angry theology that typified movement-fundamentalism with a Christian apologetic that was more attractive."[23]

Schaeffer's reckoning with the acids of modernity helped reshape evangelical thought. Like early-twentieth-century evangelicals who read Nietzsche in order to better relate their theology to modern America, Schaeffer grappled with modernist giants in order to reinvigorate fundamentalism. He also tangled with modish artists and musicians. "In the early '60s," his son bragged, "he was probably the only fundamentalist who had even heard of Bob Dylan." Schaeffer's method—what he called his "Christian apologetic," a system of thought for relating the meaning of modern cultural forms to scripture—thus gave biblical inerrancy a wider currency by certifying it for a new generation. Of course, being conversant in countercultural music did not necessarily translate into eschewing that old-time religion. Like so many other evangelical thinkers during the 1970s, including cantankerous would-be theocrats like Rushdoony, Schaeffer had an overarching philosophical mission to demonstrate the flaws in secular humanism, which he defined as "the system whereby men and women, beginning absolutely by themselves, try rationally to build out from themselves, having only Man as their integration point, to find all knowledge, meaning and value."[24]

Schaeffer believed himself to be one of the only thinkers who truly grasped the anxieties that modernity presented people with. He theorized that Western society, by adopting secular humanism as its organizing principle, had crossed a "line of despair." Modern people lived in despair because they no longer knew truth; they were mired in relativism. Prior to being pushed over this precipice, everybody, even non-Christians, could make sense of truth claims. "One could tell a non-Christian to 'be a good girl' and, while she might not have followed your advice, at least she would have understood what you were talking about," he reasoned. "To say the same thing to a truly modern girl today would be to make a 'nonsense' statement. The blank look you might receive would not mean that your standards had been rejected, but that your message was meaningless."[25]

Schaeffer contended that Western civilization had become post-Christian in its rejection of antithesis, a method of thought based on the proposition that since *this* is absolutely true, *that* is absolutely untrue. Schaeffer argued that Hegel represented the first step toward the post-Christian line of despair because Hegel theorized that synthesis, not antithesis, was the superior method of thought. Synthesis, in Schaeffer's reading of Hegel, implied relativism, since all acts, all gestures, had an equal claim to truth, in that the dialectical process would eventually envelop everything. Napoleon's conquest of Europe was to be judged not by the brutality of its individual acts but by the synthesis of the "world spirit on horseback" that Hegel famously believed Napoleon signified. Furthering his eclectic intellectual history of modernity, informed by his unique Christian apologetic, Schaeffer wrote that existentialism announced humanity's nihilistic trek across the line of despair. Sartre, Schaeffer posited, believed there was no way of knowing truth absolutely and that, given this, human existence was ridiculous. "Nevertheless, you try to authenticate yourself by an act of the will. It does not really matter in which direction you act as long as you act." An individual could choose to either help an elderly woman walk across a street or attack her and steal her purse; in either act the person was "authenticated." Although this critique of existentialism ignored some of its key facets—namely, the unrelativistic premise that an authenticating project was worthwhile only if it created space for more people to experience freedom—by reading existentialism against the grain of scripture, Schaeffer appealed to some of the young, modish Americans who voraciously read Sartre. Eventually, powerful Christian conservatives sought him out precisely because of this appeal.[26]

Although Schaeffer presented a softer side to fundamentalism, and although he avoided politicizing his theology until he was pressed into serving a growing conservative Christian movement in the 1970s, his antithesis methodology had conservative political implications. Schaeffer made clear, for instance, that he considered homosexuality an expression of modern despair. "In much of modern thinking all antithesis and all the order of God's creation is to be fought against—including the male-female distinctions." And yet despite the antihomosexual connotations of his theology, his son Frank describes his father as having been decidedly unprejudiced. "Dad thought it cruel and stupid to believe that a homosexual could change by 'accepting Christ.'" Schaeffer thought homosexuality was a sin, of course, but a sin on par with other, less politicized sins, such as gluttony. He believed all sins could be forgiven and all sinners treated with kindness.[27]

Although such parsing offered little comfort to most gays and lesbians, Schaeffer's take on homosexuality was certainly more tolerant than the demagogic antigay messages that other religious conservatives were preaching, particularly by the late 1970s, when opposition to gay rights became a cardinal standpoint of the broader Christian Right outlook. Of course ideas have consequences beyond the intentions of their authors. The modern sensibilities that Schaeffer conferred upon conservative Christianity undoubtedly attracted followers who would have otherwise remained neutral in the culture wars. But partisan operatives who had few qualms about appearing meanspirited and bigoted also took note of how Schaeffer could be used to their advantage.

Once Schaeffer gained a measure of American fame—once the families of evangelical dignitaries such as Billy Graham became regular guests at L'Abri—conservative Christian leaders identified him as the ideal conduit to a youth culture they failed to understand. "Evangelical leaders came to L'Abri," Franky writes, "so Dad could teach them how to inoculate Johnny and Susie born-again against the hedonistic out-of-control culture that had Johnny's older brother on drugs and Susie's older sister marching on the capital." After being recruited by evangelical pitchman Billy Zeoli, who enrolled wealthy conservatives like Rich DeVos, the right-wing founder of Amway, in the cause, Francis and Franky Schaeffer went into the documentary filmmaking business. Their partnership produced a thirteen-episode film series in 1976—*How Should We Then Live? The Rise and Decline of Western Thought and Culture*—which delivered Schaeffer's wide-ranging Christian apologetic to enormous American audiences.[28]

After speaking to packed houses on a film tour across America, the father-son tandem made another documentary film series in 1979 with help from C. Everett Koop, an ardently pro-life evangelical physician. This second series—*Whatever Happened to the Human Race?*—focused on pro-life issues, especially abortion. Franky says that their films gave "the evangelical community a frame of reference through which to understand the secularization of American culture." In this way, Francis Schaeffer helped conservative evangelicals adjust to modernity by preparing them for the culture wars. His emergence as the most influential evangelical theologian—as a formative Christian culture warrior—also served notice that the issues that aroused American conservatives were changing.[29]

In the 1950s and well into the 1960s, the primary political concerns of many white evangelicals, especially in the South, were related to racial desegregation. Jerry Falwell, pastor of the enormous Thomas Road Baptist Church in Lynchburg, Virginia, and one of the most recognizable evangelicals due to *The Old-Time Gospel Hour*, a ministry television program that broadcast his sermons, preached against religious leaders involved in civil rights activism. In his infamous 1964 sermon "Minsters and Marches," Falwell lectured: "Preachers are not called to be politicians, but soul winners." He also questioned "the sincerity and nonviolent intentions of some civil rights leaders such as Dr. Martin Luther King, Jr." Several evangelical churches aided massive resistance to the civil rights movement by starting Christian day schools, where whites could send their children to avoid the federally mandated desegregation of the public schools. Bob Jones University, an evangelical college located in Greenville, South Carolina, forbade blacks from enrolling until 1971, after which it prohibited interracial dating and marriage on the stated grounds that "cultural or biological mixing of the races is regarded as a violation of God's command." Given this, it was difficult to argue with the implicit rationale that informed the IRS decision to revoke Bob Jones University's tax-exempt status in 1978, logic then upheld by the Supreme Court in its 1983 ruling *Bob Jones University v. the United States*: for many white evangelicals, Christian education was a cover for perpetuating racial segregation and discrimination. Indeed, disentangling the Christian Right's moral panic from white racial panic is no easy task. Even by the 1970s, when most conservative Christians increasingly spoke about how everyone, regardless of race, was created in God's image, racial anxieties persisted in motivating many in their ranks. And yet there was more to the Christian day school movement.[30]

Between 1965 and 1975 Christian day school enrollment grew by over 202 percent, and by 1979 more than one million American children attended Christian schools. The timing of such precipitous growth suggests that it was a response to desegregation. Falwell's Lynchburg Christian Academy, for instance, opened its doors in 1967, the year Virginia's commissioner of education demanded proactive school desegregation. But Falwell, seeking to distance himself from his earlier position against civil rights, never spoke in racial terms about his school, which admitted its first black students in 1969. He, did, however, speak in religious terms, arguing that the Supreme Court's ruling on school prayer justified the Christian day school movement, "the hope of this Republic." "When a group of nine 'idiots' can pass a ruling down that it is illegal to read the Bible in our public schools, they need to be called idiots." The Christian day school movement grew in the South, but it also exploded in states far removed from the old Confederacy where desegregation was less of a concern. The California Association of Christian Schools listed 350 schools as members, including a growing network of schools in San Diego run by Tim LaHaye, who consistently made clear that his schools existed as an alternative to secular humanist schools. Indiana Baptist school principal Robert Billings's widely circulated 1971 manual *A Guide to the Christian School* summed up the reason that so many Christians were vacating the public schools: it was the "growing trend toward the secularization." In sum, the popularity of Christian day schools owed as much to fears about the secularization of curriculum as to resistance to desegregation, or at the very least showed that these two anxieties were not mutually exclusive. Christian parents sent their children to Christian schools out of a desire to have them avoid sex education, values clarification, and Darwinism, not just blacks.[31]

No matter the actual motivations of the Christian day school movement, in 1978 the IRS announced its intentions to enforce a 1970 law that empowered it to revoke the tax-exempt status of private schools proven to be racially discriminatory. The IRS stated that it would prosecute those private schools that failed to make a good-faith effort to achieve student populations comprising at least 5 percent minorities. Conservative Christians interpreted the IRS declaration as government persecution. White evangelicals in particular felt betrayed because it came under the watch of one of their own, President Jimmy Carter, a Southern Baptist who had admitted during the 1976 campaign to having a "born-again" personal redemption experience. Rather than actively seek to admit more black students in order to comply with federal law—a difficult endeavor in any case since few African American parents were inclined to send their children to white Christian day schools—evangelicals inundated the IRS with 120,000 angry letters of protest. Even though the IRS prosecuted only a few Christian day schools due to the widespread hostility its ruling provoked, Christian Right leaders attributed the politicization of evangelicals to the hazard posed by the IRS. "The IRS made us realize," Falwell claimed, "that we had to fight for our lives." Heritage Foundation founder Paul Weyrich, reflecting on his efforts to bring conservative Christians into the Republican Party fold, said he "had utterly failed" for most of the 1970s. "What changed their mind was Jimmy Carter's intervention against the Christian schools." For religious conservatives, Carter's IRS symbolized the federal government's brazen disregard for their values.[32]

Before the IRS incited a burst of evangelical political energy, conservative anxieties about how the secular state was a menace to family values had been bubbling to the surface for years. The traditional family, an idealized version of the 1950s family unit that many Americans thought to be the norm, embodied a conservative religious conception of gender roles. It encompassed one man, one woman, and children born within the confines of this heterosexual partnership. Whereas "scripture declares," according to Falwell, that the husband should "be the spiritual leader in his family," the wife was expected to accept her subordinate but ultimately more gratifying role as homemaker. Add to this the fact that religious conservatives believed that the secular state impinged upon the social roles traditionally fulfilled by the family, and the fight for family values became essential to the Christian culture wars. As Falwell declared: "It is my conviction that the family is God's basic unit in society. No wonder then, we are in a holy war for the survival of the family."[33]

Family politics were so intense during and after the 1970s because the traditional nuclear family had experienced a period of unusual stability in the 1950s, followed by an era of unprecedented instability in the 1960s. By the 1970s, signals that the traditional family was in decline were everywhere, such as higher rates of divorce and out-of-wedlock pregnancy. This was the result of several factors, including economic changes associated with deindustrialization and falling wages. The decay of the historically male "blue-collar" job market, mostly factory work that tended to be well-paying and secure due to high degrees of unionization, coincided with the explosion of the historically female "pink-collar" job market, mostly service work that tended to be low-paying, insecure, and nonunionized. Women entering the workforce in unprecedented numbers, in addition to the hardships associated with falling wages, put pressure on the traditional family model that relied upon a male breadwinner and a female caretaker.

Christian conservatives ignored such sociological explanations for the crumbling family. Instead they blamed feminists, who had indeed been critical of the sexism inherent to the traditional family well before economic transformations rendered that paradigm increasingly obsolete. As opposed to feminist solutions to family problems, which took into account the new sociological realities of the late 1970s—such as a proposal for more flexible work schedules, which would, in theory, afford working parents more time to spend with their children— Falwell offered a streamlined solution. Men and women, he argued, needed "to get in a right relationship with God and His principles for the home," implying that women needed to stay home and care for their children while men worked to earn the family wage. Falwell did not explain how American families might attain such an increasingly unattainable objective.[34]

The traditional family remained at the forefront of American politics during the 1970s not only because of its dissolution but also because of the ongoing struggle to ratify the Equal Rights Amendment (ERA). The historical struggle for the ERA, of course, predated the sixties. It had been on the agenda of woman's rights activists since shortly after ratification of the Nineteenth Amendment gave women the right to vote in 1920. Politicians from both major parties endorsed the ERA in the 1940s, but when it was first introduced in Congress in 1947, liberal and conservative opponents objected that it would negate legislation that endowed women with special protection.

The sixties feminist movement injected new life into the struggle for the ERA. As a sign of the feminist movement's success, both houses of Congress passed the amendment in 1972, sending it to the states, which were given seven years to ratify it. Thirty-eight states were required for the proposed amendment to become law, and thirty ratified the ERA in the first year of the process. But before the final eight states voted on ratification, a movement to stop the ERA gathered, ensuring its eventual demise. Although the amendment's main provision — "equality of rights under the law shall not be denied or abridged by the United States or by any State on account of sex" — sounded innocuous enough, both proponents and opponents thought it would enlist the federal government in the feminist movement's goal of total equality between the sexes. Conservatives deemed such a prospect dangerous to the traditional family.[35]

The individual most responsible for foiling the ERA was Phyllis Schlafly, a conservative activist from St. Louis who first made a name for herself with her self-published book *A Choice, Not an Echo*, widely distributed in support of Barry Goldwater's 1964 campaign for president. In September 1972, after being convinced of the need to resist the feminist movement, Schlafly founded STOP ERA. Until then she had focused her activism primarily on national defense issues. As a Catholic, she had not yet been attuned to the social issues that animated evangelicals, like school prayer. By shifting gears, Schlafly brought a large network of conservative Catholic women — those who read her *Phyllis Schlafly Report*, which had in the range of thirty thousand subscribers throughout the 1970s — into the majority-evangelical movement to defeat the ERA. In this, like Francis Schaeffer, she built ecumenical bridges to likeminded conservatives of different religious faiths.[36]

Schlafly's first shot against the ERA hit its mark, in the form of a 1972 *Phyllis Schlafly Report* essay, "What's Wrong with 'Equal Rights' for Women?" Schlafly argued that the ERA would obliterate special legal protections afforded to women, including the insulation provided by the traditional family, which "assures a woman the most precious and important right of all—the right to keep her baby and be supported and protected in the enjoyment of watching her baby grow and develop." In this Schlafly defined the parameters of the winning campaign to defeat the ERA: if men and women were legal equals, fathers had no obligation to provide for mothers. In other words, equal rights for women actually meant that special rights for mothers would be revoked. Such special rights were paramount because Schlafly believed that motherhood was a woman's most fulfilling calling, a belief that directly challenged "women's libbers" like Betty Friedan, who "view the home as a prison, and the wife and mother as a slave." Schlafly tarred feminists as enemies of motherhood, an association that stuck.[37]

As resistance to the ERA grew throughout the 1970s, the ratification process stalled. Some states that had previously ratified the amendment even reversed their votes. As it became less and less likely that the ERA would be ratified, Schlafly's reputation as the intellectual force behind the movement to defeat the ERA grew. With the 1977 publication of *The Power of the Positive Woman*, arguably the definitive antifeminist manifesto, her status as the nation's most iconic antifeminist was cemented. The first step in becoming a "positive woman," another term for a confident antifeminist in Schlafly's vocabulary, was to embrace the natural differences between men and women. Consistent with such an essentialist understanding of sexual difference, Schlafly encouraged STOP ERA activists to accentuate traditional gender roles, such as dressing particularly femininely when lobbying state legislators. To the dismay of feminists, this strategy worked to perfection. Some of the more conservative legislators, of course, hardly needed their paternalistic egos stroked in such a way. "To pass a law or constitutional amendment saying that we are all alike in every respect," argued Illinois state representative Monroe Flynn, "flies in the face of what our Creator intended." Conservative Christians like Flynn related feminist attempts to eliminate sexual difference to secular efforts to erase God from the public sphere. Schlafly snidely suggested that if feminists had a problem with sexual difference they might also have a problem with God. "Someone, it is not clear who, perhaps God," she wrote, "dealt women a foul blow by making them female."[38]

Schlafly's antifeminism had a playful side to it. When addressing conservative crowds, she often started in the following way: "First of all, I want to thank my husband Fred, for letting me come—I always like to say that, because it makes the libs so mad!" Such friskiness was an effective contrast to the humorless recriminations that feminists directed her way. During a 1973 debate on the Illinois State University campus, Friedan infamously told Schlafly: "I would like to burn you at the stake.... I consider you a traitor to your sex, an Aunt Tom." Florynce Kennedy wondered "why some people don't hit Phyllis Schlafly in the mouth." Such nastiness spoke to the fact that Schlafly had come to signify the backlash against feminism and the impending defeat of the ERA, which feminists believed was a necessary and inevitable step to full equality.[39]

Schlafly's rhetoric, of course, could also be hard-hitting, such as when she theorized about the ways feminism might empower an immoral government over and against the moral family. Describing these implications in hypothetical fashion, she wrote: "[I]f fathers are not expected to stay home and care for their infant children, then neither should mothers be expected to do so; and, therefore, it becomes the duty of the government to provide kiddy-care centers to relieve mothers of that unfair and unequal burden." Such analysis suggested that women's liberationists, in their demand for total equality, wanted to empower Washington bureaucrats to enforce social engineering programs that would undermine the traditional family. In this Schlafly helped bring together two conservative trajectories—cultural traditionalism and antistatism—demonstrating that the culture wars, rather than being an evasion of political-economic debates about how power and resources were to be distributed, represented a new way of having such debates. Exemplifying this commingling of conservative ideologies, a 1976 *Phyllis Schlafly Report* headline about a coming convention on women screamed about "How the Libs and the Feds Plan to Spend Your Money."[40]

The convention referenced in Schlafly's headline, a government-sponsored International Women's Year (IWY) conference, became a lightning rod for cultural conservatives. Schlafly described the 1977 Houston convention as "a front for radicals and lesbians." Indeed, many of those involved in organizing the IWY convention were outspoken feminists, thanks to Midge Costanza, who, as Carter's chief of the White House's Office of Public Liaison, was charged with appointing members to the IWY Commission. Costanza designated liberal New York congresswoman Bella Abzug—who once claimed "a woman's place is in the house, the House of Representatives"—to chair the commission. Pentecostal televangelist Pat Robertson, who until then, happy to have a fellow born-again Christian in the White House, had sung Carter's praises, seethed: "I wouldn't let Bella Abzug scrub the floors of any organization that I was head of, but Carter put her in charge of all the women in America, and used our tax funds to support that convention in Houston." Costanza's other selections, highlighted by feminist notable Gloria Steinem, editor of *Ms.* magazine, did little to inspire the confidence of religious conservatives, who organized to gain their share of delegates to the Houston convention. After managing to secure control of only 25 percent of the delegation, Schlafly and other conservative women decided to put on a counter-IWY conference at Houston's Astro Arena. Their Pro-Family Rally attracted some twenty thousand attendees.[41]

The IWY convention's official platform, approved by vote of the delegation, was decidedly left of center. Not only did it call for the ratification of the ERA, but it also included abortion-on-demand and gay rights planks. The staid feminism that had informed NOW at its origins had given way to a more radical vision of gender equality, signaled by Friedan's public change of heart regarding the relationship between feminism and gay rights. In 1969 she infamously called lesbianism a "lavender herring," charging that gay rights would tarnish the feminist agenda. But at the 1977 Houston convention, Friedan seconded a resolution to support gay and lesbian rights, a huge symbolic victory for the gay rights movement. Although this newly expansive alliance illustrated the power of New Left feminist sensibilities, it also played into the hands of religious conservatives like Schlafly, who believed the radicalism of the IWY platform signified "the death knell of the women's liberation movement." "The Women's Lib movement has sealed its own doom," she proclaimed, "by deliberately hanging around its own neck the albatross of abortion, lesbianism, pornography and Federal control."[42]

The national debate between feminists and the Christian Right persisted throughout the Carter administration. In the summer of 1980, another national conference, the White House Conference on Families (WHCF), generated even more controversy. During his 1976 presidential campaign Carter had promised that, if elected, he would host a conference on the American family, wrongly assuming that sponsoring such a conference would be politically safe. Since both liberals and conservatives agreed the family was in crisis, he thought both sides would be willing to convene to map out common-ground solutions. Such faulty political logic was consistent with Carter's antipartisan temperament, which, against the grain of his centrist expectations, earned him the enmity of both liberals and conservatives, both feminists and antifeminists. The disputatious Houston convention quickly disabused Carter and his advisers of the notion that a conference on the family would be uncontroversial. They delayed holding it for as long as they could without reneging on his campaign promise. They also organized it such that Carter might keep his distance: instead of one conference in the nation's capital, which might attract criticism at a time when Carter had enough problems dealing with stagflation and the Iran hostage crisis, the White House hosted three regional conferences, in Baltimore, Minneapolis, and Los Angeles. This strategy failed. In an attempt to appease feminists annoyed with him for not being an enthusiastic enough supporter of the ERA, and for stating his personal discomfort with abortion, Carter gave his consent to a plural conference title: White House Conference on *Families*. Whereas feminists believed that official recognition of the pluralistic ways an increasing number of Americans lived would help remove the stain of illegitimacy affixed to nontraditional families, such as those headed by single mothers or gay couples, the Christian Right, abiding by traditional norms, defined the family in the singular and considered the plural WHCF title an insult.[43]

The publicity generated by the battle over the WHCF gave conservatives an opportunity to advertise their own vision of the family, which they presented in the form of the Family Protection Act, first introduced in Congress in 1979 by Senator Paul Laxalt, a Nevada Republican. This proposed legislation was an effortless mix of cultural and economic conservatism. Had it passed, for example, it would have drastically cut government childcare services, a menace to both family values and antitax conservatives. Among a laundry list of conservative wishes, the Family Protection Act prominently included an antiabortion provision that sought to deny Supreme Court jurisdiction to review state laws that pertained to abortion.[44]

By the late 1970s, abortion had become a defining issue for the Christian Right. But prior to *Roe v. Wade*, the momentous 1973 Supreme Court decision that legalized most abortions in the first two trimesters of pregnancy on the grounds that a woman's right to privacy included control over her pregnant body, this was not necessarily the case. Before it was legalized, many evangelicals, like a majority of Americans, held nonabsolute views on abortion. Though they might have considered a fetus a living being, they might also have believed that a fetus's right to life should be balanced against other considerations, including the health of the woman carrying it. In short, prior to *Roe v. Wade* many evangelicals held relativistic views about abortion: they did not support an absolute right to privacy, but neither did they favor a fetus's absolute right to life. Aside from a few marginalized fundamentalists—such as far-right preacher John Rice, the longtime editor of *The Sword of the Lord*, who in 1971 wrote that he "viewed the abortion legalization campaign as the latest liberal assault on morality in a rapidly escalating culture war"—most evangelical leaders were ambivalent. The SBC even supported liberal abortion laws, a position it maintained until 1979, when conservatives ousted the moderate leadership.[45]

The movement to legalize abortion, which had been banned in most states since 1880, had ramped up in the 1950s. Doctors led the early push to overturn anti-abortion laws, believing their status as professional experts granted them the authority to decide what was best for their patients. In the 1960s some states legalized "therapeutic abortions," those deemed necessary to protect the health of pregnant women as determined by doctors. In response, Catholics, the only religious group consistently outspoken against the liberalization of abortion laws, formed the nation's first anti-abortion group in 1968, the Right to Life League. For conservative Catholics, abortion seemed like a clear-cut affront to the epistemological views that underpinned their faith. They believed that the universe had an objective moral order to which humans were bound. Abortion was murder, and murder was wrong, plain and simple. Translated into the language of conservative evangelicals, who eventually overcame their inhibitions about joining a signature Catholic cause, abortion offended God's will.[46]

Roe v. Wade forced forty-six states to liberalize their abortion laws, leading to a national debate that compelled more Americans to take a firm stance on the issue. Justice Harry Blackmun, who delivered the Supreme Court's majority opinion, recognized that the decision was fraught with peril. In his opinion he wrote: "One's philosophy, one's experiences, one's exposure to the raw edges of human existence, one's religious training, one's attitude towards life and family and their values, and the moral standards one establishes and seeks to observe, are all likely to influence and to color one's thinking and conclusions about abortion." Blackmun was certainly right about that. But he could not have predicted the degree to which abortion was to be tied up with the war for the soul of America.[47]

The day after *Roe v. Wade*, a small-town Minnesota evangelical wrote a scathing letter to the editor of her local newspaper, charging that the "diabolical" decision was "glaring evidence that our society is decaying rapidly with moral corruption." *Christianity Today*, the most important magazine of highbrow evangelical opinion, editorialized: "Christians should accustom themselves to the thought that the American state no longer supports, in any meaningful sense, the laws of God, and prepare themselves spiritually for the prospect that it may one day formally repudiate them and turn against those who seek to live by them." Although most evangelical leaders were slower to respond, the *Christianity Today* editorial anticipated the ways in which an emerging evangelical opposition to abortion would be framed.[48]

Francis Schaeffer nudged many evangelicals to oppose abortion. Jerry Falwell credited Schaeffer for convincing him to become ardently pro-life. So too did Randall Terry, who became the nation's most prominent anti-abortion activist in 1986, when he founded Operation Rescue, which premised its militant tactics on the slogan "If you believe abortion is murder, act like it's murder." Schaeffer saw abortion as evidence of the humanistic disregard for life as a moral absolute. He theorized that it was a slippery slope from abortion to euthanasia and, more broadly, to the state's having total authority over decisions regarding who gets to live and who gets to die. "In regards to the fetus, the courts have arbitrarily separated 'aliveness' from 'personhood,' and if this is so," he asked, "why not arbitrarily do the same with the aged?" In the 1979 pro-life film series *Whatever Happened to the Human Race?* Schaeffer argued that abortion was a result of a shift from a Christian-based society, in which each individual was viewed as a unique creation of God, to a secular humanist society, in which individuals were conceptualized as cogs in a larger biological machine. Franky Schaeffer writes that his father pointed "to the 'human life issue' as the watershed between a 'Christian society' and a utilitarian relativistic 'post-Christian' future stripped of compassion and beauty."[49]

Falwell, who by the end of the 1970s routinely referred to abortion

as "murder according to the Word of God," quoted Schaeffer exten-
sively whenever he discussed the topic. Like Schaeffer, Falwell believed that legalized abortion represented the tragic if logical consequence of secular humanism's negation of God. In this way Schaeffer
helped evangelicals like Falwell recognize that resistance to abortion
was of a piece with their anxieties about how a secular state was imposing its anti-Christian will on the nation. Recognizing as much com-
plicates the simplistic view held by many political observers that abortion as a stand-alone issue pushed erstwhile Democrats into voting
for the Republican Party, which has included an anti-abortion plank
in every one of its platforms since 1980. This might have been true for
some Americans, especially for anti-abortion Catholics with historical
ties to the Democratic Party. And certainly some Republican politicians have kept abortion on the national radar in order to gain electoral advantage. For example, beginning in 1976 with Congressman
Henry Hyde from Illinois, Republicans have annually proposed riders to yearly appropriations bills — the so-called Hyde Amendments —
that would prohibit federal funds from being used for abortion. But by
the end of the 1970s the vast majority of pro-life Americans were religious conservatives who would have voted Republican whether the
Supreme Court had legalized abortion or not. As demonstrated by the
Family Values Act, proposed and supported by many Republicans but
hardly any Democrats, the Republican Party was increasingly coming
to represent a Christian Right worldview in general. Opposition to
abortion was a paramount component of that worldview, but only one
ingredient of a more general antisecular perspective.[50]

Another issue that religious conservatives felt strongly about was
the gay rights movement. The Christian Right opposed gay rights on
the grounds that homosexuality flouted the will of God as expressed
in the traditional family. When the Dade County Commission in Miami, Florida, approved an ordinance in 1977 that explicitly prohibited
discrimination against gays, religious conservatives mobilized under
the leadership of Anita Bryant, the former Miss Oklahoma and popular singer who called homosexuality "a disguised attack on God." As
a countermeasure, Bryant helped place an anti–gay rights referendum on Dade County ballots, which succeeded in overturning the gay
rights ordinance by two to one. The Dade County ordinance stipu-
lation that most disturbed Bryant and her fellow conservatives was

that schools could not discriminate against gays when hiring teachers. Concerned that gay men were more likely to be pederasts and that they would recruit children to their "lifestyle," Bryant founded Save Our Children, a coalition that sought to exclude out-of-the-closet gays from the teaching profession.[51]

In 1978 California state senator John Briggs, a Bryant acolyte, introduced Proposition 6, otherwise known as the Briggs Initiative, which would have empowered California school districts to fire "open and notorious" gay teachers. Despite coming quickly on the heels of the conservative triumph in Florida, the California initiative was trounced by over one million votes. Even former governor Ronald Reagan publicly opposed the Briggs Initiative for the reason that he did not view homosexuality as "a contagious disease like the measles," perhaps a brave stance given that Reagan's impending run for the presidency was going to require religious conservative votes. Any joy that gay rights activists felt as a result of such a resounding victory was crushed three weeks later when openly gay San Francisco Supervisor Harvey Milk, the leader of the campaign to defeat the Briggs Initiative, was gunned down, along with San Francisco Mayor George Moscone, by a homophobic former colleague. Falwell, who had been campaigning with Bryant against gay rights since the Dade County referendum, deemed the Milk assassination God's judgment. To his mind, the gay rights movement was putting the nation itself at risk of divine retribution. "Like a spiritual cancer, homosexuality spread until the city of Sodom was destroyed. Can we believe that God will spare the United States if homosexuality continues to spread?"[52]

Tim LaHaye wrote a number of popular books in the 1970s and 1980s that provided readers with a framework for understanding secular humanism in relation to issues like the family, marriage, and schooling. One such book, *The Unhappy Gays*, an unsympathetic polemic against homosexuality, was published a few months before the vote on the Briggs Initiative, which LaHaye saw as necessary to "protect school children from being taught perverted sex by a homosexual." He and his wife Beverly had relocated to San Diego in 1956 from the South, where LaHaye had been a pastor since earning his bachelor's degree from Bob Jones University. In Southern California the consequences of the sexual revolution, such as casual sex and easy divorce, were more out in the open than virtually anywhere else in the nation. And yet a large contingent of religious conservatives also lived in Southern California, generating a productive friction that situated the LaHayes at the forefront of resistance to cultural radicalism.[53]

The thesis LaHaye laid out in *The Unhappy Gays*, as the title suggests, was that "homosexuals are unquestionably more miserable than straight people." LaHaye argued that the word *gay* was a deceitful "propaganda word" when used as a synonym for *homosexuality*, citing liberal historian Arthur Schlesinger Jr. for support. In a 1977 *Time* magazine article, "The State of Language," Schlesinger wrote the following passage, subsequently quoted by LaHaye: "Gay used to be one of the most agreeable words in the language. Its appropriation by a notably morose group is an act of piracy." LaHaye presented a list of reasons why "gay isn't gay," including that gay men suffered unusually high rates of depression, drug use, and suicide. In this he ignored the likelihood that the cultural stigma attached to homosexuality, which manifested in myriad forms of discrimination, was the actual cause of their unhappiness. But LaHaye's objective was not to cure discrimination. Like so many other evangelicals, LaHaye believed that committing oneself to Christianity, which affirmed heterosexuality as God's will, was the only path to personal redemption. In other words, belief in Christ was the cure to homosexuality. In this LaHaye matter-of-factly denied that homosexuality was occurring naturally. "No one," he wrote, "is born homosexual."[54]

Homosexuality was a key theme in right-wing jeremiads of that age. Like Falwell and most evangelical leaders, LaHaye believed that given social space to thrive, homosexuality would be the death of America. LaHaye introduced *The Unhappy Gays* with a fable about a trip he and Beverly took to Italy, where a guide told them that a public bath at the ruins of Pompeii was "for men only." Mentally comparing that to the public baths frequented by gay men in American cities like New York and San Francisco, he wrote: "No wonder Gibbon concluded that homosexuality was one of the moral sins that contributed to the decline of the Roman Empire." In the same ways that they pointed to *Engel v. Vitale* as the beginning of American decline, conservative Christians often alluded to Edward Gibbon's classic eighteenth-century book *The History of the Decline and Fall of the Roman Empire*, which on their reading explained Rome's collapse as the result of sexual depravity, in order to prophesy the downfall of American civilization. "A homosexually lenient society," LaHaye warned, "will incur the wrath of God." Whereas America was once great because it was a society based on biblical principles, "when sodomy fills the national cup of man's abominations to overflowing, God earmarks that nation for destruction."[55]

As opposed to those who had a more secular interpretation of American history—including most academic historians—religious conservatives held that America was founded as a Christian nation. For the Christian Right, the belief that the United States was the product of divine creation explained American exceptionalism. "I believe that God promoted America to a greatness no other nation has enjoyed," Falwell preached, "because her heritage is one of a republic governed by laws predicated on the Bible." Beyond explaining national greatness, the narrative of America's heavenly origins was also important to Christian culture warriors because it undergirded their critique of secularization by drawing a clear boundary between the nation's glorious past and its degraded present. "Either we will return to the moral integrity and original dreams of the founders of this nation," Pat Robertson cautioned, "or we will give ourselves over more and more to hedonism, to all forms of destructive anti-social behavior, to political apathy, and ultimately to the forces of anarchy and disintegration that have throughout history gripped great empires and nations in their tragic and declining years." Historian Donald Critchlow points out that this Christian Right "moral sensibility" about the nation and its history was rooted in the assumption "that free government rested upon a moral or religious citizenry whose principal civil responsibility was the protection of virtue. The sensibility upheld the belief that ultimately republican government rested on moral foundations that, if eroded, would lead to the collapse of the polity."[56]

Given the mobilization of religious conservatives during the 1970s, and given the biblical inspiration upon which their triumphant nationalism rested, the Christian Right's enthusiastic embrace of Ronald Reagan's 1980 presidential candidacy should not have been surprising. It was Reagan, after all, who famously described the United States as a "city on a hill," a metaphor he borrowed from John Winthrop, who borrowed it from Jesus. It was Reagan, not his evangelical opponent Jimmy Carter, who attended James Robison's 1980 Religious Roundtable in Dallas, where he knowingly told the gathering of adoring evangelicals: "You can't endorse me, but I endorse you." It was Reagan who promised to reinstate school prayer, who campaigned to end the alleged IRS persecution of Christian schools, who advocated for the teaching of creationism, saying that evolution was "theory only," and who vowed to overturn *Roe v. Wade*, avowing deep regret about his earlier support for pro-choice legislation. It was Reagan who said: "The First Amendment was written not to protect the people and their laws from religious values, but to protect those values from government tyranny."[57]

Reagan should hardly have been theologically palatable to white evangelicals: despite dabbling in premillennial dispensationalism, a distinctive Christian fundamentalist eschatology in which adherents sought to decode signs of the coming rapture, he also showed interest in Baha'i, astrology, and the Shroud of Turin. As one Carter supporter bitterly pointed out, Reagan was "a Hollywood libertine, had a child conceived out of wedlock before he and Nancy married, admitted to drug use during his Hollywood years, and according to Henry Steele Commager, was one of the least religious presidents in American history." Yet Reagan won nearly 75 percent of white evangelical voters in 1980—and this should not have puzzled anyone. By unambiguously aligning himself with Christian Right efforts to take God's country back, Reagan won over conservative evangelicals less interested in his theology or his personal history than in his politics.[58]

Winning over the Christian Right in 1980 was a big deal. In response to developments that they believed imperiled the nation—secularization, feminism, abortion, gay rights—religious conservatives intensified their involvement in political activism. Evangelical leaders told their congregants that it was their duty to inject their religious beliefs into the political sphere. Falwell, in an apparent reversal of his earlier claim that preachers should not participate in the civil rights movement because it was not the role God had called them to, proclaimed: "This idea of 'religion and politics don't mix' was invented by the devil to keep Christians from running their own country." Tapped by well-connected Republican operatives Paul Weyrich, Richard Viguerie, and Howard Phillips, Falwell founded Moral Majority in 1979 as part of a larger effort to bring religious conservatives into a powerful new political alliance. Falwell justified the need for Moral Majority by arguing that Christian fundamentalists like himself had more in common with similarly orthodox Jews and Catholics "than we ever will with the secularizers of this country. It is time for all religiously committed citizens to unite against our common enemy."[59]

Despite such ecumenical rhetoric, the vast majority of Moral

Majority members were evangelicals. Other than abortion, its core issues were evangelical concerns such as opposition to feminism, gay rights, pornography, and the teaching of evolution. Nonevangelical conservatives were welcome in Moral Majority: indeed, Catholics purportedly constituted nearly 30 percent of the membership at the peak of its influence in the early 1980s. But Moral Majority was immediately powerful because there was an obvious need for a political organization that would act as a vehicle for white evangelical causes. In its first year it enrolled 2.5 million mostly evangelical members and reported contributions in excess of $35 million. Moral Majority's influence increased after it was deemed to have been crucial to Reagan's victory. In the immediate aftermath of the election, one prominent headline read: "The Preachers Gave It to Reagan." Such press fed into Christian Right hyperbole, as Falwell claimed Moral Majority was the main reason Reagan got elected. Liberals reacted to the 1980 election results similarly, if from a different evaluative perspective. They fretted about an impending theocracy, comparing the Christian Right to Iranian fundamentalists who had taken American hostages, and often called Falwell the American Ayatollah.[60]

Claims about the importance of newly energized evangelicals were only half true. They ignored that even before 1980, conservative evangelicals had often organized effectively behind conservative politicians. The mistake is repeated often by historians, who tend to argue that 1980 represented the reemergence of conservative Christians in a political sphere they had deserted after the humiliation of the Scopes Monkey Trial. Nixon's 1972 reelection serves as an instructive counterexample. Neoconservatives believed Nixon's landslide represented the will of urban ethnic whites like themselves who had grown weary of a New Left they believed was dictating the McGovern campaign. Such an account, though not entirely false, ignored that the key to Nixon's victory was winning over evangelicals. Nixon did better with urban white ethnics than any Republican since the early twentieth century, thanks largely to organized labor's lack of enthusiasm for McGovern. But a startlingly high 84 percent of white evangelicals voted for Nixon in 1972. The Nixon campaign was nothing if not smart about demographic trends. The Sunbelt states were becoming increasingly populous, and evangelicals were the fastest-growing population in those states. By the early 1970s the ten largest churches in the nation, all evangelical, were located in the southern and western parts of the country. With this in mind, Nixon exploited issues that drew them to the voting booths. For instance, he leaked news that he had ordered *Portnoy's Complaint,* Philip Roth's novel about masturbation, removed from the White House library.[61]

Neoconservatives—the intellectual spokespeople for urban white ethnics—might have innovated much of the logic that informed the conservative side of the culture wars, particularly in relation to late-twentieth-century racial discourse. But the Christian Right formed the demographic bedrock of the conservative culture wars. Because of this, the war for the soul of America was as much a religious struggle between people of incompatible faiths—conservative Christians and secular liberals—as it was a fight over the nation's ethnic and racial legacies. Of course these two distinct battle lines often overlapped in the 1980s and 1990s, giving the culture wars narrative its valence.

4

The Color Line

"The problem of the twentieth century is the problem of the color line." Historians of modern American race relations are almost obligated to cite W. E. B. Du Bois's powerful declaration, drawn from his 1903 classic *The Souls of Black Folk*. "The color line," a phrase coined by Frederick Douglass in 1881 to describe the emergence of Jim Crow, is perhaps the finest metaphor for the history of American racial exclusion. The United States, after all, was founded on the dispossession of indigenous nonwhites and made rich by the enslavement of African blacks. Even after the Civil War resulted in the abolition of slavery, black Americans existed as an ostracized caste, never considered fully American. "Many whites," Ralph Ellison observed, "could look at the social position of blacks and feel that color formed an easy and reliable gauge for determining to what extent one was and was not American." Black marginalization was thrown into stark relief by the European immigrant experience, a disparity perhaps best represented by the radically different analogies for intermixing: whereas European immigrants, irrespective of ethnic background, were encouraged to mix into one big American "melting pot," an individual was removed from the American project by virtue of "one drop" of black blood.[1]

The post–World War II civil rights movement, which forced the nation to reckon with its racism, was supposed to have changed all of this. Blacks were granted formal American citizenship by the 1964 Civil Rights Act and 1965 Voting Rights Act. Martin Luther King's celebrated March on Washington speech, delivered from the steps of the Lincoln Memorial to 250,000 civil rights supporters, was to have set out the new law of the land. "I have a dream," King said, "that my four little children will one day live in a nation where they will not be judged by the color of their skin but by the content of their character." And yet color continued to handicap a person's chances of success.

In the late twentieth century, black Americans were eight times more likely than white Americans to experience chronic poverty. The schools many black Americans attended were acutely underfunded relative to those filled by white Americans. And black men were eight times more likely than white men to spend time in prison, a discrepancy one scholar calls "the new Jim Crow." Given such persistent racial inequality, that the culture wars were frequently fought from opposites sides of the color line is hardly surprising. Race, to borrow from Marx, continued to "weigh like a nightmare on the brains of the living."[2]

That the color line remained firmly intact despite the nation's formal commitment to colorblindness was a source of widespread cognitive dissonance. By extending formal freedom to all Americans, including black Americans, the nation, it seemed, had finally lived up to its stated ideals. But that racial inequality endured — that the color line often proved impervious to legal reforms — left many Americans confused. Such bewilderment, though unsettling, proved fertile grounds for intellectual innovation. American thinkers mostly agreed that post–civil rights America was not postracial, that racial disparities endured. But they often vehemently disagreed about how to diagnose and solve the array of problems stemming from this fact. A variety of theories emerged in the 1980s and 1990s to explain why the civil rights revolution had failed to relegate racial inequality to the dustbins of history. The bitter national debate over these theories functioned as a reminder that a new American identity would not easily transcend the color line. Race was a festering wound on the soul of America.

Until the 1980s, a reconstructed racial liberalism offered the most influential explanation for persistent racial inequality. The Civil Rights Act, the signature legal accomplishment of the civil rights movement, affirmed the liberal argument that appealing to legislatures and courts remained the best means for safeguarding black civil rights. Through 1965, racial liberals had supported a colorblind approach to equal opportunity, codified by Title VII of the landmark legislation, which barred discrimination and preferential treatment. But when racial inequality proved more obstinate than predicted, racial liberals adjusted their notions about proper legal redress. As most firms continued their usual practice of exclusively employing whites—since, ironically, con-travening the colorblind principle of "merit" would be a technical vio-lation of the new legal stricture against preferential treatment—many racial liberals tentatively embraced "affirmative action," a term coined by black attorney Hobart Taylor Jr. for its alliterative qualities. They became more attuned to Black Power arguments about institutional racism, arguments about how standards such as merit were embed-ded in the history of a nation that had only one hundred years earlier enslaved black people and thus was anything but colorblind. As liberal political theorist Amy Gutmann asserted: "[A] colorblind perspective fails to leave room for according moral relevance to the fact that we do not yet live in a land of fair equality of opportunity for all American citizens." A reconstructed racial liberalism favored a proactive gov-ernment that would guarantee black Americans not only "equality as a right and a theory" but also, as the nation's leading liberal Lyndon Johnson famously put it, "equality as a fact and as a result."[3]

President Johnson ditched the colorblind approach in 1965 when he issued Executive Order 11246, committing the federal government to affirmative action. Since all taxpayers, white and black, funded fed-eral construction projects, the federal government would ensure that white and black taxpayers were hired to build those projects. Such logic was applied to higher education as well, granting white and black taxpayers access to the American universities they subsidized. With this, the rhetoric about affirmative action shifted in focus from "merit" to "preference." If two candidates for a job were equal, everything else considered, the black candidate was to be given preference. In order to ensure compliance, the Equal Employment Opportunity Commis-sion (EEOC) under Johnson required that businesses that took fed-eral money count their minority employees—the first step toward es-tablishing racial quotas. Then, under Nixon, quotas became stricter with implementation of the Philadelphia Plan, a mandate that federal projects employ the same percentage of blacks as that which inhab-ited the city where the project was slated to go up. Remarkably, then, both Democratic and Republican presidents had embraced affirma-tive action. Just as remarkably, the Supreme Court made affirmative action the law of the land with its landmark 1971 *Briggs v. Duke Power Co.* case. On behalf of a unanimous court, Chief Justice Warren Burger argued: "[P]ractices, procedures, or tests neutral on their face, and even neutral in terms of intent, cannot be maintained if they operate to 'freeze' the status quo of prior discriminatory employment practices." In a nation that had long given whites preferential treatment, a new consensus held that justice demanded the opposite.[4]

Even though political elites had reached consensus by the early 1970s, affirmative action aroused condemnation from the outset. In 1968, for example, the neoconservative academic John Bunzel posed a simple but powerful rhetorical question that reaffirmed the merits of colorblindness: "Is color the test of competence?" The line that divided opponents in the affirmative action debate, then, was the line between an older colorblind racial liberalism and a newer color-conscious racial liberalism that had incorporated elements of Black Power into its theoretical framework. This split became more pronounced in 1978, when the Supreme Court heard another case on affirmative action, *Regents of the University of California v. Bakke*, about whether it was constitutional for institutions of higher education to employ racial quotas when making admissions decisions. Allan Bakke sued the University of California–Davis Medical School when his application was rejected even though his admission scores, a composite of his grade point average and his Medical College Admission Test (MCAT) scores, were significantly higher than those of several minority candidates who were accepted. Labeled the "reverse discrimination" case, *Bakke* hinged on whether "disadvantaged" candidates could be exempted from competing with a general pool of candidates.[5]

Bakke divided the nation. It also divided the Supreme Court. William Rehnquist, the most conservative member of the court, was adamant that race "may not be used at all" in university admissions decisions without violating Title VII of the Civil Rights Act. In contrast, the liberals on the court, including Thurgood Marshall and Harry Blackmun, contended that the University of California's quota system was an acceptable approach to racial discrimination. "To get beyond racism," Blackmun argued, "we must first take account of race. And in order to treat some persons equally, we must treat them differently." Marshall grounded his support for racial quotas in "the nation's sorry history of racial discrimination." He mocked the idea of a colorblind Constitution as hypocritical, given the Supreme Court's long history of taking color into consideration to the benefit of white Americans, most infamously with its 1896 *Plessy v. Ferguson* "separate but equal" decision. Splitting the difference between the starkly different conservative and liberal interpretations, the moderates on the court, including Burger, John Paul Stevens, and Lewis Powell, believed the plaintiff made a compelling case that he had been discriminated against. But unlike Rehnquist, the moderates did not wish for their *Bakke* opinion, which carried a slim majority, to overturn precedent for affirmative action. Rather, they wanted a narrow ruling that, accord to Stevens, would "enable proponents of affirmative action to distinguish this case from most of the programs that are in effect throughout the country." In his majority opinion, Powell reasoned that race could be one consideration among many in admissions decisions but that quotas violated the Civil Rights Act. As a result, affirmative action was weakened but intact. Color-conscious liberalism remained somewhat influential, but its appeal was greatly diminished. By 1981, the year Ronald Reagan moved into the White House, conservatives stood poised to fill the vacuum created by racial liberalism's increasingly steep decline.[6]

Most conservatives rejected affirmative action from the outset. Some, like Barry Goldwater, couched their arguments against it in libertarian terms, arguing that it was an unwarranted government intervention into free labor market exchanges. But more generally, conservatives found their political footing on affirmative action when they narrowed their scope to target racial quotas, which were opposed by a large majority of white Americans. Always attuned to white majority opinion, Nixon reversed his tepid support for affirmative action, including his administration's own Philadelphia Plan, in time for the 1972 campaign. Referring to his opponent George McGovern as "the quota candidate," Nixon thundered at the Republican National Convention: "You do not correct an ancient injustice by committing a new one." From then on, conservative politicians grew increasingly outspoken on affirmative action. In 1976 Republican Senator Orrin Hatch described it as an "assault upon America, conceived in lies." During the 1980 campaign, Reagan argued against affirmative action in gentler yet equally damning tones. "I'm old enough to remember when quotas existed in the U.S. for the purpose of discrimination," he said. "And I don't want to see that happen again." As right-wing rhetoric became increasingly "colorblind," conservatives anointed Alexander Bickel, the nominally liberal Yale jurist, their favorite legal scholar. In an argument entered into evidence on behalf of Bakke, Bickel contended: "Discrimination on the basis of race is illegal, immoral, unconstitutional, inherently wrong, and destructive of democratic society. Now this is to be unlearned, and we are told that this is not a matter of fundamental principle but only a matter of whose ox is gored."[7]

Reagan's appointments to sensitive civil rights positions set the tone of his administration's approach to the color line. Two conservative lawyers, Clarence Thomas and William Bradford Reynolds, were tapped respectively as chair of the EEOC and assistant attorney general for civil rights. Both men were known to disparage "race-conscious affirmative action." Thomas, a black Georgian who joined the Supreme Court in 1991, wrote in his memoir that the stigmatizing effects of affirmative action put him at a disadvantage while he attended Yale Law School. Reynolds simply called it "morally wrong." With Thomas and Reynolds taking the lead, the Reagan administration slowly chipped away at affirmative action. It raised the cap on the size of firms required to comply with federal affirmative action regulations from 50 to 250 employees—relieving tens of thousands of companies from having to hire minorities. Under Thomas's direction, the EEOC quit identifying patterns of discrimination and instead pressed a smaller number of individual discrimination cases, including a few so-called reverse discrimination cases. In short, colorblind conservatives used the power of the federal government to slow some of the signature achievements of color-conscious liberals. Reagan did his part in this cause by regularly invoking Martin Luther King as his inspiration for a colorblind America, claiming he was committed to "a society where people would be judged on the content of their character, not the color of their skin."[8]

Colorblind conservatism had its intellectual advocates, particularly Shelby Steele, author of the critically acclaimed 1990 book *The Content of Our Character*. That Steele was lumped together with a cause championed by Reagan was ironic, and not only because he was black and an English professor, two identities that tended to guarantee hostility to Reagan. Such an association was also perplexing because Steele was more honest about Reagan's rhetoric than might have been expected from the chosen champion of conservative colorblindness. "Reagan's claim of color blindness with regard to race," Steele argued, "was really a claim of racial innocence and guiltlessness—the preconditions for entitlement and power." And yet despite such misgivings, Steele thought Reagan's colorblind approach to race, his calls for "individual initiative, self sufficiency, strong families," would prove more effective in combating the color line than anything on offer from color-conscious liberals. This was because he believed that liberal policies such as affirmative action were steeped in the Black Power–infused ideology of victimhood. "Since the social victim has been oppressed by society," Steele wrote, "he comes to feel that his individual life will be improved more by changes in society than by his own initiative." In other words, by regarding themselves as victims of systematic racism and by waiting for social remedies, blacks were tragically failing to take responsibility for their own lives. In Steele's words, they were "race-holding," or making excuses for not putting in the effort needed to succeed in the American meritocracy. This represented Steele's explanation for the paradoxical persistence of racial inequality even after the victories of the civil rights movement. "If conditions have worsened for most of us as racism has receded, then much of the problem must be of our own making." It was no wonder, then, that so many conservatives, and whites in general, embraced Steele. He offered a solution to the color line that did not demand that they make sacrifices.[9]

Steele's analysis, which pinned much of the blame for the late-twentieth-century color line on black Americans, was based on the assumption that racism had in fact receded. In contrast, from the opposite end of the political spectrum, a group of mostly black academics innovated a theory that posited the persistence, or more ominously the permanence, of American racism. Critical Race Theory, as these scholars named their school of thought, emerged as perhaps the stiffest challenge to colorblind America and its institutional paragon, the American legal system. Critical Race Theory was perfectly situated to expose the contradictions of colorblind rhetoric, in part because it emerged from the crucible of Harvard University, which, in the words of Christopher Lasch, was "the foremost stronghold of meritocracy." Harvard in this way served as a proxy for the colorblind ethos thought by Critical Race Theorists to be a barrier to racial justice. It was at Harvard where the law professor Derrick Bell—the foundational Critical Race theorist—took stock of how racism manifested in an ostensibly colorblind institutional setting that operated much like the American legal system. Just as Critical Race theorists unmasked the hidden and not-so-hidden biases of the so-called Harvard meritocracy, they also leveled a sustained scholarly analysis of, in Cornel West's words, "the historical centrality and complicity of law in upholding white supremacy." Bell and his students experienced what they deciphered as a coded form of racism at Harvard. It was expressly different from the overt Bull Connor–style prejudice against which the civil rights movement fought. But it was racist nonetheless.[10]

In 1969 Harvard Law School had hired Bell, then a renowned civil rights lawyer, to placate black student protests that were part of the nationwide movement to make universities more amenable to minority student interests. In 1971 Bell became the first black American to gain tenure at Harvard Law. Bell's ability to smash through deeply entrenched historical barriers demonstrated progress. To put this in perspective, Du Bois, who in 1895 became the first black American to earn a PhD from Harvard, had been denied entry to several campus buildings during his time in Cambridge. And yet despite such tangible advances, Bell believed that his personal victory was mostly pyrrhic in a larger political sense. As the lone tenured minority at Harvard Law for more than a decade, he saw his presence there less as evidence of racial progress and more as proof of Harvard's "black tokenism policy."[11]

Bell's belief that he was the product of "tokenism" informed his single most influential contribution to legal scholarship, first elaborated in a 1980 *Harvard Law Review* article, *"Brown v. Board of Education* and the Interest Convergence Dilemma." Bell's thesis was innovative in its elementariness: "The interests of blacks in achieving racial equality will be accommodated only when it converges with the interests of whites." In constitutional terms, this meant that "the Fourteenth Amendment, standing alone, will not authorize a judicial remedy providing effective racial equality for blacks where the remedy sought threatens the superior societal status of middle- and upper-class whites." Bell later restated the "interest convergence dilemma" in the colloquial words of one of his fictional alter egos, a literary device he frequently used, the militant, über-educated black limousine driver Jesse B. Semple: "The law works for the Man most of the time, and only works for us in the short run as a way of working for him in the long run."[12]

In an empirical application of his "interest convergence dilemma," Bell advanced the argument that the 1954 landmark *Brown* decision was made possible only by Cold War imperatives. The American elite, Bell contended, concluded that Africans, Asians, and Latin Americans, those who lived opposite the global color line, might resist joining the American system if it persisted in sanctioning Jim Crow. Bell's "interest convergence dilemma" signaled his divergence from the civil rights legal tradition. "Traditional civil rights laws tend to be ineffective because they are built on a law enforcement model," as Bell put into words by way of another of his literary alter egos, Geneva Crenshaw. "But the law enforcement model for civil rights breaks down when a great number of whites are willing—because of convenience, habit, distaste, fear, or simple preference—to violate the law." Bell's rejection of civil rights legal tradition was, in turn, a rejection of the liberal narrative of progress. It fueled his pessimistic belief that racism was permanently endemic to American society, and that in changed circumstances black rights would be constrained yet again. Indeed, he assumed such backsliding was already under way. "Recent decisions, most notably by the Supreme Court," he wrote, in reference to *Bakke*, "indicate that the convergence of black and white interests that led to *Brown* in 1954 and influenced the character of its enforcement has begun to fade."[13]

Bell's courses on law and race were hugely popular among Harvard students, as was his famous 1973 casebook *Race, Racism, and American Law*. This was due to Bell's unusual and controversial methodology. In both his writing and his teaching, according to the editors of an influential Critical Race Theory anthology, "he used racial politics rather than formal structure of legal doctrine as the organizing concept for scholarly study." The first page of his casebook featured the renowned photograph of Thomas Smith and John Carlos on the 1968 Summer Olympic medal stand in Mexico City, black-gloved fists in the air. "In a subtle way," the editors wrote, "Bell's position within the legal academy—an arena that defined itself within the conventional legal discourse as neutral to race—was akin to putting up his fist in the black power salute." Bell's militancy rubbed off on his students. When he left Harvard in 1980 to become dean of the University of Oregon Law School, students organized protests to compel Harvard administrators to replace him with a minority professor. When the Harvard dons refused, on stated meritocratic grounds, students organized their own course, where they continued to read Bell's casebook. Out of that extracurricular course—taught and attended by several of the founding Critical Race Theory scholars—a school of thought was born.[14]

Critical Race Theory thus emerged in response to the machinations of the colorblind Harvard meritocracy. According to its leading thinkers, "the 'legislation' of the civil rights movement and its 'integration' into the mainstream commonsense assumptions in the late sixties and early seventies were premised on a tragically narrow and conservative picture of the goals of racial justice and the domains of racial power." Critical Race Theorists rejected the one-way assimilation of blacks into institutional settings created and controlled by whites. Prominent Critical Race theorist Patricia Williams described this process: "Blacks are the objects of a constitutional omission which has been incorporated into a theory of neutrality." Like Black Power advocates Stokely Carmichael and Charles Hamilton, Critical Race theorists did not wish "to live in a society in which to be unconditionally 'American' is to be white, and to be black is a misfortune." Rather than enlarge the circle of American identity to include blacks—the essence of the racial liberal project in both its colorblind and color-conscious iterations—Critical Race theorists thought America was irredeemable. If blacks were going to become Americans in the full sense, American identity would have to be transformed beyond recognition. It would have to be unwhitened.[15]

In 1986, after six years on the West Coast, at Oregon and then at the Stanford University Law School, Bell returned to Harvard, where he taught for another four stormy years. Soon after his return, he staged a five-day sit-in over the law school's failure to give tenure to two Critical Race theorists. The administration claimed their scholarship was substandard. In 1990, when he threatened to remain on unpaid leave until the law school hired a minority woman, Harvard fired Bell. This act of defiance undoubtedly influenced the tone of his 1992 book *Faces at the Bottom of the Well: The Permanence of Racism*, his gloomiest though best-selling work. *Faces at the Bottom of the Well* eloquently gave life to Bell's pessimistic outlook that "racism in America is not a curable aberration—as we all believed it was at some earlier point. Rather, it is a key component in this country's stability." In this Bell echoed the explanatory paradigm put forward by Du Bois in his brilliant 1935 book *Black Reconstruction in America*, in which he contended that working-class whites accepted class hierarchy because they benefited from a racial caste system. This was what Du Bois memorably called "the public and psychological wage" of being white. The comparison to Du Bois is telling: whereas Du Bois wrote about the role that race played in the making of the American class structure during the heyday of Jim Crow, Bell made his case about permanent racism in the decades after Jim Crow had been dismantled. Critical Race Theory was premised on explicating this discouraging historical trajectory. Bell wrote:

> On the one hand, contemporary color barriers are certainly less visible as a result of our successful efforts to strip the law's endorsement from the hated Jim Crow signs. Today one can travel for thousands of miles across the country and never see a public facility designated as "Colored" or "White." Indeed, the very absence of visible signs of discrimination creates an atmosphere of racial neutrality and encourages whites to believe that racism is a thing of the past. On the other hand, the general use of so-called neutral standards to continue exclusionary practices reduces the effectiveness of traditional civil rights laws, while rendering discriminatory actions more oppressive than ever.[16]

Such racial theorizing left an indelible imprint on the late-twentieth-century American academy. There Critical Race Theory was an important oppositional formation to conservative colorblindness. But beyond academia, color-consciousness was becoming increasingly unacceptable in the national political realm. No longer did the most powerful men in the nation sign off on substantial color-conscious policies, as Johnson and Nixon had done in the sixties. Rather, by 1993 a black law professor could not be named assistant attorney general for civil rights because she had expressed color-conscious views.

Lani Guinier, who taught at the University of Pennsylvania Law School, was tapped by Bill Clinton to join the Justice Department, only to be forced by the newly elected president to withdraw her candidacy after conservative critics uncovered an academic paper she had written a few years prior, titled "Keeping the Faith: Black Voters in the Post-Reagan Era." In that article Guinier argued that voting districts should be reapportioned such that blacks might achieve political representation proportional to their overall percentage of the population. A prominent report issued by a right-wing think tank contended that by rejecting colorblindness, one of "the most fundamental principles at the heart of American representative democracy," Guinier supported a "balkanized society." Based on such analysis, the *Wall Street Journal* labeled Guinier "Clinton's Quota Queen." Clinton caved to right-wing pressure, explaining his decision to terminate Guinier's candidacy in a letter to Senator Daniel Patrick Moynihan: "Over time, it became obvious to me that Ms. Guinier's confirmation hearing would engender a sustained and bitter debate over civil rights; a debate that would have been divisive and polarizing at a time when our nation needs healing."[17]

The dispute over the Guinier nomination revealed that conservatives had gained the upper hand in political struggles over the national meaning of race. Not coincidentally, it also demonstrated that conservatives had taken ownership of the rhetoric of colorblindness. This was a remarkable turnaround. Three decades prior, when colorblindness was the moral domain of racial liberalism, conservatives tended to frame their racial politics in color-conscious terms. In 1957 William Buckley Jr. editorialized that because southern whites were, "for the time being, the advanced race," they were "entitled to take such measures as are necessary to prevail, politically and culturally, where they do not prevail numerically." That conservatives had embraced colorblindness, and that liberals had adopted color-consciousness, was consistent with larger trends in the culture wars.[18]

Late-twentieth-century Americans tended to divide into opposing epistemological camps. Whereas conservatives were increasingly informed by universalistic concepts of certainty, liberals were increasingly directed by relativistic ideas about context. Most conservatives came to believe that since race did not determine character, individuals should be judged in neutral terms, without regard for color. Most liberals, in contrast, came to think that since race regrettably determined social outcomes, individuals should be afforded opportunities specific to color. Conservative conceptualizations of race grew more and more abstract; liberal interpretations grew more and more precise.

Not all conservatives were colorblind, of course. Color-conscious conservatism endured in the person of Charles Murray, arguably the most influential conservative intellectual on matters of race and public policy. Author of the 1984 bestseller *Losing Ground*, which became something of a policy handbook for conservative politicians, Murray followed in the footsteps of sixties neoconservatives like Irving Kristol when he contended that welfare cultivated dependency and a host of destructive behaviors, including drug addiction and illegitimacy—behaviors increasingly associated with a ghetto subculture of black Americans labeled "the underclass." Murray counterintuitively argued that life got worse for poor Americans in the wake of Johnson's War on Poverty, because government programs made it "profitable for the poor to behave in the short term in ways that were destructive in the long term." After calculating the costs and benefits of marrying and seeking employment, a poor couple, whom Murray imagined as rational economic actors "Harold" and "Phyllis," would have concluded that it made more sense to remain unmarried and on welfare. As he put it: "We tried to provide more for the poor, and produced more poor instead." The seductiveness of Murray's analysis was obvious, especially in an era defined by austerity: doing less appeared inexpensive, presumably achieved a better result, and let whites off the hook. At a time when urban poverty seemed more and more intractable and more and more linked to racial inequality—evident in the racialized "underclass" discourse—Murray's "benign neglect" approach proved salient, particularly since the electorate was impatient with political measures that appeared to benefit blacks.[19]

The wide acclaim that greeted *Losing Ground* underscored the centrality of race to the highly contentious struggle to redefine a normative America. A growing number of Americans, those prone to view Murray's arguments favorably, believed government handouts were an affront to traits that had made America great, namely hard work and individual responsibility. Thus many white Americans opposed affirmative action and welfare not only on the belief that such policies unfairly provided blacks with special treatment; they also increasingly rejected the very notion of government welfare as anti-American. These two strains of thought were not mutually exclusive. As Robin D. G. Kelley put it, blacks "have been the thing against which normality, whiteness, and functionality have been defined." Since legal racism had been eliminated—at least in principle—the failure on the part of poor blacks to assimilate to American values was to blame for the persistence of the color line. As a result, debates about racial inequality played out in the language of moral panic.[20]

Like most neoconservatives, Murray pitted the "new class," those who no longer used the language of individual responsibility to explain the problems of race and poverty, against commonsense Americans, those hostile to welfare on the grounds that it encouraged sloth. Murray argued that social scientists needed to take popular wisdom more seriously because, as he put it, "sticks and carrots do work." Such a microeconomic framework explained human behavior in ostensibly colorblind terms. In other words, in 1984 Murray could plausibly deny that his arguments against welfare were color-conscious, even though most readers undoubtedly imagined "Harold" and "Phyllis" as members of the black underclass. For this reason, *Losing Ground* was included in the colorblind canon, alongside Steele's *Content of Our Character*, in spite of its conspicuous deployment of racial codes. But within a decade Murray had changed his tune: he no longer considered people rational, incentive-driven animals. Instead he had come to believe that the ability or inability to make rational choices was a byproduct of native intelligence, and moreover, that race was a crucial factor in such genetically determined capabilities. Murray's transition to a much harsher form of color-consciousness reflected the hardening of conservative racial attitudes. This was made evident in the popularity of Murray and Richard Herrnstein's 1994 book *The Bell Curve*, 845 pages of social Darwinism repackaged as contemporary social science.[21]

The Bell Curve ignited an intense shouting match about the underclass and its relationship to race and IQ. On the one hand, Murray and Herrnstein, the late Harvard psychologist, characterized the world of the underclass, those who "collect at the bottom of society," in a fashion readers of *Losing Ground* would have been familiar with: "[P]overty is severe, drugs and crime are rampant, and the traditional family all but disappears." But on the other hand, their typical description gave way to an atypical explanation—atypical, at least, by late-twentieth-century standards. For them, the driving force of poverty and the bad behavior that accompanied it was a gap in cognitive ability. Dull people, those with a low IQ—which they stridently defended as an unbiased measurement—were likelier to be poor and dysfunctional. And as if this postulate was not contentious enough, Murray and Herrnstein argued that IQ was mostly genetic and, most controversially, that blacks as an "ethnic" group were inherently duller than whites.[22]

Soon after publication, more than mere book, *The Bell Curve* became a phenomenon dissected in most major national publications. Pundits of every ideological stripe weighed in on the debate. Both the liberal *New Republic* and the conservative *National Review* dedicated entire issues to Murray and Herrnstein's tome. Not surprisingly, racial liberals denounced the book. The *New York Times* columnist Bob Herbert labeled *The Bell Curve* "a scabrous piece of racial pornography masquerading as serious scholarship." "Mr. Murray can protest all he wants," Herbert mocked, but "his book is just a genteel way of calling somebody a nigger." (Herrnstein was spared such invective because he died of cancer shortly before the book was published.) Equally predictable, most conservatives rushed to Murray and Herrnstein's defense, even those who sought to distance themselves from *The Bell Curve*'s more odious color-conscious conclusions. They portrayed Murray and Herrnstein as heroes for initiating a necessary conversation on a taboo topic and lambasted media liberals, who, in the words of black conservative Thomas Sowell, focused on "the presumed bad intentions of the authors."[23]

Although many critics noted that *The Bell Curve* resembled the social Darwinism omnipresent during the late nineteenth century, hardly anyone recognized its more pertinent historical trajectory: that it was another in a long line of lurid theories about the "culture of poverty" and, of more recent vintage, the "underclass." Such unawareness was mildly surprising given that the earliest theorizing about urban black poverty sprang from liberal disgust with the gloomy genetic determinism of Murray and Herrnstein's early-twentieth-century predecessors. The influential Chicago School sociologists, for instance, sought to counter social Darwinists such as William Graham Sumner—who argued that humans were compelled to "root, hog, or die"—by explaining urban black poverty as the result of "social disorganization" born of a cultural lag that black migrants from the rural South suffered upon moving to northern cities. Since poverty stemmed from culturally conditioned behavior, Chicago sociologists proposed acclimatizing black migrants to modern industrial habits. Anthropologist Oscar Lewis carried this mode of analysis into the 1950s, coining the "culture of poverty" phrase to express his idea that poverty operated in cyclical fashion: it was passed down through generations because poor people lacked the knowledge necessary to prepare their children for any other life. Lewis, a social democrat, believed the culture of poverty justified wealth redistribution and was dismayed when his theory was recycled in order to focus attention away from such structural reforms. Moynihan ran into similar problems when his notorious 1965 report was interpreted against the grain of his liberal policy intentions.[24]

Well intended or not, twentieth-century culture-of-poverty thinking, in both its liberal and conservative guises, often buttressed genetic determinism as a legitimate form of analysis. After all, if dysfunctional behavior was thought to grow from racial distinctions, it was a small step to debate whether such distinctions sprouted from cultural or genetic differences. In the late sixties, for instance, Harvard psychologist Arthur Jensen's genetic arguments about race and IQ gained a larger than expected audience because of the groundwork laid by erstwhile liberal intellectuals like Moynihan. In his widely circulated article "How Much Can We Boost IQ and Scholastic Achievement," Jensen argued that IQ was mostly inherited and that intelligence testing was therefore a fair mechanism for channeling human talent. Herrnstein popularized Jensen's claims with his 1971 *Atlantic Monthly* article "IQ," which emphasized the political consequences of such social science. Since the United States had evolved into a true meritocracy, Herrnstein contended, the degree to which class hierarchy persevered would reflect the degree to which, simply put, "people vary." Whereas culture-of-poverty theorists like Moynihan posited that poor children failed due to their cultural limitations, genetic determinists like Jensen and Herrnstein argued that such inadequacies were in large part inherited and that IQ testing was the best way to measure such inheritance.[25]

Sociologist William Julius Wilson, author of *The Truly Disadvantaged*, published in 1987, was the most influential liberal poverty theorist of the 1980s and 1990s. Like Lewis and Moynihan before him, Wilson framed his cultural analysis in the context of economic problems—specifically, the lack of jobs for inhabitants of the deindustrialized city. He theorized that urban joblessness left poor black city dwellers socially isolated. For instance, the cognitive and linguistic skills that urban schools taught in preparation for the job market meant little when joblessness was the norm. "In such neighborhoods," Wilson wrote, "teachers become frustrated and do not teach and children do not learn." Growing up in such a situation left people hemmed in by a vicious cycle that perpetuated underclass behavior. Wilson distinguished his "social isolation" thesis from the typical culture-of-poverty framework. Whereas behavior modification was the implied solution for culture-of-poverty theorists, the remedy for social isolation was to remove the economic barriers that separated the underclass from mainstream America.[26]

In light of his stated commitment to structural economic reforms, Wilson's gratuitous focus on the usual litany of pathological behaviors—especially illegitimacy and crime—was perplexing. If he actually believed that pathological behavior would wither alongside economic barriers, as Adolph Reed Jr. asked in a stinging review, "why not define the underclass simply by its joblessness and lack of opportunity?" Wilson mentioned that one of his goals in focusing on pathology was to retake the debate from conservatives who contended that underclass behavior was cultivated by welfare dependency. But when experts like Wilson voiced concerns about the pathological behavior of poor black people, questions about the causes of such behavior proliferated—as did answers, including those provided by Murray and Herrnstein. In other words, just as the Moynihan Report sanctioned Jensen's genetic determinism, Wilson's candid accentuation of "the social pathologies of the inner city" helped create a receptive context for *The Bell Curve*. As Henry Louis Gates Jr. wrote, it was only logical that Murray and Herrnstein's genetic argument emerged when an "emphasis on behavioral causes of poverty are increasingly called upon to account for the repeating structures of black impoverishment."[27]

Biologist Stephen Jay Gould wrote the best refutation of Murray and Herrnstein's social science. As the author of the 1981 best seller *The Mismeasure of Man*, Gould was already a well-known critic of genetic explanations for social difference. According to Gould, Murray and Herrnstein's grand claims were valid only if the following four premises about intelligence were all true: it "must be depictable as a single number, capable of ranking people in linear order, genetically based, and effectively immutable." Gould believed all four presuppositions could be proved false, especially the specious notion that IQ—a recent invention of the human imagination—could be isolated as a genetic trait, like eye color. But in order to dismiss Murray and Herrnstein's most controversial contention—that blacks were on average genetically less intelligent than whites—Gould pretended, for the sake of argument, all four to be true. Even if IQ was significantly heritable within a group, such as among whites, Gould pointed out, this could not explain average differences between groups, such as between whites and blacks. He used a well-known case study of male height in a poor Central American village to illustrate this point. Two facts could be demonstrated with regard to this particular study: first, most of the Central American village men were short relative to, say, American men; second, male height was inherited, in the sense that taller village men were likelier to have taller sons than their shorter village peers. But putting these two factors together did not imply anything about group differences, such as between the poor villagers and Americans, since average male height in the village would increase over time if village nutrition more closely reflected an American diet. The same logic applied to IQ and racial groups: even if the average black IQ was less than the average white IQ, if black children's minds were nourished properly, such a gap would vanish.[28]

In addition to refuting Murray and Herrnstein's highly problematic social scientific claims, Gould highlighted the political context that validated *The Bell Curve*. Since Murray and Herrnstein's social science was easily refutable, their book's "success in winning attention must reflect the depressing temper of our time—a historical moment of unprecedented ungenerosity, when a mood for slashing social programs can be abetted by an argument that beneficiaries cannot be helped, owing to the inborn cognitive limits expressed as low IQ scores." Such left-wing criticism was not uncommon. Still more common, however, was the argument put forward by some liberals and many conservatives that even if *The Bell Curve*'s social science was wrong, its political instincts were right. Murray and Herrnstein, in other words, had to be taken seriously because they grappled honestly with an important subject that had supposedly been rendered off-limits by critics of the Moynihan Report. A spectrum of intellectuals defended *The Bell Curve* out of fear that its authors, like Moynihan, would be denounced as racists and that, as a result, scholars would ignore the fact that out-of-wedlock black births—the chief pathology addressed by the Moynihan Report—had jumped from 23 percent in 1964 to almost 70 percent by 1994. Despite the fact that white illegitimacy rates had increased in similar proportions, and given that black illegitimacy was the sine qua non of culture of poverty theories—*the* behavior that ensured the perpetuation of an underclass—*The Bell Curve* was taken seriously even in some liberal intellectual circles that had long eschewed social Darwinist explanations for racial inequality.[29]

Most conservative reviewers asserted that Murray and Herrnstein were wrong to argue that the black underclass was the product of genetic difference. But such criticism, often mild in tone, was quickly set aside so that conservatives could attend to the ways in which Murray and Herrnstein were right about one crucial trend: as a *National Review* commentator put it, "whether low intelligence is fostered by genetic inheritance or nurtured by a culture of poverty, it nonetheless passes from generation to generation." The culture-of-poverty thesis

loomed large for conservatives because it allowed them to oppose
Murray and Herrnstein's dour determinism, which disturbed their optimism about a colorblind America, while also granting them space
to agree with *The Bell Curve*'s laundry list of right-wing prescriptions.
Such a balancing act was rife with contradictions. Murray and Herrnstein's determinism was seemingly inconsistent with American norms
like hard work and merit: if Americans believed that intelligence determined social standing, they would lack incentive to work hard. Furthermore, if Murray and Herrnstein were correct about the genetic
roots of racial difference, it might make sense to advocate for a more
robust welfare state to care for those who were too unintelligent to
care for themselves. Instead, of course, Murray and Herrnstein contended that welfare was a waste of money because those who received
it lacked the intelligence necessary to find their way off it and thus
grew even more dependent. In any case, no one prescription flowed
logically from Murray and Herrnstein's theories about IQ. The same
was true of culture-of-poverty theorizing. Whereas Oscar Lewis and
William Julius Wilson saw economic redistribution as the solution to
tangled webs of pathology, others saw ending welfare dependency as
the answer. Among the latter group was President Bill Clinton, who
praised Charles Murray for his clear analysis before proceeding in
1996 to "end welfare as we know it" with his suitably titled Personal
Responsibility and Work Opportunity Act.[30]

What the politics of welfare demonstrated was that powerful coun-
terrevolutionary forces were bent on preserving the color line, in substance if not in style. The politics of crime confirmed as much as well.
Ever since Nixon leveraged "law and order" to help win the presidency in 1968, throngs of politicians have used similarly coded messages about black lawlessness to great effect. In his successful 1988
bid for the presidency, George H. W. Bush benefited from a television advertisement that targeted his Democratic opponent Michael
Dukakis by featuring a menacing mug shot of a black convict named
Willie Horton. While serving as governor of Massachusetts, Dukakis
had approved a weekend furlough program to help ease prison over-
crowding. In 1987, having failed to return to his Massachusetts prison
cell from a furlough he had been granted the previous year, Horton
raped a Maryland woman after breaking into her home and tying up
her fiancé. Bush's campaign manager Lee Atwater, who joked that if
he had his way American voters would think of Horton as "Dukakis's

running mate," hung the albatross of black criminality around Dukakis's neck. In this Atwater was following the "southern strategy" that he infamously outlined in a 1981 interview:

> You start out in 1954 by saying, "Nigger, nigger, nigger." By 1968 you can't say "nigger"—that hurts you. Backfires. So you say stuff like forced busing, states' rights and all that stuff. You're getting so abstract now [that] you're talking about cutting taxes, and all these things you're talking about are totally economic things and a by-product of them is [that] blacks get hurt worse than whites. And subconsciously maybe that is part of it. I'm not saying that. But I'm saying that if it is getting that abstract, and that coded, that we are doing away with the racial problem one way or the other. You follow me—because obviously sitting around saying, "We want to cut this," is much more abstract than even the busing thing, and a hell of a lot more abstract than "Nigger, nigger."[31]

Bill Clinton, the Democratic nominee in 1992, studiously avoided such racial pitfalls. He took a tough-on-crime stance and supported capital punishment, arguing that Democrats "should no longer feel guilty about protecting the innocent." Clinton accentuated this point during the campaign by returning to Arkansas, where he was governor, to witness the execution of Ricky Ray Rector, a mentally incapacitated black man. In a similar nod to white voter solidarity, Clinton condemned rap artist Sister Souljah for a *Washington Post* interview in which she claimed the deadly 1992 Los Angeles riots were in some measure cathartic. "If black people kill black people every day," she reasoned, "why not have a week and kill white people?" Speaking before Jesse Jackson's Rainbow Coalition, Clinton compared Souljah to white supremacist David Duke, thus insulating himself from extremists and, more important, from Jackson, whose public support for Souljah was more evidence of racial division.[32]

After Nixon, the most successful American politicians were those who mastered this racialized language of "law and order." Rudolph Giuliani, for instance, astutely leveraged white fears of black crime to become the mayor of New York City. In 1993 Giuliani won the first of two mayoral elections on the campaign slogan "One Standard, One City." As one pundit later wrote, this motto "implied that somehow black New Yorkers were getting away with something under a black mayor," a reference to Giuliani's foe, the incumbent David Dinkins. In the late 1980s and early 1990s, racial tensions flared in New York City to a degree unusual even in a city notorious for racial conflict. In 1986, as one of many such examples, a group of white teenagers brutally assaulted three black men whose car had broken down in Howard Beach, a white ethnic enclave of Queens. One of the black men, Michael Griffith, was hit by a car and killed while attempting to flee the white mob. Widespread protests compelled even Mayor Ed Koch—not exactly beloved by black New Yorkers—to compare the incident to a lynching.[33]

Such racial tensions were captured to perfection by Spike Lee's controversial 1989 film *Do the Right Thing*, which Lee claimed he made as an explicit response to Howard Beach. The film's story, set in a single block of a Bedford-Stuyvesant neighborhood in Brooklyn, takes place over the course of the hottest day of the summer. The two main characters are Mookie, an immature pizza deliveryman played by Lee himself, and Sal, the paternalistic owner of Sal's Famous Pizzeria, played by Danny Aiello. Mookie and Sal barely seem to get along even though they have mutual interests in maintaining a good relationship: Mookie needs Sal for employment, and Sal needs Mookie as a liaison to his predominantly black customer base. Mookie and Sal's tenuous bond represents the fragile state of race relations in New York City; when it splinters, festering racial tensions explode in violence. Toward the end of the sweltering day, a fight breaks out in the pizzeria between Sal and a few of his black customers, including Radio Raheem, a proxy for Black Power who stalks the streets with his ghetto blaster cranked to Public Enemy's "Fight the Power." When white police arrive at the scene of the melee, they kill Raheem while trying to subdue him with what Lee called the "Michael Stewart chokehold," alluding to graffiti artist Michael Stewart's 1983 death while in police custody. After witnessing Raheem's murder, Mookie throws a trash can through Sal's window, setting off rioters who besiege the pizzeria, burning it to the ground. As police disperse the crowd with water cannons, the mob chants, "Howard Beach."[34]

Upon first glance, the characters in *Do the Right Thing* come across as depthless racial stereotypes. Mookie, for instance, refuses to make a commitment to his girlfriend Tina, a blunt Puerto Rican played by Rosie Perez, despite the fact that she is the mother of his son—thus he is a stand-in for black illegitimacy. Sal's son Pino, played by John Tur-

turro, who hurls racial epithets with ease and frequency, personifies white ethnic resentment. Such cartoonish depictions reach an apex during a series of monologues in which several characters rattle off a succession of base racial insults. Yet although most of Lee's characters are caricatures, taken as a whole, his film is nuanced. Most of the characters do the *wrong* thing—the film's title is meant to be ironic—but not because they are evil people. Even when they do the wrong thing, such as when Sal calls Raheem "nigger" or when Mookie destroys Sal's storefront window, the characters evoke sympathy. They are responding to a set of less-than-ideal circumstances beyond their control. In the words of Roger Ebert, one of the few mainstream critics who gave the film a favorable review, *Do the Right Thing* "comes closer to reflecting the current state of race relations in America than any other movie of our time." It struck a chord with late-twentieth-century Americans conditioned to think about racial identity in zero-sum terms. As Henry Louis Gates argued, "the film is an allegory of the melting-pot myth," a parable for the pessimistic 1980s.[35]

Unlike Ebert and Gates, most critics failed to notice that *Do the Right Thing* was a profound meditation on American race relations. Instead, they worried that black audiences would interpret it as an incendiary call to arms. *Newsweek*'s Jack Kroll described Lee's movie as "dynamite under every seat." David Denby, writing in *New York*, accused Lee of creating a "dramatic structure that primes black people to cheer the explosion as an act of revenge." "If some audiences go wild," Denby concluded, "he's partly responsible." In the same issue of *New York*, Joe Klein contended that Dinkins, who was running against Koch in that year's mayoral elections, would "pay the price for Spike Lee's reckless new movie about a summer race riot in Brooklyn, *Do the Right Thing*, which opens in June 30 (in not too many theaters near you, one hopes)." Reminiscing about Klein's article more than a decade later, Lee asked: "What the fuck is that? What he's saying is, 'Pray to God that this film doesn't open in your theater, because niggers are gonna go crazy.'" Klein thought *Do the Right Thing* had only two messages for black audiences: "the police are your enemy" and "white people are your enemy." More astutely, Lee pointed out Klein had only two messages for his white readers: white property was more valuable than black life, and black audiences were too dumb to understand the difference between art and reality.[36]

Do the Right Thing was destined for a controversial reception. White critics and audiences could not help but view it through the lens of black criminality—the same lens through which they increasingly viewed politics. Giuliani's 1993 campaign promise to restore order to the "Ungovernable City," a label for New York City popularized by Nathan Glazer in a 1961 *Commentary* article, traded on a collective siege mentality in which white New Yorkers, "already harassed at every turn by squeegee men, trash storms, and peddlers," as a Giuliani critic put it, "were on the verge of losing control of the city entirely—maybe even at the precipice of some sort of apocalyptic racial massacre." Despite the fact that Dinkins had already begun systematically suppressing low-level crime—the visible effects of poverty—the narrative of disorder rose to the status of moral panic. As Richard Cohen argued in the *Washington Post:* "Aside from the deranged, there's not a single Gothamite who thinks it has gotten better under Dinkins—no matter what his statistics say." On the watch of a permissive black mayor, blacks had gotten away with murder. It was time to restore "one standard" for "one city." Giuliani's colorblind rhetoric, which doubled as easily discernible racial code-speak, won the day. For conservatives, the racialized politics of "law and order" dovetailed nicely with their colorblind mission to restore personal responsibility as the national ethos.[37]

Getting tough on crime was more than a rhetorical gesture. Legislators from both national parties generally took draconian anticrime prescriptions, which dominated conservative thought, very seriously. An important 1982 *Atlantic* article written by neoconservative criminologists George Kelling and James Q. Wilson—"Broken Windows: The Police and Neighborhood Safety"—typified right-wing conceptualizations about crime. Kelling and Wilson's argument was deceptively simple: "[I]f a window in a building is broken and is left unrepaired, all the rest of the windows will soon be broken." As they put it: "[O]ne unrepaired broken window is a signal that no one cares, and so breaking more windows costs nothing." Kelling and Wilson maintained, counterintuitively, that their "broken windows" theory of crime was true no matter the neighborhood. They premised this claim on a 1969 experiment in which a sociologist abandoned two cars in distinctly different neighborhoods: one in gritty Bronx, the other in posh Palo Alto. The car left in the Bronx was hastily stripped and vandalized. The car abandoned in Palo Alto was left untouched, at first. But after the experimenter took a sledgehammer to the windshield, the floodgates were opened to vandals, who quickly trashed the car. From this Kelling and Wilson determined that "vandalism can occur anywhere once communal barriers—the sense of mutual regard and the obligations of civility—are lowered by actions that seem to signal that 'no one cares.'"[38]

The "broken windows" theory, more than a mere explanation for high crime rates, was an argument about how liberal permissiveness was hurting those it was designed to help, namely, poor blacks. Seen in this light, Kelling and Wilson proffered a culture-of-poverty explanation for the underclass. "Untended behavior," they contended "leads to the breakdown of community controls." In other words, allowing pathological behavior to go undisciplined invites more such conduct. Even the slightest threat to order, such as "otherwise harmless displays of subway graffiti," is a slippery slope to anarchy: "the proliferation of graffiti, even when not obscene, confronts the subway rider with the inescapable knowledge that the environment he must endure for an hour or more a day is uncontrolled and uncontrollable, and that anyone can invade it to do whatever damage and mischief the mind suggests." As a prescription, Kelling and Wilson proposed the recriminalization of bad behavior, even that which does not outwardly harm others, such as public drunkenness. "Arresting a single drunk or a single vagrant who has harmed no identifiable person seems unjust, and in a sense it is," Kelling and Wilson wrote. "But failing to do anything about a score of drunks or a hundred vagrants may destroy an entire community." They wanted to return to an earlier era in American criminal justice, when the proper role of the police was enforcing order. Thus Kelling and Wilson gave social-scientific cover to what was in most contexts a moral argument about appropriate public behavior. It made no sense for a criminal justice system to ignore bad behavior like public drunkenness—behavior that, when condemned, was usually done in moralistic tones—"because it fails to take into account the connection between one broken window left untended and a thousand broken windows." In short, enforcing normative America was good criminology.[39]

Gertrude Himmelfarb, the neoconservative historian of Victorian Britain, added historical weight to policy arguments about how a permissive welfare state was creating an "underclass" of deviants. Himmelfarb's scholarly oeuvre was nothing less than a celebration of Victorian culture, or, more specifically, of what the Victorians called "virtue."

Himmelfarb credited Victorian culture with shaping a healthy, orderly, austere, chaste, and humble society. She attributed this realization of a better society to the Victorian habit of speaking a language thick with values, exemplified by the ways in which Victorians framed poverty. Someone might have been "poor," but because the term did not imply dependency, it was not taken to be pejorative. However, there was shame in being a "pauper," because the word was associated with dependency. Himmelfarb contrasted this Victorian moral code with our value-neutral language, which, in her view, contributed to spikes in deviant behavior. She argued that it is our "reluctance to speak the language of morality, far more than any specific values, that separates us from the Victorians." The value-neutral ways in which Americans spoke about poverty had, as the title of a famous 1993 Moynihan article phrased it, "defined deviancy down."[40]

In sum, by the late twentieth century most conservatives, and some liberals, took an unfavorable view of collective efforts to solve racial inequality. Liberal stalwarts such as sociologist Frances Fox Piven, who continued to make the case that a more robust welfare state was the best approach to ameliorating racial inequality, were distinctly in the minority. Instead, the national discussion about race oscillated between the behaviorist prescriptions of those like Wilson and Himmelfarb and the eugenicist assumptions of those like Murray and Herrnstein. Given such constraints, it was little wonder that more optimistic theories about race, such as racial liberalism and its offshoot, cosmopolitanism—the idea that people might identify with specific groups but at base were part of a larger human community—had difficulty gaining traction, particularly in comparison to pessimistic conceptions such as Critical Race Theory. In an increasingly bitter racial climate, many black intellectuals closed ranks.

Afrocentrism, the best example of black thought that, in the face of the persistent color line, forewent the American project, exploded as an alternative mode of inquiry on several campuses across the country. Afrocentrism, or what Molefi Kete Asante, founding chair of the African American studies program at Temple University, called "Afrocentricity," rooted black American culture squarely in African history instead of American or European history. Afrocentrism had important epistemological consequences: academic "objectivity," as Asante argued in his formative 1987 book *The Afrocentric Idea*, was "a kind of collective subjectivity of European culture." Rather than a normative framework, Afrocentrism was a perspective grounded in the specifics of black identity. "I have the insight that comes from having been born black in the United States," Asante posited. "That fact puts me in a critical mood within the intellectual and social milieu I share with Eurocentrists." In addition to its implications for knowledge formation, Afrocentrism had important political consequences: unlike Eurocentrism, which treated blacks as objects, Afrocentrism assumed that blacks had agency. In this way Afrocentrism was meant as a form of empowerment. Black Americans were not merely the sons and daughters of slaves, so much clay in the hands of their white oppressors. Rather, blacks were the cultural legatees of a once proud African civilization.[41]

If Asante represented the pluralist side of Afrocentrism—Asante did not entirely dismiss the value of other identities and forms of knowledge, even those that supposedly originated in Europe—Leonard Jeffries Jr., who directed the black studies program at the City College of New York, embodied the extremist side of Afrocentrism. Jeffries believed not only that black Americans should be proud of the African civilization from which they descended but that Europe or "the West" stole nearly all of its ideas from Africa, the cradle of civilization. This idea helped shape the Afrocentric curriculum that was adopted by schools in various regions of the country—including in Portland, Oregon, where students learned not only "black history" but also "black mathematics" and "black science." Jeffries took the rhetoric of Afrocentrism to an extreme degree. Echoing Elijah Muhammad, the founder of the Nation of Islam, Jeffries expanded on racialist melanin theories by dividing all humans into "Ice People," whites who are inherently evil and cruel, and "Sun People," blacks who are naturally good and caring. In 1995 Jeffries told an interviewer he would like to leave his children a world where "there aren't any white people."[42]

Americans became more aware of Afrocentrism in 1996 when the Oakland, California, board of education passed a so-called Ebonics resolution requiring its teachers, mostly white, to learn their mostly black students' patterns of speech. The Oakland board designated Ebonics not a deviant dialect but a legitimate language in its own right. If blacks spoke differently it was because of a long history of racism and segregation. Forcing them to meet a white standard of language was an act of blaming the victim. It also denied their cultural heritage and agency rooted in their African past. Critics of the Oakland Ebonics measure were numerous. The *New York Times* editorialized that Ebonics was merely "black slang," or the "patois of many low-income blacks," and argued that learning Standard English would empower black students. Black reporter Rachel Jones wrote in *Newsweek* that "mastery of Standard English gave me a power that no one can take away from me." In contrast, famed left-wing linguist Noam Chomsky put the debate in the context of power dynamics: "If the distribution of power and wealth were to shift from southern Manhattan to East Oakland, 'Ebonics' would be the prestige variety of English and [Wall Street bankers] would be denounced by the language police." To underscore this point, a disproportionate number of black students had long been categorized as academically unfit, or as one North Carolina school district labeled its weaker students, "educable mentally handicapped," due in part to "linguistic deviances." Ebonics, then, was not only about blacks celebrating their own cultural difference and agency. It was about their resisting an American norm that discriminated against them. Standard English, it seemed, was another product of the color line. Ebonics was an Afrocentric response.[43]

Martin Bernal's 1987 book *Black Athena: The Afroasiatic Roots of Classical Civilization* endowed Afrocentric claims with a confidence born of historical proof. *Black Athena* engaged the long-standing debate over which peoples formed ancient Greece: Indo-Europeans (proto-Aryans) or Egyptians and Phoenicians (proto-Africans and Asians). Ancient Greece's fabled status as the seedbed of democracy — the fount of Western civilization — raised the stakes of this dispute well beyond the typical academic disagreement. The Aryan-origins argument, paradigmatic for much of the nineteenth and twentieth centuries, had served as an ideological facade for European imperialism in Africa and elsewhere. Bernal's thesis, in contrast, accentuated the nonwhite origins of ancient Greece. Extant sources demonstrated that Africans and Asians peopled ancient Greece, he contended, and arguments to the contrary were in part the product of lingering racism.[44]

Many black Americans devoured Bernal's tome. It confirmed their budding Afrocentric presuppositions about how blacks developed civilized ideas before whites. Caught between these poles, several classicists maintained that the best scholarship on the subject had downgraded all such racialist formulas as anachronistic, given that race was socially constructed long after the fact of ancient Greece. But such criticism was often as much about politics as about methodology: Molly

Myerowitz Levine, a classicist who wrote an important critique of *Black Athena*, labeled Bernal's book "dangerous" for reopening nineteenth-century questions about racial origins. "Misapplied," she wrote, "it can be the match that ignites the tinderbox of neo-racist theories of origins. It can become the 'who gave what to whom' that leads to the 'who took what from whom,' which culminates in the 'who stole what from whom.'" In other words, *Black Athena* played to the zero-sum assumptions that governed racial discourse in late-twentieth-century American thought. Whereas many conservatives mocked Afrocentric history as a misguided attempt to build black self-esteem—including Irving Kristol, who contended that "genuine self-esteem comes from real-life experiences, not from the flattering attention of textbooks"—Levine worried about much more insidious consequences. By framing ancient black history as a "stolen legacy," she fretted, Afrocentrists had adopted "the nineteenth-century sounds of a racist Kulturkampf." Such a posture rendered late-twentieth-century racial reconciliation unlikely.[45]

Levine's critique of *Black Athena* signified a stark challenge to ontological conceptions of race—and to all theories of race that presupposed immutable qualities, whether biological, cultural, or historical. In this she joined a small but eminent group of cosmopolitan thinkers, including philosophers Charles Taylor and Kwame Anthony Appiah, intellectual historian David Hollinger, and literary theorist Henry Louis Gates Jr., who analyzed race as a way to undermine its political power and to bridge the color line. Cosmopolitan thinkers posited that because race was a social construction, it was malleable and could be politically reconstructed to reflect a multicultural society like the United States. Cosmopolitanism was thus a much more optimistic reading of race than most of the other theories that sought to explain the post–civil rights persistence of racial inequality. That it existed only at the margins of racial discourse during the 1980s and 1990s illuminated the steadfastness of the color line.[46]

Charles Taylor historicized one of the more controversial by-products of racial liberalism's demise: identity politics, the concept that political attitudes necessarily flow from self-identified social groups, including racial groups. From a critical if sympathetic vantage point, Taylor argued that identity politics—including Afrocentrism, perhaps its quintessential expression—arose as a plausible, perhaps even necessary response to centuries of racial inequality. In this Taylor followed the lead of Franz Fanon, who theorized in *The Wretched of the Earth* that the most powerful weapon of the colonizer, more than military might, was the collective inferiority complex of the colonized—an inferiority engendered by the colonial condition. Taylor transposed such logic onto an American political context, where the long and brutal history of racism had conditioned many blacks to a wretched view of themselves. Given this history, identity politics, or what Taylor called a "politics of recognition," a politics that treated all cultures as intrinsically valuable, was a rational response. Taylor argued as much despite his skepticism of relativist claims that all cultures were equal. He contended that Americans, who often judged minority cultures unfavorably due to prejudice and arrogance, had a limited view of the world and their place in it. The solution, Taylor argued, was "a willingness to be open to comparative cultural study of the kind that must replace our horizons in the resulting fusions." In other words, when ethnocentric views were challenged, a better cultural framework might emerge. Framing cosmopolitanism in this way, Taylor vehemently opposed the racial arrogance of Saul Bellow's infamous statement "When the Zulus produce a Tolstoy we will read him." Taylor argued against Bellow not only on the grounds that the Zulus might have produced a Tolstoy that had yet to be discovered but also from the standpoint that Zulu culture likely evaluated merit differently and that Americans would have benefited from learning its evaluative system. This was what he meant by replacing narrow horizons with a vision formed by cultural fusion. It was his "dialogic process," a process aligned with the proposals of various other cosmopolitan thinkers.[47]

Kwame Anthony Appiah, though more critical of identity politics than was Taylor, was similarly sympathetic in his recognition that racial inequality distorted liberal politics grounded in universally recognized rights and freedoms. Appiah believed that in a multicultural society like the United States, identities, insofar as they governed political behaviors and expectations, should ideally be based on individual choice. But he was sensitive to the fact that identities were often ascriptive and that some ascriptive identities were more coercive than others. Blacks, for instance, had little choice but to be identified as African Americans. And a much more coercive set of norms were ascribed to the African American identity than to a less visible, more voluntary ethnic identity such as Irish American. Appiah made clear that positive racial identification was "a predictable response" by blacks in at least two ways: it gave them a sense of racial solidarity in their struggles with a racist society, and it reminded whites of their unearned racial privilege. But such benefits did not come without costs. "If, in understanding myself as African-American, I see myself as resisting white norms, mainstream American conventions, the racism of 'white culture,'" Appiah asked, "why should I at the same time seek recognition from these white others?" In other words, blacks could not reject normative America with one hand while asking to be included in it with the other. Appiah's solution to this quandary was for people to reject forced racial ascriptions altogether. Instead, people needed to "live with fractured identities; engage in identity play; find solidarity, yes, but recognize contingency, and, above all, practice irony." In sum, Americans should live by the recognition that racial identity was a social construct. This was the bridge across the color line.[48]

David Hollinger's historical explorations of American racial identity similarly emphasized distinctions between voluntary and forced ascriptions. Hollinger sought to transcend discourses that assumed the immutability of racial identity. Instead, he embraced a more individualistic and voluntary conception of identity, what he described as "affiliation by revocable consent." This was Hollinger's vision for a "postethnic America," the title of his widely read 1995 book. However, like Taylor and Appiah, Hollinger recognized the power of coercive ascription, which operates by the logic of what he termed a "political economy of solidarity." Solidarity, for him, was "a commodity distributed by authority," especially when tied to the nation-state. "Central to the history of nationalism, after all, has been the use of state power to establish certain 'identities,' understood as performative, and thus creating social cohesion on certain terms rather than others." For Hollinger, this raised the question: was the American nation the appropriate place to invest solidarity in the hopes of a more encompassing justice? The nation, in this sense, had always had a dialectical relation to justice. Though it was "capacious enough to act effectively on problems located in a large arena," conversely, Hollinger contended, it was "poorly suited to satisfy the human need for belonging." But the alternative, to form solidarities based on smaller circles of identity, such as race or religion, though "tight enough to serve the need for belonging, cannot be expected to respond effectively to challenges common to a larger and more heterogeneous population." The knottiness of this dialectic did not, by Hollinger's reckoning, render the American nation incapable of serving the ends of justice. Despite his hesitations, mostly related to the persistent racial injustices suffered by the descendants of African American slaves, Hollinger defended the American nation as a proper place to seek justice. "A stronger national solidarity enhances the possibility of social and economic justice within the United States," he contended. "This is a simple point, but an extremely important one. Any society that cannot see its diverse members as somehow 'in it together' is going to have trouble distributing its resources with even a modicum of equity."[49]

Henry Louis Gates Jr. did not perfectly fit the cosmopolitan mold. But, being more hopeful on the question of racial identity than were most other black literary theorists, Gates was much closer to Taylor, Appiah, and Hollinger than he was to Afrocentrists like Asante or Critical Race theorists like Bell. As the United States grew more diverse, Gates believed, the "cultural impulse" of African Americans "represents the very best hope for us, collectively, to forge a new, and vital, common American culture in the twenty-first century." In positing culture as something that could be fashioned anew, Gates joined cosmopolitans in theorizing that racial identity was a subjective enactment of hybridity. And yet he also recognized that such an optimistic reading was often unwarranted: thinking about racial identity "in terms of its practical performative force doesn't help me when I'm trying to get a taxi on the corner of 125th and Lenox Avenue. ('Please sir, it's only a metaphor.')" Gates rebuffed those who used the social constructedness of race as an excuse for refusing the political legitimacy of black identity. Here he had in mind colorblind conservatives like Linda Chavez, Reagan's secretary of labor, who maintained that "any attempt to systematically classify human beings according to race will fail, because race is an arbitrary concept." Whereas white Americans had no need to declare themselves white because they were assumed American, black Americans could neither declare themselves black nor be assumed American. While rejecting racial ontology in the same terms as Taylor, Appiah, and Hollinger, in this way Gates also highlighted the political problems that accompanied such an antiracial epistemology: it drew attention away from the negative consequences of racism. This was the irony of colorblind America. Toni Morrison, the Nobel Prize–winning author of *Beloved*, a novel about a runaway slave who murders her daughter rather than allow her to be returned to slavery, put this paradox as follows: "The people who invented the hierarchy of 'race' when it was convenient for them ought not to be the ones to explain it away, now that it does not suit their purposes for it to exist."[50]

Gates understood cosmopolitanism, then, in appropriately perplexing terms. Since racial identities were constructed—since they were performative—they were malleable enough to suit a more enlightened racial order. But because most people understood racial identities in ontological terms, and because the racist regime from which such understandings emerged had yet to be dismantled, political battles about racial inequality had to be fought on older terms. The cosmopolitan theory of voluntary affiliation was undercut by inequality, racial and otherwise. The fact that the United States grew less and less economically equal after the 1970s and that economic inequality often reinforced racial inequality—as seen in the "underclass" discourse—undermined the likelihood that American culture would embrace the cosmopolitanism of Taylor, Appiah, Hollinger, and Gates. Hollinger seemed to realize as much when he qualified his hopes for a postethnic America by pointing out that "a society that will not take steps to help its poor citizens of all ethno-racial groups will have little chance to find out how successful have been its efforts to overcome the racist attitudes empowered by whites." Although the civil rights movement had left the nation much less sadistic, the color line would persist so long as Americans' racial nerves were frayed by deindustrialization, urban blight, and economic inequality.[51]

5

The Trouble with Gender

At a swanky party in Washington, DC, on June 30, 1982, fifteen hundred right-wing activists gathered to celebrate the defeat of the ERA. Much to the delight of the guests, who included prominent conservatives like Phyllis Schlafly, Jesse Helms, and Jerry Falwell, a rendition of "Ding, Dong, the Witch Is Dead" marked the official passing of the deadline to ratify the amendment. The Christian Right, it seemed, had risen from the ash heap of history to reclaim the nation from feminists and secular humanists. As President Reagan optimistically pronounced two years later: "Americans are turning back to God."[1]

This "backlash," as the journalist Susan Faludi titled her best-selling book about antifeminism, grew into an incredibly powerful movement by the 1980s. Feminists and gay rights activists were frequently put on the defensive, as antifeminist reactionaries often dictated late-twentieth-century American sexual politics. The Christian Right, it seemed, had finally gained the upper hand in its campaign to uphold the traditional nuclear family of one man, one woman, and many children—a norm that religious conservatives generally rooted in Christian ideals and specifically grounded in the America of the 1950s.[2]

But there was no going back to the 1950s. The antifeminist backlash was constrained by historical changes set in motion by the feminist and gay rights movements. In the same way that the civil rights movement had fundamentally challenged normative white Americanism, the feminist and gay rights movements had upended matter-of-fact sex roles. Standard American expectations for male and female behavior, once prescribed by powerful cultural norms, were no longer widely considered the natural order of things. Seemingly fixed identities were being destabilized by new and increasingly widespread sensibilities about sex, sexuality, marriage, fertility, and family. A new category—gender—emerged to distinguish the biological from the cultural and political. Differences between men and women that were obviously natural, such as the fact that only women could become pregnant, were deemed sexual. But most other distinctions, such as the notion that men should earn wages while women cared for children, were deemed gendered. And gender was malleable. If traditional gender norms were manifestations of male domination, then new norms could be forged in unison with feminist goals to ensure equality between the sexes.[3]

In the eyes of feminists, those who defended traditional gender roles were defenders of male supremacy. But to many conservatives, disregard for traditional gender roles entailed grave consequences. As one anti-ERA flyer warned: "Society can be good or depraved, civilized or uncivilized. It either possesses order or chaos depending on the degree in which the male and female sex roles are accepted or rejected." For conservatives, gender differences were sacred; a world shorn of them would be a world devoid of meaning.[4]

In his influential 1973 book *Sexual Suicide,* the conservative writer George Gilder charted antifeminist arguments about sexual difference that proved influential to the backlash. Gilder contended that sexual difference was "our most precious heritage," because it was divined from God and because it had long ordered Western civilization. The revolution in sexual morality, including the scrambling of gender roles, was destroying the institution of marriage, an ominous development since Gilder believed marriage was the bedrock of any good society.[5]

Sexual Suicide spread blame widely, including to those men who intentionally avoided the obligations of marriage. But Gilder fixated on feminism, which, as he saw it, sought to liberate women from the family, the only institution capable of channeling men's primal urges in nondestructive ways. Gilder's ideas about sexuality served as an all-explanatory social theory: Because women bore children, sex was more gratifying to them than to men, whose sexual pleasures were fleeting. Thus female identity was bound up in a woman's reproductive roles. But in modern society, where physical strength no longer accrued social standing to men, male identity was yoked to a man's capacity to earn a family wage. Take that away and men were adrift, "more prone to masturbation, homosexuality, voyeurism, gratuitous

sexual aggression, and other shallow and indiscriminate erotic activity." In short, Gilder conceptualized sexual difference as a civilizing
agent.[6]

Gilder was a conservative activist. His 1981 book *Wealth and Poverty*, arguably the definitive brief for Reagan's mixture of supply-side
economics and conservative cultural politics, contended that work,
family, and faith, not government, created wealth. But antifeminism
proved so powerful because it had a wide ideological range. Gender
trouble was troubling to a lot of people. For example, the historian
Christopher Lasch, formerly one of the New Left's leading thinkers,
joined Gilder in his opposition to feminism.[7]

Lasch's 1977 book *Haven in a Heartless World*, a history of how social scientists had validated the assault on the family, was hardly an
antifeminist polemic on the order of *Sexual Suicide*. But it had some
traditional gender implications, leading conservatives to praise it despite Lasch's anticapitalist gestures about how "the sanctity of the
home is a sham in a world dominated by giant corporations."[8]

Lasch ascribed his anxieties about the crumbling traditional family to his experiences as a parent, which exposed him to "our society's indifference to everything that makes it possible for children to
flourish and grow up to be responsible adults." In raising questions
about feminist goals vis-à-vis the family—especially the stated objective that women and men should be equally unconstrained from marital obligations—Lasch was merely drawing attention, he thought,
to the needs of children. "The trouble with the feminist program is
not that economic self-sufficiency for women is an unworthy goal,"
he contended, "but that its realization, under existing economic conditions, would undermine equally important values associated with
the family." In this elocution, Lasch sought to transcend the shouting
matches over family values. "While defenders of the family need to
acknowledge the justice of the central feminist demands," he argued,
"feminists for their part need to acknowledge the deterioration of care
for the young and the justice of the demand that something be done
to arrest it." Lasch's explanation for this turn of events was deeply historical. He argued that soon after control of economic production was
wrested away from workers and given to corporate management—
the disciples of Frederick Taylor—Americans were also compelled to
abdicate family management to those so-called experts employed in
what Lasch derisively termed the "helping professions." He character-

ized this process as a cycle of dependency. "The diffusion of the new ideology of social welfare had the effect of a self-fulfilling prophecy." Persuading the housewife "to rely on the advice of outside experts," Lasch argued, "undermined the family's capacity to provide for itself and thereby justified the continuing expansion of health, education, and welfare services." Here *Haven in a Heartless World* paralleled conservative arguments about how feminism and the welfare state formed an unholy alliance. Feminists had paved the way, in Lasch's view, for the outsourcing of parental authority to state welfare agencies.[9]

Fears about feminism, whether voiced by a conservative writer like Gilder or by a more heterogeneous thinker like Lasch, were far from baseless. Feminism was arguably the most successful sixties movement. In addition to its achievements in upsetting oppressive gender norms, the movement chalked up several concrete political victories. Thanks to feminism, to cite one example, American society became less hospitable to men who abused women. This was due in large part to grassroots feminist efforts to open shelters for battered women across the nation. It was also thanks to feminist legal activism, which by the late 1970s forced most states to adopt rape shield laws. Such laws made it easier to prosecute and convict rapists, since they rendered inadmissible a victim's sexual history, exposure of which had been the accused's most effective strategy to embarrass and delegitimize his accuser.[10]

Since few people openly defended the rights of wife beaters and rapists, conservatives were mostly mute on these feminist-inspired shifts. Yet even these unobjectionable changes hinted at the growing capacity for women to live independently of men, a trend that, taken as a whole, proved troubling to conservatives. Conservatives were particularly threatened by female economic autonomy because they deemed it a direct threat to the traditional family. As a Census Bureau demographer confirmed in 1985, women who work "gain greater confidence, expand their social circles independent of their husbands' friends, taste independence and are less easy to satisfy, and more likely to divorce." In other words, working women threatened the traditional family model clung to by conservatives.[11]

Liberal feminist groups like NOW improved the economic opportunities afforded to many women by compelling the EEOC to expand its enforcement of laws that ensured "equal pay for equal work" to include women. Sex discrimination in the workplace persisted to vary-

ing degrees, as the 1980 movie *9 to 5* parodied. But that it was possible for a Hollywood film shot through with feminist themes to be
commercially successful signified a new receptivity to feminist logic.
9 to 5 pitted three heroic working-class women, played by Lily Tom-
lin, Jane Fonda, and Dolly Parton, against a villainous sexist employer,
performed by Dabney Coleman. The three protagonists live out a cathartic revenge fantasy when they take their cruel misogynist boss
captive, harnessing him in leather and chains. In his absence from the
workplace, the women implement changes amenable to female staff,
including a flexible scheduling scheme, a job-share program, and an
in-office daycare center. At the film's conclusion, the company president sweeps in to laud the new management style, crediting it for
ramping up productivity, the implication being that women could
enter the workforce in greater numbers if only the workplace were
more female-friendly. Such themes had disquieting implications for
conservatives.[12]

It was against the backdrop of feminist success, and cultural representations like *9 to 5* that incorporated feminist messages, that the
antifeminist backlash emerged as a formidable counterforce in both
politics and culture. Faludi's systematic documentation of the backlash included an analysis of antifeminist tropes that dominated the
media, such as the notion that women were unhappy with their liberation, what Gertrude Himmelfarb called the "cultural contradictions of
liberation." "Many women," Himmelfarb wrote, "having gained entry
into the workplace, lost their secure place in the marital home." According to the host of an ABC special titled *After the Sexual Revolution,* "the price of the feminist revolution is loneliness and depression."
The acclaimed 1987 film *Fatal Attraction,* starring Michael Douglas as a
family man who has an affair with a seductress played by Glenn Close,
epitomized this antifeminist motif. When Douglas's guilt-ridden character attempts to end the illicit relationship, Close's character rebuffs
him, screaming: "I'm thirty-six years old! It may be my last chance to
have a child!" Damaged by postfeminist sensibilities that leave her obsessed with nostalgic visions of domesticity, the spurned lover morphs
into a stalker prone to irrational behavior and violence, made evident
when she memorably boils a pet rabbit to send an angry message to
her ex-lover. The Douglas character's wife, played by Anne Archer,
symbolizes the traditional family. Her acts of forgiving her husband
and, in the film's climax, killing the psychotic home-wrecker bring the

family's triumph over the derangements of postfeminist sexual morality. To emphasize the poignancy of *Fatal Attraction*'s appropriation of
backlash themes, Faludi described watching the film in a theater full
of angry men screaming for Douglas's character to "kill that bitch."[13]

The feminist revolution of the sixties that helped upset American gender norms divided the American political landscape, pitting
conservatives against liberals; traditionalists against feminists. It also
fractured feminist discourse. Although feminists were typically united
in their opposition to conservatives, they fought among themselves
over the best way to frame new understandings of gender. In particular, they debated the tricky problems of sexual difference and sexual equality. As historian Mary Jo Buhle phrases it: "The definitional
axis of feminism swings between *difference*, meaning an emphasis on
the qualities that distinguish 'woman' from 'man' and determine the
distinctive roles, rights, and identities of each; and *equality*, meaning
a claim to autonomy and justice based on the common humanity of
men and women." This puzzle mirrored a contradiction intrinsic to
the larger American project summed up by the Latin phrase *E Pluribus Unum*: Could the United States be both diverse and unified? Could
feminism value difference and equality? That such knotty questions
could be asked about both feminism and Americanism illustrates why
the fight over feminism's legacy was so critical to the larger culture
wars. Did feminism enhance the American promise of equality, or
did it boost the equally American assurance that difference will be
respected?[14]

Whereas equality was the linchpin of the sixties feminist movement,
a focus on sexual difference shaped some of the most influential feminist thought of the late 1970s and early 1980s. This attraction to what
came to be known as "difference feminism" worked in tandem with
a renewed feminist interest in psychoanalysis and Freud's suggestion
"that human beings consist of men and women and that this distinction is the most significant one that exists." Nancy Chodorow led the
way in this regard. In her pathbreaking 1978 book *The Reproduction
of Mothering: Psychoanalysis and the Sociology of Gender*, Chodorow
suggested that gender traits, deeply burrowed in the psyche, emerged
in order to complement social roles. In her expansive 1989 follow-up
book *Feminism and Psychoanalytic Theory*, Chodorow argued that "our
experiences as men and women come from deep within, both within
our pasts and, relatedly, within the deepest structures of unconscious

meaning and the most emotionally moving relationships that help constitute our daily lives."[15]

In contrast to the biological determinism and theological fatalism of conservatives, Chodorow's feminist psychoanalysis focused on "the relational and situated construction of gender difference." This applied even to how people understood the body, the most tangible evidence that men and women were, in fact, different. Chodorow wrote that "we cannot know what people would make of their bodies in a nongender or non-sexually organized world, what kind of sexual structuration or gender identities would develop." In other words, bodily difference might have seemed obvious, but how we conceptualized and used the body was not self-evident outside of culturally specific ways—outside of gender relations. But recognizing the social constructedness of gender differences did not lead Chodorow to dismiss the potential for such differences to play a role in liberation from patriarchy. Because men were expected to work in the cutthroat public sphere, the male psyche was habituated to rugged individualism. But since women were required to stay in the home as mothers, the female psyche was conditioned to cooperation and empathy. Feminist utopia was a society organized around the values integral to motherhood.[16]

Carol Gilligan, author of the 1982 book *In a Different Voice: Psychological Theory and Women's Development*, was more explicit than Chodorow in declaring that female mores were superior to male values. *In a Different Voice*, which practically became the bible of difference feminism, was written as an act of academic patricide: Gilligan's argument was pitched as a direct challenge to her teacher the psychologist Lawrence Kohlberg, who posited that women were less rational than men because they were overreliant on interpersonal relations. Gilligan did not contradict Kohlberg's idea that women were more social than men. She even supported such a view by citing a number of studies that found women did not value success as much as men when one person's success corresponded to another's failure. But whereas psychologists like Kohlberg and Erik Erikson had long argued that such studies indicated that the male psyche was normative and the female psyche was inferior or partial, Gilligan interpreted the evidence to make the opposite point. Masculine values, she wrote, "reflect a conception of adulthood that is itself out of balance, favoring the separateness of the individual self over connection to others, and leaning more toward an autonomous life of work than toward the interdependence of love and care." In other words, Gilligan flipped a malecentric evaluative scheme on its head: she argued that if any gender-specific psyche should be the norm, it should be the female psyche—that the differences between men and women demonstrated that female ethics were a better model for humanity.[17]

The feminist debate over sexual difference was more than academic. This was made plain by fascinating testimony offered by Rosalind Rosenberg and Alice Kessler-Harris, two historians of American women, during 1985 appellate court hearings on the *EEOC v. Sears* case. The opposing arguments put forward by Rosenberg and Kessler-Harris outlined the terms of the debate over difference and equality and also demonstrated the tangible stakes involved. The EEOC charged Sears, Roebuck with sexual discrimination based on its record of not hiring a proportional number of women to fill the company's well-paid sales positions. Testifying on behalf of Sears, Rosenberg argued that the meager number of female sales representatives was not necessarily proof that the retail giant had discriminated against women. "Men and women differ in their expectations concerning work, in their interests as to the types of jobs they prefer or the types of products they prefer to sell," Rosenberg stated. "It is naive to believe that the natural effect of these differences is evidence of discrimination by Sears." Rosenberg's testimony was consistent with the defense Sears had mounted more generally: it was difficult to find qualified female salespeople because women were largely uninterested in such positions.[18]

Historian Alice Kessler-Harris, the EEOC's expert witness, countered that such logic rested on the faulty assumption that women had always been afforded equal opportunity. "What appears to be women's choices, and what are characterized as women's 'interests' are, in fact, heavily influenced by the opportunities for work made available to them," Kessler-Harris testified. "Where opportunity has existed, women have never failed to take the jobs offered." Kessler-Harris continued: "Failure to find women in so-called non-traditional jobs can thus only be interpreted as a consequence of employers' unexamined attitudes or preferences, a phenomenon which is the essence of discrimination."[19]

Despite Kessler-Harris's best efforts, the court found in favor of Sears. To those feminists who emphasized equality, such a result was another sign that the backlash was winning. Even more alarming, however, was the fact that Sears grounded its defense in the logic of difference feminism. The backlash, it seemed, was so pervasive that it had colonized feminist theory itself. As Faludi wrote: "'Difference' became the new magic word uttered to defuse the feminist campaign for equality."[20]

Arguments about equality and difference also played out in high-profile disputes about pornography. By the 1980s, due in part to the 1969 Supreme Court decision *Stanley v. Georgia*, which established an implied right to privacy by invalidating state laws that criminalized possession of obscene materials, pornography had become ubiquitous. So, too, had debates about pornography. Some feminists argued that pornography offered men *and* women erotic pleasure and that, given this, those against pornography upheld a sexual double standard that feminists had worked hard to overcome. These self-described "sex-positive feminists" contended that women, like men, had sexual agency and that women and men could be sexual equals. In contrast, some of the most prominent feminists, most notably Andrea Dworkin and Catharine MacKinnon, insisted that sex highlighted how men were different from women. More to the point, sex was about men dominating women, and pornography was about men flaunting their sexual violence against women. In her 1979 book *Pornography: Men Possessing Women*, Dworkin called pornography "inextricably tied to victimizing, hurting, exploiting," representative of a social system in which "the only choice for the woman has been to embrace herself as a whore." She attributed the precipitous growth of pornography not to its legalization, which was merely a symptom of something much more sinister, but rather to the violent male backlash against feminist gains. Dworkin described pornography as "the propaganda of sexual terrorism."[21]

MacKinnon made clear her assumption that sexual difference was less natural than most people assumed but that such difference, whether constructed or not, had long shaped gender relations and was thus crucial to how feminists should think about pornography. "Feminists do not seek sameness with men," MacKinnon explained. "We more criticize what men have made of themselves and the world that we, too, inhabit." Specifically, men had made a world of pornography, which had made women the objects of their violent sexual desires. As a law professor, MacKinnon focused on how pornography was legitimized as speech. Just as Critical Race theorists sought to unmask how supposedly neutral legal concepts were in fact deeply embedded in American history and were thus inextricably racist, MacKinnon sought to show that "free speech" could not be abstracted from long-standing patriarchal norms and was thus, in the form of pornography, a cover for sexual inequality. MacKinnon extended this theory to the act of sex itself in order to critique sex-positive feminists. "The belief that whatever is sexually arousing is, ipso facto, empowering for women is revealed as a strategy in male rule." Although she mischaracterized arguments put forward by sex-positive feminists, who maintained sex could be more enjoyable to women only in the context of gender equality, MacKinnon's views highlighted the importance that left-wing culture warriors placed on identity. Identity politics was not just about group solidarity, in this case female solidarity. It was about how one viewed power and hierarchy in America. MacKinnon theorized that women were at a huge disadvantage because American institutions were historically conditioned to discriminate against them. In the abstract, this framework aligned her with those on the left side of the culture wars spectrum. But on the specific issue of pornography, MacKinnon and Dworkin discovered that religious conservatives were their most reliable political allies.[22]

Dworkin and MacKinnon needed all the help they could muster as they took their fight against pornography out of the seminar room and into city hall. When they drafted antipornography statutes that they submitted to the Minneapolis and Indianapolis city councils in 1984, conservatives lined up in support. Their proposed ordinance was grounded in the presumption that pornography violated women's civil rights because it was "discrimination on the basis of sex." By avoiding the rationale that the First Amendment did not protect pornography because it was obscenity, an argument that the courts no longer accepted as a given, Dworkin and MacKinnon sought to avoid legal challenges that would have likely ended in defeat. Instead, their ordinance would have allowed women who could prove their lives had been damaged by pornography to sue for restitution. The Minneapolis city council twice passed the statute, but Mayor Donald Fraser vetoed it each time. Dworkin and MacKinnon had more luck in conservative Indianapolis, where their ordinance became law until the courts overturned it on free speech grounds.[23]

The strange alliance between conservatives and antiporn feminists was on full display during a 1985 episode of William Buckley Jr.'s famed public affairs show *Firing Line* that featured Dworkin as a guest. The episode also illustrated that the alliance was little more than a by-product of political convenience. Buckley, for instance, introduced the topic of the day by declaring that he was in favor of banning pornography but was lukewarm to Dworkin's thesis that it infringed on women's civil rights. He preferred the older rationale that pornography was obscenity and thus not legally protected. Buckley believed that a long-standing American tradition of allowing infringements on dangerous speech permitted the American people to ban pornography should they will it. But that was the rub: Buckley fretted that the liberation movements of the sixties, particularly feminism, had corrupted the American soul, sapping Americans of the willpower necessary to fight pornographers. He and Dworkin wanted the same thing—they wanted to ban pornography—but they had vastly different explanations for how pornography had become a problem of such magnitude. Buckley asked Dworkin: "How do you account for the evolution of a spread of pornography, *pari passu*, with the evolution of women's rights?" Buckley believed that pornography was one of the "cultural contradictions of liberation" and that if women did not want to be subjected to it they needed special legal treatment of the sort feminism had helped obliterate. Dworkin responded by resorting to her frequently made claim that pornography was an expression of the antifeminist backlash, consistent with the legal case that it violated women's rights. The implication of this line of reasoning was that feminism would achieve its aims only once pornography was outlawed.[24]

Although Buckley sought to distance himself from Dworkin on the issue of pornography, intellectually if not politically, the logic of antiporn feminism influenced the Christian Right. As a Southern Baptist leader put it, pornography "depersonalizes individuals and makes things of them." An antiporn alliance between feminists and religious conservatives should have been formidable, particularly since their most outspoken opponent was *Hustler* publisher Larry Flynt, who, as part of a campaign "to push my First Amendment rights as far as I can," sent free copies of his hypergraphic magazine to all the male members of Congress. But even with an adversary whom most Americans deemed reprehensible, antipornography efforts stalled in the courts, where speech rights were interpreted in increasingly expansive ways. Antiporn forces thus took a new line of attack: refuting a

1970 presidential commission that concluded there was no causative link between pornography and violence, they contended that consuming pornography made men more likely to commit violent acts. That John Hinckley Jr., the deranged lone gunman who shot Reagan in 1981, had a porn cache seemed like prima facie evidence of such an association, and all the motivation Reagan needed to make pornography a national issue.[25]

Reagan's attorney general Edwin Meese formed a Commission on Pornography in 1985. Meese made it clear that his commission would take a much different tone from that of its 1970 predecessor when he appointed Henry Hudson as his chair. As assistant attorney general of Virginia, Hudson had notoriously established a "vice squad" that all but banished pornography from the city of Arlington. Meese and Hudson stacked the commission with social conservatives such as James Dobson, a psychologist and outspoken evangelical. Meese's conservative pornography commission painted a picture of how he envisioned America: "The Commission is an affirmation of the proposition that the purpose of a democracy involves not simply the functioning of its political system but also the achievement of the good life and the good society."[26]

After a year spent traveling the nation, visiting porn outlets and interviewing self-styled victims of pornography, the Meese Commission released a 1,960-page report, including an extensive appendix that listed the titles of magazines and films ranging from *A Cock between Friends* to *69 Munching Lesbians*. The report's main conclusion was that pornography caused violence and should thus be treated like a social threat.[27]

Many Americans agreed. Serial killer Ted Bundy later invited Dobson to conduct the one and only television interview with him because reading the Meese Report convinced him that his addiction to pornography had fueled his murderous rampage. But critics objected that the Meese Commission could reach such a conclusion only by ignoring the overwhelming majority of social scientists who found no correlation between pornography and violence. In fact, Judith Becker, one of only two social scientists on the commission, dissented from the report's findings, outlining her disagreement during internal deliberations about how a victim of pornography should be defined. After one member stated that such a victim was "someone who has been raped," Becker highlighted the speciousness of such logic by countering that someone who has been raped "is a victim of the crime of rape," not pornography. A much more plausible claim could have been made, she joked, that a victim of pornography is "someone who sustains a paper cut while turning the pages of a sex magazine." Hudson deflected such criticism by countering that social science could not measure human dignity. Decency alone demanded that degrading depictions, such as those "involving inanimate objects being used to penetrate the genitalia of another person," be outlawed. In other words, although the Meese Commission sought scientific cover in the rationale that pornography caused violence, in the final tally it rested its case on moral grounds. From a different evaluative perspective, Barry Lynn of the ACLU described the Meese Report as "little more than prudishness and moralizing masquerading behind social science jargon."[28]

The national pornography debate was one of the few instances during the culture wars when left and right partisanship was scrambled. It was certainly one of the only instances of feminists aligning with antifeminists. This highlighted the contradictions built into the fact that the feminist and sexual revolutions emerged from the sixties as twin movements but were often at odds from the outset. If any one individual personified these paradoxes, it was the fiery cultural critic Camille Paglia. In the positions she took Paglia did not neatly fit any one paradigm. She was an atheist and a lesbian, labeled herself a feminist, and favored legal access to many of the things the Christian Right sought to prohibit, including abortion, pornography, and prostitution. And yet she was branded the "bête noire" of feminism, described by Naomi Wolf as "the nipple-pierced person's Phyllis Schlafly who poses as a sexual renegade but is in fact the most dutiful of patriarchal daughters." In short, Paglia demonstrated that the antifeminist backlash made for strange bedfellows.[29]

Paglia skyrocketed to fame with her first book, *Sexual Personae: Art and Decadence from Nefertiti to Emily Dickinson*, a contentious, unfashionable 712-page work of literary criticism. A perverse reading of English and American literature that characterized William Blake as the British Marquis de Sade and described Walt Whitman and Emily Dickinson as "self-ruling hermaphrodites who cannot mate," *Sexual Personae* became a *New York Times* best seller, no doubt because of its provocative thesis that human nature has a primal sexual side to it. Paglia argued that humans created civilization out of our Apollonian inclinations in order to contain our Dionysian forces, which were best left to the bedroom, the modern sexual equivalent of the wilderness.[30]

After *Sexual Personae*, Paglia turned her talent for polemics to writing essays about sex, sexuality, and feminism. One such long piece, titled "No Law in the Arena: A Pagan Theory of Sexuality," made clear why feminists considered Paglia a traitor to their cause. In it she outlined her vision of a libertarian countercultural feminism that stood diametrically opposed to mainstream feminism. Representative of "bourgeois codes" and "authoritarian totems," feminism, according to Paglia, had become the new moralism, replacing the sexual conformity of the 1950s that the sixties counterculture had toppled. Paglia argued that "in the absence of sexual violence, sexual conduct cannot and must not be legislated from above, that all intrusion by authority figures into sex is totalitarian." She viewed consensual sex, including prostitution and pornography, in the same way that libertarians understood a labor contract: as a mutually beneficial exchange. Although many feminists conceptualized prostitution and pornography through the lens of patriarchal exploitation, she might have found common ground with those feminists, fewer in number, who accorded all women agency, including prostitutes and porn actors. Paglia contended that by equating pornography with rape—by heeding Robin Morgan's dictum that "pornography is the theory, and rape is the practice"—feminists had trivialized legitimate acts of sexual assault.[31]

Even if she might have found some feminist allies in the debates about pornography, Paglia extended her analysis of rape in ways that made her few feminist friends. Concurring with some of the more controversial evolutionary biologists, she maintained that men were biologically motivated to rape because they were sexually aggressive, or Dionysian, and that the purpose of modern society was to contain such aggression with Apollonian controls. In sum, whereas many feminists believed that contemporary mores inculcated a culture of rape, Paglia argued that modern society was all that stood between men and their female rape victims. Expanding upon this already disputable thesis, Paglia made the incendiary claim that date rape was a myth because women who did not want sex should know better than to go behind closed doors with men, where Apollonian protections gave way to Dionysian temptations. "Too much of the date-rape and sexual harassment crisis claimed by white middle-class women is caused partly by their own mixed signals," Paglia wrote. Although her critique of feminism was secular, she agreed with religious conservatives on the immutability of sexual difference. Nobody, including feminists, could change the fact that in the privacy of the bedroom, men were instinctively disposed to find their way inside women.[32]

Paglia was not the only self-described feminist who saw it as her mission to rescue feminism from feminists. Disputes about equality and difference had taken their toll on the fragile unity of the larger feminist movement. Philosopher Christina Hoff Sommers—author of the 1994 book *Who Stole Feminism? How Women Have Betrayed Women*—harshly criticized those feminists who perceived "revelations of monstrosity in the most familiar and seemingly innocuous phenomena." Sommers distinguished between her classic liberal brand of feminism, which limited its agenda to the simple demand that women enjoy "the same rights before the law that men enjoyed," and post-sixties feminism, which more ambitiously waged a culture war against patriarchy. Whereas Sommers was a sex-blind feminist in her belief that people should be afforded equal treatment before the law based solely on their actions, most feminists contended that it was impossible for women to be evaluated by the same standards as men because gender relations shaped even supposedly neutral institutions like the courts and schools. This conceptual divide, between those who believed society was best organized around neutral principles that people could aspire to as individuals and those who thought that society was weighted down by historical patterns that could be overcome only by finding solidarity in groups, marked an important front in the culture wars. This bifurcation also shaped how people understood their nation and world. For instance, feminists developed an epistemology of victimization, a more relativistic, femalecentric model for knowing the world. Sommers, of course, lambasted the notion that there were "female ways of knowing," likening it to the "idea of a Republican epistemology or a senior citizens' epistemology." However, the feminist epistemology of victimization was more than merely one partial view among many, no better, no worse. Since oppression offered a better vantage point from which to understand the world, as many feminists believed, an epistemology of victimization fundamentally challenged long-cherished American standards.[33]

No doubt many feminists remained aloof from epistemological debates. Plenty continued to join groups like NOW, which prioritized classic liberal goals such as equal pay for equal work. But in the ivory tower, where feminism remained robust into the 1980s and 1990s, theories about how patriarchy shaped everything, including how women perceived the world, proliferated, particularly in women's studies programs. Such theorizing about patriarchy made women's studies programs targets for right-wing vigilantes like David Horowitz, whose magazine *Heterodoxy* dedicated many reams of paper to documenting the "war against men" waged by the antimale ideologues flourishing on the nation's college campuses. But the two most important critics of women's studies emerged from its own ranks, once again demonstrating that the backlash was not restricted to religious and conservative activists.[34]

Daphne Patai and Noretta Koertge, authors of the 1994 exposé *Professing Feminism: Education and Indoctrination in Women's Studies,* were unsparing in their allegation that women's studies programs fostered habits of mind inimical to academic values. "Logic, the analysis of arguments, quantitative reasoning, objective evaluation of evidence, fair-minded consideration of opposing views—modes of thinking central to intellectual life," they wrote, "were dismissed as masculinist contrivances that served only to demean and oppress women." In other words, since even a seemingly objective concept like reason was inseparable from the patriarchal society from which it emerged, women's studies professors dismissed it as irredeemably repressive. According to Patai and Koertge, campus feminists rated "feelings" as more constitutive of female knowledge, a theory premised on the "consciousness-raising" tactics of the women's liberation movement. To their sex-blind feminist ears, such an epistemological orientation sounded consistent with antediluvian stereotypes about how women were inherently unsuited for complex thinking. "The characterizations of male and female have not changed," Patai and Koertge wrote. "Instead, the plus and minus signs associated with each gender have been reversed."[35]

The partisans in the national debate over pornography, and in the more rarefied dispute about women's studies, did not always line up as expected. Meanwhile, the abortion struggle, despite being even more contentious than the battles over pornography and women's studies, operated along a more predictable and intelligible spectrum. Although some liberal Catholics opposed abortion for reasons of faith—for the same reasons that they opposed the death penalty—most abortion warriors tended to align with their political and moral brethren. In this way abortion, perhaps more than any other issue, illustrated the alternative epistemological universes that separated the two sides of the culture wars. Some Americans—liberal, secular, and feminist— had a relativistic view of the world in which circumstances matter greatly in distinguishing right from wrong. Some other Americans— conservative, religious, and traditionalist—had a more orthodox or fundamentalist view of the world in which truth is universal no matter the context. Applying the relativistic view to abortion, liberals argued that every pregnancy has its own set of circumstances and that a pregnant woman is the only person in a position to understand the best thing for her and her fetus. Liberals also tended to balance the well-being of the mother against a naturalistic assumption that a seven-month-old fetus is closer to being human than a microscopic, newly conceived embryo. Conservatives contended, simply, that a fetus is a person from conception, as God intended, and, as such, has an inviolable right to life that overrides the concerns of a pregnant woman.

In short, the abortion dispute was also a proxy for a larger philosophical debate about the meaning of life and personhood. Liberals maintained life had meaning when it was conscious and rational. Conservatives contended God gave life meaning from inception. Feminists maintained that women, as self-determining persons, should decide for themselves whether or not to carry a pregnancy to term. Antifeminists contended that women, bound by God to be dutiful wives and mothers, should bear the burdens of pregnancy. Feminists saw the anti-abortion movement as another indication of the backlash. Anti-abortion activists deemed women who had abortions sinners three times over: they sinned when they had nonreproductive, often extramarital sex; they sinned when they rejected their predetermined role as mothers; and they sinned when they killed their babies.[36]

The law could not possibly hope to reconcile such diametrically opposing claims. For their part, anti-abortion activists saw *Roe v. Wade* as a scourge that unleashed a holocaust. It was impossible to know how many more abortions *Roe* resulted in, since many if not most abortions performed prior to 1973 were illegal and thus unrecorded. But the number of abortions performed in the United States during the 1980s and 1990s—well over one million per year—was a figure of such magnitude that it was no wonder conservatives committed to the cause with fervor. Anti-abortionists traveled the country in vans with evocative images of aborted fetuses plastered along the sides. They urged all Americans to watch *Silent Scream*, a 1984 video that included clips of an ultrasound film depicting an actual abortion, during which the narrator solemnly calls the fetus's open mouth a "silent scream." And even though most anti-abortion activists were nonviolent, the movement as a whole grew increasingly violent. In 1982 the first abortion clinic was bombed. By the end of the Reagan administration, 77 had been bombed, 117 had been burned, and many more had been burglarized and vandalized. Anti-abortion violence culminated in the assassination of at least six abortion providers. A passion for the lives of unborn children together with a hypermasculine hatred of feminism proved a toxic mix. Randall Terry, a Pentecostal preacher who founded Operation Rescue—an anti-abortion group famous for employing the nonviolent techniques of the civil rights movement but which had links to violent militants—hated birth control and premarital sex almost as much as abortion. He considered the abortion battle the major front in the war against those who would remove "virtually every vestige of Christianity from our laws, morals, institutions, and, ultimately, our families." Terry's millenarian rhetoric on abortion, which undoubtedly roused some of those willing to bomb abortion clinics and kill abortion providers, flowed from his belief in the natural goodness of patriarchy.[37]

Anti-abortionists were not the only ones dissatisfied with how the law addressed the issue of abortion. Many legal feminists, including eventual Supreme Court justice Ruth Bader Ginsburg, were unhappy with *Roe v. Wade*'s constitutional rationale. They were irked that the decision was based on the due-process clause of the Fourteenth Amendment, stipulating that a woman could not be barred from obtaining an abortion, instead of on the equal protection clause, which would have ensured women equal access to abortion. In other words, a woman's right to an abortion was dependent on her proximity to an abortion clinic, not to mention her ability to afford such an expensive procedure, a precedent that opened a window to anti-abortion efforts. Disappointed by their inability to overturn *Roe*, anti-abortionists were consoled by their success in making an abortion difficult to obtain in most places. By 1991, 83 percent of counties nationwide had no abortion provider, and women from as many as twelve states had to travel to another state to receive an abortion. In states where anti-abortion forces gained a foothold, particularly in the South and Midwest, myriad laws that curtailed abortion were upheld by the Supreme Court, including laws that forbade the use of state funds for abortions, which meant that poor women would have more difficulty obtaining an abortion; laws requiring parental consent; laws mandating that doctors provide patients with information about alternatives to abortion; and laws requiring that women seeking an abortion wait twenty-four hours—a "cooling-off" period—before being allowed the procedure. *Roe* remained an important symbol of a women's constitutional right to an abortion, but because it did not guarantee that right, anti-abortion forces were able to chip away at it. Neither feminists nor anti-abortionists were happy with this stalemate. Both sides looked to the Supreme Court to remedy the situation once and for all.[38]

It was in this context that Reagan nominated Robert Bork to join the Supreme Court in 1987. Before sitting on the US Court of Appeals for the District of Columbia from 1982 to 1988, and before serving as solicitor general from 1973 to 1977, where, on orders from Nixon, he infamously fired Watergate special prosecutor Archibald Cox, Bork made a name for himself as a professor at Yale Law School. In that capacity, he helped shape how conservatives thought about the Supreme Court and American jurisprudence. In 1968, for example, he wrote an article for *Fortune* titled "The Supreme Court Needs a New Philosophy" in which he articulated the case for judicial restraint by rejecting the Warren Court's decision-making philosophy of ruling "not according to the criteria they cite but according to their social and political sympathies." Bork's critique of the Warren Court, which was responsible for such landmark liberal decisions as *Brown v. the Board of Education* and *Miranda v. Arizona*, led him to embrace the doctrine of "originalism," that legal interpretation should be constrained by the original intent of those who framed the Constitution. Only original intent, he argued, "can give us law that is something other than, and superior to, the judge's will." Bork contended that originalism was a more democratic judicial philosophy than that which informed the liberal activism of the Warren Court—and the later Burger Court, which ruled on *Roe*—because it "confines judges to areas the Framers assigned to them and reserves to democratic processes those areas of life the Framers placed there." And Bork's analysis of the Supreme Court was ultimately rooted in neoconservative "new class" thought: he maintained that it was composed of liberal elitists who disdained American traditions.[39]

Bork applied his originalist judicial philosophy to several rulings during his stint as a circuit court judge. In the 1984 case of *Dronenburg v. Zech*, involving an enlisted sailor who sued that his right to privacy was violated when the navy discharged him for homosexual conduct, Bork wrote the majority opinion that rejected the suit. In general, he maintained that jurists were not obligated to take Supreme Court decisions that gave people new rights as precedents. In particular Bork rejected the right to privacy, a precedent set by the 1965 Supreme Court decision *Griswold v. Connecticut*, which had invalidated laws that restricted the sale of contraceptives. But more to the point of those who opposed Bork's nomination to the Supreme Court, including the vast majority of feminists, by rebuffing the privacy precedent Bork was rejecting the legal grounds upon which *Roe v. Wade* stood. From this viewpoint Bork's nomination was of a piece with the 1984 Republican Party platform, which promised to appoint Supreme Court justices who would be sworn to uphold "the sanctity of innocent human life." In the words of a Reagan administration attorney, "the opposition to Judge Bork's elevation to the Supreme Court appears to be based largely upon the fear of many that he will provide the one vote presumably necessary to reverse the *Roe* decision." Indeed, Bork had described *Roe* as a "classic instance" of the sort of judicial activism he abhorred, "a serious and wholly unjustifiable judicial usurpation of State legislative authority."[40]

Even though some liberals liked Bork, less for his politics than for his intellectual bona fides, the most powerful among them lined up to sink his confirmation. Senator Joseph Biden, who had designs on the Democratic presidential nomination and who was chair of the powerful Judiciary Committee, led the charge by compiling an unfavorable assessment of Bork's views that became known as the "Biden Report." He was joined by stalwart liberal Senator Ted Kennedy, who gave a speech on the day Reagan nominated Bork that stands as one of the quintessential instances of culture wars rhetoric:

Robert Bork's America is a land in which women would be forced into back alley abortions, blacks would sit at segregated lunch counters, rogue police could break down citizens' doors in midnight raids, school children could not be taught about evolution, writers and artists could be censored at the whim of government, and the doors of the federal courts would be shut on the fingers of millions of citizens for whom the judiciary is—and is often the only—protector of individual rights that are the heart of our democracy. America is a better and freer nation than Robert Bork thinks. Yet in the current delicate balance of the Supreme Court, his rigid ideology will tip the scales of justice against the kind of country America is and ought to be.

The Senate Judiciary Committee rejected Bork's nomination by a 9–5 vote, followed by a 58–42 vote against him by the entire Senate. "To Bork" entered the American political lexicon as a verb to describe partisan efforts to squash judicial and political appointments. At a 1991 NOW conference, Florynce Kennedy gave a speech on the imperative to defeat Clarence Thomas's nomination to the Supreme Court. "We're going to Bork him," she declared. "We're going to kill him politically!"[41]

Shortly after the disappointment of his failed Supreme Court confirmation hearings, Bork quit the bench and joined the American Enterprise Institute as a resident scholar, a perch that gave him an audience willing to listen to him retell the story of his losing battle with American liberalism. "I can offer you a unique perspective," he quipped. "Who wouldn't like George Armstrong Custer's version of events at the Little Bighorn?" Bork, of course, claimed he was the victim of slander. His critics, he charged, had misread his record on *Roe* and much else. But given his later writings on the topic of abortion, Bork's opponents were right to defeat his nomination. In his 1996 book *Slouching towards Gomorrah: Modern Liberalism and American Decline*, Bork wrote that he "objected to *Roe v. Wade* the moment it was decided, not because of any doubts about abortion, but because the decision was a radical deformation of the Constitution." Applying his originalist lens, Bork thought *Roe* a clear-cut case of judicial overreach. "The Constitution has nothing to say about abortion, leaving it, like most subjects, to the judgment and moral sense of the American people and their elected representatives." Bork compared *Roe* to the notorious 1857 *Dred Scott v. Sandford* ruling that people of African descent were not American citizens. "Just as *Dred Scott* forced a southern pro-slavery position on the nation," Bork contended, "*Roe* is nothing more than the Supreme Court's imposition on us of the morality of our cultural elites."[42]

Slouching towards Gomorrah mapped the antifeminist backlash onto conservative anxieties about the obliteration of American norms. Feminism and the other sixties liberation movements, Bork argued, had ushered in a pervasive nihilism that had destroyed long-standing values of decency. "The rough beast of decadence," he wrote, "a long time in gestation, having reached its maturity in the last three decades, now sends us slouching towards our new home, not Bethlehem but Gomorrah." The relativistic theory that reality is "socially constructed," Bork contended, had crystallized with New Left efforts to replace traditional standards with a countercultural philosophy suggested by the slogan "If it feels good do it." These were hardly rules everybody could live by, particularly when applied to traditional gender roles, abortion, and human life. In postulating that the vast majority of women who sought abortions did so as a simple matter of convenience—because it "felt good"—Bork contended that abortion was "a way for women to escape the idea that biology is destiny, and from the tyranny of the family role." It was in this way that Bork understood feminism as a threat to civilization: by challenging deeply ingrained expectations that women should prioritize their roles as wives and mothers, feminists had degraded the sanctity of human life. By ranking the needs of a woman over the right of an embryo to live, Bork believed, feminists had redefined human life in dangerously relativistic fashion. Just because a pregnant woman was more sentient and more capable than her fetus of living without the assistance of others did not privilege her life over that of the fetus. The right to life, Bork wrote, "must lie in the fact that you are alive with the prospect of years of life ahead. That characteristic the unborn child has." He maintained that abortion "deepens and legitimates the nihilism that is spreading in our culture and finds killing for convenience acceptable." In sum, Bork equated feminism and modern American liberalism with Nazism, the catchall analogy for a nihilistic disregard for human life.[43]

Feminism was not the only sixties liberation movements that threatened time-honored American standards for gender relations. Its close cousin the gay rights movement, judging by the fearful conservative reaction to it, was equally menacing to gender norms, although it had not reshaped American political culture to the same degree as feminism had. This is not to say that gay rights had not made important strides since it first gained national renown with the 1969 Stonewall Riots. Annual gay pride parades were growing in popularity, especially in large, cosmopolitan cities like New York and San Francisco.

Gay rights organizations like the Gay and Lesbian Advocates and Their Defenders (GLAD) had been founded to do the grubby legal work of a movement that was slowly but surely establishing its permanence on the American political scene. GLAD procured modest funds for its occasionally successful court battles against those who sought to prohibit gays and lesbians from adopting children and from teaching in public schools. But such incremental rewards came with risks. In 1982 arsonists burned down the offices of the *Gay Community News*, a Boston-based weekly journal that served as an important voice of the movement. Gays and lesbians who were open about their sexuality, whether activists or not, were highly vulnerable to homophobic-inspired violence. If feminism represented a potential danger to the sexual order, then open homosexuality signified its downfall. If feminism weakened the traditional family by granting women some independence from men, then gay rights obliterated it by eradicating heterosexual obligations. In a 1987 *Gay Community News* piece, gay rights activist Michael Swift promised that the gay rights movement would abolish the traditional family, which he described as "a spawning ground of lies, betrayals, mediocrity, hypocrisy and violence." The Christian Right took such warnings seriously and responded in kind.[44]

As if convincing Americans to accept homosexuality was not difficult enough, gay men were overwhelmingly among the first victims of a strange and deadly new infectious disease that emerged in the early 1980s. Homophobes interpreted this "gay plague," officially labeled Autoimmune Deficiency Syndrome, or AIDS, as evidence that public health concerns, even God, sanctioned their homophobic prejudices. "The poor homosexuals," Patrick Buchanan said, "they have declared war upon nature, and now nature is exacting an awful retribution." With less sarcasm, Jerry Falwell stated: "AIDS is the wrath of God upon homosexuals." The cover of the July 1983 issue of Falwell's *Moral Majority Report* depicted a family wearing surgical masks under the headline "Homosexual Diseases Threaten American Families." Linking homosexuality to public health was a convincing way for conservatives to argue that gay men should not be afforded a right to sexual privacy and that the courts should uphold antisodomy laws, which had come under attack in states such as Texas and Georgia. Psychologist Paul Cameron, author of *The Medical Consequences of What Homosexuals Do*, based his testimonies in favor of sodomy laws on his findings that infectious diseases afflicted gay men at much higher rates because they were more promiscuous than heterosexuals and because they engaged in risky sexual practices. Conservatives often cited Cameron because he provided social-scientific cover for their moral prejudices. Of course Cameron's scholarship was shaded by his religious beliefs. He referred to himself as "a servant of Christ" who sought to do a "Christlike job of the homosexual issue." "The truths the social sciences have uncovered," he maintained, "do little damage to the cause of Christ, and, in fact, buttress the validity of the Judeo-Christian point of view." In short, whether expressed in religious or scientific language, rightwing hostility to homosexuality was rampant during the early days of the AIDS epidemic. Even some public officials felt safe expressing frank antigay sentiments. Morton Blackwell, whose purpose on Reagan's White House policy staff from 1981 to 1984 was to serve as the administration's liaison to the Christian Right, was openly contemptuous of gay rights groups. Blackwell declared that federal subsidies to groups that offered counseling to troubled gay teenagers, symbolic of how antifamily forces had co-opted government, were enough to make his "blood boil."[45]

Originally, AIDS was difficult to diagnose because its first victims died from a variety of random infections and tumors, due, it was eventually discovered, to the fact that AIDS ruthlessly attacks the immune systems of those it infected. Throughout the 1980s and well into the 1990s, before medical researchers discovered ways to temper its effects, an AIDS diagnosis was almost always a death sentence. Because AIDS was so lethal and because it was infectious, a debate arose about the best ways to reconcile public health concerns with the civil rights of those afflicted. Since AIDS victims tended, at least originally, to be members of a stigmatized group, many sought to tilt the debate in favor of a supposed greater good. During a 1985 episode of *Firing Line*, Buckley implied that he supported efforts to restrict the movement of AIDS victims due to public health concerns. But he also favored limiting the civil rights of gay men due to his sense that many AIDS victims were morally culpable. Buckley's guest, legal scholar Alan Dershowitz, responded that the baggage AIDS carried with it distorted the debate. In other words, if most AIDS victims had been heterosexual—which was soon the case, particularly as AIDS spread to the less-developed world—the national discussion would have been more rational. In making this point, Dershowitz singled out conservatives like Pat Buchanan for relishing the fact that their "predispositions somehow proved out medically." Dershowitz was against a "teleological approach that nature somehow supports morality." This was not to say that he was a homophile. "I have no particular liking for the homosexual act," he told Buckley. Rather, he thought it necessary to separate his personal homophobia from a naturalistic and constitutional handling of a health crisis.[46]

Many conservatives were less willing to set aside their prejudices. This helps explain the Reagan administration's scandalously slow response to the AIDS crisis. Reagan did not attend a meeting on the subject until 1983, and in that meeting Blackwell advised him to respond to the AIDS epidemic by shuttering gay bathhouses and publicly condemning homosexuality. Reagan ignored this advice. But until 1985 he also ignored the AIDS crisis altogether. In the interim, AIDS research and education languished, and AIDS victims continued to die by the thousands. Moreover, because Reagan overlooked the issue, religious conservatives like Blackwell and Gary Bauer were empowered to shape the federal message, if not Reagan's rhetoric. In 1986 Bauer, serving as chair of Reagan's Working Group on the Family, sought to implement an educational approach to AIDS grounded in the logic that the best way to stop its spread was to teach young Americans moral sexual behavior. In this vein, Secretary of Education William Bennett said that "young people in our schools must be told the truth—that the best way to avoid AIDS is to refrain from sexual intercourse until as adults they are ready to establish a mutually faithful monogamous relationship." Some conservatives had harsher recommendations. Republican House member William Dannemeyer thought the federal government should make it a crime for those infected to knowingly engage in high-risk sexual activities. "The AIDS virus does not have rights," Dannemeyer reasoned, "and the rights of individuals who persist in engaging in certain activities are outweighed by the rights of those unsuspecting persons whose lives are placed at risk."[47]

Because Reagan's response to AIDS was halting at best, gay rights activists and their political allies were thoroughly convinced that he was a cruel homophobe. Larry Kramer, who helped found the highly effective direct-action group AIDS Coalition to Unleash Power, better known by its acronym, ACT UP, referred to Reagan as "America's Hitler." Democratic House member Henry Waxman said: "In the long run, Ronald Reagan will not be remembered for 'Star Wars,' for his tax bill, or, perhaps, not even for the Iran-Contra affair, but for his continued and stubborn refusal to support AIDS efforts." Lacking the president's support did not discourage a renewed commitment to gay solidarity in the face of an awful disease. It also did not diminish the playfulness of gay rights activism. Activists devised a "Falwell game" in which they called Moral Majority's toll-free phone numbers by the thousands, tying up lines and harassing those who manned the phones. In response to North Carolina senator Jesse Helms's persistent homophobia—he likened homosexuality to "a battle against American values"—ACT UP raised an enormous inflatable condom over his home. In short, AIDS motivated both sides of the culture wars over homosexuality. Religious conservatives saw AIDS as a chance to intensify their backlash against gay liberation. But gay rights activists worked overtime to deny Christian Right efforts to make them into pariahs.[48]

When Reagan nominated C. Everett Koop to be the US surgeon general, liberals and feminists reacted with horror. Likewise, gay rights activists were pessimistic that the surgeon general would break with the prevailing Reagan administration approach to AIDS. Koop, after all, was a renowned evangelical and anti-abortionist. He was the author of the 1976 book *The Right to Live, the Right to Die*, and he had helped Francis Schaeffer make his 1978 anti-abortion film series, *Whatever Happened to the Human Race?* Religious conservatives rejoiced at Reagan's choice of the Philadelphia surgeon. They logically assumed that Koop would align with them on homosexuality and AIDS. But Koop proved everyone wrong. Because he saw it as his ethical duty to respond to the AIDS crisis with both sound science and compassion, he submerged any antigay prejudices he might have had. Koop became the face of the federal government's U-turn on AIDS and in the process elevated the standing of the surgeon general's office. This achievement did not come easily.

During Reagan's first four years in the White House, Koop's tentative suggestion that he be allowed to coordinate a federal response was ignored. But by late 1985, as critics of the administration's record on AIDS grew bolder, Reagan requested that the surgeon general write a special report on the subject. Almost everyone expected that Koop's report would tout the conservative line about how promoting abstinence and monogamy, not safe sex, was the key to fighting the spread of AIDS. But the surgeon general's report on AIDS, released

in the fall of 1986, advocated instead for a more honest and comprehensive approach to sex education, one that included teaching about
condom use. In perhaps the most telling and controversial passage,
Koop wrote:

> Many people—especially our youth—are not receiving information
> that is vital to their future health and well-being because of our ret-
> icence in dealing with the subjects of sex, sexual practices, and ho-
> mosexuality. This silence must end. We can no longer afford to side-
> step frank, open discussions about sexual practices—homosexual
> and heterosexual. Education about AIDS should start at an early age
> so that children can grow up knowing the behaviors to avoid to pro-
> tect themselves from exposure to the AIDS virus.[49]

In reaction to the surgeon general's report on AIDS, conservatives
reprimanded Koop. In an editorial titled "Flying the Koop," the *Washington Times* called the report "one doozy of a bomb for his old supporters." Bennett termed Koop's approach to sex education "straight
homosexual propaganda." Another Christian Right leader characterized it as "selling the gospel of sodomy to the entire country." Yet another countered that teaching children about homosexuality would
engender "a rise in homosexual sex among teenagers." Countercharg-
ing that his erstwhile allies had not only abandoned him but forsaken
Christian compassion altogether, Koop was emboldened by the negative response. He had twenty million copies of his report distributed,
and he went on a speaking tour, outlining his plan for audiences across
the nation. In 1988 Koop sent an eight-page condensed version of the
report to every household in America, 107 million in total, the largest
single mailing in American history. Thanks in no small part to Koop's
efforts, Reagan finally spoke publicly about AIDS on May 31, 1987. By
then 36,058 Americans had been diagnosed with AIDS, and 20,849
had died of the horrible disease.[50]

Compelling the federal government to take more robust action was
a huge victory for AIDS activists. Researchers soon discovered drug
treatments that rendered AIDS much less deadly, and the educational
campaign set into motion by Koop made the disease, and homosexuality more generally, less of a stigma. Of course these successes hardly
signaled the end of the gay rights movement's struggles against the
Christian Right. In 1992, for instance, Colorado voters passed Amend-

ment 2, designed to prevent local municipalities from recognizing gays and lesbians as a protected class of citizens, by more than one hundred thousand votes. The Christian Right, which had a stronghold in Colorado Springs, a rapidly growing city south of Denver, had been effective in outraging voters with details from cities where so-called gay ordinances had passed. For instance, conservatives highlighted tales from gay-friendly Madison, Wisconsin, where a judge ordered two women to undergo sensitivity training because they refused to rent a room to a lesbian, and where school libraries were stocking their shelves with "homosexuality-promoting children's books like *Heather Has Two Mommies*."[51]

In 1996 the Supreme Court overturned Amendment 2 with *Romer v. Evans*, more evidence in the eyes of conservatives that the court represented a liberal "new class" that sought to redefine morality for the nation's majority. As Bork wrote in response to the *Romer* decision: "Modern liberalism tends to classify all moral distinctions it does not accept as hateful and invalid." Conservative Supreme Court Justice Antonin Scalia argued in his dissenting opinion that Amendment 2 was "a rather modest attempt by seemingly tolerant Coloradoans to preserve traditional sexual mores against the efforts of a politically powerful minority to revise those mores through the use of laws." Scalia contended that the *Romer* decision "places the prestige of this institution behind the proposition that opposition to homosexuality is as reprehensible as racial or religious bias."[52]

That last bit of Scalia wisdom, about how gays and lesbians, much like racial and religious minorities, had gained official recognition as a protected class of citizens, highlighted the ironic and counterintuitive ways in which the two sides in the homosexuality debates framed their arguments. Conservatives, ignoring the colorblind philosophy that had informed their approach to contentious racial matters such as affirmative action, argued that unlike racial and ethnic minorities, who were born black or brown, sexuality was a choice. In the words of one of the architects of the Amendment 2 campaign, "gay individuals can change their sexual orientation" and thus did not merit special legal protection. Many evangelical churches and organizations offered counseling services that promised to help gays and lesbians go straight. In contrast, gay rights activists often articulated a biological essentialist argument about homosexuality. Defying the logic of the sixties gay liberation movement—that sexual identity was

freer when it was an individual choice—many gay rights activists in
the 1980s and 1990s, perhaps as a strategic rejoinder to the Christian
Right, contended that people did not choose to be gay but rather were
born gay.[53]

Much as the politics of pornography had shaken up the moral al-
legiances that typified the culture wars, the politics of homosexuality
had jumbled the assumptions of both those for and those against gay
rights. Where did nature end and nurture begin? Did culture or biology determine sexual and gender identities? What was the relationship between political identity and the individual? What did it mean
to be a woman? to be gay? In the wake of the feminist and gay rights
revolutions, answers to such questions were elusive. Nothing seemed
certain. But out of such uncertainty was born a range of innovative
theories.

Some of the leading feminist thinkers of the early 1990s conceptualized a theoretical approach unprecedented in its radical assault on
gender norms. Lead amongst them was the philosopher Judith Butler,
whose 1990 book *Gender Trouble*, read widely in academic and activist circles, took the social constructionist theory of gender to drastic
new heights, well beyond an earlier paradigm expressed by those like
Kate Millett and Carol Gilligan. Whereas before Butler many prominent feminists thought it necessary to counter patriarchy with a politics of female solidarity—identity politics—Butler posited that "there
is no gender identity behind the expressions of gender; that identity
is performatively constituted by the very 'expressions' that are said to
be its results." In other words, Butler contended that the female "self,"
or individual, was nonexistent apart from the culture that had created it. More important to the feminist debates about difference and
equality, Butler argued against an essential feminist subject—and, as
such, against utopian visions of matriarchy—on the grounds that such
a position adhered to entrenched patriarchal norms. "Is the construction of the category of women as a coherent and stable subject," she
asked, "an unwitting regulation and reification of gender relations?
And is not such a reification precisely contrary to feminist aims?" Just
as Nietzsche and Foucault theorized there was no humanist self that
presupposed political culture, Butler opposed the idea that there is a
pregendered subject. Butler thought that the best approach to subverting "masculine hegemony and heterosexist power" was to make
"gender trouble," or to render all gender boundaries unintelligible.

Such an idea, no matter how philosophically interesting, was politically confusing. "Feminists of the world, transgress the boundaries!" was hardly a winning manifesto.[54]

And yet *Gender Trouble* provided feminist theorists with a new sense of confidence that their intellectual labors mattered. A new generation of feminist academics came of age believing they could disrupt the usual practices by which gendered languages were transmitted and that in so doing they could transform gender relations. Poststructuralist feminist theory, they believed, held the key to liberating people from oppressive patriarchal norms.

Given that Butler's theory destabilized the categories of "woman" and "man," it proved useful not only to feminist thought but also to what would come to be known as "queer theory," an extension of the antinomian implications of poststructural feminism to gay liberation. In its epistemological anarchism, queer theory was arguably even more radical than Butler's brand of feminism, particularly in the hands of Eve Kosofsky Sedgwick. Coming fast on the heels of *Gender Trouble*, Sedgwick's 1991 book *Epistemologies of the Closet* suggested there were two ways to conceptualize homosexuality. First, there was what she termed the "minoritizing view," which held that there existed a "relatively fixed homosexual minority" of people who "really are" gay. This was the view maintained by those who thought the best approach to destigmatizing homosexuality was to argue for its naturalness. It was also consistent with the tone of mainstream depictions of homosexuality, such as the *Time Magazine* cover story about popular actor Ellen DeGeneres coming out of the closet, summed up by the title "Yep, I'm Gay!" The second way to think about homosexuality, according to Sedgwick, was what she called the "universalizing view," the "queer" idea that sexual desire fluctuates and that even "apparently heterosexual persons" have homosexual tendencies. Gore Vidal best summed up this "universalizing view" when he wrote that "there is no such thing as a homosexual or heterosexual person, there are only homo- or heterosexual acts."[55]

Following Foucault's highly influential *History of Sexuality*, Sedgwick theorized that by the twentieth century everyone was compelled not only to identify in terms of gender, as either man or woman, but also in terms of a sexuality, as either homo or hetero. Such a genealogical understanding, that "homosexual" as a distinct sexual identity was a social construction of recent vintage, favored the universalizing

view and transcended gay rights. To Sedgwick, the fact that sexuality
had been placed "in a more and more distinctively privileged relation to our most prized constructs of individual identity, truth, and
knowledge" meant that the language of sexuality had transformed all
human relations. Therefore Sedgwick sought to "queer" sexuality in
the same way that Butler had "troubled" gender. She sought to show
how gender relations were shaped by binary ideas about sexuality.
Still, she was attentive to how queer theory mapped unevenly onto
the gay rights movement: if there were no unambiguously gay people,
then there could hardly be a movement specific to gay rights. In other
words, even though Sedgwick privileged "constructivist over essentialist, universalizing over minoritizing, and gender-transitive over
gender-essentialist understandings of sexual choice," she understood
that gay rights activism often demanded different priorities. In short,
her theoretical unmasking of the hetero-homo binary, however insightful, was not always the most suitable approach to curbing the repressive, often violent effects of homophobia. A homosexual political
subject remained necessary, if not academically fashionable.[56]

Just as Sedgwick was hesitant about the possible effects of queer
theory, some feminist theorists worried that the death of the feminist
subject, as heralded by Butler, would prove problematic to political
feminism. One of the most convincing among such feminists was political theorist Nancy Fraser, whose breakthrough 1989 book *Unruly
Practices* theorized that without a firm ethical framework grounded in
equal rights for women as women, realigning the political coordinates
of sex and gender was impossible. Fraser demonstrated her skepticism with regard to subjectless feminism by way of a critical look at
Foucauldian politics. She summed up Foucault's theory of power as
follows: power was too diffuse to be contained by the agency of sov-
ereign subjects. In other words, Foucault rejected liberal norms about
how individual subjects might construct a defense against illegitimate
forms of power. This was similar to how Butler overturned the idea
that female identity might act as a barricade against patriarchy. But for
Fraser, rejecting the political subject rendered political liberation impossible. The political enemies of feminism would not quit identifying
women *as women* just because feminist theorists had argued that female identity was an expression of patriarchy. Reconstituting a female
political subject out of the ashes of patriarchy was necessary even if

he female subject could not help but be understood in gendered or sexist terms. Women had to either fight for their rights as women, and gays as gays, or else surrender. In sum, even though partisans in the culture wars tended to gravitate toward their political *and* epistemological comrades—in fact, this was one of the overarching features of the culture wars—there were those who dissented from this trend. There were exceptions that proved the rule. Fraser and Butler might have positioned themselves similarly on specific political questions, such as a woman's right to be hired to fill jobs historically reserved for men, but they fundamentally disagreed on the philosophical rationale for such a politics.[57]

As feminists debated the political intricacies of a destabilized female identity, male identity was also in the process of being dislodged from its seemingly secure foundations. Men, including conservative Christian men, were equally compelled to adjust to new conceptions of gender. In fact, if social critic Barbara Ehrenreich was right, the male "flight from commitment," as symbolized by *Playboy* magazine's celebration of bachelorhood, was even more responsible than feminism for weakening the traditional family. Men, not feminist women, were the ones who had rebelled against American norms. Ehrenreich's counterintuitive claim, forwarded in her 1987 book *Hearts of Men*, made some sense in light of the fact that so many American women aligned, it seemed, against their own interests and with the backlash. "Ironically," she wrote, "by choosing independence, feminists could make common cause with the male rebels of our generation, while the antifeminists could represent themselves as women's true defenders against the male rebellion." Although Ehrenreich's claims were overstated, given the undeniable impact of feminism, one thing was clear. Nobody, men included, could escape the transformations to late-twentieth-century American gender relations.[58]

Susan Faludi recognized as much when she followed up *Backlash* with *Stiffed*, her impressive 1999 book about "the betrayal of the American man." Faludi argued that men, like women, had been misshapen by gender expectations that no longer matched reality. After attending a meeting of convicted spousal abusers, those who seemingly represented an out-of-control masculinity that had become the subject of so much social speculation, Faludi reported that "the men had probably felt in control when they beat their wives, but their

everyday experience was of feeling controlled—a feeling they had n
way of expressing because to reveal it was less than masculine, woul
make each of them, in fact, no man at all."[59]

The combined historical forces of feminism, which provided
women with some economic independence from men, and deindustrialization, which replaced a stable factory-based labor market with
a tenuous service economy, killed the male breadwinner model. In a
world in which more and more women worked, and in which more
and more jobs looked like women's work, men could no longer be
certain about their roles. American masculinity was in tatters. Like it
or not, American men had to adjust to a new gender landscape. Ironically, those men who clung most fiercely to traditionally prescribed
gender roles were best positioned to reconstitute American masculinity in ways that cohered with new economic imperatives while leaving
patriarchy intact.

As historian Bethany Moreton shows in her cultural history of
Walmart, the company born in the evangelical Ozarks that revolutionized the national retail market, a new patriarchal archetype emerged
that reconciled conservative gender expectations with the service
economy. Walmart managers, typically conservative evangelical men,
resigned themselves to service, with Jesus as their role model, on the
condition that they were afforded some degree of paternalistic authority over their mostly female workforce. Moreton argues that this new
interpretation of Christian manliness reshaped gender relations across
the Christian Right more broadly, including in the home. As conservative evangelical women entered the workforce in growing numbers,
the servant-authority mindset freed men to help with housework and
childcare duties while still retaining their grip on patriarchal authority.
Secure in the knowledge that their wives respected their God-given
authority, men remained kings of their castles even as they occasionally changed dirty diapers.[60]

Against this new gender backdrop, religious conservatives fought
out the culture wars in different terms. Jerry Falwell's fire-and-
brimstone style slowly gave way to a gentler antifeminism that better
fit the servant-authority sensibility. The Promise Keepers, a Christian organization for men founded in 1990 by University of Colorado
football coach Bill McCartney, embodied this new and gentler antifeminism. The Promise Keepers, according to Faludi, had a "vision of
founding manhood on spiritual principles" which might allow men

"to reclaim respect, appreciation, and authority at home as devout husbands and fathers." Many reporters, and most feminists, thought the Promise Keepers were merely yet another branch of the antifeminist Christian Right, a connection made plausible by the rhetoric of some of their spokesmen. Tony Evans, for example, implored Promise Keepers who filled stadium after stadium to make clear to their wives appropriate gender dynamics: "Honey, I've made a terrible mistake. I've given you my role. I gave up leading this family, and I forced you to take my place. Now I must reclaim that role." But Faludi, attuned to male gender trouble, emphasized those Promise Keepers qualities that helped men adjust to postindustrial America. For instance, when not thundering about a man's duty to rule over his wife, even Evans proclaimed that Christian men needed to reject macho attitudes and embrace their sensitive side by crying and talking about their feelings. Faludi described the Promise Keepers she interviewed as polite, wistful, and nonthreatening, a stark contrast to the angry men whom she had encountered watching *Fatal Attraction* a decade earlier. In this way Faludi thought the Promise Keepers offered a brilliant personal solution to the dilemmas men faced. "Once men had cemented their identity to Jesus," she wrote, "they could reclaim a new masculine role in the family, not as breadwinners but as spiritual pathfinders." Leading the family in God's path became a viable way to express manhood. As McCartney told Faludi, such a role was "mandated."[61]

If the Promise Keepers were more about reckoning with the crisis of masculinity than about fighting feminism, James Dobson showed that it was possible to do both—that it was possible to mix a softened Christian masculinity with an unreconstructed antifeminism. In fact, Dobson's therapeutic brand of Christian psychology, which helped millions of Christian Americans adjust to postfeminist cultural patterns, proved more effective than Falwell's wrathful style at waging the culture wars against feminism.

In the late 1970s Dobson left his position as a psychologist at the University of Southern California School of Medicine and Children's Hospital, where he "saw firsthand how divorce, abuse, and other forms of familial strife were tearing their lives apart," convinced that his life's purpose was to defend the traditional family unit. He thus founded Focus on the Family to help reverse the sexual revolution, which he starkly characterized as "a "sudden disintegration of moral and ethical principles such as has never occurred in the history of mankind."

Dobson and Focus on the Family hosted a radio program of the same name that distinguished itself from the firebrand shows that dominated the Christian airwaves by routinely taking calls from men who broke down and cried on the air.[62]

Although Dobson signaled that hypermasculinity was no longer a prerequisite for Christian manhood, his brand of Christian wisdom attracted an audience that was mostly female. In fact, so many women trusted Dobson that they sent him letters by the truckload asking his advice on various personal matters. He hired a team of female "correspondents" to respond to this overwhelming amount of mail, and he set up telephone hotlines for women to dial for advice. By the time Dobson moved Focus on the Family to Colorado Springs in 1991, his army of letter and phone correspondents numbered in the thousands. Such counseling services enabled Focus on the Family's sophisticated fundraising enterprises: letter-writers and callers were more likely to pay membership fees, and they purchased mountains of Focus on the Family advice literature, much of which was written by Dobson himself.

Dobson explicitly related the counseling component of Focus on the Family to the organization's political advocacy. For instance, women who sought advice about their cheating or porn-obsessed husbands found sympathetic correspondents. But they also received lessons about how their husbands' infidelities resulted from a cultural rot that had weakened the traditional family. Guidance on how best to rehabilitate the family, with instructions for how to submit to their husbands, was often included as part of the lesson plan. "Please understand that I believe firmly in the Biblical concept of submission, as described in the Book of Ephesians and elsewhere in the Scripture," Dobson explained. "But there is a vast difference between being a confident, spiritually submissive woman and being a *doormat*." His patriarchal advice was thus couched in terms that empowered women. As opposed to those conservative evangelicals who wanted wives to obey husbands and not ask questions, Dobson preferred that women submit on better terms.[63]

In 1987 the Christian Right's favorite psychologist published a marital advice book—*Love for a Lifetime*—that combined a folksy, therapeutic style with a traditionalist message. Dobson thought that by helping married couples achieve "the mystical bond of friendship, commitment, and understanding," he might mitigate against the rising divorce rate, a "tragedy" that had befallen the nation. Like all marriage counselors, he advised that couples determine their compatibility prior to marriage. But Dobson's version of such otherwise banal counsel was shaped by a hyperessentialist view of sexual difference. He believed that recognizing sexual difference, which he called a "biological foundation," was the key to marital bliss. "Genesis tells us that the Creator made *two* sexes, not one, and that He designed each gender for a specific purpose." Dobson asserted that gender-specific purposes were not only biological, in the obvious ways that men and women "fit" together, but also psychological: whereas a woman needed daily affirmation from her husband that he loved her, which "is why flowers and candy and cards are more meaningful to her than to him," a man needed his wife to create a haven from the cutthroat workplace. "God put greater toughness and aggressiveness in the man and more softness and nurturance in the woman—and suited them to one another's needs." In short, healthy marriages rested on the recognition of difference. For Dobson, this was an exciting prospect: "How boring it would be if the sexes were identical, as the radical feminists have tried to tell us!"[64]

Given that millions of religious conservatives embraced Dobson's traditional ideas about marriage, including his notion that marriage was made happy by those who welcomed strict gender roles, it was no wonder so many Americans loathed Hillary and Bill Clinton. Hillary, the personification of liberal feminism, was the prototypical successful career woman. When she led a task force on healthcare reform in her capacity as First Lady, conservatives responded with outrage, not only because they opposed a more socialized healthcare system but also because they hated it that Hillary did not assume the matriarchal role expected of those in her position. Bill, for his part, cut his political teeth working on the "acid, amnesty, and abortion" campaign of George McGovern. Although many political commentators correctly placed the Arkansas Democrat in the center of the political spectrum, particularly on crime and the economy, Clinton's feminist-infused cultural liberalism, including his support for legal abortion, was alien to a Christian Right in no mood to appease him. When the newly elected president's intentions to lift the ban on gays in the military were made public in 1993, conservative evangelicals swamped Congress with nearly half a million calls. When his surgeon general Joycelyn Elders provocatively stated that teaching masturbation in schools would be appropriate, conservatives riding high on their 1994 midterm successes compelled the president to fire her. And when news leaked that Bill had oral sex with a young White House intern by the name of Monica Lewinsky and then committed perjury by denying the affair during grand jury testimony, apoplectic conservatives in the House impeached him. In a book that purported to document Clinton's serial pattern of corruption, William Bennett defended independent prosecutor Kenneth Starr, whom McGovern called the "prosecutor-at-large of presidential sex," on the grounds that a political leader's private moral compass was predictive of his or her commitment to the public good. Bennett disdained the argument made by Clinton's defenders, that "America needs to become more European (read: 'sophisticated') in its attitude towards sex," describing such logic as "an assault on American ideals."[65]

A majority of Americans disagreed with Bennett's judgment of events. So, too, did a majority in the Senate, which narrowly found Clinton not guilty of perjury and obstruction of justice, allowing him to remain president. Many Americans were also inclined to agree with Hillary Clinton's famous statement that the attack on her husband's presidency was the work of a "vast right-wing conspiracy." In any case, the Clinton-Lewinsky scandal that rocked the nation in 1998 and 1999 represented an armistice of sorts in the perplexing, decades-long national wars over sex and gender. Millions of Americans rejected the premises of feminism and the sexual revolution. Yet even more Americans had come to terms with some, if not all, of the legacies of these sixties cultural earthquakes and had come to see those who opposed such changes as reactionaries who stood outside the American mainstream. Everyone had visions about who and what represented American sexual norms. But these visions were often separated by vast political and moral gulfs.

6

The Sacred and the Profane

In 1992 Patrick Buchanan wrote one of his typically fuming essays warning about the threat posed by the leftists who had captured the commanding heights of American culture. To drive home his point, he offered up an outrageous analogy: "Stalin, who was partial to Chicago gangster films, thought that if only he had control of Hollywood, he could control the world." In similar if less playful terms, conservative art critic James Cooper fretted that the nation's political leaders focused their attention on foreign wars "while failing to realize the war is also raging on the battlefield of the arts within our own borders." American conservatives, it seemed, had reached the conclusion that cultural representations had grave political consequences. In fact, such a notion—that culture was power—had become a staple of late-twentieth-century conservative common sense.[1]

Ironically, it was the New Left that did the most to popularize a theory about the power of culture. The radical activists of the sixties believed they could forge new political arrangements by transforming American culture. But by the 1980s and 1990s, many American liberals, with some notable exceptions, argued that cultural representations were relatively powerless. For example, they contended that the profane images of Robert Mapplethorpe's art, or the pornographic lyrics of the rap group 2 Live Crew, had little effect on American sexual behavior. Such artistic renderings, liberals argued, should not be judged in moral or ethical terms and were socially instrumental only to the degree that they demonstrated the nearly infinite diversity of free expression. In short, liberals had a relativistic approach to art: who were they to criticize artistic expressions that some people found meaningful? This perspective stood in stark contrast to that put forward by conservatives, who claimed that vulgar cultural representations, which they deemed objectively immoral, corrupted the American soul. In the face of such a grave threat, conservatives ignored arguments about the unqualified merits of free expression. Rather, they openly touted the necessity of censorship.[2]

In this fight for American culture, conservatives were explicit about what type of artistic representations they opposed. They were against hostile portrayals of religion and people of religious faith, just as they were against favorable portrayals of extramarital sex and homosexuality. Such cultural expressions violated the normative America that conservatives sought to affirm. In contrast, conservatives forwarded a cultural ideal that journalist Sidney Blumenthal isolated as "the neokitsch aesthetic": a nostalgic, irony-free celebration of traditional American greatness, which often took the form of 1950s pastiche. This was an America when John Wayne was king, an America when families closely resembled the Cleavers of the television program *Leave It to Beaver*, a time when television programming was, in the words of conservative film critic Michael Medved, "innocent and decent." "Apparently," as Blumenthal put it, "kitsch in black and white was traditional culture."[3]

Nostalgia for the 1950s was not unique to conservative thought. It had been a persistent feature of American pop culture since the sixties. That such nostalgic renderings of the 1950s appeared by the early 1970s suggests the vast cultural distance the nation had traveled during the transformative sixties. George Lucas's 1973 film *American Graffiti*—about two high school graduates enjoying one last night of cruising in their cars before real life begins—depicts the last gasp of innocence in Modesto, California, circa 1962. The 1978 Hollywood film *Grease*—about a mismatched couple who fall in love—portrays 1958 as a simpler time when trauma was limited to heartbreak, even for working-class white ethnic teenagers. And the popular television show *Happy Days*, which first aired in 1974—about the Cunninghams, a happy, normal white middle-class family living in 1950s Milwaukee—validates normative America by contrasting it with looming threats like the sexual revolution. Such cultural productions were not didactic in an overtly conservative fashion. But they represented a yearning for an earlier, safer, happier, more harmonious America—for an America that made sense. As historian Jill Lepore writes, 1950s nostalgia represented "a remembrance of childhood, a yearning for a common past, bulwark against a divided present, comfort against an uncertain future."[4]

The further the culture got from the 1950s, literally and figuratively, the more alarming were the cries of conservatives. "For those who create the popular culture," Ronald Reagan said in his 1989 farewell address, "patriotism is no longer in style." Buchanan was more direct. Calling Reagan's lament a "dramatic understatement," he said: "America's art and culture are, more and more, openly anti-Christian, anti-American, nihilistic."[5]

Buchanan's pronouncement had a grain of truth. American art and popular culture had indeed been transformed by the transgressive ethos that grew out of the sixties. Television programming increasingly showcased sex, from 1970s situational comedies like *Three's Company* to 1980s primetime soap operas like *Dallas* and *Dynasty*. One of the most popular situation comedies of the 1980s and 1990s, *Married with Children*, portrayed the traditional family, in the disapproving words of Medved, "as a comically outmoded and beleaguered structure that creates endless difficulties for those enslaved to it."[6]

As if this was not bad enough for conservatives, American film made television seem tame by comparison. When Jack Valenti took over the presidency of the Motion Picture Association of America (MPAA) in 1966, the film industry abandoned the Hays Production Code that had enforced relatively staid norms since the 1930s. The MPAA instead adopted a ratings system that allowed much more graphic depictions of sex and violence, on condition that such films were rated R, as in "restricted" to adults. Such a regulatory adjustment, which codified cultural shifts, led to an astonishing run of Hollywood films that seemed designed to mock American taboos. A "New Hollywood" came into being, led by a group of young directors who reached large audiences by emphasizing sex, violence, and disrespect for authority. Violent, irreverent films like *Bonnie and Clyde* (1967) paved the way for films like Oliver Stone's *Natural Born Killers* (1994), movies of the type that Medved described as an orgy of "ugliness, horror, and depravity."[7]

Popular music also broke with the "innocent and decent" culture of 1950s America. This was especially true of heavy metal, a genre of rock 'n' roll that featured distorted electric guitar riffs and tribal drumbeats. Heavy metal musicians, mostly men with long, flowing hair, ironically mixed gender-bending imagery with hypermasculine

messaging. Gene Simmons, lead singer of Kiss, personified the paradoxes of heavy metal by combining a flamboyant stage persona, which
included a heavy application of makeup to his face, with a misogynistic boastfulness about his notoriously active sex life. Simmons told
public radio host Terry Gross: "If you want to welcome me with open
arms, I'm afraid you're also going to have to welcome me with open
legs." The ubiquity of heavy metal, and its legions of adoring, headbanging fans, led to a minor moral panic in the mid-1980s. Historian
of heavy metal Ian Christe nicely captures the genesis of these anxieties: "Headbangers appeared in public everywhere, milling around
strip malls with long, unkempt (and often kempt) hair and sporting
T-shirts that bore the frequently frightful names and imagery of bands
like Ratt, Def Leppard, Iron Maiden, and Venom. America's authority figures were starting to feel greatly antagonized." The ABC news
program *20/20*, which was never reluctant to report on moral panic,
dedicated an episode to heavy metal in 1987. Intoning about "lyrics
obsessed with sex, devil worship, suicide," *20/20* pondered whether
heavy metal contributed to teenage suicide. Indeed, the heavy metal
band Judas Priest was sued in 1990 by Nevada parents who claimed
the group's supposedly subliminal messages had convinced their teenage sons to attempt suicide.[8]

The heavy metal scare, like most American moral panics, became
the subject of congressional hearings in 1985 at which the Senate
heard testimony on the subject of "porn rock." Such hearings were
made possible by the tireless efforts of Tipper Gore, wife of Senator Al
Gore, and her fellow "Washington wives," the patronizing title given
to the four women who founded the Parents' Music Resource Center (PMRC). Gore picked a fight with the music industry after over-
hearing the Grammy-award-winning musician Prince's song "Dar-
ling Nikki," about a girl masturbating in a hotel lobby, playing on her
eleven-year-old daughter's stereo. In order to caution parents about
explicit content, Gore and the PMRC convinced record companies
to place warning labels on such "filthy" albums. "Tipper Stickers," as
the labels came to be called, were not meant to censor art, according to Gore, who considered herself a liberal Democrat and "a strong
believer of the First Amendment." Rather, the labels were merely intended to educate consumers, especially those parents too busy to do
their own research about the music their children listened to. Such a
strategy was all the more urgent, in Gore's view, given that the mu-

sic industry no longer exercised self-restraint—given that it was more and more difficult to raise "PG kids in a X-rated society," as she titled her 1987 book. Republican Senator Paula Hawkins put it this way in her statement before the "porn rock" hearings: "Much has changed since Elvis' seemingly innocent times. Subtleties, suggestions, and innuendo have given way to overt expressions and descriptions of often violent sexual acts, drug taking, and flirtations with the occult." Those who protested Elvis Presley's pelvic gyrations on *The Ed Sullivan Show* could not have anticipated what was to come in succeeding decades.[9]

To give the Senate audience a taste of "porn rock," the PMRC presented a small sampling of music videos at the congressional hearings. In general, music videos fed anxieties about heavy metal, since videos meant that displays of rebelliousness could no longer be contained in concert halls. A new cable channel, Music Television, better known as MTV, made the music and imagery of heavy metal a fixture in American homes. One of the videos shown in the Senate hearings was Twister Sister's hit "We're Not Gonna Take It," in which the hairy band members, symbols of heavy metal's negative influence on American youth, storm through an idyllic suburban neighborhood and embolden a teenage boy to stand up to his obnoxious authoritarian father. The video depicted violence, but of the cartoonish type. Dee Snider, Twisted Sister's ghastly-looking lead singer, said it "was simply meant to be a cartoon with human actors playing variations on the Roadrunner / Wile E. Coyote theme." Given that it was an obvious parody, even slapstick comedy, the "We're Not Gonna Take It" video hardly constituted a dire threat—its violent, gender-bending, antiauthoritarian protagonists notwithstanding. To many observers, using that particular video and that particular band—Snider testified that he was a Christian who abstained from tobacco, alcohol, and drugs—demonstrated that the heavy metal scare was overblown. More transgressive heavy metal acts existed—acts that better matched PMRC cofounder Susan Baker's warnings about bands that "promote and glorify suicide, rape, sadomasochism." But popular acts like Twisted Sister were hardly emblems of such evil.[10]

The "porn rock" congressional hearings featured testimony from several artists who opposed PMRC efforts, including Snider and, perhaps surprisingly, folk musician John Denver, who was "strongly opposed to censorship of any kind." The most confrontational testimony came from musician and composer Frank Zappa, who argued that the PMRC warning label scheme was "an ill-conceived piece of nonsense which fails to deliver any real benefits to children, infringes the civil liberties of people who are not children, and promises to keep the courts busy for years dealing with the interpretation and enforcement problems inherent in the proposal's design." Zappa believed "porn rock" was a red herring; the real issue, in his view, was that the record industry was pressuring Congress to pass antipiracy legislation that would have criminalized the common practice of making duplicate recordings using tapes in one's home. Record companies "didn't agree to this stickering of albums on moral grounds," Zappa charged, "but business ones." The record industry recognized that warning labels were a painless way to appease moral conservatives like Senator Strom Thurmond, whom they needed to support their antipiracy legislation. In fact, rather than hurt record sales, "Tipper Stickers" often improved them by making otherwise unremarkable albums seem like forbidden fruit.[11]

To musicians, Tipper Gore had become a foil and a muse. The heavy metal band Danzig wrote a hit song about Gore titled "Mother"—"Mother, tell your children not to hold my hand!" And the provocative hip-hop star Ice-T rapped: "Yo Tip, what's the matter? You ain't gettin' no dick? You're bitchin' about rock 'n' roll, that's censorship, dumb bitch. The Constitution says we all got a right to speak. Say what we want Tip, your argument is weak." And yet to conservatives, Gore did not go far enough in her efforts to limit the reach of heavy metal. She could not win.[12]

Right-wing pundit George Will argued that rock music—"a plague of messages about sexual promiscuity, bisexuality, incest, sado-masochism, satanism, drug use, alcohol abuse and constantly, misogyny"—had to be reined in lest the American experiment in self-government perish. The biggest problem with "porn rock," Will contended, was that it had desensitized young people. Offensive acts no longer elicited shame and embarrassment. Echoing venerable conservative understandings about how democracy demanded virtuous citizens capable of self-restraint, Will wrote: "A public incapable of shame and embarrassment about public vulgarity is unsuited to self-government." Put another way, hedonism had slipped into the mainstream of American culture, thus driving a nail into the coffin of the Protestant ethic that had been the bedrock of American civilization.

"Perhaps the coarsening of a public is irreversible, especially when the coarsening concerns a powerful and pleasurable appetite such as sex." But Will's declension narrative was not entirely fatalistic. He believed that it was still possible for American culture to "move away from coarseness toward delicacy of feeling." The question, of course, was how. How could opponents limit the reach of a depraved music industry? How could they make American culture wholesome again?[13]

William Buckley Jr. had a candid answer to such questions. Consistent with his long-standing position that the First Amendment did not license unrestricted free expression, and echoing arguments he made in that era's pornography debates, Buckley contended that government censorship was an appropriate solution. Communities, he thought, had a right to set and enforce standards. "At the Yale University Library," Buckley said, "you can't get a book by Marquis de Sade without getting a special clearance from the graduate school." Appearing on a 1988 episode of Buckley's *Firing Line* dedicated to the subject of "dirty rock lyrics," Gore insisted, again, that the PMRC did not seek a new role for government, that such censorship efforts would violate the civil liberties of musicians, and that warning labels were perfectly consistent with the First Amendment. Buckley called that position untenable. The rock lyrics in question, he argued, were a form of child abuse, and therefore the state was duty-bound to intervene. In other words, Buckley and Gore agreed in their assessment that explicit music was a danger to society, but they disagreed over how to balance that recognition with an implied right to free expression. Buckley embraced censorship. In contrast, even as the public face of the PMRC, Gore was at pains to describe herself as a liberal, a free-speech advocate, and a fan of rock music. But such defensiveness was to no avail. When punk rocker Jello Biafra told Oprah Winfrey that the PMRC was a front for the Christian Right, "for people like Jesse Helms and Phyllis Schlafly," he was stating a common assumption: only conservatives believed explicit content was bad for society. No matter how hard she tried, Gore was unable to shed the notion that she was in cahoots with conservative censors. Of course such a connection was fitting: Gore and the PMRC, intentionally or not, helped pave the way for a government censorship campaign that gained considerable traction once the targeted music shifted from rock to rap — once the targeted musicians shifted from white to black.[14]

Rap music, also called hip-hop, emerged from the black neighborhoods of New York City and Los Angeles to take the nation by storm in the 1980s. Rap lyrics, typically chanted in time to looping beats and mixed samples of rock, funk, jazz, and rhythm and blues, tended to describe a dystopian vision of ghetto life. Joseph Saddler, better known as the rapper Grandmaster Flash, gave radio listeners across America a taste of life in the Bronx with his 1982 hit "The Message":

> Rats in the front room, roaches in the back
> Junkies in the alley with the baseball bat
> I tried to get away, but I couldn't get far
> Cause a man with a tow-truck repossessed my car.

Chuck D of the hugely successful hip-hop group Public Enemy, which intermingled Black Power messaging with an aesthetics of the street—"911 is a joke in yo town, late 911 wears the late crown"—called rap the "CNN of the ghetto." Ice-T, who achieved fame in the 1980s for his clever, sexually explicit raps, and then gained even more notoriety for his 1992 song "Cop Killer," said his role was to "bring out how brothas on the corner talk." Many music critics agreed. Arthur Kempton described rappers as "the pre-eminent young dramaturgists in the clamorous theater of the street." Nelson George of *Village Voice* argued that the role of artists like Ice-T was to "describe the reality of the world they live in." In a debate with Tipper Gore on *The Oprah Winfrey Show*, George reversed the PMRC script: "The music represents society, not the other way around." In other words, rap music had redeeming value not because it shaped behavior but because it told the otherwise untold stories of black urban America. In this way, Ice-T's music was comparable to *Native Son*, Richard Wright's 1940 novel that had been banned in at least eight states for its violent portrayal of life on Chicago's South Side.[15]

Whether or not Ice-T was a literary naturalist on par with Richard Wright, his music, and rap more generally, sold millions of records, and not only to black consumers. Once computerized scanning allowed for the systematic tracking of record sales, replacing a haphazard system that overemphasized records purchased in highly visible music stores and deemphasized records bought in the suburbs, a remarkable thing happened. As the journalist David Samuels wrote: "America awoke on June 22, 1991 to find that its favorite record was not *Out of Time*, by aging college-boy rockers R.E.M., but *Niggaz4life*, a musical celebration of gang rape and other violence by N.W.A., or Niggers With Attitude, a rap group from the Los Angeles ghetto of Compton whose records had never before risen above No. 27 on the Billboard charts." Marketing rappers as violent black criminals was a surefire way to sell lots and lots of records to suburban white Americans. As Samuels argued: "Rap's appeal to whites rested in its evocation of an age-old image of blackness: a foreign, sexually charged, and criminal underworld against which the norms of white society are defined, and, by extension, through which they may be defied." In other words, rap music was normative America's great taboo, and as with most taboos, people gravitated toward it, especially young people. As Ice-T said: "The white kids in suburbia are buying N.W.A. records and their parents don't know what to do about it." Indeed, the commonplace sight of white college students rapping along to N.W.A.'s song "Fuck tha Police" no doubt engendered widespread cognitive dissonance. N.W.A. rapper Ice Cube's lyrics hardly described the life of the typical white fraternity brother:

> "Fuck tha Police" coming straight out the underground
> A young nigger got it bad 'cause I'm brown
> And not the other color. Some police think
> They have the authority to kill the minority . . .
>
> A young nigger on the warpath
> And when I'm finished, it's gonna be a bloodbath
> Of cops, dying in L.A.
> Yo, Dre I've got something to say: "Fuck tha Police."

So-called gansta rap seemed bent on making a mockery of Reagan's America.[16]

Conservatives would have censored N.W.A. if violent lyrics had been illegal. Instead conservatives went after sexually explicit rap, which proved an easier target due to the continued legal wrangling over obscenity laws. The primary recipient of right-wing censorship efforts was 2 Live Crew, a Miami rap band whose 1986 debut album, *The 2 Live Crew Is What We Are*, took, in the words of one music critic, "sexually explicit rap lyrics to a new level of nastiness." That album, which included the notorious track "We Want Some Pussy," went gold. The band's next album, *As Nasty as They Wanna Be*, which

featured the wildly popular single "Me So Horny," was released in 1989
to even more commercial success. *As Nasty as They Wanna Be* placed
2 Live Crew at the center of a firestorm that made the moral panic over
heavy metal seem tame by comparison. Conservatives thought "Tipper Stickers" were inadequate warning for the depravities contained
within 2 Live Crew albums. To be sure, 2 Live Crew's lyrics left little
to the imagination. "Me So Horny" included sexist passages like the
following:

> Girls always ask me why I fuck so much
> I say "What's wrong, baby doll, with a quick nut?"
> 'Cause you're the one, and you shouldn't be mad
> I won't tell your mama if you don't tell your dad
> I know he'll be disgusted when he sees your pussy busted
> Won't your mama be so mad if she knew I got that ass?
> I'm a freak in heat, a dog without warning
> My appetite is sex, 'cause me so horny.[17]

In 1989 Jack Thompson, a lawyer affiliated with right-wing media
activist Donald Wildmon's organization, the American Family Association (AFA), convinced Florida governor Bob Martinez that *As
Nasty as They Wanna Be* met the legal classification of obscenity. In
turn, after Martinez persuaded local law officials to pursue the case, a
Broward County sheriff warned that there was probable cause to arrest anyone who sold 2 Live Crew albums. As a countermeasure, the
band filed a lawsuit, but a US district court judge ruled that *As Nasty
as They Wanna Be* was indeed obscene and thus illegal to sell. Un-
dercover police arrested several record storeowners, and 2 Live Crew
band members were arrested after performing at a Miami nightclub.
No guilty verdicts ever came of the arrests, and the obscenity ruling
was overturned in 1992. But the legal dispute fed a national controversy that was further fueled by the dimension of race.[18]

Most of those who publicly fought to criminalize 2 Live Crew argued that censorship was a necessary step because there was a causal
nexus between sexually explicit music and the sexual abuse of women
and children. Conservatives maintained that the music of 2 Live Crew
was the equivalent of pollution and the government had a right to regulate it out of existence. George Will neatly summed up this view by
way of a common analogy: "We legislate against smoking in restau-

rants; singing 'Me So Horny' is a constitutional right. Secondary smoke is carcinogenic; celebration of torn vaginas is 'mere words.'" 2 Live Crew's lyrics were indeed more graphic than most. But popular music of many kinds was awash in sex, making it plausible that race was a contributing factor to the seemingly disproportionate legal response to rap. Phil Donahue, who dedicated several episodes of his daytime talk show to the issue of music censorship, wondered aloud about why 2 Live Crew was singled out: "We've got to wonder about racism." During one such episode, with 2 Live Crew rapper Luther Campbell as a guest, Donahue played a Madonna video from her "Blind Ambition" concert performance of "Like a Virgin," which included scenes of her gyrating and stroking herself, and asked, "If we arrest Luther how come we're not arresting Madonna?"[19]

One of Donohue's audience members answered his rhetorical question by declaring that 2 Live Crew's music "isn't even art, it isn't even music, it's rap." In other words, Madonna was granted some leeway, at least in this particular debate, because, unlike rappers, she was a musician and an artist. Cultural gatekeeper Robert Bork put it like this: "[R]ap is generally little more than noise with a beat, the singing is an unmelodic chant, the lyrics often range from the perverse to the mercifully unintelligible. It is difficult to convey just how debased rap is." Such a position ignored the fact that millions of Americans considered rappers artists worthy of their patronage. As Jello Biafra hilariously responded to the Donahue audience member who denied rap was music: "Not everyone wants to hear Lee Atwater sing the blues."[20]

Whereas conservatives contended that 2 Live Crew was a threat to American sexual norms, most liberals, to the degree that they defended 2 Live Crew against censors, did so merely out of their stated support for the principles of free expression. Very few liberals argued that 2 Live Crew's music was culturally redeeming. Henry Louis Gates Jr. was one of the few exceptions. Gates testified on behalf of 2 Live Crew at their criminal trial—testimony that likely helped get the band off on all charges—and he also later testified before the appeals court that overturned the original obscenity ruling. In his testimony, Gates did much more than merely defend 2 Live Crew's First Amendment rights. He argued that 2 Live Crew needed to be understood in the context of the long history of African American cultural resistance. "For centuries," Gates wrote in the *New York Times*, "African Americans have been forced to develop coded ways of communicating to protect them from danger. Allegories and double meanings, words redefined to mean their opposites (bad meaning 'good,' for instance), even neologisms (bodacious) have enabled blacks to share messages only the initiated understood." In short, 2 Live Crew lyrics were not literal. Even its most sexist lyrics—*especially* its most sexist lyrics—needed to be understood at the level of parody. As Gates put it: "These young artists are acting out, to lively dance music, a parodic exaggeration of the age-old stereotypes of the oversexed black female and male. Their exuberant use of hyperbole (phantasmagoric sexual organs, for example) undermines—for anyone fluent in black cultural codes—a too literal-minded hearing of the lyrics."[21]

Not everyone agreed with Gates. Conservatives viewed his argument as another example of how "new class" intellectuals used tortuous logic to rationalize bad behavior. Many feminists and some leftists argued that 2 Live Crew needed to be critiqued because they profited from sexism. Left-wing media critic Ben Bagdikian wrote a letter to the *New York Times* editor in response to the Gates article and contended that 2 Live Crew's songs were different from previous African American cultural expressions, not only because they were more misogynistic but also because they were "not performed as a sequestered inside joke, but mass marketed in the hope of making money rewards precisely because they are promoted to be sensational and clearly understood." Anticipating such a response, Gates called 2 Live Crew's sexism "troubling," but also wrote that it was so over the top "that it almost cancels itself out in a hyperbolic war between the sexes." Perhaps more to the point, Gates accentuated the racial hypocrisy of those who singled out 2 Live Crew: "Is 2 Live Crew more 'obscene' than, say, the comic Andrew Dice Clay? Clearly, this rap group is seen as more threatening than others that are just as sexually explicit. Can this be completely unrelated to the specter of the young black male as a figure of sexual and social disruption, the very stereotypes 2 Live Crew seems determined to undermine?" Understood in this way, 2 Live Crew was merely a convenient prop for a moral panic colored by racial overtones.[22]

Whether or not 2 Live Crew was intentionally spoofing the dominant culture—whether or not they were the conscious heirs to black comedian Redd Foxx—was not very important. More pertinent was that 2 Live Crew had come to represent the exaggerated totems of American racial and sexual anxieties. Its music was popular, in part because, yes, "sex sells," but also in part because, consciously or not, it tapped into a rich discourse about race and masculinity that was compelling to white and black audiences alike, often for very different reasons. Of course 2 Live Crew was not the only musical group of the era to touch such raw nerves.

Despite Madonna's white skin and iconic status, she became the subject of a culture wars controversy in 1989 when Pepsi-Cola canceled its commercial starring the world-famous pop star. Pepsi paid Madonna $5 million to make the advertisement, set to her song "Like a Prayer," but aired it only twice due to pressure from conservative groups like Wildmon's AFA, which threatened the soda company with a boycott. Conservatives were irate about the MTV version of "Like a Prayer," which mixed religious symbolism with sexual imagery. As Camille Paglia, Madonna's biggest admirer, described the video: "Madonna receives the stigmata, makes love with the animated statue of a black saint, and dances in a rumpled silk slip in front of a field of burning crosses. This last item, with its uncontrolled racial allusions, shocked even me." It was no wonder Pepsi backed away from the commercial. Arguably more surprising was that Pepsi chose Madonna as the face of its product in the first place. Sure, she was one of the most recognizable people in the world—as Michael Medved wistfully wrote, "[T]here are Amish kids in Pennsylvania who know about Madonna." But conservatives had long worried about her singing about taboo subjects like virgin sex—"touched for the very first time"—and teenage pregnancy—"papa don't preach, I'm in trouble deep." "Asked about how to diminish illegitimacy," Bork wrote, "a woman who worked with unmarried teenage mothers replied tersely: 'Shoot Madonna.'"[23]

Madonna's "Like a Prayer" video was provocative not only because of its overt racial and sexual imagery but because it used such imagery as a way to break down the barriers between the sacred and the profane. In other words, religion mattered. The video highlighted the animalistic, grotesque, pagan side of Christian iconography—blood, flesh, and lust—in ways that religious conservatives deemed blasphemous. Raised an Italian American Catholic, Madonna had long used her music as a way to probe the meaning of a religion that seemed dead to her. The ironic stage name she gave to herself—Madonna—rejoined the Virgin Mary with the whore Mary Magdalene. In this Madonna was a lot like filmmaker Martin Scorsese, another Italian American Catholic fascinated with the iconography of his religious upbringing but frustrated by its seeming irrelevance to modern life. Madonna, of course, was keenly aware of this similarity: the title of her contentious video "The Last Temptation of Madonna" was a play on Scorsese's divisive 1988 film *The Last Temptation of Christ*, which engendered the quintessential episode in the culture wars.[24]

The Last Temptation of Christ, a lightning rod well before it was released in theaters, was based on Nikos Kazantzakis's 1955 novel *The Last Temptation*, which had been controversial in the United States since the early sixties, when conservatives fought to have the English translation removed from several public libraries. Consistent with the existentialist angst of the postwar era, the novel painted Jesus as a "Nietzschean hero," as God-in-the-making. *The Last Temptation* reversed the traditional Christian script—humanity does not need God; rather, God needs humanity—making it one of a growing number of literary reinterpretations of Jesus's life that by their very definition violated the terms of the sacred. Salman Rushdie, author of the 1988 novel *Satanic Verses*, a literary reinterpretation of the Prophet Muhammad that propelled the Ayatollah Khomeini to issue a call for Rushdie's death, explained why such an approach to a sacred figure was bound to incite: "Whereas religion seeks to privilege one language above all others, one set of values above all others, and one text above all others, the novel has always been about the way in which different languages, values and narratives quarrel, and about the shifting relations between them, which are relations of power." In late-twentieth-century America, the same could have been said more generally about art in its relation to conservative Christianity.[25]

After Scorsese secured the film rights to the Kazantzakis novel, he hired Paul Schrader, his collaborator on *Taxi Driver* and *Raging Bull*, to write the screenplay for what came to be titled *The Last Temptation of Christ*. Schrader, who grew up in a chiliastic Dutch Calvinist family, was, like Scorsese, intrigued by the idea of reimagining Jesus for the big screen, particularly a Jesus tempted by the sins of the flesh. One of the most contentious aspects of the novel was that Kazantzakis's Jesus constantly struggles with the bipolar nature of his existence, split between the human and the divine. While on the cross, Jesus is confronted with one final temptation, in which he vividly imagines a full human life for himself, including a marriage to Mary Magdalene and lots of sex. Jesus reawakens from this dream—his last temptation—to find himself back on the cross, finally prepared to make the ultimate sacrifice for humanity, to embrace his divine side. In his original screenplay Schrader pushed the envelope on Jesus's temptations by accentuating sex, the greatest test of Jesus's faith.[26]

With a script in hand, and with a major studio in Paramount backing production, Scorsese was set to begin filming *The Last Temptation of Christ* in 1983. But Paramount canceled production before filming got under way, in large part because the studio decided it was a bad idea to anger the conservative groups that threatened to boycott it and its parent company, Gulf + Western. By the time it stopped production, Paramount and Gulf + Western were receiving five thousand angry letters per week. Scorsese was devastated by Paramount's decision, but he was undeterred. He had long been obsessed with making a film that would "push the concept of Jesus into the twenty-first century," a film that would make Jesus come alive for a corrupted world, and he was convinced that Kazantzakis's novel was the perfect vehicle for fulfilling this objective. *The Last Temptation of Christ* was to be Scorsese's most personal film.[27]

Stopping *The Last Temptation of Christ* was the personal obsession of the equally irrepressible Donald Wildmon. A Methodist pastor, Wildmon quit the ministry in 1976 and moved to Tupelo, Mississippi, where he founded the National Federation for Decency. From the outset of his career as a media activist, Wildmon deployed boycotts against companies that advertised their wares on television programs he deemed unsuitable. In 1978, for example, he organized a successful boycott against Sears, persuading the department store chain to quit advertising on sexually explicit shows like *Charlie's Angels* and *Three's Company*. On the heels of such victories, Wildmon convinced Jerry Falwell to share Moral Majority's enormous mailing list with him, multiplying his reach exponentially. With this new platform he launched a campaign against Proctor and Gamble, compelling the consumer goods company to pull advertising from several supposedly offensive programs. As his power grew, Wildmon expanded his scope beyond sexually explicit programming. He began focusing more and more on Hollywood's seeming hostility to Christianity. Thus it was only logical that Wildmon would target *The Last Temptation of Christ*.[28]

In 1986 Universal bought the rights to produce *The Last Temptation of Christ*, largely because Tom Pollack, the new president of the studio, wanted Scorsese among his stable of directors. In response, Wildmon quickly sprang his newly named organization, the AFA, into action. Letters poured in to Universal and its parent company MCA. But unlike Paramount, Universal held strong in the face of this adversity, allowing Scorsese to bring *The Last Temptation* to completion. As the film's release date approached, the studio hired Tim Penland, an evangelical media consultant, to convince religious conservatives to wait until they saw the movie before they waged war against it. Penland, who sincerely believed he could bridge the widening chasm between Hollywood and the Christian Right, persuaded Wildmon and other religious conservatives to hold their fire. Hedging its bets, Universal also hired Josh Baran, a liberal media consultant who specialized in defending free expression against, in his words, "the forces of the reactionary right." Convinced that the film "was going to be the most controversial film ever released by any studio in the history of the movie business," Baran was flabbergasted that Universal had allowed Scorsese to make it. With such expectations in mind, Baran employed Susan Rothbaum to write a robust defense of the film on First Amendment grounds. In her report, a summary of which served as a full-page advertisement that ran in all of the nation's major newspapers, Rothbaum wrote: "The American way of life depends on the free expression of many voices, many points of view."[29]

With this Baran and Rothbaum aligned Universal with Hollywood liberals like Normal Lear, the eminent television producer who founded People For the American Way (PFAW) in 1981 in order to reclaim the mantle of Americanism for liberalism. The American way, by the standards of Hollywood liberals, dictated that Scorsese had a right to make the film and consenting adults had a right to see it. Whether or not *The Last Temptation of Christ* was blasphemous was open to interpretation and beside the point.[30]

Conservatives were unmoved by the free-expression defense. Angry that Universal broke its promise to allow them to view *The Last Temptation* before its release, right-wing activists swung into action in the months leading up to the film's August 1988 opening. Unable to contain his Christian Right allies, Penland severed ties with Universal and joined the attack, describing Scorsese's movie as "a sex film about Jesus Christ." Wildmon, who called the film the most "blatant attack on Christianity" in the history of Hollywood—even before he had seen it—distributed thousands of copies of an unofficial script that included the highly sexual passages from Schrader's first script, passages that never made the final cut. Most major Christian Right leaders joined Wildmon's movement against *The Last Temptation*. Bill Bright of Campus Crusade for Christ wanted to "make this the last temptation of Universal to make a film that is going to defame the name of Jesus Christ." James Dobson, after admitting he had not seen the film, told his massive radio audience that it "would appear to be the most blasphemous, evil attack on the church and the cause of Christ in the history of entertainment." For a whole host of reasons, including their growing animus toward Hollywood, religious conservatives determined, often sight unseen, that *The Last Temptation of Christ* was a grave offense to their Christian faith.[31]

Scorsese's depiction of Jesus Christ, though less provocative than Kazantzakis's revision, was bound to anger many Christians. Practicing Christians understood Jesus as both human and divine. However, conservative Christians tended to accentuate the divine side of Christ, since Christ's divinity was more aspirational for those living in a fallen world. *The Last Temptation* portrayed a Christ, played by Willem Dafoe, who seemed more human—more flawed—than divine. Scorsese's Christ was driven nearly insane by human temptations, particularly his intense sexual desires. As Buckley complained, Scorsese "gives us a Christ whose mind is distracted by lechery, fancying himself not the celibate of history, but the swinger in the arms of the prostitute Mary Magdalene." Such a response baffled many liberal theologians. "How can you say Jesus 'sacrificed' his life," asked Unitarian minister Maurice Ogden, "if he had no attachment to life?" If Jesus was to be a model for those who would resist temptation, his temptations had to be real, and what was more tempting to a young man than sex? Although Universal never granted conservatives their wish to watch *The Last Temptation* prior to its grand opening, the studio gathered together a group of liberal Christian leaders for an early screening. At the film's conclusion, they gave Scorsese a standing ovation. Several argued that it affirmed their faith. Robert Thompson, a Baptist from Illinois, thought it was the perfect instrument for shaking up people's preconceptions about Jesus, "the path to truth and growth."[32]

Scorsese received an Oscar nomination for Best Director. But *The Last Temptation* was not widely acclaimed. Many assumed that the Academy of Motion Picture Arts and Sciences recognized Scorsese less for the merits of the picture than for his dogged refusal to cower before the Christian Right. For critics the film was too long, moved too slowly, and deviated too far from the epic biblical film genre. Indeed,

Scorsese's deliberate transposition of his beloved New York streets onto the Palestinian desert landscape had a jarring effect. For Scorsese, of course, this was the point. In order to make the Jesus story relevant to late-twentieth-century moviegoers, he had insisted on depicting the disciples as working-class everymen to whom contemporary audiences could relate. For this reason he had been adamant that Harvey Keitel play the role of Judas, who is the hero in this revisionist account—in the film Judas betrays Jesus only on Jesus's orders. As Medved panned: "With his thick Brooklyn accent firmly intact, braying out his lines like a minor Mafioso trying to impress his elders with his swaggering, tough-guy panache, Keitel looks for all the world as if he has accidentally wandered onto the desert set from a very different Martin Scorsese film." For Medved, it was "the height of irony that this level of controversy could be generated by a film this awful."[33]

Most conservatives were less troubled by whether *The Last Temptation of Christ* was a good movie and more concerned with ensuring that Hollywood quit making films that insulted their faith. In the month prior to the film's release, MCA received over one million pieces of mail, mostly angry pleas from religious conservatives. On August 11, 1988, the day before the film's grand opening, thousands of religious conservatives marched on Universal Studios in protest, holding aloft signs such as "Scriptures Not Scripts" and "Holy Word Not Hollywood." Explaining why so many people felt compelled to attend such a protest, Wildmon said: "M.C.A./Universal planned, the very next day, to release a movie which portrays the Lord Jesus Christ as a liar, a fornicator and a weak, confused, fearful individual unsure of who he is." Universal strategically opened the film in nine cities unlikely to attract more outpourings of evangelical anger: New York, Los Angeles, Chicago, Washington, DC, Seattle, Minneapolis, San Francisco, Toronto, and Montreal. And yet protestors found their way to these hubs of cosmopolitanism, where they were treated like curiosities, making the opening of *The Last Temptation* a spectacle on the order of the Scopes Monkey Trial.[34]

As with so many other cultural controversies of the era, the added attention helped *The Last Temptation* at the box office, at least initially. It opened with sold-out shows, as urbanites waited in long lines to see the much ballyhooed film. Such commercial success might have led conservatives to some soul searching about the effectiveness of their tactics had they not achieved a noteworthy consolation prize when

Blockbuster, the nation's largest chain of video stores, refused to carry the movie. Moreover, the campaign against Scorsese's movie was a fundraising boon for organizations like Wildmon's AFA. In short, *The Last Temptation of Christ* proved an ideal proxy for a greater crusade against Hollywood. Conservatives were not about to relent.[35]

The Christian Right's mounting hatred for Hollywood was a result of the film industry's tentative embrace of the sixties cultural revolutions. Its animosity was also the product of institutional changes that relegated religious conservatives to the margins of movie production. Religious groups, including the Catholic Church, had helped write the Hays Production Code and during the Hays Code era had had some control over film content. But as the Hays Code era came to an end, religious conservatives could no longer expect to be the nation's moral guardians with respect to movies, and Hollywood filmmakers grew increasingly willing to push boundaries with respect to Christianity. Of course Hollywood remained unwilling to cross some lines. Conservatives wondered why it was acceptable to make a film based on Kazantzakis's *The Last Temptation*, which was deeply insulting to Christians, but not a movie based on Rushdie's *Satanic Verses*, which was deeply insulting to Muslims. As Medved wrote: "When it came to the prospect of enraging the Islamic faithful, the instinct for self-preservation took precedence over the commitment to controversial religious explorations, but the Universal bosses felt no corresponding compunctions when it came to offending Christians."[36]

In their battle against Hollywood double standards, conservatives found a champion in Michael Medved. Medved, a film critic and co-host of the television show *Sneak Previews*, gained renown in the late 1980s for his increasingly bleak perspective on the entertainment industry. His best-selling 1992 book *Hollywood versus America: Popular Culture and the War on Traditional Values*, cemented his status as the premier anti-Hollywood polemicist. The book's first sentence set the tone: "America's long-running romance with Hollywood is over." According to Medved, millions of Americans viewed Hollywood as "an alien force that assaults our most cherished values and corrupts our children." He argued that the film industry's oft-noted financial woes stemmed from its disregard for American tastes. More Americans would spend their hard-earned cash on movie tickets if the films better reflected their values. Hollywood, it seemed, was more interested in spreading transgressive messages than in making money. To

emphasize this point, Medved asserted that the only thriving segment of the entire entertainment industry was country music: "with
its earthy and unpretentious attempts to connect with the everyday
concerns of Middle America, [it] provided one of the few bright spots
in the general gloom of the music business." Although his argument
was problematic—movie ticket sales suffered largely because video-
cassette players had become commonplace in homes across America,
and country music, though popular, could not compete with the commercial success of rap—his book nicely articulated the vast chasm that
separated the Hollywood and conservative cosmologies.[37]

Medved believed the soul of Hollywood was sick. Echoing conservative arguments about liberalism more generally, he contended that
Hollywood's gravest problem was its moral relativism, which had led
to a complete disregard for standards. "The politically correct, properly liberal notion is that we should never dig deeper—to consider
whether a given work is true, or good, or spiritually nourishing—or
to evaluate its impact on society at large." Whereas conservatives believed cultural representations had the power to shape society, liberals
appreciated cultural works in more limited ways. And whereas conservatives saw censorship as a necessary tool, liberals defended the
right to free expression even for offensive cultural content. As Medved
complained: "[T]hose who defend contemporary rap music, with its
extravagantly brutal and obscene lyrics, do not generally condone the
conduct described in the songs; they suggest, rather, that it is inappropriate to judge such material on a moral basis."[38]

Medved also pointed out that the liberal defense of free expression
was hypocritical. For instance, Hollywood liberals would never have
defended the right to make a film that favorably depicted Holocaust
deniers. Boundaries existed for everyone; the question was where to
draw them. Medved argued: "The perspectives of the loony left, for
example, are robustly represented in Hollywood—as evidenced by
the triumphal career of Oliver Stone—while the outlook of the radical
right is all but invisible." He wanted Hollywood to quit hiding behind
the First Amendment and admit that its movies helped shape American society, for better or worse, usually worse. Medved assumed that
a more honest debate would allow Americans to choose sides and set
standards.[39]

This cultural dispute also played out in more highbrow realms of art
in the late 1980s. Conservatives were quick to judge and censor profane

art. Liberals were quick to suspend judgment and defend free expression. The art wars heated up in 1988, when conservative groups discovered that the National Endowment for the Arts (NEA) had subsidized the artist Andres Serrano's *Piss Christ*, a photograph of a plastic crucifix submerged in the artist's urine. The fact that NEA money found its way to Serrano only indirectly—the NEA had granted seventy-five thousand dollars to the Southeastern Center for Contemporary Art, which then awarded Serrano fifteen thousand—hardly satisfied conservative critics. When the Virginia Museum of Fine Arts in Richmond displayed *Piss Christ*, an outraged museumgoer wrote a letter to the *Richmond Times-Dispatch:* "The Virginia Museum should not be in the business of promoting and subsidizing hatred and intolerance. Would they pay the KKK to do a work defaming blacks? Would they display a Jewish symbol under urine? Has Christianity become fair game in our society for any kind of blasphemy and slander?" Just as Medved highlighted Hollywood duplicity in its willingness to insult Christians but not other racial and religious groups, conservative Christians wondered why artists were keen on offending them but no one else. Why not *Piss Mohammed*? Wildmon fumed: "*The Last Temptation of Christ* presented Jesus as a tormented, deranged, human-only sinner; Madonna represented Christ having sex with a priest in her new video *Like a Prayer*; and now a crucifix submerged in urine and titled *Piss Christ*." He advised his followers to take a stand lest they be future victims of anti-Christian pogroms.[40]

Serrano's intentions were not as straightforwardly anti-Christian as his conservative critics assumed. Raised in an immigrant family—his mother was Afro-Cuban and his dad was Honduran—Serrano had grown up attending an Italian American Catholic church in Brooklyn. Thus like that of Madonna and Scorsese, his art was a commentary on a religious upbringing that engendered a fascination with Catholic iconography. By 1986 his work also revealed a growing captivation with bodily fluids, a common preoccupation among New York artists during the AIDS crisis. For Serrano, bodily fluids worked nicely with religious imagery since blood was so prominent in the Bible—indeed, since Christians felt compelled to drink the blood of Christ every Sunday morning. *Piss Christ* was thus similar to *The Last Temptation of Christ* in the way it juxtaposed the sacred and the profane. The crucifix symbolized Christ's otherworldliness. The urine demonstrated that religion was of this world. "The Church is obsessed with the body and blood of Christ," Serrano said. "At the same time, there is the impulse to repress and deny the physical nature of the Church's membership. There is a real ambivalence there." Sister Wendy Beckett was one of the few people who found *Piss Christ* constructive as a critique. A British nun and art critic, Beckett declared that *Piss Christ*, though sensationalist, correctly evoked the lack of reverence given to Jesus. "His great sacrifice is not used," Beckett said. "We live very vulgar lives. We put Christ in a bottle of urine—in practice."[41]

In contrast to Beckett's favorable analysis, most liberals simply defended Serrano's right to express himself in his art, and they maintained that the NEA, representing the national community of art experts, should be free to decide which art merited funding. As Senator Edward Kennedy said: "The American people strongly support public funding of the arts and reject the know-nothing censorship the right wing is trying to impose." In contrast, conservative politicians proclaimed that public funds should never support art that disrespected the nation's Christian majority. Senator Jesse Helms, who led the congressional battle against blasphemous art, took personal offense to Serrano's work. "He is not an artist," Helms asserted. "He is a jerk. And he is taunting the American people, and I resent it." Senator Alphonse D'Amato tore up a reproduction of *Piss Christ* on the Senate floor. "This so-called piece of art," D'Amato roared, "is a deplorable, despicable display of vulgarity." Predictably, the controversy was good for Serrano's career. "I feel when people attack a work of art to such a great extent," Serrano said in an interview; "they imbue it with a far greater power than when they ignore it and, in that, I'm flattered that they think it deserves such attention."[42]

The conservative vilification of Andres Serrano paled in comparison to the right-wing demonization of the artist Robert Mapplethorpe, who became the Christian Right's bête noire. "Mao is dead," as Todd Gitlin pithily wrote. "Now Mapplethorpe is the devil king." Mapplethorpe's distinctive black-and-white photos were the focus of two highly public museum controversies in 1989 and 1990. And due to the fact that Mapplethorpe, like Serrano, had been the recipient of NEA funds, the controversy swirling around his art helped advance conservative efforts to regulate and defund the NEA. Coincidentally, all of this happened after Mapplethorpe died of AIDS in March 1989, at the age of forty-two. Before then his renown was mostly limited to the avant-garde art scene. In that milieu Mapplethorpe was celebrated for his skill in blurring the boundaries between high cultural forms, with his highly stylized black-and-white prints, and mundane subject matter, which included representations of flowers and nude men. Some of his nudes were depictions of homoerotica and sadomasochism. Like Madonna, Scorsese, and Serrano, Mapplethorpe was raised a Catholic and claimed that he took pictures of little altars as an homage to his religious upbringing. But his years spent with his close friend the punk rocker Patti Smith and his years spent in New York City's gay subculture likely contributed more to his aesthetic than his years spent in a Long Island Catholic church.[43]

The first hullabaloo over Mapplethorpe's work ensued in the summer of 1989—just a few months after his death—when the Corcoran Gallery in Washington, DC, canceled plans to display *The Perfect Moment*, a traveling exhibit of 175 of Mapplethorpe's photos. Although the Institute of Contemporary Art in Philadelphia had already displayed *The Perfect Moment* without incident, Corcoran officials anticipated a different response. Situated next door to the White House, the Corcoran played host to a more staid clientele than that of the Institute of Contemporary Art, which sat on the University of Pennsylvania campus and was frequented by urbane art consumers conditioned to the transgressions of the avant-garde. Corcoran patrons included conservative politicians who held the purse strings to NEA funds that the Corcoran relied upon. Indeed, Helms's staff repeatedly made threatening phone calls to Corcoran officials in the months prior to the planned Mapplethorpe exhibit.[44]

Artists considered the Corcoran decision to cancel *The Perfect Moment* an act of censorship. As a reprisal, Washington-area artists staged a slide show of Mapplethorpe's most explicit photos, projecting them onto the Corcoran building late one June night. And in order to give Washington-area art fans a chance to see Mapplethorpe's work, the nonprofit Washington Project for the Arts (WPA) displayed *The Perfect Moment* to record crowds for three weeks in July and August 1989. Of the 175 pieces that made up *The Perfect Moment*, only seven were from Mapplethorpe's provocative *X-Portfolio*. Five of those seven prints were depictions of homosexual sadomasochism, including a self-portrait of Mapplethorpe in leather chaps plunging a bullwhip into his anus, and another depicting a finger being inserted into a penis. The other two eyebrow-raising pieces were nonpornographic pictures of nude children—taken in the presence of consenting parents.

These seven images, isolated from the rest of the exhibit in order to give patrons fair warning about the explicit content, drew the longest lines. The WPA received only a few complaints, some more serious than others. As one visitor ironically wrote on the registry: "I've been here four times already and this show disgusts me more each time I see it."[45]

Mapplethorpe's photography became the subject of another controversy in 1990, when Cincinnati officials closed down an exhibit of *The Perfect Moment* at the Cincinnati Contemporary Arts Center. Law enforcement indicted the museum and its director, Dennis Barrie, on charges of obscenity and child pornography, the first instance in American history that charges had been brought against a museum for an art display. Although such an unprecedented indictment shocked the art world, it was unsurprising that it happened in Cincinnati, "a city," as a reporter for the *New York Times* wrote, "that casts itself as a bulwark in the war against pornography." Cincinnati was home to the National Coalition Against Pornography, and no X-rated theaters or strip clubs operated within city limits. As Cincinnati chief of police Lawrence Whalen stated: "The people of this community do not cater to what others depict as art." Indeed, not a single Cincinnati movie theater had dared show *The Last Temptation of Christ*. During the trial, in order to prove that Mapplethorpe's prints were not obscene, the defense built a case on the aesthetic merits of his work. Barrie enthusiastically took up this task, calling Mapplethorpe "one of the most important American photographers and the pre-eminent classical photographer of the last two decades." "His images," Barrie continued, "derive their power from a consistent aesthetic vision—one of proportion, balance, directness and clarity, which are the essential attributes of classical art." Mapplethorpe was an artist, not a pornographer. Much to the relief of artists and curators around the nation, a jury acquitted Barrie and the museum on all charges. But the art battles lingered.[46]

The Serrano and Mapplethorpe controversies provided conservative cultural critics with a platform to voice their grievances about the contemporary state of art. Such critics tended to conceptualize art in terms derived from Matthew Arnold, the nineteenth-century British cultural critic. Arnold and his twentieth-century American followers believed that cultural representations should be judged art only if they constituted "high truth," if they ennobled or inspired. George Will wrote that art must "elevate the public mind by bringing it into contact with beauty and even ameliorate social pathologies." By this criterion, Mapplethorpe's works did not qualify.[47]

But not everybody shared these standards. The late-twentieth-century avant-garde believed art was at its best when it when it disrupted social conventions. Such "postmodern art" was, according to Irving Kristol, "a politically charged art that is utterly contemptuous of the notion of educating the tastes and refining the aesthetic sensibilities of the citizenry. Its goal, instead, is deliberately to outrage those tastes and to trash the very idea of an 'aesthetic sensibility.'" The conservative art critic James Cooper characterized contemporary art in more acidic terms: "[M]odern art—long ago separated from the idealism of Monet, Degas, Cezanne, and Rodin—had become the purveyor of a destructive, degenerate, ugly, pornographic, Marxist, anti-American ideology." Unlike liberals, who, perhaps disingenuously, maintained that contemporary artists like Mapplethorpe had no agenda beyond the individual imperatives of free expression, conservatives argued that Mapplethorpe and his ilk sought to subvert all that was good about American culture.[48]

Camille Paglia agreed with conservatives that Mapplethorpe had a subversive agenda. But Paglia parted ways with conservatives in her evaluation of his work and agenda. Paglia argued that the Corcoran did the right thing when it canceled its exhibition of *The Perfect Moment*, but such an argument served as criticism of the Corcoran, not Mapplethorpe, whom she considered her "spiritual brother." "Mapplethorpe was an avant-garde outsider, a sexual outlaw, a night rider," Paglia wrote. "It dilutes him to enshrine him in a national landmark." Paglia hated it that liberals defended Mapplethorpe's art on the grounds that it was beautiful and harmless. She wrote: "We must frankly face the mutilations and horrors in Mapplethorpe's sexual world and stop trying to blandly argue them away as fun and frolics of 'an alternative lifestyle.'" Sadomasochism, she pointed out, had never been sanctioned by any society, anywhere, and was thus matter-of-factly subversive. "Mapplethorpe's liberal supporters do not understand him. His work is a scandal to all their progressive humanitarian ideals." Mapplethorpe showed that some taboos remained and that avant-garde art still had a role in revealing such taboos to a dismayed public. To conservatives, taboos were taboo for a reason, and those who traded in the "devil king" had to be stopped. For Paglia, making art taboo again was

an achievement that elevated Mapplethorpe into the pantheon of artists who revealed the Dionysian underbelly of Western civilization.[49]

The Mapplethorpe controversies, coming on the heels of the Serrano hullabaloo, led to a crisis for the NEA. House Republican Dick
Armey, who lambasted the NEA for showcasing those "artists whose
forte is ridiculing the values of Americans who are paying for it," coauthored a threatening letter that 105 House members sent to the NEA in
response to disclosures that the agency had subsidized *The Perfect Moment*: "If the NEA has enough money to fund this type of project, then
perhaps the NEA has too much money to handle responsibly." Despite
describing himself as a lover of art, no politician worked harder than
Jesse Helms to punish the NEA for subsidizing profane art. "We have
ten or twelve pictures of art, all of which I like," Helms said, "but we
don't have any penises stretched out on the table," a reference to a
postcard of an *X-Portfolio* print that Helms kept in his pocket in order
to illustrate Mapplethorpe's depravity on a moment's notice. In the
month after the Corcoran controversy, Helms sought to persuade the
Senate to pass an amendment to the NEA budget that would have imposed restrictions on the type of art the endowment could sponsor.
The Helms amendment would have specifically prohibited the NEA
from subsidizing works that depicted homoeroticism, sadomasochism, and sexual exploitation of children. It never got enough votes to
pass. Instead, Congress reauthorized the NEA budget in 1990 with
a vaguely worded decency clause that went as follows: "Artistic excellence and artistic merit are the criteria by which applications are
judged, taking into consideration general standards of decency and
respect for the diverse beliefs and values of the American people."[50]

The NEA crisis raised an important question: when politicians limited the types of art funded by the NEA, did they violate the First
Amendment rights of artists? Artists, of course, contended that the
decency clause was an unconstitutional form of censorship. They insisted that artistic freedom demanded autonomy from politicians,
who were unqualified to judge art. Artists wanted the tried-and-true
peer review system to maintain control of the NEA grant-making
process, independent of political interests: experts should determine
what art was worthy of government subsidization. Conservatives, in
contrast, argued that taxpayers should never be forced to foot the bill
for profane art and that government's unwillingness to fund an artist
was not a violation of that artist's rights. As House Republican Dana

Rohrbacher said: "Artists can do whatever they want on their own time and with their own dime." Conservatives believed that government should fund only art that aligned with American norms and that those artists who insisted on transgressing such norms should subject their work to the market. Ironically, some transgressive artists had long enjoyed commercial success, particularly Robert Mapplethorpe, whose art did well on the market even before the culture wars rendered it nearly priceless. But other, less renowned avant-garde artists were more reliant upon NEA funds and thus interpreted the decency clause as government censorship.[51]

John Frohnmayer, whom Bush appointed as chair of the NEA in 1989, was charged with implementing the decency clause. He inserted a "loyalty oath" into NEA grant applications: in order to receive NEA funds, artists had to pledge not to use such funds to create obscene work. Although Frohnmayer promised he was "not going to be the decency czar," that was precisely what he became in the eyes of the artists. Four such avant-garde artists—Holly Hughes, Karen Finley, John Fleck, and Tim Miller, the so-called NEA Four—sued the NEA after Frohnmayer overturned a favorable panel recommendation and denied them a grant. Frohnmayer objected to funding the NEA Four because their work depicted sex and sexuality in ways he deemed obscene. The case eventually went all the way to the Supreme Court. In *Finley v. NEA*, the Supreme Court decided in favor of the NEA: in denying the four artists money, the NEA had not violated their constitutional right to free expression.[52]

Even though Frohnmayer angered artists by enforcing the decency clause, the Christian Right was infuriated that the Bush administration had not taken a stronger stance against the NEA. When asked why he never endorsed the Helms amendment, Bush responded that even though some of the "filth" the NEA funded was deeply offensive to him—particularly "the sacrilegious, blasphemous depictions that are portrayed by some to be art"—he was opposed to "getting the federal government into telling every artist what he or she can paint, or how he or she might express themselves." In other words, Bush tried to straddle the center. But this was a center that would not hold. Heading into the 1992 Republican primaries, Bush was vulnerable to a challenge from his right on cultural issues such as the NEA crisis. Patrick Buchanan proved to be an ideal challenger.[53]

Although Buchanan's insurgent campaign never seriously threat-

ened Bush's incumbency, Buchanan was a powerful spokesperson
for those religious conservatives who were dismayed that Bush failed
to support their war against the NEA. Buchanan was a refreshing
voice to many conservatives, who thought cultural liberals needed
to be resisted much more aggressively. He had long been a critic of
the NEA, which he described as an "upholstered playpen of the arts
and crafts auxiliary of the Eastern liberal establishment," and he ridiculed avant-garde artists who wanted to be honored by a society that
they loathed. Plus Buchanan was unapologetically homophobic: he
straightforwardly equated homosexuality with "barbarism," mocking
"poor, pathetic Robert Mapplethorpe" and the photographs of "the
degraded acts by which he killed himself." When the Republican primaries moved south, the Buchanan campaign ran a thirty-second television advertisement that included excerpts from a Marlon Riggs–
directed documentary film about gay black men, *Tongues Untied*. The
advertisement featured leather-and-chain-clad men dancing in slow
motion while a narrator grimly pronounced that such footage was
taken from a Bush administration–funded film that extolled homosexuality. Although this smear campaign did not win Buchanan many
delegates, it did compel Bush to fire Frohnmayer. And Buchanan's
campaign more generally convinced Bush to allot Buchanan a prime
slot on the Republican convention stage, where he delivered his infamous culture wars speech. Moreover, the 1992 Republican platform
condemned "the use of public funds to subsidize obscenity and blasphemy masquerading as art" and declared that "no artist has an inherent right to claim taxpayer support for his or her private vision of art
if that vision mocks the moral and spiritual basis on which our society
is founded."[54]

Buchanan was not alone among conservative politicians fighting
the culture wars during the 1992 presidential campaign. That year Vice
President Dan Quayle issued a public critique of Murphy Brown, the
title character of a CBS situation comedy played by Candace Bergen.
Quayle lambasted the "poverty of values" depicted by the *Murphy
Brown* plot: Brown, a powerful television reporter, decided to have a
baby and raise it as a single mother. *Murphy Brown*, in Quayle's assessment, "mocked the importance of fathers" and treated single motherhood as "just another life-style choice." Although liberals in turn
mocked Quayle's attack on a television character, many conservatives
came to his defense. "In a thousand ways," the conservative critic

Mona Charen wrote, "the *Murphy Brown* show snidely implies that only middle-American dunderheads believe you ought to be married before getting pregnant." Charen continued: "Surely even the sun-dazed Southern Californians can look beyond their hot tubs every now and then and see the wreckage that family breakdown is creating in American life."[55]

Quayle and Charen made these charges in the context of debates about the causes of that year's Los Angeles Riots. Sidestepping the glaring issues of poverty and police brutality, conservatives assumed that the violence perpetrated by young black males during the riots resulted from the historically damaged black family and culture. Such reasoning, which harked back to the tired logic that undergirded the Moynihan Report and decades of "culture of poverty" theorizing, was less interesting than the implicit recognition that cultural representations evince power. It was more interesting that Quayle thought *Murphy Brown* had the capacity to shape the national family structure, for better or worse. The fact that the vice president of the United States believed it was worthwhile to attack a fictional character revealed how much stock conservatives put in the power of culture. Buchanan ex-emplified such a theory with his explanation of the LA Riots:

> Does it make a difference that school kids in L.A., who never heard of Robert Frost, can recite the lyrics of Ice-T and 2 Live Crew? Where did that L.A. mob come from? It came out of the public schools from which the Bible and Ten Commandments were long ago expelled. It came out of drugstores where pornography is everywhere on the magazine rack. It came out of movie theaters and away from TV sets where sex and violence are romanticized. It came out of rock concerts where rap music extols raw lust and cop-killing. It came out of churches that long ago gave themselves up to social action, and it came out of families that never existed.[56]

Even after the conservative movement had long captured the Re-publican Party, and even after a conservative Republican Party had controlled the White House for twelve years, right-wing culture warriors were insecure about their power. The national culture—art, music, film, and television—seemed to have slipped from their hands, signaling that the America of the conservative imagination was dead or dying.

7

God, State, and Curriculum

Robert Simonds, a spokesperson for the National Association of Christian Educators, declared in 1983 that "a great war" gripped the land. "Atheism, in the cloak of an acceptable 'humanitarian' religious philosophy," he warned, "has been subtly introduced into the traditional Christian American Culture through the public school system." In making such a claim, Simonds echoed conservatives across the nation who worried that a liberal educational establishment was relentlessly smuggling secular humanism into the schools.[1]

That the public schools were home to a major front in the culture wars should not have been a surprise. Quarrels about education have long accompanied American cultural conflict. The schools, after all, have been the institution most counted on to ensure the reproduction of American norms—norms that in and of themselves have been the object of bitter dispute. In this way, debates about education have long acted as a proxy for arguments about whose values will shape the nation's future. Walter Lippmann explained this struggle in succinct terms at the beginning of the twentieth century: "It is in the school that the child is drawn towards or drawn away from the religion and the patriotism of his parents."[2]

By the end of the twentieth century, when a Christian Right pamphleteer fretted that the nation's system of education was training "children for a new social system where they will be developed for use as resources of the federal government's choosing," the battle for the American school had grown more heated than ever. As the government institution Americans most entered into on a regular basis, the school came to be thought of by millions of conservatives as a spearhead for the secularist forces they so feared.[3]

Religious conservatives sought to reverse secular tendencies that had erased God from the public schools. Because they believed that the American republic demanded citizens made virtuous by Christian values, religious conservatives viewed secularization as dangerous to the survival of the nation. They blamed cultural degeneration, in the form of violence, drug use, and extramarital sex, on the 1962 Supreme Court decision *Engel v. Vitale,* which ruled school prayer unconstitutional. They believed that the removal of religion from the schools was unfair, even antidemocratic, given that the vast majority of Americans, 96 percent according to one Gallup poll, believed in God. With such dissonance in mind, legal scholar Stephen Carter likened the secularization of the American public sphere to collective schizophrenia. "We often ask our citizens to split their public and private selves," Carter wrote, "telling them in effect that it is fine to be religious in private, but there is something askew when those private beliefs become the basis for public action."[4]

While conservatives saw recent educational developments as catastrophic, cosmopolitan-minded educators believed it their job to solidify civil rights gains by making antiracism manifest in the curriculum. To do so, they took it upon themselves to replace curriculum materials that, as one left-leaning educator put it, "tend to perpetuate images of white, middle-class, suburban families living in traditional bliss." Many educational leaders had internalized the pedagogies of liberation championed by the sixties movements. This shift in consciousness reshaped the priorities of the nation's largest teachers' union, the National Education Association (NEA). The NEA Human and Civil Rights (HCR) Division, the sixties movement arm of the teachers' union, published pamphlets and hosted conferences dedicated to themes such as race relations, ethnic studies, and affirmative action. In the early 1970s, HCR officials spoke with an implicitly revolutionary vocabulary, critiquing racism in the institutional terms set forth by Black Power theorists. HCR director Sam Ethridge openly discussed the United States in the most pessimistic of ways, hinting that white America might try to wipe out its black citizens the way Germany did its Jews. At the HCR's 1971 conference, keynote speaker John Gibson, a Tufts University political scientist who wrote about civic education, advocated teaching "black math." Instead of posing problems in language that made sense only to affluent white students, such as "stocks and bonds or the flight of planes," math equations should be framed in accordance with the experiences of black students. Gibson used the following example of an appropriately "black math" problem: "If a cockroach is running at one mile an hour, and a rat is running at 15 miles an hour, at what time T will cockroach A meet rat B?"[5]

Most teachers across the country did not warm to pedagogies inspired by analyses of institutional racism. This included many of the teachers in the Albert Shanker–led American Federation of Teachers (AFT), which promoted a relatively traditional curriculum. That said, a key segment of the nation's educational leadership was indeed radical, whether housed in the NEA or the nation's teachers' colleges, where Brazilian radical Paolo Freire's 1970 book *The Pedagogy of the Oppressed*—a pedagogical companion to Frantz Fanon's anticolonial *Wretched of the Earth*—was increasingly assigned to teachers-in-training. This despite the fact that the political trends of the 1970s dampened the enthusiasm of radical pedagogues. When the conservative educational movement gained ground as a counterforce to New Left educators, the NEA exchanged its revolutionary rhetoric for a defensive posture. The 1979 HCR conference was organized on the stated need to close ranks against a rising conservatism that had put "human and civil rights in jeopardy." In his opening remarks, NEA president John Ryor proclaimed that he was "paranoid" about the conservative attack on public education. Panels at the 1979 conference were dedicated to understanding "neo-Right campaigns," including efforts to undermine affirmative action and censor books.[6]

By the early 1980s, as a result of this shift in focus—and as a tribute to the power of the conservative reaction to left-leaning curriculum reforms—the HCR quit challenging institutional racism. Instead it focused its energies on promoting a safer antiracist curriculum that would be amenable to more people. A 1983 NEA pamphlet exemplified this gentler approach: "As Americans, we have a unique opportunity to celebrate people, for our borders are filled with a precious assortment of cultures, each one contributing to history and seeking appreciation." The new name for this curriculum was "multiculturalism." In schools across the country, students were taught to recognize the value of the many different racial and ethnic cultures that popu-

lated the United States. Each little platoon of society was to be represented in the curriculum. In this way multiculturalism allowed radical educators, those still interested in pedagogies that grew out of
sixties liberation movements, to teach about black identity as distinct
from normative white American identity. But since multiculturalism
was more about representing diversity than about challenging institutional hierarchy, it appealed to a wider array of teachers and allowed it
to become the implicit ethos of the national curriculum.[7]

But, as students learned more and more about race and ethnicity,
they learned less and less about religion. As multiculturalism took
hold, religion was essentially erased from the curriculum, so much so
that Clinton issued a directive in 1995 meant to clarify the constitu-
tionality of teaching about religion: "Public schools may not provide
religious instruction, but they may teach *about* religion, including the
Bible or other scripture." Even more disconcerting to conservatives,
many public schools were disallowing public expressions of religion
for fear of violating the laws of the land. "It appears that some school
officials, teachers and parents," Clinton observed, "have assumed that
religious expression of any type is either inappropriate, or forbidden
altogether, in public schools."[8]

That educators deemed religion a topic too controversial to teach
about, and that school administrators thought public expressions of
religion illegal, despite the fact that the vast majority of their students
were growing up in religious households, was bound to breed hostility. On his popular television show *The 700 Club*, Pat Robertson told
viewers in characteristically hyperbolic fashion that the American
government was "attempting to do something that few states other
than the Nazis and Soviets have attempted to do, namely, to take the
children away from the parents and to educate them in a philosophy
that is amoral, anti-Christian and humanistic." His fellow televangelist
Jimmy Swaggart, equally caustic, fretted that "the greatest enemy of
our children today in this United States is the public school system. It
is education without God."[9]

Without God, perhaps, but not without religion. Christian conservatives argued that secular humanism—the philosophy that they believed informed the public school curriculum—was more than an ideology. Secular humanism was a religion in its own right. Tim LaHaye
dedicated his 1983 book *The Battle for the Public Schools: Humanism's
Threat to Our Children* to "the growing army" of parents "who realize

that secular humanism, the religious doctrine of our public schools," is to blame for "the origin of rampant drugs, sex, violence, and self-indulgence in our schools, which are not conducive to the learning process." LaHaye aimed his rhetoric against an educational establishment that he believed was "determined to jam atheistic, amoral humanism, with its socialist world view, into the minds of our nation's children and youth, kindergarten through college." He listed the traits that he thought defined a religion and argued that secular humanism, "the official doctrine of public education," evinced all of them, including "a stated dogma," "a priesthood," "seminaries," and "open acknowledgment of its position." During 1982 hearings on the issue of secular humanism in a local Oregon school district, a conservative school board member summed up the Christian Right sense that the public schools offered religious instruction of the wrong kind: "[T]he humanists have church services in the schools five days a week, Monday through Friday."[10]

In making secular humanist schools a culture wars issue, religious conservatives partook in a venerable right-wing ritual of invoking the specter of John Dewey as an explanation for all that was wrong with American education. In the late 1980s, Mae Duggan, founder of Citizens for Educational Freedom, argued that the "schools have deteriorated under the influence of John Dewey and his secular humanist philosophy." Prominent conservative theologian Richard John Neuhaus made a similar argument, even while begrudgingly admitting that he admired Dewey, particularly compared to his disciples. "Dewey was both wiser and more candid than much of today's public educational establishment," Neuhaus wrote. "He made no bones about the fact that education required religion and, in his view, the religion required is the religion of humanism." Neuhaus was mostly correct about Dewey's epigones. Every now and then a progressive teacher would honestly state the ideological stakes of public education. The author of a 1983 article published by *The Humanist*, for example, argued that "the classroom must and will become an arena of conflict between the old and the new—between the rotting corpse of Christianity, together with all its adjacent evils and misery, and the new faith of humanism." But for the most part, educators sheathed their liberal curriculum designs in a cloak of professionalism. This was nothing new. During the West Virginia textbook controversy of the early 1970s, for instance, the NEA sent a panel to intervene on the premise that teachers sought

"objective thinking in children" as opposed to the "subjective deter-
minations" of those parents who protested. Locals saw through this
fig leaf. One minister told NEA representatives that he was "deeply
concerned about those who hide behind professionalism" while hyp-
ocritically stamping the curriculum with what he determined was an
anti-Christian dogma. Conservatives understood their battle for the
American school as a culture war against an immoral ideology, not as
an attack on professionalism.[11]

Conservative politicians were attentive to constituents' anxieties
about secular humanist schools. Republican Senator Orrin Hatch
responded with a "Protection of Pupil Rights" amendment that he
added to the 1978 reauthorization of the Elementary and Secondary
Education Act. The Hatch Amendment, as it became known, required
that educational materials produced by the federal government be
made available to parents before being used in the classroom. It also
stipulated that parents had the right to shield their children from any
such materials that they found objectionable. The Hatch Amendment,
broadly interpreted, was grounded in the conservative "family values"
rationale that parental rights took priority over the needs of the state.
It was meant to ensure that parents, not Jimmy Carter's newly created Department of Education, had the final say in what their children
learned about. Evincing this logic at a 1982 "Family Forum," Reagan's
first secretary of education Terrel Bell exclaimed that "education is
a family matter. The parent is the foremost teacher, the home is the
most influential classroom, and the schools should exist to support the
home." Phyllis Schlafly's book *Child Abuse in the Classroom*—a collection of selected testimonials from 1984 hearings about Hatch Amendment regulations—sought to demonstrate "how schools have alienated children from their parents, from traditional morality such as the
Ten Commandments, and from our American heritage." Schlafly complained that the public schools had replaced basic cognitive education
with "a system of changing the child's values." In one Hatch Amendment hearing, a parent protested that a guidance counselor regularly
visited her child's classroom to probe students about whether they
believed in God. Another parent was outraged that his child's school
used the MACOS teaching guide, which he described as "a very subtle
way of teaching our children genocide, homosexuality, euthanasia."[12]

Conservative parents believed that the schools violated their fundamental right to religious freedom. In this elocution, which implied

that secular humanism was "the religious doctrine of our public schools," religious conservatives thought they had legal precedent on their side. In the landmark 1961 Supreme Court decision *Torcaso v. Watkins*, which helped codify the secularization of the public sphere by reaffirming that government employees could not be held to a religious test, Hugo Black hid away an afterthought about secular humanism in a footnote to his opinion: "Among religions in this country which do not teach what would generally be considered a belief in the existence of God, are Buddhism, Taoism, and secular humanism." Even though Black was referring to an actual humanist church—the Fellowship of Humanity—his aside bulked large in Christian Right logic about secular humanism more broadly construed.[13]

Similarly, religious conservatives interpreted a 1965 Supreme Court decision, *United States v. Seeger*, as judicial recognition that secular humanism was, in fact, a religion because it allowed for conscientious objection on moral grounds unrelated to religious affiliation. In sum, designating secular humanism a religion, and arguing that its dominion over the public school curriculum was a violation of the First Amendment, proved an innovative tactic in the Christian Right's legal struggles to influence public education during the 1980s. And yet such efforts were largely unsuccessful. In the church-state rulings about public education throughout the decade, the courts largely treated secular humanism as functionally nonreligious in dealing with Christian Right challenges to public school curricula. But this was not for lack of effort and creativity.[14]

During the 1980s, an imaginative and feisty federal judge by the name of W. Brevard Hand became an ally of the Christian Right in its fight against secular humanist schools. In a 1983 case, *Wallace v. Jaffree*, Hand declared that the First Amendment did not bind states. If Alabamans saw fit, Hand argued, their public schools could offer religious instruction. This argument served as an important precursor to the right-wing embrace of judicial originalism, the theory that jurisprudence should be constrained by the original intent of those who framed the Constitution. Originalism, as such, stood in opposition to incorporation, a process by which portions of the Bill of Rights, including the First Amendment, were applied at the state level—the logic that prevailed in *Engel v. Vitale*.[15]

Anticipating that the Supreme Court would reject his argument, which it did in 1985, Hand constructed an alternative legal rationale by using the incorporation precedent against itself: he contended that secular humanism was the established religion of the public schools and thus violated the religious freedom of Christians. Applying such logic to a 1987 case, *Smith v. Board of School Commissioners*, Hand ruled against Alabama textbooks on the grounds that they "affect a person's ability to develop religious beliefs and exercise that religious freedom guaranteed by the Constitution." Hand's opinion was over-ruled at the appeals level, but not before leaving a lasting mark on con-servative understandings of public schooling.[16]

Even if Hand's legal logic proved unconvincing, the political impli-cations of his argument, that the public schools alienated a good por-tion of Christian America, was patently true. By the 1980s Americans routinely ranked *Engel v. Vitale* as the single most unpopular Supreme Court decision. Countless Christian Right leaders made it the focus of their elegies to a once great nation. Bill Bright, founder of Cam-pus Crusade for Christ, called the *Engel v. Vitale* decision "the darkest hour in the history of the nation." Bright attributed the "escalation of crime, disintegration of families, racial conflict, teenage pregnancies and venereal diseases" to the abolition of school prayer.[17]

Such widespread sentiments no doubt motivated Reagan's deci-sion to side with religious conservatives in the school wars, includ-ing his support for the Christian Right's quixotic effort to amend the Constitution to legalize school prayer. In the words of his religious adviser Gary Bauer, Reagan championed "the restoration of family values in American education" by taking "the side of parents, even against the powerful education establishment." As Reagan put it, he wanted "to end the manipulation of school children by utopian plan-ners, and permit the acknowledgment of the Supreme Being in our classrooms just as we allow such acknowledgements in other public institutions." He told a Chicago Catholic school audience in 1982: "I don't think God should ever have been expelled from the classroom." Public prayer, he argued, was "part of our American heritage and a privilege which should not be excluded from our schools." The clos-est the school prayer amendment ever got to advancing to the ratifica-tion stage of the amendment process was in 1984, when fifty-six sen-ators voted in favor of it, ten votes short of the necessary two-thirds. Failure, of course, did not persuade religious conservatives that their goals were unworthy. Rather, it convinced them the nation and its schools were that much more in need of redemption.[18]

An important component of the Christian Right campaign to take back American schools was the movement to curb the teaching of evolution. As a result of such efforts in the early 1980s, the national debate about evolution heated up to a degree not felt since the Scopes Monkey Trial of 1925. After Scopes, most biology textbooks, especially those used in the South, disregarded evolution, avoiding even a mention of Charles Darwin. But following the *Sputnik* scare of 1957, alarm about scientific literacy slowly but surely led to an uptick in teaching about evolution.[19]

Conservative evangelicals, who tended to be fervently anti-Darwinist, reacted with alarm. They believed the integration of evolution into the biology classroom to be of a piece with an all-embracing secularism. So they fought back. Their main tactic was to inject creationism into the biology curriculum, arguing that it should be taught alongside evolution as an equally plausible theory of human origins. Although these new-breed creationists, like the old breed, were almost uniformly religious fundamentalists, they challenged evolutionary biology on supposedly scientific grounds. Recognizing that their curriculum would be ruled illegal if they rationalized its need in religious terms, conservative activists instead drew upon an emerging body of research known as "creation science." The Institute for Creation Research (ICR), a think tank housed in Southern California, produced the bulk of the literature on "creation science." In 1981 the Arkansas state legislature overwhelmingly passed the Balanced Treatment for Creation Science and Evolution Science Act, legislation based almost exclusively on ICR publications. Despite its scientific pretensions, the act became law due to overwhelming support from evangelicals. Voting in favor of the Arkansas law, as one Arkansas legislator put it, was a "vote for God." "When you get a mass of phone calls in favor of a bill," he remarked, "and when it appears to be in support of motherhood, apple pie, and the American way of life, it is hard to vote against it." The ACLU challenged the law, and a federal district court struck it down on the grounds that "creation science" advanced religion.[20]

Predictably, most scientists scoffed at the premise of "creation science," which they deemed oxymoronic. Scientists assumed that religious fundamentalism, the epistemological formation that informed creationism, was antithetical to science. Although such views were understandable, creationists were not, strictly speaking, antiscience.

Rather, they adhered to a pre-Darwinian scientific method. Like Francis Bacon, whose philosophy of science governed Western scientific practice well into the early nineteenth century, creationists believed that science was limited to that which can be observed firsthand. Unlike contemporary scientists, late-twentieth-century creationists did not include speculative hypotheses—theories unverifiable by direct observation—in their "true" scientific method. Henry Morris, a foremost creationist thinker, exemplified such an approach. "Since it is impossible to make observations or experiments on the origin of the universe," he argued, "the very definition of science ought to preclude" any such discussions. In short, for creationists, evolution could not explain human origins, much less the origins of the universe, in scientifically valid ways. Evolution was a theory concocted by wildly imaginative scientists. It was not fact.[21]

Scientists admonished doubters with the simple claim that evolution was indeed fact. As evolutionary biologist Stephen Jay Gould worded it, creationists held "a vernacular misunderstanding of the word 'theory.'" Speaking to a group of evangelicals about evolution, Reagan exemplified just such a misunderstanding: "It is a scientific theory only, and it has in recent years been challenged in the world of science—that is, not believed in the scientific community to be as infallible as it once was." Ironically, creationists often cited Gould as one of a growing number of scientists who questioned evolution. Indeed, Gould and his colleagues pioneered "punctuated equilibrium," a concept that challenged Darwin's theory of natural selection by positing that evolution was even more random and more rapid than Darwin had it. Gould theorized that evolutionary trends "cannot be attributed to gradual transformation within lineages, but must arise from the differential success of certain kinds of species." But as Gould stressed, the fact that he contested Darwin's theory of evolution did not also mean that he questioned the fact of evolution. He believed Darwin was right about the fact that all living beings emerged from earlier forms, even if Darwin's theory to explain the mechanism of this process was wrong. When Gould and his fellow scientists debated competing theories, facts did not evaporate. "Einstein's theory of gravitation replaced Newton's in this century, but apples didn't suspend themselves in midair, pending the outcome." Evolution, then, was both fact and theory: "humans evolved from ape-like ancestors whether they did so by Darwin's proposed mechanism or by some other yet to be discovered."[22]

Although Gould clearly explained the scientific meaning of the word *theory*, which he defined simply as "structures of ideas that explain and interpret facts," creationist readers who happened upon Gould no doubt remained unconvinced. Putting aside their unobservable faith in the existence of God, creationists argued that the world could be understood only insofar as it could be immediately observed. Such an outlook was far removed from the modern, scientific view that speculative interpretation gets us closer to accurate understandings of the world. The two sides of the culture wars often split along this epistemological gulf: one side increasingly relied upon newer and newer paradigms for explaining our world and its problems; the other returned again and again to the tried and true.[23]

Following the lead of scientists, few jurists in the nation were convinced of the merits of "creation science." As with efforts to remove reading materials deemed secular humanist, the courts impeded conservative attempts to insert creationism into the public school science curriculum. In its 1987 decision *Edwards v. Aguillard*, the Supreme Court overturned a Louisiana law mandating that biology teachers include creationism in their lessons on evolution, objecting that the law's sole purpose was to "advance the religious viewpoint that a supernatural being created humankind."[24]

Despite such legal setbacks, conservatives had a great deal of public support on the issue. Gallup polls in the 1990s consistently showed that over half of Americans rejected evolution. One such 1992 poll revealed that 82 percent of American adults believed that God created humans, and a majority of these believed specifically in the Genesis account. These staggering numbers placed enormous pressure on biology teachers in many parts of the country. The National Academy of Sciences (NAS), the leading professional association of scientists, fought back against widespread creationist sentiments and sought to aid biology teachers with the publication of two pamphlets in the 1990s: *Teaching about Evolution and the Nature of Science* and *Science and Creationism*. The NAS pamphlets represented some of the clearest explanations about the science of evolution and some of the best refutations of creationism.[25]

Despite their scientific and pedagogical lucidity, the NAS pamphlets were less sensible about curricular politics. They implied that opposition to the teaching of evolution on religious grounds was misplaced because most "major religious denominations have taken official positions that accept evolution." This was small consolation to those fundamentalist Christians who could not reconcile their faith with Darwinism. What the NAS pamphlets underestimated was the very real threat their curriculum posed to millions of conservative Christians. Such underestimation extended to professional educators more generally. Many liberal educators failed to recognize that whereas the schools were growing more tolerant of racial and ethnic diversity, they were becoming *less* tolerant of religious expression, particularly of the fundamentalist variety. Such a discrepancy was highlighted by the conservative appropriation of multicultural argumentation. Insinuating that Christians were a victimized group, Judge Hand compared "the state denial of the history of religion in the textbooks to the state activity in denying black history and its contributions in these texts."[26]

In the 1990s the Christian Right implemented a new technique in its fight against secular schools. Activists ran stealth campaigns for local school boards, campaigning only amongst their coreligionists, who were expected to vote in high numbers. "We're trying to generate as large a voter turnout as possible among our constituency," the Christian Coalition's Ralph Reed explained, "by communicating with them in a way that does not attract the fire of our opponents." The plan worked to perfection in Vista, California, a suburb of San Diego, where conservatives gained a three-person majority on the five-person school board in 1992. The new board rapidly gained national attention with radical curriculum mandates, such as adding "secular humanism" to the list of topics taught in the district's comparative world religions class, in order to establish it as a religion. John Tyndall, one of the newly elected conservatives who worked as an accountant for the ICR, attracted controversy when he asked a committee of district science teachers to review a creationist text—*Of Pandas and People: The Central Question of Biological Origins*—for inclusion in the curriculum. Soon after the committee predictably rejected the book, the conservatives on the board rewrote the local science standards to include the following clause: "To enhance positive scientific exploration and dialogue, weaknesses that substantially challenge theories in evolution should be presented." In response to this and the board's actions more generally, the local teacher's union, allied with moderate parents who found the overtly conservative politicization of their schools distasteful, organized a successful recall of the conservative Vista board members in 1993.[27]

In 1999 conservatives in control of the Kansas board of education fostered an international scandal when they revised state science standards by deleting references to biological evolution and the origins of the universe. The Kansas conservatives maintained that the science standards, which had been newly revised in 1998 by a committee of science educators, aimed at indoctrinating students in what they called "a quasi-religious philosophy" that defined science in purely naturalistic terms. As the pro-creationist authors of a pamphlet about the Kansas controversy wrote: "Under this radical redefinition of science, no scientist would be allowed to conclude, on the basis of scientific evidence, that God played a role in the creation of the world." Indeed, some of the language in the 1998 standards seemed intended to marginalize students skeptical of evolution for religious reasons. In the event that students raised "a question in a natural science class that the teacher determines to be outside the domain of science," teachers were instructed to "explain why the question is outside the domain of natural science and encourage the student to discuss the question further with his or her family and clergy." In response to this, the Kansas conservatives claimed they merely sought standards that prevented discrimination "against students who believe the scientific evidence warrants a theistic rather than a naturalistic interpretation of origins." But more to the point, conservatives saw themselves as challenging a smug "new class" of experts who held religious values in disdain. Writing in the *New Republic*, Gregg Easterbrook neatly expressed such a view: "Once you weren't supposed to question God. Now you're not supposed to question the head of the biology department."[28]

As in Vista, the Kansas conservatives were eventually voted off the school board, and the science standards were reinstated. Similarly, in Lake County, Florida, religious conservative board members were voted out after sensational attempts to mandate the teaching of "patriotic" history. And in rural Blissfield, Michigan, evangelical anger failed to block a local school-improvement plan. Thus the effect of religious conservative educational activism seemingly proved fleeting. But however unsuccessful in these specific instances, such efforts created broad discord that helped spur hundreds of thousands of Christians to migrate out of public schools. Antipathy to the trajectory of public education led to a massive expansion of Christian day schools. In 1977 the three largest Christian day school networks combined enrolled approximately 350,000 students. By 1992 this number had mushroomed to an estimated 775,000 students; by 2002 there were over 880,000 Christian day school students.[29]

Many religious conservatives sent their children to Christian day schools because they loathed the secularism of the public schools. Such secularism, Christian Right educators believed, was on display beyond biology classes that taught evolution and social studies classes that taught anthropological curricula such as MACOS. Secular humanism was also demonstrable in history courses, where students were increasingly taught to think about the past through a lens that challenged the historical inevitability central to fundamentalist eschatology. Students in Christian day schools were not taught to think critically about history but were rather taught to accept it on faith that things happened by God's design. Bob Jones University Press, which met the increasing demand for providential-history textbooks arising from the growth of the Christian day school movement, published books, such as *U.S. History for Christian Schools*, that mixed historical fact with biblical doctrine.[30]

In addition to a preference for such religious content, many conservative parents favored the strict instruction style of Christian schools. Since evangelicals believed that humans are inherently sinful, they often thought children needed draconian discipline in order to become godly. Such pedagogical authoritarianism stood in marked contrast to child-centeredness, a pedagogy that, to varying degrees, had helped shape public school sensibilities since the early twentieth century. Child-centeredness was premised on the idea that children instinctively know what was best for themselves and should thus should have some say, directly or indirectly, in their curriculum. Hoary right-wing assaults on John Dewey were as much about his child-centered philosophy as about his political liberalism. More to the point, conservatives conceptualized child-centeredness as a branch of liberalism, which was reasonable since Dewey himself theorized that the liberal value of "open-mindedness means retention of childlike attitude." As the antidote to Deweyan child-centeredness, many Christian educators turned to Rouhas John Rushdoony and his 1985 book *Philosophy of the Christian Curriculum*. Rushdoony described the implications of a child-centered pedagogy as follows: "Instead of being accountable to God, parents, teachers, and society, the pupil can assert that God, parents, teachers and society are responsible to him." Rushdoony's theocratic doctrine that God's laws take precedent over man's laws doubled as a strike against child-centeredness. Since children had to be made to conform to the immutable truth of God, their subjective longings had to be quashed.[31]

In the 1980s and 1990s, a growing number of religious conservatives pulled their children not only out of public schools but out of schools altogether, and the ranks of the homeschooled grew precipitously. In 1985 there were about 250,000 homeschooled children. By 1999 well over one million American children were schooled at home. An estimated 90 percent of those who homeschooled their children were evangelicals, who increasingly believed they were commanded by the Bible to educate their own children. Public educators were understandably dubious about homeschooling. "If anyone can teach," warned John Cole, president of the Texas Federation of Teachers, "teaching will, indeed, no longer be a profession." More idealistically, Robert McClure of the NEA worried that homeschooling would undermine the promise of American pluralism; he argued that "it's important for children to move outside their families and learn how to function with strangers." Local school boards across the country were also suspicious and tended to reject home-school applications. Some parents, especially well-educated liberals, gained approval by convincing school boards that their child had special needs that they could best attend to. But religious conservatives were almost always refused such permission—undoubtedly a result of the chasm that separated how the average school board member conceptualized the public schools from how the typical evangelical thought about what were derisively termed "Satanic hothouses." When conservative parents failed to receive permission to homeschool their children, they often took their cases to court, where they had a great deal more success. Lawyers with the Homeschool Legal Defense Association convinced judges all over the country that a parent's right to determine his or her child's life, codified by previous interpretations of the Fourteenth Amendment right to privacy, was more compelling than compulsory school attendance laws. Owing to such efforts, homeschooling was legal in every state of the union by the 1990s.[32]

The upshot of this considerable movement out of the public schools was that whereas the de facto national curriculum remained liberal, only a shrinking percentage of the nation's schoolchildren were exposed to it. The Christian Right ultimately reduced the impact of secular schools not by changing them to reflect their values but by abandoning them altogether.

Of equal consequence, religious conservatives helped foster the popular notion that the public schools were in crisis. Neoconservative education reformers like William Bennett, secretary of education during Reagan's second term in the White House, used this fractured educational landscape to their advantage.

Resistance to liberal curricular reform, perhaps more than any other sphere in the culture wars, revealed the perplexities of a conservative movement that housed both religious conservatives and neoconservatives. Religious conservatives railed against the state as an agent of secularism. Yet they formed alliances with neoconservatives who sought to reshape the national curriculum more to their liking from within the hallowed halls of government—specifically within the administrations of Ronald Reagan and George H. W. Bush.

Although neoconservatives were not unsympathetic to Christian Right concerns about the role of religion in society, their primary complaint with the nation's educational system was that standards were deteriorating. The schools, they argued, were failing to provide American children with a basic education. Neoconservatives believed that a focus on educational equity had been to the detriment of educational excellence. In this they learned their lessons from a massive government study written by sociologist James Coleman in 1966—officially titled *Equality of Educational Opportunity* but more famously known as the Coleman Report—which found that school funding had little bearing on educational achievement and thus efforts to achieve equity were wasteful. The Coleman Report, based on a survey of the verbal ability of 645,000 students in four thousand schools across the country, argued that schools "bring little influence to bear on a child's achievement that is independent of his background and social context." Such a conclusion had no clear political valence. In his 1972 book *Inequality*, leftist scholar Christopher Jencks extrapolated from Coleman Report findings to contend that economic redistribution was a better route than educational reform to achieving a more equal society. But neoconservatives used it to argue that pushing for educational excellence measurable by standardized tests was the best method to improve schools. Chester Finn, an influential neoconservative who served in Reagan's department of education, often spoke about how "holding schools to account for their students' academic achievement" was the only educational policy that made sense in a "post-Coleman" world. Though educational policy could not create a more equal society, by setting high standards it could compel schools to strive for academic excellence.[33]

These notions about excellence resulted in a neoconservative approach to school reform distinct from the Christian Right's: whereas religious conservatives organized at the grassroots level and often distrusted federal intervention in education, neoconservatives sought to implement top-down solutions from their perches in the federal government. For example, neoconservative educational thinkers originated a reform called "outcome-based education" as a way to emphasize excellence as opposed to equity. For them, outcome-based education simply meant that educational progress was to be measured by what students produced (outcomes) rather than by what resources were put into schools (inputs). Paradoxically, outcome-based education became the target of conservative venom in 1994. What was particularly ironic was that the neoconservative former secretary of education Bennett led the charge against outcome-based reforms, calling them "a Trojan horse for social engineering." Finn, meanwhile, contended that conservatives were wrong to oppose outcome-based education, though he made this argument with an important "devil lurks in the details" qualification, contrasting his vision with how liberal educators in the Clinton era implemented it. "Rather than itemizing the basic skills and knowledge that well-adjusted children should be able to demonstrate in core academic subjects," Finn lamented, "the lists of outcomes that were actually drafted had more to do with social attitudes, ideological positions, and interpersonal relations."[34]

In short, though neoconservatives aligned themselves with Christian conservatives against liberal curriculum reform, conservatives as a whole were far from monolithic in their approaches to instituting a conservative curriculum. Neoconservatives pushed for a set of centralized national educational reforms. Christian conservatives, on the other hand, sought to break all ties with a federal educational establishment that they deemed hopelessly secular. But these differences in means often paled in comparison to agreement over ends. Religious conservatives and neoconservatives agreed that the post-sixties upending of the traditional curriculum had been disastrous.

Bennett believed that his education reform agenda was ideally suited to bring religious conservatives and neoconservatives together under one big conservative tent. He thought his demand that the nation's schools focus on basic knowledge was popular across much of the political spectrum. Such a view stemmed from Bennett's own ecumenical political background. When he joined the Reagan administration in 1981 as the chair of the National Endowment for the Humanities (NEH), Bennett considered himself a Democrat. But while directing the National Humanities Center in North Carolina, Bennett had distinguished himself as a scathing critic of the academic Left. For this reason, influential neoconservatives, including Irving Kristol, championed his NEH nomination. Bennett's cause was also helped by the fact that Reagan's first choice, Mel Bradford, a so-called paleoconservative known for his celebration of antebellum southern culture, had written about Lincoln as a "dangerous man" comparable to Hitler for his executive power grab and his brutal invasion of the South. This did not sit well with neoconservatives, who had no problem with Lincoln's means of destroying slavery, a retrograde way of life that had been ripping the nation apart. In contrast to Bradford, Bennett had written a doctoral thesis in political philosophy that included an appreciative study of Lincoln and Martin Luther King Jr.[35]

Although Bennett's chief priority as secretary of education was to compel public schools to impart basic education, a goal heading the neoconservative education agenda since the Coleman Report, he also believed the curriculum should inculcate moral character. In his view, these were the two most important tasks traditionally assigned to the schools. But the sixties had warped the nation's educational mission. During and after the sixties, the nation had experienced, in his words, "a sustained attack on traditional American values and the place where those values had long had a comfortable and congenial home—the school." As with basic education, Bennett thought moral instruction had widespread support. Indeed, a 1987 Gallup Poll showed that nearly 60 percent of Americans desired a national curriculum that included compulsory moral instruction. Citing a 1986 study of twelve high school students concluding that students with conservative moral values performed significantly better, Bennett deduced that basic education and moral instruction were mutually reinforcing and therefore that his reform efforts were intellectually consistent.[36]

To the degree that Bennett supported traditional moral instruction, his views meshed well with the Christian Right's argument that education should be guided by religious values. Speaking before the Knights of Columbus in 1985, Bennett maintained that the Supreme Court had "failed to reflect sufficiently on the relationship between our faith and our political order," a speech that earned him the title "Secretary of Evangelization" among liberals. But many conservatives did not trust Bennett.[37]

For paleoconservatives, such bad feelings stemmed from the aggressiveness with which neoconservatives had lobbied in favor of Bennett and against Bradford. The NEH chair flap helps explain the harshness of paleoconservative Stephen Tonsor's 1986 analogy for the larger conservative movement's taking its cues from neoconservatives. "It is splendid when the town whore gets religion and joins the church," Tonsor seethed. "Now and then she makes a good choir director, but when she begins to tell the minister what he ought to say in his Sunday sermons, matters have been carried too far." More generally, religious conservatives were suspicious of the faith Bennett seemed to place in the secular state. Such reservations were confirmed when Bennett spoke out against parents who wanted to remove their children from classes due to objectionable content. "The effort to achieve a consensus in what should be taught," Bennett stated, "should not be undercut by allowing people to opt out of discussions of these things if they have disagreements with this or that." As the author of a 1987 *National Review* article explained, Bennett's "messianic effort to save the country by means of a national consensus on education and morals" deemphasized parental rights. This concerned the Christian Right. "After all, who can guarantee that Deweyites will never again replace Bennettites as arbiters of good citizenship?"[38]

In spite of such conservative discord, neoconservatives had success with their key reform efforts. This was especially true of their push for national standards, which they believed would compel schools to return to basic education. In making the case for standards, neoconservatives counted on support from powerful economic and political actors. The American elite almost uniformly understood the state of American public education through the lens of *A Nation at Risk*, a widely publicized 1983 report arguing that American schools, by failing to offer a basic education, undermined the nation's ability to compete in an increasingly global economy. *A Nation at Risk* set off a national education scare unlike any since 1957, when the Soviets launched the *Sputnik* satellite, proving once again Hannah Arendt's aphorism that "only in America could a crisis in education actually become a factor in politics." More than a crisis, *A Nation at Risk* ushered in an era of systematic education reform. The influential report represented Reagan's signature education legacy, which was ironic given that at first Reagan had wanted nothing to do with it.[39]

Reagan had entered the White House with a Christian Right view of public schools. Not only did he support a school prayer amendment, but he also contended that parents should have unrestricted rights to educate their children as they saw fit. Reagan believed that the government should underwrite educational "choice" with tax credits or vouchers, a market-based education policy innovated by Milton Friedman in the 1950s that would have allowed parents to send their children to any school they wished, including Christian day schools, on the taxpayer dime. But beyond subsidizing parental rights, Reagan thought the federal government had no role to play in education. While campaigning in 1980, he promised that if elected he would abolish the Department of Education, which his predecessor Jimmy Carter had created as a concession to the NEA. Once elected, Reagan took an easier route: rather than seeking to abolish the Department of Education, which would have instigated a contentious political battle, he simply starved it of the funds necessary to make it effective. Such neglect led an otherwise supportive Chester Finn to charge that Reagan's education policies signaled a "failure of leadership."[40]

Secretary of Education Terrel Bell sought to prove his boss wrong by showing that the Department of Education could be useful in setting a conservative agenda. Seizing on complaints from the nation's business leaders about poorly performing schools—grumbles of the type that unfailingly emerge in bad economic times, as was the case during the "Reagan Recession" of the early 1980s—Bell suggested the formation of a presidential blue-ribbon commission on education. Reagan rejected the idea. Going forward without the White House imprint, Bell created the National Commission on Excellence in Education, consisting of eighteen prominent business leaders, academics, and government functionaries. Echoing elite anxieties, this commission's report, *A Nation at Risk*, evinced an alarmist tone. "The educational foundations of our society," the report notoriously cautioned, "are presently being eroded by a rising tide of mediocrity that threatens our very future as a Nation and a people." Within a year of its publication, millions of copies of *A Nation at Risk* were in circulation.

Several other publications soon followed, including Ernest Boyer's *High School*, Theodore Sizer's *Horace's Compromise*, and John Goodlad's *A Place Called School*, all of which, to varying degrees, traded in the trope that the nation suffered from a crisis of educational mediocrity.[41]

Attuned to the fact that Bell's commission had struck a nerve, Reagan claimed responsibility for *A Nation at Risk*. On the 1984 campaign trail, he peppered his speeches with quotes from it, emphasizing the role government might play in achieving educational excellence. Reagan endorsed the report's main prescriptions, giving legs to one of the most successful education reform movements in American history. Several states quickly enacted sweeping education reform laws that put American schools to work testing its students like never before. In addition to tests, *A Nation at Risk* convinced policymakers of the need for a nationwide core curriculum to ensure unvaryingly high academic standards in every region in the country. A 1989 meeting of state governors in Charlottesville, Virginia, called by President Bush, who dubbed himself "the education president," made setting standards in five core subject areas, including history, de facto national policy. Although national standards were to be voluntary and the responsibility for implementing them was to remain in the hands of state and local policy makers, the trend toward nationalization had been set into inexorable motion. The logic that undergirded *A Nation at Risk* had proven intoxicating.[42]

Attempts to create a national curriculum led to heated controversies, especially surrounding the *National History Standards* (analyzed in chapter 9). Such conflicts revealed the paradoxical nature of the conservative movement's culture wars on the public schools. In the first place, a decades-long Christian Right assault had weakened the public's trust in the schools, leaving them vulnerable to neoconservative reformers who wished to standardize basic education. In the second place, the neoconservative push for standards engendered even more conflict over the curriculum, since liberal educators were positioned by their professional standing to direct the production and implementation of such standards. Indeed, even though millions of religious conservatives rejected the content taught in the public schools, conservatives continued to lose the battle for the American curriculum, which persisted in reflecting a post-sixties paradigm: secular, relativistic, and multicultural. Sensing defeat, many religious conservatives abandoned the battlefield by joining the Christian day school and home-school movements.

But while religious conservatives lost the struggle for content, neo-conservatives won the battle for educational form, as arguments about standards became the new national paradigm. And yet many religious conservatives continued to resist the government role in education, even joining forces with liberals in opposing some neoconservative reform efforts. This was perplexing, given that Christian Right anxieties about the liberal curriculum and neoconservative concerns about standards had long been mutually reinforcing. It highlights the irony of the historical alliance forged between religious conservatives, who sought to reassert local control, and neoconservatives, who worked to command the federal educational establishment. Both groups wanted to reverse the post-sixties liberal curriculum, but the means by which the neoconservatives succeeded in doing so alienated many of their erstwhile Christian right allies.

8

The Battle for the American Mind

Syndicated conservative columnist George Will declared in 1991 that well-publicized disagreements over the American university curriculum were "related battles in a single war, a war of aggression against the Western political tradition and the ideas that animate it." Given such high stakes, Will endowed Lynne Cheney with a weightier title than her already prestigious one as chair of the National Endowment for the Humanities (NEH). She was the "secretary of domestic defense." In that role, Cheney was more crucial to the survival of the nation than her spouse, who happened to be the actual secretary of defense. "The foreign adversaries her husband, Dick, must keep at bay are less dangerous, in the long run, than the domestic forces with which she must deal."[1]

Impassioned debates about higher education, which reached their apex in the early 1990s, highlighted long-standing attempts by conservatives to differentiate themselves from what they considered an unscrupulous, anti-American "new class" of elitist intellectuals. They succeeded in tweaking the popular imagination regarding the nation's institutions of higher learning, which many people came to think of as leftist redoubts where standards were destroyed and the best of Western civilization had been replaced by a "politically correct" mishmash of multicultural nonsense. An exposé genre flourished—with titles including *The Closing of the American Mind, Cultural Literacy, Illiberal Education, Tenured Radicals,* and *Telling the Truth*—helping to harden tropes about university professors, especially in the humanities, as both out of touch and, paradoxically, on the march.[2]

And yet to the ears of many thoughtful listeners, the conservative critique of academia—distilled to its essence by George Will's shrill warnings about "domestic forces"—sounded hyperbolic. Whether Stanford University ought to assign John Locke or Frantz Fanon, a debate that played out on the *Wall Street Journal* editorial page in 1988, hardly seemed like a battle upon which the nation's fate rested. At the same time, the notion that innovative techniques for interpreting texts would help usher in a more progressive society—by freeing "people from ideological mystifications and aberrancies," as one prominent English professor announced—struck most commentators as mere fantasy. Rather than transform the American political system, the Left "marched on the English department while the right took the White House," as Todd Gitlin put it with his pithy metaphor for academic solipsism in the face of conservative triumph. The culture wars in higher education appeared to be a mere tempest in a teapot, fought out by equally hysterical partisans.[3]

Of course the history of the culture wars in higher education during the 1980s and 1990s is more complex than such appearances suggest. Whether the battles over academia had political consequences is debatable. But that they had enduring historical significance is inarguable. Shouting matches about academia reverberated beyond the ivory tower to lay bare a crisis of national faith. Was America a good nation? Could the nation be good—could its people be free—without foundations? Were such foundations best provided by a classic liberal education in the humanities, which Matthew Arnold described as "the best that has been thought and said"? Was the "best" philosophy and literature synonymous with the canon of Western civilization? Or was the Western canon racist and sexist? Was the "best" even a valid category for thinking about texts? Debates over these abstract questions rocked the nation's institutions of higher education in the 1980s and 1990s, demonstrating that the culture wars did not boil down to any one specific issue or even a set of issues. Rather, the culture wars often hinged on a more epistemological question about national identity: How should Americans think?

In grappling with this all-important question, many influential American academics turned to France for answers. Specifically, they incorporated theoretical frameworks informed by French philosophers like Michel Foucault, Jacques Lacan, and Jacques Derrida—frameworks that in various ways relativized truth and morality as expressions of power. Of course importing French theory was not entirely necessary to such a task, since early-twentieth-century American pragmatists had anticipated the French invasion in their idea that knowledge is radically tenuous. "The 'true,'" as William James wrote in his 1907 book *Pragmatism*, "is only the expedient in the way of our thinking, just as 'the right' is only the expedient in the way of our behaving." But in the austere 1970s, French theory proved more alluring, more exotic, and thus more marketable for those seeking to outcompete rival scholars for scarce funds. "Lacan, Derrida, and Foucault are the academic equivalents of BMW, Rolex, and Cuisinart," as Camille Paglia glibly phrased it. "French theory is like those how-to tapes guaranteed to make you a real estate millionaire overnight. Gain power by attacking power! Call this number in Paris *now*!"[4]

Trendiness aside, the new forms of thought that dominated academic interchange, whether spoken in a French dialect or not, were often insightful. Literary criticism, for instance, was rejuvenated by persuasive theories about the ways text, meaning, and even language are specific to circumstance. Such theorizing went beyond Marxist critic Fredric Jameson's famous imperative to "always historicize!" Even within a given historical context, multiple meanings could be extracted from any text based on who was doing the reading and for what purposes. "The only way that we can hope to interpret a literary work," explained renowned literary theorist Stanley Fish, "is by knowing the vantage from which we perform the act of interpretation—in contemporary parlance, where we're coming from." By the 1980s Duke University English Department's star-studded faculty, which included Fish as its chair, Jameson, Frank Lentricchia, Barbara Herrnstein Smith, Jane Tompkins, and briefly Henry Louis Gates, had become the vanguard of this mode of literary interpretation. The Duke literary scholars—nicknamed "the Fish tank"—did more than merely refine literary criticism. By undermining notions about the stable meaning of texts, they fundamentally challenged the commonsense idea that literature has timeless value. And thus the Duke literary critics and their academic epigones across the nation made the Western canon a culture wars issue.[5]

Fish did arguably more than anyone else to make avant-garde methods grounded in French theory usable for a new generation of literary scholars. The rhetorical question that served as the title of his 1980 book—*Is There a Text in This Class?*—challenged traditionalist literary critics like E. D. Hirsch, who contended that texts held constant as units of knowledge. Hirsch wrote an influential article in 1980—a preview of his 1987 best-selling book *Cultural Literacy*—in which he argued that texts are repositories of discrete facts that readers need to accumulate in order to be properly educated Americans. *Cultural Literacy* even included an appendix listing the many units of knowledge—names, dates, places, and sayings—that he believed illustrated literate Americanism. For Fish, in contrast, a text was not set in stone. Rather, a text was "the structure of meanings that is obvious and inescapable from the perspective of whatever interpretative assumptions happen to be in force." For the critic, then, the object of study was not the text in and of itself but rather the interpretative assumptions that give meaning to texts. To the anger of traditionalists, this had the effect of elevating the importance of theory. It was not enough for literary critics to analyze literature alone.[6]

Fish's purpose was to explode all false binaries that continued to govern the way people thought about texts. In a move that must have seemed familiar to readers of Derrida, he collapsed distinctions that separate object from subject, reader from text. Everything was worthy of interpretation; everything was a text. In his mission to blur all boundaries, Fish and his colleagues also pulled down the barricade that stood between literature and ordinary language—a barricade that traditionalists had long manned as the aesthetic gulf that separated the sublime from the vulgar. "Literature is a conventional category," Fish argued. "All texts have the potential of so counting, in that it is possible to regard any stretch of language in such a way that it will display those properties presently understood to be literary." Black literary critic Houston Baker put this in more colloquial terms when he argued that standards for ranking texts were "no different from choosing between a hoagy and a pizza." Textual hierarchies were conventions of time, place, circumstance, and power. The Western canon, as with all canons, was a social construction. The implications of such thinking were potentially monumental: if the very notion of a canon could be thrown into question, Fish argued, then so too could "the whole idea of 'Americanness.'"[7]

Transgressing literary standards was more than merely a matter of textual interpretation for many academic leftists. "It is a struggle among contending factions," Jane Tompkins told a reporter from the *New York Times* in 1988, "for the right to be represented in the picture America draws of itself." Many scholars believed that revising the canon by adding books authored by women and minorities would expand normative conceptions of Americanism to include women and minorities. This was a reading of French theory particular to post-sixties American cultural politics. Whereas Foucault theorized that seemingly objective statements were in fact true only within linguistic contexts, his American devotees reduced this concept to a more immediately applicable formulation: they argued that universal claims about truth and objectivity represent the particular interests of the powerful. And whereas Fish theorized that texts signify socially situated interpretive assumptions, many academics condensed this insight to suit the needs of progressive identity politics: they contended that the Western canon was the embodiment of white male supremacy. In sum, achieving a better country meant winning the canon wars.[8]

William Bennett was the first prominent conservative to issue a public outcry about this state of affairs. In 1984, while serving as chair of the NEH, Bennett authored a pamphlet—*To Reclaim a Legacy: A Report on the Humanities in Higher Education*—with the intention of generating a controversy on par with that created by *A Nation at Risk*. Bennett held a traditionalist vision of the humanities. He believed the Western canon—which he defined in the terms of Matthew Arnold as "the best that has been said, thought, written, and otherwise expressed about the human experience"—should be the philosophical bedrock of the nation's higher education. "Because our society is the product and we the inheritors of Western civilization," Bennett matter-of-factly wrote, "American students need an understanding of its origins and development, from its roots in antiquity to the present." But to his dismay, curricular anarchy, having replaced a coherent curriculum grounded in the Western canon, reigned supreme. Like his fellow neoconservatives, Bennett pinpointed the disruptive sixties as the beginning of this slide into pedagogical chaos. In the face of demands by militant students who wanted a curriculum tailored to their various interests—interests that often stemmed from radical political positions—faculty and university administrators had experienced a "collective loss of nerve and faith." As a result, "the curriculum was no longer a statement about what knowledge mattered."[9]

Even though Bennett believed threats to the Western canon first emerged in the sixties, he blamed contemporary professors for making matters worse. It was their fault, he argued, that the humanities were dying, a trend he extrapolated from the decline in the number of students who majored in disciplines like English and history. Professors had become too specialized and were thus unqualified to teach with the breadth required by a curriculum based on the Western canon—the type of curriculum that once attracted a great many more students. But even more egregious than overspecialization, in Bennett's view, was the politicization of the curriculum. "Sometimes the humanities are used as if they were the handmaiden of ideology," he wrote, "subordinated to particular prejudices and valued or rejected on the basis of their relation to a certain social stance." This was Bennett's way of criticizing the hold that identity politics had on the study of literature and history, institutionalized in the new programs founded in the sixties like black, ethnic, and women's studies. He believed the politicized expansion of the canon to include texts authored by minorities and women violated universal aesthetic standards. But that was not the worst of it. There were influential professors, those like Fish, who believed the humanities have "no inherent meaning because all meaning is subjective and relative to one's own perspective." Bennett concluded that these two types of humanities scholars— those who hailed from the identity politics school of thought and those who adhered to relativistic modes of literary interpretation— were equal threats to the Western canon. The one sought to revise it without regard for the recognized categories of distinction that made the Western canon a repository of "the most powerful and pervasive influences on America." The other sought to dismiss distinction altogether. Given that conservatives believed the Western canon unlocks the wisdom upon which a free society is based, this was an alarming development.[10]

Conservative unease that the canon was under siege became a full-fledged panic in the late 1980s when Stanford University, at the behest of some of its students, revised its core curriculum. Prior to the changes, all Stanford first-year students were required to read the same fifteen texts as part of its Western Civilization program, including the Bible and selections from Homer, Plato, Augustine, Dante, More, Machiavelli, Galileo, Luther, Voltaire, Marx and Engels, Darwin, and Freud. In 1986 Bill King, president of the Stanford Black Student Union, formally complained to the academic senate that the core reading list was "racist." "The Western culture program as it is presently structured around a core list and an outdated philosophy of the West being Greece, Europe, and Euro-America is wrong, and worse," he contended, "it hurts people mentally and emotionally in ways that are not even recognized." Stanford's academic senate agreed to examine the issue. Students who opposed the Western Civilization curriculum continued to exert pressure while the senate deliberated over the next two years. In early 1988 students held a rally and marched alongside Jesse Jackson while notoriously chanting, "Hey hey, ho ho, Western culture's got to go." Later that year the academic senate voted 39–4 to modify the first-year core curriculum. The new curriculum, retitled "Culture, Ideas, and Values," or CIV for short, was the senate's attempt at a compromise. Instead of using a fixed list, the professors who taught the course would annually reach consensus over which texts to assign based on a loose set of standards. For example, under the new rubric students were required to read at least one "Enlightenment thinker," which in practice simply meant that Rousseau could be assigned instead of Voltaire. The only rule governing the CIV reading list that radically departed from the previous Western Civilization list was that a small number of authors representing minority, female, and non-Western perspectives were required. Other than that, CIV was not that different, a fact that hardly satisfied critics.[11]

The Stanford canon became an international cause célèbre. Glossing over the fact that the new CIV program hardly departed from the old Western Civilization curriculum, media sensationalism made Stanford's revisions seem like a proxy for the death of the West. *Newsweek* titled a story on the topic "Say Goodbye Socrates." Conservatives fanned the flames of this narrative. In a debate with Stanford president Donald Kennedy, Bennett, who was by then the secretary of education, charged that the Stanford revision had resulted from "an unfortunate capitulation to a campaign of pressure politics and intimidation." "The West is the culture in which we live," he asserted. "It has set the moral, political, economic and social standards for the rest of the world." Bennett proclaimed that by abdicating its authority to a group of unruly student militants, "a great university was brought low by the very forces which modern universities came into being to oppose: ignorance, irrationality and intimidation." Allan Bloom wrote a letter to the *Wall Street Journal* editor in 1989—two years after his book *The Closing of the American Mind* made a rigorous if eccentric case for a classic liberal education rooted in the Western canon—in which he argued that the Stanford revisions were a travesty. "Stanford students are to be indoctrinated with ephemeral ideologies and taught that there can be no intellectual resistance to one's own time and its passions," Bloom contended. "This total surrender to the present and abandonment of the quest for standards with which to judge it are the very definition of the closing of the American mind, and I could not hope for more stunning confirmation of my thesis."[12]

The Stanford debate stoked the fires of the culture wars in higher education. It gave Bennett, Bloom, and other conservative defenders of the Western canon cause to air their grievances about American higher education. Of course the conservative reaction to Stanford's revised curriculum was exaggerated. Not only were changes to the first-year reading list less extensive than conservative rhetoric implied, but the idea that the Western Civilization course represented a long-standing tradition was patently false. Bliss Carnochan, who directed the Stanford Humanities Center during the controversy, sought to demystify this idea: "[I]t can hardly be emphasized strenuously enough or often enough," he pleaded, "how far from truth and into demagoguery the legend strays, so fragile, partial, and short-lived was any prior consensus." Stanford's core curriculum, like all canons, was a highly contested body of knowledge. To begin with, the Western Civilization course was a recent American invention. Prior to World War I Americans had sought to distinguish themselves from Europeans, a desire the nation's humanities curriculum tended to echo. But when American politicians committed the United States to war in Europe, American curriculum builders followed suit, hitching the nation's cultural fate to Europe. By World War II the sensibilities expressed by Carlton Hayes in his widely used 1932 Western Civilization textbook had become so common as to seem natural: "Europe has been the seat of that continuous high civilization which we call 'western,' which has come to be the distinctive civilization of the American continents as well as of Europe."[13]

But mere decades after World War I gave birth to Western Civilization, the Cold War signaled its death knell. New imperatives called for specialized knowledge and area studies. Barely afloat through the first few decades of the Cold War, by the late sixties most universities quit mandating that students complete a Western Civilization course. In 1969 Stanford dumped the required course, a victim to student demands that they be given more freedom to tailor coursework to their specific needs and interests. Many professors were happy to oblige. The director of the Stanford Western Civilization program claimed at the time that he and many of his colleagues "are no longer convinced that there is a standard or specifiable body of knowledge or information necessary for a liberal education." Thus no core curriculum in the humanities existed at Stanford during the 1970s.[14]

But in 1980 a growing number of Stanford professors who had come to believe that the humanities curriculum needed more coherence reinstituted a version of the Western Civilization course that included the famous core reading list. In retrospect, those responsible claimed they did not intend for the list to be canonized. Their goal was rather more humble. They believed, perhaps naively, that if all first-year students read the same books, it would give them something meaningful to discuss with each other in their dormitories and cafeterias. In short, the course that became the subject of international scandal—and the reading list that conservatives deemed sacred—had been back on campus for a mere eight years; and those who revived it, far from being messianic defenders of the West, simply wanted students to value their university experience as something more worthwhile than vocational training.[15]

Yet the arguments that conservatives put forward in the canon wars, however bombastic, however overstated, and however ahistorical, should not be understood as having been made in bad faith. Conservatives were reacting to fundamental changes that had left many Americans bewildered. There is no other way to explain, for example, the popularity of *The Closing of the American Mind*, which spent more than a year on the *New York Times* best-seller list after publication in 1987. Such astronomical sales were a surprise to everyone, including its author. Bloom, a professor of philosophy at the University of Chicago who specialized in Plato and Rousseau, did not set out to write a best seller. A book that included a seventy-page chapter titled "From Socrates' *Apology* to Heidegger's *Rektoratsrede*" was not designed to sell eight hundred thousand copies in its first year, and over 1.2 million total. The book's commercial success was in part the product of its timeliness: subtitled *How Higher Education Has Failed Democracy and Impoverished the Souls of Today's Students*, it hit bookstores just as the Stanford canon war was heating up, putting the politics of higher education on the front pages of newspapers and magazines. And Hirsch's *Cultural Literacy* was second only to Bloom's atop the 1987 nonfiction best-seller lists.[16]

But such immediate relevance was not the sole explanation for the rate at which Bloom's jeremiad flew off the shelves. *The Closing of the American Mind* struck a chord with Americans struggling to make sense of the ruptures that had been altering social arrangements since the sixties—especially the changes to the nation's landscapes of race and gender, changes that were highly noticeable on college campuses. Just as these changes led some to question the epistemological foundations of the old order—often in the guise of the canon—others grasped for what they knew to be good, natural, true, and timeless. Into this milieu walked Bloom, who offered his readers a powerful vocabulary—a "meditation on the state of our souls"—with which to ward off the barbarians at the gates.

The Closing of the American Mind had a little something for everyone. For instance, both traditionalists and academic leftists could get behind Bloom's argument that a liberal education should provide students with "four years of freedom," which he described as "a space between the intellectual wasteland he has left behind and the inevitable dreary professional training that awaits him after the baccalaureate." But at its most explicit, *Closing* was red meat for conservatives. It was an angry, if sophisticated, denunciation of relativism in all its forms: philosophic, moral, cultural, and educational. Bloom believed relativistic thought had spread through American culture like a cancer. "There is one thing a professor can be absolutely certain of," Bloom observed: "almost every student entering the university believes, or says he believes, that truth is relative." But to make matters worse, the university reinforced relativistic "openness," as students were taught that "indiscriminateness" was "a moral imperative because its opposite is discrimination."[17]

As opposed to "indiscriminateness," Bloom supported discrimination in the service of truth and beauty. Such a stance translated into an array of positions at odds with conventional academic wisdom. For instance, he thought it entirely appropriate to celebrate works of philosophy, art, and literature that in their genius rose above the chains of time and place. Bloom believed the human condition is anchored by ineluctable essentials that transcend specific historical contexts. "What each generation is," he argued, "can best be discovered in its relation to the permanent concerns of mankind." Such a platonic theory of history ran counter to the radical forms of contextualization that held wide sway in the humanities. But whereas most conservative critics of the university understood the impulse to contextualize as an effect of the movements that swept up campuses in the sixties—and although Bloom loathed that decade, describing it as an "unmitigated disaster"—he understood relativistic thinking as inherent to modernism more broadly, particularly in the thought of Nietzsche, modernism's most honest spokesperson. Following a long line of philosophic absolutists, Bloom theorized that all forms of relativistic thinking led down the slippery slope to nihilism. This is why Bloom begrudgingly praised Nietzsche, not for any love of nihilism but for Nietzsche's unblinking recognition that the mere hint of relativism logically concludes in the death of God. But in spite of his affinity for Nietzsche's frankness, Bloom disdained the distorted importation of Nietzsche into American thought, especially the premise "that man is a value-creating, not a good-discovering, being"—a premise inherent to the forms of literary interpretation that collapsed text and reader.[18]

Bloom made only one reference to Foucault and Derrida in his 382-page book, toward the very end, while lamenting the way French theory had misshaped the American study of literature, especially the notion that "there is no text, only interpretation." And yet Bloom's lengthy, multilayered analysis of Nietzsche might just as well have been about Foucault. For Nietzsche, as for Foucault, there is no escape from relativism: morality, to cite Nietzsche's most famous argument, is merely a contextual mode of understanding human behavior that, because it seems timeless, tends to mask its "will to power." For Bloom, then, Nietzsche's relativism was nihilistic because in a world where nothing matters—where nothing is good, nothing is true, and God is dead—anything goes. Yet for Americans, Bloom argued, the death of God did not equate to meaninglessness; rather it entailed that they could find meaning in their true selves. He called this "nihilism with a happy ending," "nihilism without the abyss," "a Disneyland version of the Weimar Republic." But Bloom contended that in the real world there are no happy endings for those who "pursue happiness in ways determined by that language." The language of nihilism left Americans spiritually impoverished. Sloppy thinking threatened the American soul. Or, as Bloom put it by way of reference to Plato's legendary cave allegory: "merely methodological excision from the soul of the imagination that projects Gods and heroes onto the wall of the cave does not promote knowledge of the soul; it only lobotomizes it, cripples its powers." Americans had killed God without a suitable replacement for the truth.[19]

Bloom used Weimar Germany as an analogy for the dangers presented by sixties America, a comparison common to neoconservative declension narratives. "Whether it be Nuremberg or Woodstock," he proclaimed, "the principle is the same." Weimar analogies were particularly a fetish of those, like Bloom, who had studied with German émigré Leo Strauss, the esoteric political philosopher who detected nihilism lurking around every modern corner. Bloom left unanswered the question whether another Hitler was right around the corner of sixties America. But he was sure of one thing: "The American university in the sixties was experiencing the same dismantling of the structure of rational inquiry as had the German university in the thirties. No longer believing in their higher vocation, both gave way to a highly ideologized student populace." Repeating academic leftist assumptions that an antifoundational epistemology was tightly linked to progressive political views, Bloom thought relativistic thinking helped "highly ideologized" students marshal left-wing politics on campus. Paraphrasing academic doctrine, he rhetorically asked: "Who says that what universities teach is the truth, rather than just the myths necessary to support the system of domination?" Bloom specifically decried the prominent argument, articulated most forcefully by Black Power activists, that standards merely offer cover for institutional forms of racism. Such thinking, he contended, validated claims that blacks were less successful on campus due to deeply rooted power structures. "Black students are second-class not because they are academically poor but because they are forced to imitate white culture," Bloom wrote, with no effort to hide his sarcastic tone. "Relativism and Marxism"—those modes of thinking most responsible for sacrificing universal truth at the altars of context and perspective—"made some of this claim believable."[20]

Bloom's antipathy to Black Power was informed by his experience while teaching at Cornell University during the campus upheaval of 1969, when militant black students infamously brandished guns to magnify their demands for affirmative action and the implementation of black studies. As gadfly writer Christopher Hitchens later wrote: "Chaos, most especially the chaos identified with pissed-off African Americans, was the whole motif of *The Closing of the American Mind*." That is, Bloom was not only concerned about the philosophical anarchy that marked a relativistic culture. He was also anxious about the more tangible disorder that seemingly overwhelmed universities in

the wake of sixties liberation movements. In this Bloom was not unusual. On the contrary, such anxieties underwrote the culture wars in
higher education. And yet *Closing* was more elitist than many conservative culture warriors should have been comfortable with. William
Bennett, a more mainstream conservative, believed that *all* Americans should read the canon as a recipe for freedom. Bloom, however—
despite protesting during a 1987 television interview that he was "not
a snob"—waxed nostalgic for a time when a liberal education was the
preserve of the select few. *Closing* epitomized a theory made famous
by Strauss: all good texts reveal one meaning for the masses and another for those savvy enough to read between the lines. Read in this
way, *Closing* was a deeply paradoxical account of higher education. As
Hitchens pithily worded it: "the American mind was closed, because
it had become so goddamned open." Opening the American mind did
not involve opening the gates of American higher education to the
barbarian hordes.[21]

Bloom's influence was circumscribed by his elitism, and his book
had only limited success as a manifesto for how to remake the university. Such a task would be left to more practical-minded conservatives.
Somehow, though, Bloom's elitism did not diminish his appeal—an
incongruence recognized by some of his harshest critics, including
political theorist Benjamin Barber, who gave Bloom the title "philosopher despot." "He claims the country has deserted the university and
blames democracy for the debacle, so the country adopts him as its favorite democratic educator," Barber wrote, bemused by the irony. *The
Closing of the American Mind*, then, influenced conservative culture
warriors not because of its elitism but because it helped them form
a rhetorical defense against cultural trends they deemed dangerous.
Bloom's material success demonstrated to a new generation of conservative activists that an antirelativist critique of the professoriate was a
useful mechanism for leveraging partisan objectives. William Kristol,
son of Irving and at that time assistant to Secretary of Education Bennett, wrote in the *Wall Street Journal* that the conservative movement
should take as "one of its guides this extraordinary book."[22]

Beyond the fact that it helped conservatives fashion a powerful argument against the state of American higher education, *Closing* became a cultural phenomenon because of the persona Allan Bloom cut
in the public imagination: a caricature of the chain-smoking, sherry-
sipping professor, grumbling about the latest fads. Playing the churl-

ish eccentric to perfection, Bloom complained about the popularity of rock 'n' roll, describing it as a "gutter phenomenon," worse than earlier romantic expressions that found redemption in the unconscious impulses of savages: instead of somewhat noteworthy literature, all we got from our more recent "voyage to the underworld" was "Mick Jagger tarting it up on stage." Insulting the cultural form that represented the very essence of modern America hardly seemed like a successful strategy for winning over modern Americans. Yet it made Bloom all the more fascinating. When his newfound fame garnered him an appearance on *The Oprah Winfrey Show*—the true measure of pop-cultural significance—Bloom's hatred of rock 'n' roll was mentioned not as a serious issue that might lead anyone to think twice about his antimodernism but rather as an amusing aside that revealed his quirkiness. Such a reaction was perhaps inevitable. Hardly anyone put before Oprah's cameras seemed to understand his argument, including the host herself, who believed her audience's inability to correctly answer simple historical trivia questions was evidence of Bloom's thesis that, as she put it, America was "raising a generation of dummies."[23]

The Oprah conversation briefly became more substantial—or at least more familiar to the ongoing debates in the academy—when Bloom read a famous passage from W. E. B. Du Bois's *Souls of Black Folk* about how reading great books is akin to "sitting with Shakespeare," the implication being that classic texts transcend the constraints of circumstance, including those imposed by race. Northwestern literature professor Gerald Graff, invited on the show to disagree with Bloom, countered that Du Bois read classic texts as political tools in his fight against racism. Whether those in the audience understood the nuances of this distinction was unclear. What was clear is that, as opposed to Graff, whose dictums about how learning is a "process" likely struck most viewers as meaningless professional jargon, Bloom radiated a larger-than-life aura of someone who knew a lot about a lot of really important things. Indeed the culture wars in higher education did not flower from the deep roots of American anti-intellectualism, strictly speaking. Rather, most Americans seemed to prefer one type of intellectual to another: they preferred an idealized renaissance man who spoke with the gods to a hackneyed agent of the "new class" who butchered sacred cows with his profane ways or, worse yet, with his banal language.[24]

Saul Bellow depicted this larger-than-life Bloom in his novel

Ravelstein, a memoir-style rendering of his close friend's unconventional form of genius published in 2000, eight years after Bloom had died of AIDS. Bellow's Professor Ravelstein, a cartoonish depiction of Bloom, was credible because Bloom already loomed large in the American imagination as a caricature of himself. Bellow, in fact, had a lot to do with such Bloom lore, even well before he wrote *Ravelstein*. He also authored the renowned foreword to *Closing*, announcing in the first sentence: "Professor Bloom has his own way of doing things." According to Bellow, Bloom refused to stoop to the level of his philistine contemporaries, preferring instead to keep company with the likes of Aristotle. By encouraging readers to think of Bloom as a renegade genius, Bellow also invited mockery. Philosopher Robert Paul Wolff playfully suggested that Bloom was a figment of Bellow's literary imagination.

> Saul Bellow has demonstrated that among his other well-recognized literary gifts is an unsuspected bent for daring satire. What Bellow has done, quite simply, is to write an entire coruscatingly funny novel in the form of a pettish, bookish, grumpy, reactionary complaint against the last two decades. The "author" of this tirade, one of Bellow's most fully-realized literary creations, is a mid-fiftyish Professor at the University of Chicago, to whom Bellow gives the evocative name "Bloom." Bellow appears in the book only as the author of an eight-page "Foreword," in which he introduces us to his principal and only character.

The idea that helped make Bloom a cultural marvel—the notion of him as a sage among boors, sent from some distant past to rescue civilization from the abyss—was also what helped make him an easy target for ridicule. For better or worse, this perception also secured *Closing of the American Mind*'s place as the most important text of the culture wars—the culture wars' über-text—even though Bloom insisted it belonged "to neither political party."[25]

Of course, *Closing* was also significant for reasons of substance; it attracted plenty of critics more concerned with Bloom's argument than with his aura. The most common point of substance made against Bloom was that his antimodernist philosophy stemmed from his discomfort with the demographic changes in higher education. Historian Lawrence Levine wrote an entire book on this premise, appropriately titled *The Opening of the American Mind.* "As the university becomes more open to and representative of the diverse peoples, experiences, traditions, and cultures that compose America," Levine contended, "its impulse to find explanations for those parts of our history and our culture we have ignored grows proportionately." In relating curricular revision to demographic transformation, Levine sought to ease concerns about relativism. He argued that most American academics were not "Nietzscheanized" leftists who espoused a radical form of moral relativism. Rather, they were mild cultural relativists who believed that people who live in a multicultural society like America should be broad-minded. In short, most academics were multiculturalists. But, Levine argued, multiculturalism was the very thing that Bloom feared. "Bloom's anxiety was not relieved by the fact that what cultural relativism commonly taught students is not to make a simple-minded equation between everything as equal," he wrote, "but rather to be open to the reality that all peoples and societies have cultures which we have to respect to the extent that we take the trouble to understand how they operate and what they believe."[26]

A less common critique, but one that had equally important implications for the culture wars in the academy, was that tight linkages between epistemology and political ideology, whether assumed by a traditionalist like Bloom or an academic leftist like Levine, make no sense. In other words, philosophic relativism does not necessarily correlate to leftism any more than philosophic absolutism equates to conservatism. In philosopher Richard Rorty's memorable metaphor, one could display an abiding interest in both "Trotsky and wild orchids," as Rorty did as an adolescent, but that does not then entail that an attraction to leftist politics has anything to do with an aesthetic appreciation for noncultivated flowers. "Disagreements among intellectuals as to whether truth is timeless," Rorty argued in a critical review of *Closing,* "or whether the 'inalienable rights' of the Declaration are 'grounded' in something non-historical, or are instead admirable recent inventions (like education for women, or the transistor), are just not that important in deciding how elections go, or how much resistance fascist takeovers encounter." In other words, Rorty echoed Todd Gitlin's assessment that the politics of the English department have nothing to do with the politics of the White House—but with a twist. Rorty thought there was no plausible way to rationalize a political position by recourse to philosophic or aesthetic foundations. He willingly admitted that his defense of social democracy was entirely arbitrary.[27]

In contrast to Rorty, Gitlin believed that leftist demands for equality were grounded in universal impulses. Given this, even though the former president of SDS was far from conservative, Gitlin's purpose in fighting the academic culture wars was to put a stop to those academic leftists whose emphasis on relativistic notions of identity represented the "twilight of equality." In this Gitlin was far from alone. One major fault line in the culture wars, though largely unnoticed beyond the ivory tower, was between two Lefts. On the one hand was an academic Left interested in either identity politics or theories that delegitimize universal claims to truth. On the other hand was a political Left that believed their causes were better served when grounded in universal assertions about justice and human agency.[28]

One of the more famous academic scandals of the era, the so-called de Man affair, illustrated these complexities. In 1987, four years after his death, a researcher discovered that Paul de Man, the most famous deconstructionist this side of Derrida, had written hundreds of articles for a Belgian newspaper operated by Nazi collaborators during World War II. In one such essay de Man claimed that "a solution to the Jewish problem that would aim at creation of a Jewish colony isolated from Europe would not result, for the literary life of the West, in deplorable consequences." Although de Man's other wartime articles were devoid of such blatant anti-Semitism, the fact that he offered his literary talents to a collaborationist newspaper meant that he helped whitewash Nazi crimes. No doubt inferring as much himself, de Man hid his collaborationist past as he climbed the academic food chain to become perhaps the most renowned professor in the English department at Yale University, a department full of famous scholars. His many friends and admirers were stunned by the revelations. But for his detractors, de Man's disturbing past operated as the smoking gun that demonstrated the nihilism of his deconstructionist theories. Or worse yet, it was evidence that his radical form of literary relativism was merely a retroactive excuse for the sins of his past. To make this charge stick, de Man's critics repeatedly quoted two sentences from his 1979 book *Allegories of Reading*: "It is always possible to excise guilt because the experience always exists simultaneously as fictional discourse and as empirical event and it is never possible to decide which one of the two possibilities is the right one. The indecision makes it possible to excuse the bleakest of crimes."[29]

By the late 1980s *deconstruction* had become a generic if pretentious signifier for much of what went for academic inquiry. In the words of one critic, it was "the squiggle of fancy French mustard on the hot dog of banal observations." And yet deconstruction did indeed offer a new theoretical elocution, particularly in the writings of French philosopher Jacques Derrida. Although de Man was the best-known American deconstructionist, the theory became synonymous with Derrida, who cast a huge shadow over the humanities in the United States. Derrida's sway was evident at the annual meetings of the Modern Language Association (MLA), where he was the most frequently cited scholar during the 1980s. At its most basic level, Derrida's theory was that all Western philosophical concepts are false, grounded as they are in metaphysical oppositions between mind and body, subject and object, reader and text. When Derrida notoriously wrote that "there is nothing outside the text," his intention was not to deny physical reality. Rather, he argued that there is no way of knowing such reality unmediated by texts. This might seem like a liberating insight, particularly to those theorists equipped with the interpretive tools necessary to decode texts. But, Derrida cautioned, incommensurability is a problem inherent to language. De Man put this in simple terms: "Sign and meaning can never coincide." De Man also put it in terms that imply an existential crisis: "Death is a displaced name for a linguistic predicament." In other words, humans will never have words for communicating the quandary of their existence. So deconstruction not only signaled the death of the author; it also heralded the end of all norms. If every attempt to understand fellow humans is doomed to failure, standards cannot be conceived as anything other than arbitrary.[30]

Conservatives rejected deconstruction as an attack on the very idea of meaning, and therefore on the very idea of America. Right-wing columnist Charles Krauthammer wrote in 1990 that deconstruction "poses a threat that no outside agent in this post-Soviet world can match." But the deeply pessimistic implications of deconstruction also frustrated several on the Left. For example, David Lehman, a professor of poetry, wrote a popular book about the de Man affair in which he fretted about the effect deconstruction had on the liberal quest to expand knowledge about a common humanity. Since deconstruction held that "language is inherently a slippery medium," he argued, it logically "follows that any attempt to represent other people and places must be held suspect." This deconstructionist theory of difference called into question the very premise of humanist disciplines like anthropology. "To the deconstructively minded anthropologist," Lehman wrote, "description is necessarily infused with ideology, and reports from the field of a third world country may, whatever the writer's intentions, help perpetuate a colonialist perspective." In other words, since the only way to describe another culture is through signs, and since signs never convey meaning in ways intended by their author, it is impossible to do justice to another culture, particularly as a privileged outsider. This aspect of deconstruction helped shape postcolonial theory, a related school of thought that sought to show how the colonizer can never know the colonized on any other terms. Deconstruction, understood as such, was simply another in a long line of theories about how observer and observed can never be understood in isolation from one another. But for those liberals like Lehman who wanted their knowledge to contribute to the cause of a more just world, deconstruction seemed to have a paralyzing effect. By militating against the possibility of intelligible communication, it limited the prospects for justice, which demands agreed-upon conceptions of the good life. In short, deconstruction negated the utopian possibilities that had long inspired a universalist left.[31]

Such skepticism regarding deconstruction informed the approach many left-leaning writers took after de Man's collaborationist essays were unearthed. They included historian Jon Wiener, author of a 1988 article published in *The Nation*, "Deconstructing de Man," the most widely cited piece on the affair. Wiener quoted several leftist scholars who "argued that the presuppositions of deconstruction—that literature is not part of a knowable social and political reality, that one must be resigned to the impossibility of truth—make it at worst nihilistic or implicitly authoritarian and at best an academic self-indulgence." Building on this, most leftist critics of deconstruction sought to somehow link de Man's early collaborationism and his later deconstructionism. Historian Anson Rabinbach argued that such connections were not to be found "in their content, which is quite different." Rather, he more modestly argued that such associations were located "in the attitude of exhaustion in the face of politics, the feeling of despair at the possibilities that history offers." Others went further. Jeffrey Mehlman, a professor of French, contended the revelations about de Man's past opened up "grounds for viewing the whole of deconstruction as a vast amnesty project for the politics of collaboration in France during World War II." In other words, these critics rejected Rorty's premise about the lack of a correlation between political ideology and epistemology: it seemed Trotsky and orchids, or in this case, Vichy and deconstruction, indeed went hand in glove.[32]

In contrast, noted deconstructionist J. Hillis Miller, de Man's colleague at Yale, told Wiener that he saw "no connection between de Man's collaborationist writings and deconstruction." More specifically, Miller argued that in de Man's deconstructionist works "there is no trace remaining of the nationalist and organicist ideas" evinced by his World War II–era texts. Derrida agreed, insisting that his late friend "had broken radically" with whatever ideology he possessed during the war: "[T]here was no trace to my knowledge either in his life or in his remarks or in his texts that allows one to think the opposite." Yet rather than stopping there, Miller, Derrida, and most of de Man's advocates also argued that deconstruction was an implicit repudiation of fascism. In other words, deconstructionists defended their school of thought not by following the logic of Rorty's entreaty about Trotsky and orchids but rather by reversing the terms laid out by their left-wing critics. Whereas the early de Man's belief that aesthetic forms grow organically from national cultures made him susceptible to anti-Semitic and fascist thought, they contended, the later de Man's antiessentialism made him a champion of democratic freedom. Deconstruction in this way was a bulwark against the rigid ideologies that make totalitarianism possible. According to his followers, it was the means by which de Man atoned for the sins of his youth.[33]

Although both critics and apologists overstated the relationship between de Man's collaboration and his deconstruction, that the debate was fought on such philosophical grounds highlighted one of the defining questions of the culture wars: could the United States have a national purpose in the absence of foundational principles? Many intellectuals on both the Right and the Left viewed deconstruction with alarm precisely because they believed foundations necessary in their quest to align the nation with higher ideals. They worried about the apparent decline of principles that once bound Americans together in common cause. And their declension narratives usually started with the sixties. For example, Paul Berman, one of the more prominent liberal critics of the academic Left, contended that the New Left's post-1968 revolt against Enlightenment values spawned relativistic academic discourses such as deconstruction, which he otherwise described as "extravaganzas of cynicism." Such theories, he argued, fit perfectly in the post-sixties academy, where it was widely assumed that dead white men achieved world domination "by using terms like rationalism, humanism, universality, and literary merit to persuade other people of their own inferiority."[34]

The nation that made sense to those like Berman seemed to be coming apart at the seams. The philosophical anarchism they detected in deconstruction was but one symptom of this larger national crisis. Another warning sign was the tribalism of identity politics, also born in the sixties. Todd Gitlin's critique of identity politics, refracted through the lens of 1969, when SDS suffered a traumatic schism over whether or not to focus its activism on third world revolutionary movements, exemplified the political Left's antipathy to the academic Left. For Gitlin, warring factions of the post-1969 New Left represented a fork in the road between "good" and "bad" sixties activists—between those committed to the common American good and those dedicated to racial and ethnic separatism. The latter, Gitlin argued, helped give birth to the "twilight of common dreams," the tribal condition of the Left that otherwise went by the name of identity politics. "The cant of identity underlies identity politics," Gitlin explained, "which proposes to deduce a position, a tradition, a deep truth, or a way of life from a fact of birth, physiognomy, national origin, sex, or physical disability." Gitlin, Berman, and other liberals saw fragmentation as inherently conservative. They argued instead that an Enlightenment appeal to common humanity was the best response to discrimination. For conservatives, however, discrimination was not the dilemma. Rather, in their view the hyperattention paid to racial and sexual discrimination was the central problem with those who controlled the nation's institutions of higher education.[35]

As a result of such conservative concerns, an evocative new meme wormed its way into American political discourse in the early 1990s. It went as follows: An elitist class of intellectuals sought to police the thought of those American citizens whom they believed clung to racist, sexist, jingoistic, and other atavistic attitudes. In policing language, it was believed that the American professoriate endangered free speech in the name of what came to be known as political correctness, "PC" for short. President George H. W. Bush gave life to this convincing narrative in a May 4, 1991, commencement address at the University of Michigan. "Ironically, on the 200th anniversary of our Bill of Rights, we find free speech under assault throughout the United States, including on some college campuses," Bush warned. "The notion of political correctness has ignited controversy across the land. And although the movement arises from the laudable desire to sweep away the debris of racism and sexism and hatred, it replaces old prejudices with new ones. It declares certain topics off-limits, certain expression off-limits, even certain gestures off-limits."[36]

To the degree that political correctness was a genuine phenomenon, it took shape due to historical exigencies: latent racial and sexual tensions surfaced as a result of the post-sixties integration of diverse peoples and perspectives into the American system of higher education. Given this, conflict on college campuses was unavoidable, and the fact that universities instituted speech codes prohibiting discriminatory language was unsurprising. Simply put, university administrators believed that regulating racially and sexually charged words would reduce racially and sexually charged violence. Academic leftists defended speech codes on more rarefied grounds. Consistent with their theories about the determinative power of language, they believed preventing colloquial language that conveyed racial and sexual hierarchies would help end discrimination. Such an instrumental theory about the power of language and culture was the opposite of the position taken by liberals in censorship debates over art and popular culture, demonstrating perhaps that cultural theory often flowed from political positioning, rather than vice versa.[37]

Conservatives believed that speech codes—the quintessential expression of political correctness—generated an atmosphere of campus repression comparable to McCarthyism. Some liberals agreed. Gitlin, for instance, believed that "a bitter intolerance emanates from much of the academic left." Such "bitter intolerance" seemed to be one of the driving forces in the campaign to deny conservative literary critic Carol Iannone's 1991 appointment to the National Council on the Humanities, an advisory body to the NEH. The putative rationale given by those who opposed Iannone was that she was unqualified for such a lofty position. In a widely circulated letter sent to Democratic senator Edward Kennedy, chair of the Committee on Labor and Human Resources that would determine Iannone's fate, Phyllis Franklin,

the executive director of the MLA, argued that a scholar of "such junior standing and slim scholarly production" was not a good candidate
to advise Lynne Cheney, the chair of the NEH. Iannone was less than
a decade removed from receiving her doctorate, and her only teaching
position until then was as a nontenured visiting professor at a community college. Cheney, who nominated Iannone, countered with a
populist appeal: Iannone should not be disqualified merely because
her teaching experience was at a community college. Rather, Cheney
argued, such experience would serve her well in an advisory capacity.
The NEH needed more input from scholars not cloistered off in elite
research universities.[38]

Of course, more to the point than Iannone's experience, or lack
thereof, was Iannone's ideological orientation. That she helped found
the National Association of Scholars (NAS), established in 1987 in order to oppose "liberal bias" in academia, burnished her appeal with
conservatives like Cheney. In turn, academic leftists objected to Iannone primarily because of her political biases. Franklin's letter to
Kennedy noted disapprovingly that Iannone's curriculum vitae publications consisted almost exclusively of articles published in the neoconservative magazine *Commentary*. One such piece, "Literature by
Quota," asserted that prizes bestowed upon Alice Walker for her novel
The Color Purple "seemed less a recognition of literary achievement
than some official act of reparation." Franklin charged, bluntly, that
Iannone's *Commentary* essays were "not contributions to scholarship." In response, Senator Daniel Patrick Moynihan expressed dismay over the snide allegation that Iannone was "merely a *Commentary*
writer." "In London, Paris, Rome, Stockholm, to say of a professor of
literature that his or her principal work has appeared in *Commentary*
is," he proclaimed with rhetorical flourish, "to say that this is a critic
of the first rank. In the tradition, say, of Lionel Trilling."[39]

Moynihan's use of the Senate floor to defend a magazine was a curious move, even if his old friend Norman Podhoretz edited the magazine in question. Moynihan took such an extreme measure because he
was viscerally offended that the nation's supposed cultural gatekeepers
deemed *Commentary* unworthy. To him it defined the pinnacle of the
American literary imagination. In a similar vein, Gertrude Himmelfarb wrote to Kennedy that Iannone would be a welcome presence on
the National Council on the Humanities precisely because she wrote
for *Commentary*. Himmelfarb argued that Iannone would "bridge the

gap between the academy and the literate public. With the rise in recent years of highly specialized, almost arcane modes of academic discourse in the humanities, that gap has approached the dimensions of a chasm." Despite such a rousing defense by well-respected figures, the Kennedy-led Senate committee rejected Iannone's nomination by a 9–8 vote entirely down party lines. Orrin Hatch, one of the Republicans who voted in Iannone's favor, reacted with an angry rhetorical question: "If this isn't political correctness, what the hell is it?"[40]

Cheney may not have liked the outcome of that particular brawl over the direction of the NEH. But her overt politicization of the NEH, which was unparalleled even in comparison to her predecessor Bennett, created a context for such partisanship. Even though Cheney failed to secure Iannone a seat on the NEH, she was generally successful in surrounding herself with like-minded lieutenants. Moreover, Cheney used her pocket veto to scuttle nearly all proposals that included mere mention of race or gender—scribbling on the margins of such proposals, "not for me!"—even when her conservative council voted to endorse some such projects on their merits. One example among many: Cheney rejected a proposal from the Fowler Museum of Cultural History at the University of California at Los Angeles to help fund an exhibit on Haitian vodou. Cheney also removed the NEH label from the critically acclaimed PBS series *The Africans*, a project the endowment had already funded. Instead of works tinged with race and gender analysis, or works that reflected critically on American culture, Cheney green-lighted safer projects such as Ken Burns's mawkish PBS series *The Civil War*. For such actions, academics in the humanities came to loathe Cheney. In their eyes, she had hijacked a crucial and honorable government agency, making it an arm of the conservative movement.[41]

When Bill Clinton took the White House in 1993, conservatives were reluctant to concede control of the NEH, which they had enjoyed control of for twelve years under the leadership of Bennett and Cheney. Many of them opposed Clinton's nominee to chair the NEH, Sheldon Hackney, president of the University of Pennsylvania. In the months leading up to Hackney's confirmation hearings, several prominent conservative pundits, including Rush Limbaugh, George Will, and Charles Krauthammer, targeted him as an example of all that was wrong with higher education. Ralph Reed, executive director of the Christian Coalition, dubbed Hackney "the Pope of Political Correctness." John Leo, who wrote about higher education for *U.S. News and World Report,* created a "Sheldon Award" for cowardly university presidents.[42]

Hackney came in for this abuse due to high-profile PC scandals that rocked Penn during his tenure as president. Such hullabaloos were thanks in no small part to the *Daily Pennsylvanian,* the student-run newspaper, which persistently aggravated racial tensions. One of its regular columnists, conservative Gregory Pavlik, wrote a piece in which he agreed with libertarian provocateur Lew Rockwell's statement that the number of blacks lynched in American history paled in comparison to the number of whites murdered by blacks. Black students and faculty lodged several formal complaints, but since the *Daily Pennsylvanian* operated independently of university administration, Hackney's hands were tied. Dissatisfied, a group of black students committed a mild act of civil disobedience on April 15, 1993, by attempting to steal every copy of that day's print of the *Daily Pennsylvanian.* Some of the students were caught in the act and arrested by campus police. No doubt aware of the situation's precariousness, university officials let the students off with what amounted to a slap on the wrist. Insulted by such inaction, the *Daily Pennsylvanian* editorialized that Hackney had violated its freedom of press, establishing a plot line picked up by conservatives around the nation.[43]

Against the backdrop of Hackney's struggles with a politically incorrect student newspaper, an even greater controversy—what became known as "the water buffalo incident"—stained his presidency. On a late night in January 1993, a group of black female students were on the campus quad celebrating the founding of their sorority when male students from a nearby dormitory began shouting insults, including, allegedly, "nigger bitches." When campus police arrived at the scene, only one of the men, Eden Jacobowitz, admitted to having screamed what sounded like a racial epithet. "Shut up, you water buffalo. If you want to have a party, there is a zoo over there," Jacobowitz admitting to shouting while pointing in the direction of the Philadelphia Zoo north of campus. Jacobowitz, an Israeli, defended his choice of words by explaining that, translated into Hebrew, "water buffalo" was slang for a loud or rowdy person. Despite this rationale, the university judicial inquiry officer charged Jacobowitz with racial harassment. Conservative Penn history professor Alan Kors, a charter member of NAS, asked Hackney to intervene on Jacobowitz's behalf.

Hackney declined, claiming that he did not have such authority. Jacobowitz and Kors then took their case to the conservative press. On April 26, 1993, the *Wall Street Journal* ran an editorial titled "Buffaloed at Penn." "A freshman, the latest victim of the ideological fever known as political correctness, goes on trial at the University of Pennsylvania today," the *Journal* editorialized. "It's not irrelevant to note that the head of this institution, Sheldon Hackney, is President Clinton's nominee to head the National Endowment for the Humanities and a man, university spokesmen insist, committed to free speech."[44]

The "water buffalo incident" made headlines during another high-profile media blitz about another politically correct Clinton nominee, Lani Guinier, the so-called quota queen. Clinton selected Guinier to be his assistant attorney general for civil rights before withdrawing his nomination in a capitulation to right-wing demonization. However, Clinton stuck by his nomination of Hackney, who seemed more willing to say what was necessary to quiet critics. Asked about political correctness at his confirmation hearing, Hackney warned that it could be a "serious problem if it were to capture a campus, if it were to become the orthodoxy shutting out other points of view." In further testimony, he proclaimed that "it would, of course, be disastrous if a university, or if higher education in general, were to be captured by the extreme postmodern position." Hackney had first made his mark in academia as a historian of the American South whose methodologically traditional scholarship bore no mark of the hyperrelativistic modes of thinking that had become influential in the humanities. And yet it is doubtful Hackney would have matter-of-factly dismissed such academic trends in the context of, say, a seminar room discussion. That he did so in the halls of Congress was no doubt because he thought his successful confirmation depended on it. In his memoirs, written after his four-year term as chair of the NEH, Hackney was far more astute in his analysis of what actually represented a "serious problem" in higher education. "Nothing appeared on the crisis calendar during my years as president of Penn more than matters of race and cultural diversity, and I don't think Penn was peculiar in that regard," he wrote. "One of the lessons of the 1960s is that the stresses and strains of the broader society are going to crop up more quickly on college campuses than elsewhere."[45]

Many conservative critics of the academy also recognized that the politics of race, and sex, were at the heart of culture wars in American higher education. The brash young writer Dinesh D'Souza was a case in point. If Bloom's *The Closing of the American Mind* was only implicitly about race and sex, D'Souza's 1991 best seller *Illiberal Education* was much more up front about such matters, made patently clear by the book's subtitle: *The Politics of Race and Sex on Campus.* Even though *Illiberal Education* borrowed heavily from previous conservative books about higher education, including *Closing,* D'Souza helped clarify the terms of the debate in ways that Bloom could not. D'Souza wrote a clear narrative that not only described the many sins of the academic Left, including political correctness, multiculturalism, affirmative action, and literary relativism, but also managed to tie these phenomena together in convincing fashion. In short, *Illiberal Education* was nicely packaged, helping to explain its considerable impact. Of course D'Souza's success was also predicated on the precipitous growth of right-wing foundations and think tanks, which by the 1980s formed a veritable counteracademy. D'Souza was the prize product of this new world of conservative ideas. As an undergraduate at Dartmouth College, D'Souza had edited the *Dartmouth Review,* one of a growing number of student newspapers funded by the conservative Olin Foundation. His work at the *Dartmouth Review,* where he habitually poked fun at left-wing academic shibboleths, caught the attention of the American Enterprise Institute, which awarded him a fellowship to fund the research that would become his book on higher education.[46]

Illiberal Education targeted what D'Souza termed the "victim's revolution" that had transformed American campuses in the wake of the sixties—a revolution "conducted in the name of those who suffer from the effects of race and gender discrimination in America." D'Souza argued that the special dispensations afforded to minority and women students, in the form of affirmative action, violated the very premise of America. University admissions, he believed, should align with the universal standards codified by the founding fathers: equal opportunity and equal responsibility. Quotas obliterated uniform standards of justice, a dangerous development since, "as Aristotle observed," such uniformity was "the only lasting basis for community." D'Souza also applied this framework to the university curriculum, which increasingly taught students that "justice is simply the will of the stronger party; that standards and values are arbitrary, and the ideal of the educated person is largely a figment of bourgeois white male ideology."

In this way, the victim's revolutionaries had joined forces with the relativistic literary theorists schooled in Foucault and Derrida. "Because the old notion of neutral standards corresponded with a white male faculty regime at American universities," he wrote, "minority and feminist scholars have grown increasingly attached to the *au courant* scholarship, which promises to dismantle and subvert these old authoritative structures." Whereas generations of scholars celebrated the transcendent genius of Shakespeare, a new generation of scholars taught overtly ideological texts such as *I, Rigoberta Menchu*, the autobiography of a Nobel Prize–winning Guatemalan activist. D'Souza believed that the new literary theorists, rather than make the case for multicultural texts on their aesthetic merits, sneaked substandard works into their classrooms with claims that the very idea of the canon was illegitimate, a cover for white supremacy and patriarchy.[47]

Another well-worn idea that D'Souza relied upon was the neoconservative trope about an adversarial "new class" that threatened the fabric of American cultural norms. Such a notion, which had a long history, became increasingly popular in the 1990s. As neoconservative critic Roger Kimball wrote in his 1990 book *Tenured Radicals*: "Academia (like other aspects of elite cultural life), has reneged on its compact with society." Impugning an elitist "new class" provided conservative critics of the academy with populist credentials. Siding with "the people" against the "special interests"—in this case, against a professoriate that sought to advance a hodgepodge agenda that Kimball called "left eclecticism"—was a better approach to political success than elitism. And yet, ironically, one of the central criticisms conservatives made about "new class" professors was that their modish theories had a leveling effect. Complaining that academics had embraced "the degraded and demotic world of pop culture," Kimball bemoaned that "Aristotle's *Metaphysics*, a television program, and a French novel" were all treated equally, as part of some unified "general text." In other words, even though Kimball belittled academic snobbery with the best of right-wing populists, he also preserved the right of the critic to differentiate the sublime from the vulgar. He was a traditionalist who held the quaint idea that some aesthetic forms are better than others because they get us closer to the truth. And even though he wrote that the "truth does not play political favorites," deep down Kimball surely believed that conservatives had a better read on it.[48]

Cheney, always the partisan, made the truth a partisan issue in her

1995 book, nonironically titled *Telling the Truth*, a summary of the academic culture wars that she played such a key role in. Cheney critiqued academic leftists, the bane of her existence while she chaired the NEH, for their "view that there is no truth." She scorned the fashion of reading power and hierarchy into everything, even canonical texts. "The humanities are about more than politics, about more than social power," Cheney argued. "What gives them their abiding worth are truths that, transcending accidents of class, race, and gender, speak to us all." Cheney blamed faulty academic thinking on the importation of Foucault's "relativism without recourse." Where Cheney saw truth, Foucault saw "regimes of truth." Although Cheney's antirelativism was a common feature of the conservative critique of the academy, she used such notions to score partisan political points to an unprecedented degree. While arguing that presidential campaigns had devolved into contests between two competing "regimes of truth," she particularly condemned Clinton's "postmodern presidency" and the biased press that enabled it. "That a liberal bias became evident then suggests," she argued, "that the kind of thinking so common on campuses—the idea, for example, that objectivity is an illusion that only the foolish value—was beginning to have a significant impact on journalism." If the press judged Clinton favorably, relativistic modes of interpretation must have been at work. To this extent, postmodernism was a liberal plot.[49]

By the 1990s *postmodernism* had become the preferred label to describe the many fashionable modes of academic thought that had been at the center of a decade-long cultural conflict. The culture wars in higher education, then, were fueled by anxieties about postmodernism. Conservatives believed that too many Americans were succumbing to postmodern ways of thinking that denied the truth about American goodness. They fretted that postmodern America was splintering into tribal factions, each with its own claim to the truth. Fears that had long been expressed about modern America had taken on a panicked tone. As Gertrude Himmelfarb eulogized: "The beasts of modernism have mutated into the beasts of postmodernism—relativism into nihilism, amorality into immorality, irrationality into insanity, sexual deviancy into polymorphous perversity."[50]

Some leftists, echoing concerns they expressed about deconstruction during the Paul de Man affair, joined conservatives in agonizing about the effects of postmodernism. One such leftist, physicist Alan

Sokal, submitted a hilarious, intentionally nonsensical paper to *Social Text*, an elite journal of cultural studies that specialized in postmodern analysis. Remarkably, the *Social Text* editors published Sokal's hoax essay, titled "Transgressing the Boundaries: Toward a Transformative Hermeneutics of Quantum Gravity." Sokal made a number of ridiculous arguments in the article. In pretending to deconstruct the laws of physics, he argued: "[T]he π of Euclid and the G of Newton, formerly thought to be constant and universal, are now perceived in their ineluctable historicity; and the putative observer becomes fatally de-centered, disconnected from any epistemic link to a space-time point that can no longer be defined by geometry alone." As if this were not enough, Sokal concluded his faux piece with a Derrida-like overstatement: "[P]hysical 'reality,' no less than social 'reality,' is at bottom a social and linguistic construct." After he revealed that his article was a ruse, Sokal's hoax was reported on the front page of the *New York Times*. Sokal confessed that he pulled his prank as "an unabashed Old Leftist who never quite understood how deconstruction was supposed to help the working class." He insisted that he was not against historical or sociological investigations of the production of scientific knowledge, but he maintained that such research, however compelling, had "no bearing whatsoever on the ontological question." Put differently, the nucleus of an atom can be made to split no matter the "militaristic orientation of American science" that led to such a discovery.[51]

Fredric Jameson—who practically set the terms for discussing postmodernism with his 1984 article "Postmodernism, or The Cultural Logic of Late Capitalism"—also fretted about the political possibilities of postmodernism. He believed that postmodernism limited the possibilities for emancipatory change by rendering human solidarity impossible. Fracture, whether political, in the form of identity politics, or epistemological, in the form of postmodernism, was not liberating. Rather, it was a product of political reaction. Whereas the modern era of capitalism ushered in mass movements that made the world a better place, the postmodern era brought atomization that saw the weakening or even dissolution of such working-class cohesion. For Jameson, then, the culture wars were symptomatic of the postindustrial transformation of capitalism.[52]

This is not to say that the culture wars were merely a sideshow to politics proper, something navel-gazing English professors did while more serious-minded people strategized about how to take back the White House or, better yet, how to organize the working class into a revolutionary vanguard. No, the implication of Jameson's analysis was that the culture wars were unavoidable. To the degree that a consensus about how to think about America ever existed, there was no going back. The culture wars were the new American norm. The culture wars were the defining narrative of postmodern America.

9

The Contested American Past

History was all the rage for late-twentieth-century Americans. Genealogical research became increasingly common, museum and monument construction boomed, and Civil War reenactment mushroomed into a veritable national pastime. In 1995 the A&E Television Networks launched the History Channel, which immediately drew high ratings for a programming schedule that included a hefty dose of shows about World War II, particularly about Hitler.

The Walt Disney Company sought to cash in on this obsession in the early 1990s with a theme park dedicated to American history. Disney's America was to have been part heritage, part amusement, a mix of "serious" and "fun." Similar to other living history museums such as Colonial Williamsburg, Disney's America was to simulate momentous events in American history. But in contrast, Disney's America patrons would get a taste of authentic history from the vantage point of amusement park rides. Disney CEO Michael Eisner highlighted the serious side of the park by proclaiming that it would reject a "Pollyanna view" of American history. He promised to "show the Civil War with all its racial conflict" and even discussed tackling the Vietnam War. Such an approach attracted criticism from all over the political map. Liberal political cartoonist Tom Toles ridiculed the idea by superimposing Goofy on a mock-up of the iconic image of a naked girl, badly burned by napalm, fleeing US-sponsored South Vietnamese soldiers. Conservative William Kristol argued that if Disney was "going to have a schlocky version of American history, it should at least be a schlocky, patriotic, and heroic version." Alas, Disney scrapped its plans for a history theme park due in part to such widespread skepticism.[1]

The Disney history flap demonstrated that although Americans were taking an extraordinary interest in the nation's past, they disagreed fervently about how it should be represented. History wars gripped the nation. Growing numbers of Americans took to heart George Orwell's truism that "who controls the past controls the future." For conservatives, history would redeem the nation from all that had gone wrong since the sixties. History would especially help Americans overcome the trauma of the Vietnam War. Norman Podhoretz argued that the history of America's role in that war, which had been relegated to "the forensic equivalent of an unmarked grave," needed to be revised and that the health of the nation depended on it. This became evident to Podhoretz when, during the 1980 presidential campaign, Ronald Reagan called the Vietnam War a "noble cause." Although pundits characterized Reagan's historical revision as a blunder, Podhoretz wrote that "Reagan's gaffe was closer to the truth" than most assumed. He contended that the United States had failed to win the war in part because too many Americans denied that it was morally just. This "stab in the back" elocution served as the crux of how conservatives thought history might redeem the nation. If the United States of America was to return to being the world's indispensable nation—a city upon a hill— conservatives had to win the struggle over its historical meaning.[2]

For those on the Left, history was no less important. The left-wing interpretation of American history, like the right-wing version, often acted as a form of redemption. The greater attention paid to the history of blacks, Native Americans, Chicanos, immigrants, women, and workers was in part a means of redeeming the humanity of people previously swept away by traditional historical narratives that focused on the role of powerful white men. But left-leaning Americans also understood the purpose of history as a tool for social transformation. Howard Zinn, who did more than any single individual to popularize a leftist version of American history, advised that historians could encourage radical change by giving voice to history's voiceless. This was Zinn's overriding purpose for writing *A People's History of the United States*, which has sold more than two million copies since it was published in 1980. Zinn's magnum opus was an alternative to those traditional textbooks that told stories of unbending, elite-driven progress. *A People's History* was explicitly framed from the perspective of the downtrodden. Zinn's haunting descriptions of suffering—by the dispossessed, slaves, factory workers, and victims of war—were meant to evoke empathy for the subjugated. But perhaps more important than highlighting those who suffered at the hands of a pitiless elite, *A People's History* emphasized those Americans who resisted injustice. Zinn sought to connect the past to the present in a fashion that he believed would prove useful in the promotion of "justice and brotherhood." Writing an alternative American history was, for Zinn, planting the seeds out of which an alternative American future might flower.[3]

Most Americans who read *A People's History of the United States* undoubtedly considered it a major revision. But in fact Zinn's book was a work of synthesis made possible by a growing body of scholarship, known as social history, which had already unearthed the histories of peoples long neglected by a discipline overattuned to political and economic elites. Social historians sought to prove that even oppressed peoples helped determine the warp and woof of history—that even the wretched had "agency." Gary Nash's groundbreaking 1974 book *Red, White, and Black: The Peoples of Early America* argued that the history of American Indians and black slaves was more than merely a by-product of forces set into motion by European settlers. Rather, the inarticulate hordes actively participated in the forging of a new world. "Africans were not merely enslaved. Indians were not merely driven from the land," Nash explained. "To include them in our history in this way, simply as victims of the more powerful Europeans, is no better than to exclude them altogether. It is to render voiceless, nameless, and faceless people who powerfully affected the course of our historical development as a nation."[4]

Social historians maintained that their nontraditional subject matter allowed for a more accurate reading of the past. American Indians, after all, made up a majority of the population of North America during the colonial era. Not accounting for their influence was simply bad history. Of course the historians who resisted their claims on the discipline—those who saw social historians as barbarians at the gates—often invoked the specter of objectivity. In the pages of the *American Historical Review*, Irwin Unger charged that social historians were motivated by an "exaggerated present-mindedness," "not by the natural dialogue of the discipline but by the concerns of the outside cultural and political world." Social historians responded by claiming the very mantle of professional standards that their critics accused them of subverting. Jesse Lemisch, who helped usher in "history from the bottom up" with his groundbreaking work on merchant seamen during the Revolutionary War, scolded the traditionalists: "We will simply not allow you the luxury of continuing to call yourselves politically neutral. We are in the libraries, writing history, trying to cure it of your partisan and self-congratulatory fictions, trying to come a little closer to finding out how things actually were." In other words, even though social historians were revising the American narrative in radical ways, they shared the methodological and epistemological assumptions of the traditionalist historians with whom they did battle. Whether studies of the founding fathers got us closer to the historical truth than investigations of Revolutionary-era proto-lumpenproletariat was up for debate, not whether or not it was possible to decode objective historical truth in the first place.[5]

Even though social historians believed themselves purveyors of truth, they also tended to be explicit about their political positioning. This was because they were hyperattentive to how their scholarship was a radical departure in the discipline. As Nash argued, historians could no longer deny the simple fact that "we read, think, and write selectively and in ways that reflect our cultural biases." The key to this recognition was that social historians were not the only biased scholars. Their traditionalist adversaries were equally compromised, if not more so for their refusal to recognize their own prejudices. Following in the footsteps of those who pioneered black, ethnic, and women's studies, social historians helped normalize the idea that historical writing, like all forms of knowledge, was value laden. The title of Zinn's autobiography, *You Can't Be Neutral on a Moving Train*, was the perfect metaphor for such conscious subjectivity. With a growing number of people entering the historical discipline admitting that their work was given direction by ideological considerations, historical knowledge fragmented. For leftist historians, this was an unavoidable consequence of their challenge to traditional historians, those who judged solely the deeds of rich white men to be the stuff of history. In this way social historians, perhaps unintentionally, undermined the premise of objectivity by revealing that historical narratives are always partial—historical interpretations are always political. As historians Joyce Appleby, Lynn Hunt, and Margaret Jacob put it: "It is as if the social historians with their passion for breaking apart the historical record had dug a potentially fatal hole into which history as a discipline might disappear altogether."[6]

Given that junior scholars were being conditioned into a discipline with competing schools of thought about what, if anything, counted as historical truth—and given that a growing number of them, like their counterparts in English departments, were reading antifoundationalists such as Foucault—it is easy to see, in retrospect, how historical interpretation increasingly became a consciously relativistic enterprise. It is also easy to see how the social turn was quickly followed by a cultural turn. Instead of excavating marginalized human experiences in order to revise an empirical historical narrative about America, cultural historians decoded the contextually specific meaning of cultural practices in order to understand how human beings adjusted to their unique situations. In addition to exhuming the social archive, such as legal records, to explain how marginalized people helped shape history, cultural historians sought out ephemera, such as images, to theorize about desire and other such intangible phenomena. In short, conceptualizations of power, always crucial to historical interpretation, had changed. Whereas social historians, like traditional political historians, understood power as palpable, as something people took and had taken from them, cultural historians understood power as protean, as something embedded in routines such as language and habits of consumption. Thus cultural historians investigated the ways in which cultural practices regulated hierarchical categories such as race and gender. In fact, demonstrating how supposedly neutral classifications like race and gender masked power became *the* project of cultural history. The rise of cultural history did not relegate politics to the margins of the discipline. Rather, everything historical was fair game for political analysis. Cultural history, in this way, should be thought of as a scholarly application of the sixties feminist slogan "The personal is political"—it should be considered part and parcel of the Left's cultural turn.[7]

The politicization of historical subjects beyond the purview of traditional political history infuriated traditionalist scholars like Gertrude Himmelfarb. In the 1980s, as she was gearing up for retirement from her position at the City University of New York, where she had taught history since 1965, Himmelfarb turned her considerable literary talents to fighting the history wars. Broadly speaking, she rejected the application of theoretical frameworks informed by Foucault and other Continental thinkers that relativized morality as an expression of power. More specifically, Himmelfarb objected to the politicization of history that she believed went hand in glove with the discipline's anachronistic hyperattentiveness to the "race/gender/class" holy trinity. "Any part of that trinity," she wrote, "involves a considerable revision of the past, but the whole requires nothing less than its deconstruction." Himmelfarb criticized the scholarship of feminist historian Joan Scott as representative of tendencies to politicization. Scott sought to "decode" the past for its implicit sexism, even or especially in situations where contemporaries failed to see sexism. Himmelfarb insisted that privileging gender was an ahistorical imposition of present concerns. "Contemporaries may have thought that their history was shaped by kings and statesmen, politics and diplomacy, constitutions and laws. New historians know better," Himmelfarb wrote. "They know that 'high politics' are ephemeral and epiphenomenal, to say nothing of being elitist and sexist." Unlike cultural historians, who viewed their historical subjects through the eyes of cultural historians, Himmelfarb allowed her historical subjects to speak for themselves, and she often liked what she heard, especially when writing about Victorian England, her primary area of expertise. Himmelfarb contrasted the moral certainty of Victorian English culture with the moral relativism of postmodern American culture. The latter was neatly represented by what she called "New History."[8]

In a 1989 *American Historical Review* roundtable that featured Himmelfarb's critique of disciplinary trends, Joan Scott countered Himmelfarb by quoting the American Historical Association (AHA)'s founding motto—"history is past politics and politics present history"—as a defense of New History. She believed the AHA maxim nicely described how cultural historians conceptualized politics beyond "formal operations of government" to include "contests that involve power in Michel Foucault's sense—power not only as a relationship of repression or domination but also as a set of relationships or processes that produce positive effects." Such a notion of power, in which people were understood to have acted on desire as much as on fear, implied that even the repressed were invested in "meanings of truth" that kept them in their allegorical shackles. Traditionalist historians like Himmelfarb objected to such a theory as an imposition of the historian's biases and thus as a relativistic distortion of the truth. Such complaints demonstrated to Scott that traditionalist historians, like the elite they venerated, mistakenly believed their particular views of the world were universal. She thought that traditionalist anxieties about relativism served as a cover for reactionary responses to the democratization of the historical enterprise. Attacks on new forms of historical interpretation were often motivated, consciously or not, by objections to the fact that New Historians focused on women and minorities. New History threatened, Scott wrote, "the uniformity, continuity, and homogeneity that orthodox historians have traditionally sought to impose." Historian Lawrence Levine put it in similar terms: "[T]he primary criticism of contemporary historiography has little to do with what kind of history we practice and almost everything to do with the subjects of that history."[9]

Even if traditionalists often conflated relativism with multiculturalism, plenty of historians, including those with leftist political commitments, fretted about a lack of concern for "telling the truth about history," as Appleby, Hunt, and Jacob titled their 1994 book. These three historians, although somewhat sympathetic to New Historians, nevertheless charged them with neglecting the long-standing purpose of historical craft: shedding light on truth. Indeed, Hayden White, one of the most prominent American theorists of new historical techniques, provocatively claimed that the work of the historian was no more than "a verbal structure in the form of a narrative prose discourse." In other words, for a cultural historian like White, historical truth was unknowable and, frankly, irrelevant. Historians, as such, were not that different from novelists. Both constructed narratives. Eschewing such an antinomian position, Appleby, Hunt, and Jacob argued in favor of "a democratic practice of history [that] encourages skepticism about dominant views, but at the same time trusts in the reality of the past and its knowability." Significant political stakes were involved in such a fight against epistemological anarchists like White. "It is as if higher education was opened to us—women, minorities, working people," worried Appleby, Hunt, and Jacob, "at the same time that we lost the philosophical foundation that had underpinned the confidence of educated people." The struggle for representation was in part a struggle for intellectual authority, the very premise of which had been undermined by relativistic theories of history and power. With this in mind, the authors of *Telling the Truth about History* believed a calculated if limited defense of traditional historical practice necessary. "Rather than underlining the impossibility of total objectivity or completely satisfying causal explanation, we are highlighting the need for the most objective possible explanations as the only way to move forward, perhaps not in a straight line of progress into the future, but forward toward a more intellectually alive, democratic community, toward the kind of society in which we would like to live." Of course conservatives, especially those outside the academy, considered any left-wing variant of American history heretical, even those offering "the most objective possible explanations."[10]

To outsiders, disputes within the historical discipline often seemed prosaic. But the history debates of the late twentieth century reverberated beyond the ivory tower. This was the result of contradictory factors. Because Americans were arguably more invested in the past than ever before, professional historians were granted large platforms from which to disseminate their expertise. Nevertheless, the gulf between how professional historians explained the nation's history and how most Americans understood it grew to immense proportions. Sheltered by academic freedom, historians were relatively unconstrained in investigating the past in ways that complicated the traditional narrative of American exceptionalism. But most Americans continued to learn about the nation's past, in schools, museums, national parks, and movies, as they always had, as a tale of national greatness and unbroken progress. Most Americans did not follow the historical discipline's social and cultural turns. When professional historians sought to interject these new forms of historical knowledge into the public world beyond the ivory tower—when they sought to extend their scholarship into museums and into the school curriculum—a clash of cultures ensued, a clash that meshed with the wider culture wars. The history wars did not alter intellectual life within the historical discipline in any significant fashion other than giving historians added fodder for their teaching and scholarship. Historiographic debate, after all, had long been the lifeblood of professional history. But beyond the academy, the history wars mattered. Powerful conservative interests with little respect for academic norms vigorously contested academic knowledge that challenged normative America.

Some of the most intense history skirmishes grew out of contentious exhibits on display at the Smithsonian Institution. For most of its history, the purpose of the Smithsonian—the "nation's attic"—had been to enshrine objects of the heroic American past. But by the 1980s curators increasingly used Smithsonian artifacts as vehicles for historical interpretations about social relations. Such a shift in priorities was in part a result of the economic recession of the 1970s, which had hit higher education particularly hard. An increasing number of academically trained historians, unable to obtain positions as professors in an impossibly tight job market, instead got hired on by museums. Consequently, trends in public history began to follow trends in academic history. More and more public historians who worked as museum curators, including those at the Smithsonian, evinced the same cultural Left sensibilities that had become so prominent on college campuses. They sought to disturb the triumphalist American story that museums had long been accustomed to telling. This could be seen in such exhibits as *Field to Factory*, a social history of the Great Migration of millions of blacks out of the South, and *A More Perfect Union*, which focused on the internment of Japanese Americans during World War II. Although neither of these exhibits, displayed at the Smithsonian's American History Museum beginning in 1987, generated much controversy, they signaled the changes in public historical practice that inevitably brought the culture wars into the "nation's attic."[11]

The first major Smithsonian controversy erupted in 1991 over an exhibit at the National Museum of American Art titled *The West as America*. The exhibit's curators used wall texts to narrate the paintings of illustrious nineteenth-century American artists—Thomas Cole, George Catlin, Frederic Remington, and Thomas Moran, among others—such that viewers might think critically about the art's subtexts. Specifically, the curators wanted visitors to reflect on how the art represented the romanticization of manifest destiny. Elizabeth Broun, who directed the National Museum of American Art, held that the purpose of *The West as America* was to subvert conventional understandings of westward expansion. "That American society still struggles to adjust to limitations on natural resources, to grant overdue justice to native populations, to locate the contributions of ethnic minorities within a mainstream tradition, and to resolve conflicts between unbridled personal freedom and the larger social good," Broun wrote, "tells us that we have ignored our history far too long, accepting the images of the last century as reality." William Truettner, the lead curator of *The West as America* collection, contended that this particular "corps of talented artists" aided the federal government's efforts to subdue the land and peoples of the West. For example, Albert Bierstadt's 1868 *Among the Sierra Nevada Mountains, California*, an enormous painting of a picturesque mountain landscape, cast the American West "as a new Eden, announcing its scenic wonders and publicizing its staggering resources." Bierstadt and the other painters displayed in *The*

West as America, according to Truettner, helped sell the West as "an aggressively fabricated national anthem."[12]

Not surprisingly, *The West as America* had plenty of detractors. The *New York Times* art critic Michael Kimmelman called the exhibit "art-historical revisionism." Although not unsympathetic to the notion that the paintings of Bierstadt and others helped sell manifest destiny, Kimmelman argued that the exhibit was too didactic, too unambiguous, too laden with "forced analyses and inflammatory observations." Historian Daniel Boorstin, who had been librarian of Congress from 1975 to 1987 and whose scholarship doubled as a celebration of the American pioneer spirit, charged that *The West as America* was "perverse, historically inaccurate, and destructive." The *Wall Street Journal* editorialized that the exhibit was "an entirely hostile ideological assault on the nation's founding and history." Charles Krauthammer called it "the most politically correct museum exhibit in American history." Predictably, bad press helped sell tickets—60 percent more than the museum had sold to the previous year's special exhibit. Controversy also created an unusual level of participation on the part of museum patrons, who waited in long lines to sign the comment books. Some of the comments, later published in the *New York Times*, were supportive. "Don't let the politicians deter you," wrote one visitor. "They don't cope too well with reality, anyway." Other guests panned the exhibit. "Never have I seen such simpleminded, ignorant, and mean-spirited interpretations of brilliant art that stands on its own," one offended patron wrote. "Jesse Helms has surely been right all along about our tax money supporting vile, anti-American propaganda." One thing was certain: by questioning the premises of westward expansion, so central to American mythology, *The West as America* exposed the raw nerves of a nation's fragmented understanding of its past.[13]

As the history wars heated up in the museums, so too did they gather momentum in the schools. In the early 1990s a special committee for the New York commissioner of education released a ninety-seven-page report on history curricula that triggered a national debate. *One Nation, Many Peoples: A Declaration of Cultural Independence*, which counseled an approach to teaching history that emphasized America's racial pluralism, set a confrontational tone in its very first sentence: "African Americans, Asian Americans, Puerto Ricans/Latinos, and Native Americans have all been the victims of an intellectual and educational oppression that has characterized the culture and institutions of the United States and European American world for centuries." The way out of such oppression was to teach the history of minorities—a method that the New York special committee believed would resonate with new attitudes regarding racial identity. No longer contented "with the requirement, common in the past, that they shed their specific cultural differences in order to be considered American," most Americans, especially non-white Americans, affirmed a right to cultural diversity, and even perhaps autonomy. History, in sum, should no longer reflect a normative American identity. To the contrary, it should be taught so as to challenge such tyrannical norms.[14]

Not every member of the New York special committee agreed with the report. The most famous dissent was authored by the venerable liberal historian and Democratic Party house intellectual Arthur Schlesinger Jr., who expanded his disagreements into a best-selling book about the culture wars, *The Disuniting of America*. Schlesinger sought to cut a "vital center" path through the culture wars, similar to the trail he famously blazed through the early Cold War. Outflanking both Left and Right played extremely well with the mainstream literary public, which, in its mood of fighting back against the "cult of ethnicity" that "belittles *unum* and glorifies *pluribus*," embraced *The Disuniting of America*. Schlesinger's book was favorably reviewed in the most prominent newspapers, magazines, and literary publications, from the *New York Times* to *Time Magazine* to the *New York Review of Books* to the *New Republic*. In the British conservative weekly *The Spectator*, historian Raymond Carr ranked it the best book he had read that year. "It is a courageous onslaught by a committed liberal on the craven surrender by educators to current ethnic fads," Carr wrote, "and shows how in so doing they cross the fatal line between a legitimate cultural pluralism and a divisive ethnocentrism, committing the historical absurdity of denying America's historical heritage."[15]

Schlesinger's centrism was most explicit in his analysis of race. Although he generally disdained identity politics, he was more willing than conservatives to admit that the identity ethos stemmed from his beloved nation's blemishes. For this reason he begrudgingly softened his critique of black hyperattention to identity, which informed the approach to history advocated by the New York report. "Like other excluded groups before them," Schlesinger wrote, "black Americans invoke supposed past glories to compensate for real past and present injustices. Because their exclusion has been more tragic and terrible than that of white immigrants, their quest for self-affirmation is more intense and passionate." But in other instances, his rhetoric was indistinguishable from that of conservative critics who lambasted the academic Left for replacing traditional knowledge with, in Schlesinger's words, "a compensatory literature, inspired by group resentment and pride." The very title of Schlesinger's book, premised on the notion that the United States had once been united, was a deeply conservative assumption grounded in the normative Americanism of the 1950s.[16]

Staking such a position put Schlesinger in the crosshairs of black studies scholars like Houston Baker Jr., who harshly responded to a Schlesinger piece against multiculturalism that ran in the *Wall Street Journal.* In a letter to the editor, Baker suggested "that what Professor Schlesinger is really after is a return to the single-bathroom, exclusive, country-club version of an academy that did, perhaps, mark the 1950s in the life and work of Professor Schlesinger himself." In contrast to Schlesinger, Baker thought the multicultural historical curriculum "the most energetic, innovative, and potentially salvific feature of the project called 'America.'" Schlesinger responded, in a personal letter to Baker, "that belated justice should not degenerate into racial cheerleading at the expense of serious history." He went on to explain that he believed the Western tradition "is almost unique in that it provides the means of its own reform." "My concern," Schlesinger continued, "is that you are saying to young blacks that this great tradition is not for you. I can't imagine anything more damaging to the psyche. Nor do I believe that Balkanization is a useful future for America. Do you?"[17]

Schlesinger did not deny American racism. Rather, he thought it stemmed from Americans' not living up to their stated ideals. When white Americans murdered American Indians to clear the land for white settlers, this was a violation of the spirit of America rather than endemic to it. The same went for Western thought more broadly. Schlesinger took pleasure in pointing out "that the assault on the Western tradition is conducted very largely with analytical weapons forged in the West." He asked: "What are the names invoked by the coalition of latter-day Marxists, deconstructionists, poststructuralists, radical feminists, Afrocentrists?" Schlesinger provided the obvious answer: "Marx, Nietzsche, Gramsci, Derrida, Foucault, Lacan, Sartre, de Beauvoir, Habermas, the Frankfurt 'critical theory' school—Europeans all." In cleverly calling attention to this paradox, Schlesinger smartly anticipated counter-arguments made by the likes of historian Robin D. G. Kelley, who maintained that it was impossible to disentangle the Enlightenment from its imperial origins when "the primitive mind was constructed as the very opposite of Reason: atavistic, regressive, barbaric."[18]

What worried Schlesinger most about multiculturalism was that American public schools no longer served as "the great instrumentality of assimilation and the great means of forming an American identity." To him, the multicultural curriculum repudiated "the historical theory of America," about how people from any racial or ethnic background could conform to American culture based on common ideals as opposed to common ancestry. Here Schlesinger exaggerated the dangers that multiculturalism poses to national unity. No matter how revisionist, multiculturalism was grounded in an American project. Schlesinger's alarmism stemmed from the fact that he conflated multiculturalism with Afrocentrism. Multiculturalists, unlike Afrocentrists, believed America was redeemable, if flawed. Schlesinger's overstatements notwithstanding, there was no denying that the version of the American past taught to late-twentieth-century schoolchildren was different from that taught to previous generations. There was also no ignoring the resistance to such change, which had been building throughout the 1980s.[19]

Late in that decade, a number of scholars made sweeping claims about a disaster in the nation's history education. For this contention they relied upon a 1986 survey of a representative sample of eight thousand eleventh graders, sponsored by the US Department of Education and administered by the Educational Testing Service (ETS), revealing that American high school students had serious gaps in their knowledge of basic US history. Over 30 percent of those assessed failed to properly identify the significance of the Declaration of Independence, and over 65 percent placed the Civil War in the wrong half-century. For the traditional-minded authors of this growing body of crisis literature, such as Chester Finn and Diane Ravitch—authors of *What Do Our 17-Year-Olds Know?*—the survey results represented "a devastating indictment of U.S. high schools." Lynne Cheney, author of *American Memory*, another book in this crisis genre, lectured that by not teaching young people the traditional American narrative, "we do to ourselves what an unfriendly nation bent on our destruction might." Thanks to the left-wing history that had come to dominate

the public school curriculum — or worse yet, the left-wing social studies approach, which accentuated contemporary problems to the neglect of historical study—Americans no longer had a shared sense of
the American past. This was a dangerous development in the eyes of
those who believed that the nation's heroic history was the best means
by which to instill moral and civic duty. Putting aside whether or not
there was any political merit in such a vision of history education,
what Cheney and her fellow traditionalists ignored was that such sur-
veys had always garnered poor results. Americans, in other words,
never really knew their history. In 1943, decades before the social and
cultural turns transformed the history curriculum, a similar survey
showed that only 25 percent of first-year college students—an elite
cohort by 1943 standards—knew Abraham Lincoln was president
during the Civil War.[20]

The supposed crisis in history education propelled curriculum reforms in several states that differed markedly from the New York proposal. The history standards put into effect in California in 1988, *The
History-Social Science Framework*, authored by Ravitch and Professor of Education Charlotte Crabtree, were the best known of such reforms and, unlike the New York curriculum, became something of a
national model. The *Framework* was designed to transcend the culture
wars, or, more modestly, it was meant to rise above the long-standing
debates between those who advocated for a history-centered curriculum and those who pushed for a more generic social studies method.
Ever since the 1930s many schools had deemphasized historical learning and had instead implemented a social studies approach, which focused on contemporary problems. Proponents of social studies had
long argued that since Eurocentrism had tainted the study of history,
teaching students how to think critically about the present was a better and more relevant method for inculcating democratic values in a
multicultural society. The *Framework* repositioned history at the center of the curriculum. Moreover, it restored formerly prominent aspects of the history curriculum, such as the history of religion, which
publishers and teachers had long avoided for fear of offending a religiously diverse student population.[21]

For these reasons, some conservatives, including Cheney and
Chester Finn, applauded the *Framework*. They believed it offered a
remedy to the social studies approach, which, in their view, was a left-
wing technique for ignoring the nation's exalted history. Although the

new California history curriculum recognized the legitimacy of multiculturalism as one factor among many that shaped the nation's historical narrative, some conservatives supported the *Framework* because it also accentuated that which bound Americans together in common cause. Students were to "realize that true patriotism celebrates the moral force of the American idea as a nation that unites as one people the descendants of many cultures, races, religions, and ethnic groups." Due to such language, Schlesinger believed the California approach, unlike the later New York plan, resolved "the conflicting commands of our national motto, *E Pluribus Unum*. Out of many, one."[22]

In spite of the support it garnered from conservative culture warriors like Cheney, Finn, and Schlesinger, the California history curriculum included plenty of features that offended traditionalist sensibilities. Yes, the *Framework* focused on history, but not the celebratory type that conservatives revered. Students were to learn a set of historical thinking skills designed to engender a critical perspective on conventional interpretations of the American past. In this way the *Framework* opened up the curriculum to the modes of historical analysis that had reshaped the historical profession in the wake of the sixties. Furthermore, the *Framework* set up a sequence of courses that mandated three years of US history *and* three years of world history—at a time when most states offered only one year of world history, if any. Thus the *Framework* shifted the trajectory of history education away from the traditional Western civilization curriculum that linked the contemporary United States with ancient Greece as part of a great chain of enlightened civilization. This was a bold move that sought to close the gap between how university historians conceptualized their craft and how history was taught in the nation's public schools: a decentralized world history curriculum, which university historians had been developing since the 1970s, was explicitly intended to blunt the Eurocentric biases that had long colored how Americans thought about the world beyond their nation's borders. In short, although the *Framework* was in some ways designed to sidestep the culture wars, in other ways it set the stage for one of the archetypal skirmishes in the war for the soul of America—the battle over the *National History Standards*.[23]

In her role as chair of the NEH, and in her enthusiasm for history standards, in 1987 Cheney requested proposals for a research center that would build bridges between academic historians and public school teachers. A group of scholars at the University of California–Los Angeles (UCLA) responded to the request, won a grant of $1.6 million, and established the National Center for History in the Schools (NCHS) in 1988. The grant stipulated that NCHS would need to be a collaboration between academics from a school of education and a history department; thus Crabtree, the coauthor of the California *Framework* and the first director of NCHS, was brought together with renowned social historian Gary Nash. NCHS quickly set to the task of gathering data about how history was taught across the nation, while also establishing a national network of history educators. After a 1989 meeting of state governors in Charlottesville, Virginia, made the creation of national standards in five core subject areas, including history, de facto national policy, NCHS was ideally situated. On the basis of what it had already accomplished, Cheney pushed to have NCHS take the lead in writing national history standards.[24]

With such federal support, NCHS convened a diverse group of scholars, educators, and policy makers. The ambitious goal: create national history standards. Aware that history standards had the potential to spark controversy, NCHS sought to foster a broad consensus. This was not an easy task. For instance, the National Council for Social Studies (NCSS) was hesitant to join the project out of fear that history-centered standards might deemphasize the social studies. Professional historians were also skeptical, not because they opposed more uniformity in the national history curriculum but rather due to suspicions about Bush administration objectives. But both the NCSS and the major historical associations, including the American Historical Association (AHA), came around. NCSS officials were convinced that the standards would emphasize a skills-based methodology consistent with the social studies approach, and they also recognized that national standards were going forward with or without them, so they might as well have a say in the process. The concerns of historians were allayed by the fact that Nash was serving in a lead role at NCHS, an indication that the standards would indeed cohere with modern professional historiography. Thus with most major constituencies aboard—aside from Afrocentrists and conservative Christians, who were deliberately left out of the process for fear that their historical visions could never be reconciled—and with financial backing from the NEH and the Department of Education, the National History Standards Project was launched.[25]

To get the ball rolling, NCHS created task forces to write standards for three separate curricula: history for students from kindergarten through fourth grade (K–4 History); US history for students from fifth through twelfth grade (5–12 US History); and world history for students from fifth through twelfth grade (5–12 World History). These groups, in consultation with advisory committees, worked for almost three years to create comprehensive standards and teaching examples. During deliberations among the advisory committees, which were charged with setting criteria for the task forces, several contentious issues were debated, sometimes testily. Not surprisingly, multiculturalism in particular arose as a thorny issue for those setting criteria for US history standards. Some members of the committee lobbied for a robust account of the African American contribution to the national narrative. Cynthia Neverdon-Morton of the Association for the Study of Afro-American Life quoted Du Bois — "Would America have been America without her Negro people?" — to make her case that the standards should consider "the centrality of the Afro-American experience." James Gardner, the deputy executive director of the AHA, told the committee that the AHA would support only standards rooted in multicultural awareness. "We don't see this as an option or an alternative but the reality of our past." From the opposite vantage point, Mark Curtis of the Atlantic Council of the United States feared that "the so-called multicultural agendas in history threaten to balkanize American society." The majority favored a multicultural curriculum and drafted a list of criteria that included the following language: "Standards for United States history should reflect the nation's diversity, exemplified by race, ethnicity, social status, gender, and religious affiliation." But, consistent with the mission to foster a broad consensus, another criterion emphasized that standards should illustrate "our common civic identity and shared civic values." In short, like the California *Framework*, the national US History Standards were intended to avoid the pitfalls of the culture wars.[26]

Achieving a consensus on world history standards proved more difficult. On one side of the debate stood those professors who had helped revolutionize the teaching of world history, including the pioneer of such an approach, William McNeill, who argued that as westerners we "are a minority in the world and ought to know it." Peter Stearns, another important scholar in the field, contended that the World History Standards "must stress not only European ideas and political institutions but also the big changes—demographic, social, economic, technological, and so on—that have shaped and been shaped by human endeavor." World historians posited that culture is not essential or specific to any one civilization or nation. Such a theory of history flew in the face of those who wanted the standards to reflect the tried-and-true Western Civilization curriculum, which emphasized the transmission of enduring values—values that supposedly served as the bedrock of free and democratic societies like the United States. Finn contended that Western Civilization was the superior model because "the full story of democracy, neither disguising nor apologizing for its innate superiority to other forms of government, should be the centerpiece of our teaching of history." In contrast to such a curriculum, Finn believed that world history was culturally relativistic, and as such was dangerous because it would not provide American students with a proper appreciation of the superiority of their nation's democratic system of government. The first draft of World History Standards criteria tilted in favor of the Western Civilization proponents, but in response to strenuous objections levied by representatives of the AHA, the world historians carried the day. The World History Standards, like the California *Framework*, represented a major revision in how Americans were to learn about the world beyond American borders.[27]

In October 1994 the *National History Standards*, the result of a collaboration unprecedented in size and scope, went to press. Most of those responsible for the creation of the standards considered the final product a remarkable achievement. Their document, they believed, would help bridge the gulf between the historical discipline's best practices and the public school curriculum taught to millions of American schoolchildren. Because the deliberation process had been relatively smooth during the creation of the K–4 History Standards and the 5–12 US History Standards, hardly anyone suspected these two sets of standards might cause an uproar. Those involved in the process of crafting the 5–12 World History Standards recognized potential dangers, since their negotiations had been far more contentious. And yet since nearly everyone involved in the project understood that creating and implementing history standards was a fluid process, even those disappointed in the results seemed resigned to supporting the larger mission. There was reason to be optimistic.

Such rosy expectations were premature. Controversy engulfed the release of the *National History Standards*. Due to the ironies of education reform, perhaps controversy was inevitable. NCHS had gained a foothold because a powerful conservative—Lynne Cheney—wanted to reposition the traditional American narrative at the center of the curriculum. And yet those responsible for creating the standards had been key players in the movement against traditional history. Gary Nash, one of the most influential practitioners of social history—which upended the traditional narrative to account for women, blacks, Native Americans, and other subaltern groups—served as associate director of NCHS during the project, and was instrumental in helping to shape the 5–12 US History Standards. This paradox would later haunt the *National History Standards.* But at the time of his initial appointment Nash did not raise red flags with Cheney and the other traditionalists involved, largely because he helped author a Houghton Mifflin textbook series that aligned with the California *Framework.* In fact, for those earlier efforts Nash was targeted by a group of San Francisco State University students, largely Afrocentrists, who took control of Oakland and Berkeley school board meetings in 1991 to demand that the textbooks be kept out of schools. The students labeled the textbooks that Nash coauthored racist for their failure to properly celebrate all minority ethnic groups. Nash was "stunned" by the implication that he was racist. Indeed, that he was on the receiving end of an attack by leftist students, for writing a textbook not multicultural enough, was perplexing given his scholarly record.[28]

Even as the *Standards* document was about to go to press—at the precise moment when those who created the *Standards* were most confident about the integrity of their product—warning signs were present. A complaint registered by Chester Finn should have, in retrospect, served as a cautionary tale. Upon reading the final version of the *Standards,* Finn wrote a memorandum stating various objections. Given "its valiant effort to gain the approbation of innumerable constituencies within the education and history communities whose blessings have been thought desirable," he wondered, in contrast, how the *Standards* might be interpreted by groups not involved in their creation, such as legislators, the Chamber of Commerce, the American Legion, and "callers to the Rush Limbaugh show." Finn himself viewed the *Standards* unfavorably: "What can only be termed 'political correctness' and 'relativism' rear their unlovable (but increasingly familiar) heads in too many places. Sometimes this takes the form of an unwarranted emphasis on various victim groups, overwrought attention to certain minorities, the inflating of the historical contribution of minor figures who happen to have the proper characteristics, and other such slightly overwrought efforts at after-the-fact egalitarianism." Finn's complaints were specifically about the 5–12 US History Standards, which became the primary target of right-wing criticism. This was perhaps surprising, since, as noted, the advisory committee for US history standards had reached a consensus much more easily than those who debated the world history standards, which were largely ignored during the national shouting match that ensued. The traditional narrative of American history, it seemed, had become more sacrosanct than even the Western Civilization curriculum.[29]

Even after all she had done for the *National History Standards*, including lavishing federal money on NCHS, Cheney was the first person to publicly attack them. She launched her assault with an October 20, 1994, piece in the *Wall Street Journal* titled "The End of History," in which she fretted that the *Standards* portrayed American history as "grim and gloomy." She complained that "those pursuing their revisionist agenda no longer bother to conceal their great hatred of traditional history." Journalist Frank Rich wondered in the *New York Times* whether Cheney's second thoughts about the *Standards* were motivated by her desire "to be a major player in the Gingrich order." Rich continued: "The evidence suggests that she deliberately caricatured her own former pet project as politically correct so it might be wielded as a Mapplethorpe-like symbol to destroy the agency she so recently championed." In this view, Cheney attacked the *Standards* out of political opportunism: she recognized that condemning the *Standards*, and the National Endowment she had only recently chaired, was a good way to ingratiate herself with Newt Gingrich and the new Republican House majority.[30]

Of course, it was equally probable that Cheney turned against the *Standards* out of her disappointment that they failed, in the end, to promote the traditional political narrative she thought American students so desperately needed. Such anxieties certainly shaped the angry conservative response. In the weeks following Cheney's opinion piece, the *Wall Street Journal* published a number of fuming letters to the editor. One such writer asked, simply: "Are we prepared to allow the haters of America to dictate how American history will be taught to our children?" Right-wing AM radio phenomenon Rush Limbaugh denounced the standards created by "Gary Nash and a select group from UCLA" as a "bastardization of American history" that should be flushed "down the sewer of multiculturalism." "History is real simple," Limbaugh explained. "You know what history is? It's what happened. It's no more." Diane Ravitch joined the right-wing chorus, even though the California *Framework* that she coauthored had served as a model for the *Standards*; she critiqued the *Standards* for overstating the importance of a "struggle by the oppressed to wrest rights and power from white male Protestants." Ravitch argued that such an emphasis downgraded the status of democratic ideals to "a hollow façade, like storefronts in a Hollywood western, while greed, racism and corruption appear to be the real commonalities of American history."[31]

Historian John Patrick Diggins offered one of the livelier conservative critiques of the *Standards*. Diggins had long been one of the more cantankerous critics of the New Left's seeming hold on academia, arguing that such influence demonstrated that "the New Left is an idea whose time has passed and whose power has come." "A white male conservative who admired Madison more than Marx," Diggins cheekily wrote, "had about as much chance of getting hired on some faculty as Woody Allen of starting as point guard for the Knicks." In 1995 Diggins sent a letter to Schlesinger, which was then widely disseminated, seeking to convince him to reject the *Standards* on the grounds that its supporters were "all staunch multiculturalists; and you are their enemy." Diggins compared the New History that informed the *Standards* unfavorably to Schlesinger's celebrated scholarly works *The Age of Jackson* and *The Age of Roosevelt*. "The way history is written today by academics who came out of the sixties," Diggins grumbled, "no single personality can be said to stand for or speak for an age or an era." Instead, he complained, the masterpiece of contemporary historiography was *The People's History of the United States*. In the historical profession's rejection of the "great man" theory of history, it also dismissed the history of ideas as elitist. To Diggins this was unfortunate. "At least when one does intellectual history," he wrote, "one must defer to those thinkers who are our superiors, must get straight what they thought and believed." In contrast, by the logic of those who authored the *Standards*, "the historian is almost free to impose his or her thoughts on workers, slaves, and other subalterns of the past who have no voice of their own." In other words, Diggins argued that social history might claim to be "history from the bottom up," but it is in fact elitist, not to mention arrogant, because "it is present-day scholars who now claim to speak for the silent dead." Diggins chalked up such an approach to "ideological desperation."[32]

One of the central gripes that conservatives had with the *Standards* was that they downgraded the importance of great American men such as George Washington while upgrading the significance of less crucial Americans. For instance, Cheney charged that the *Standards* insufficiently spotlighted traditionally important figures such as Ulysses Grant and Robert E. Lee while lavishing attention on supposedly marginal figures such as Harriet Tubman. Conservative journalist John Leo complained that Ebenezer McIntosh, who led the Stamp Act Riots, was included as a teaching example for the American Revolution standard because he "fits right in as a sort of early Abbie Hoffman or Jerry Rubin." "U.S. history," Leo wrote, "is now being written from the counter-cultural perspective by oppression-minded people who trashed the dean's office in the 1960s (or wish they had)." He continued: "By the allocation of the text, America today seems to be about 65 percent Indian, with most of the rest of us black, female, or oppressive." Of course such criticism was deceptive in that it focused on the teaching examples, which were merely intended to illustrate how teachers might apply the *Standards* in the classroom. Lazy members of the media, particularly television reporters, repeated such deceptive claims again and again. As a result, phone lines at the Department of Education were clogged by calls from livid citizens asking misinformed questions such as "Why are the Feds telling our schools that our kids can't learn about George Washington anymore?"[33]

In spite of the conservative campaign against the *National History Standards*, schools, libraries, teachers, and various other Americans purchased copies by the thousands. NCHS had trouble meeting the demand. Moreover, many of those who took the time to read the *Standards* for themselves, including some journalists, recognized their value. Most major metropolitan newspapers defended them. As the *New York Times* editorialized: "Reading the standards and support materials is exhilarating." Even those who recognized that the *Standards* bucked traditional history offered praise. Historian David Kennedy wrote that they symbolized the "seismic upheavals in American society" that had taken place since the sixties and that, as such, they paid "considerably more attention to analyzing the messy practice of democracy than to explicating those ideals." In response to those like Limbaugh who critiqued the *Standards* with the simpleminded claim that history was only about facts, US Representative Dale Kildee, a Democrat from Michigan, said: "History isn't like math where two plus two equals four. It's a lot more than facts, and they don't always add up to the same sum."[34]

Not all national politicians saw eye to eye with Kildee. Senator Slade Gorton, a Republican from Washington, denounced the *Standards* in a January 18, 1995, speech from the Senate floor that was written by conservative scholar John Fonte, a close associate of Cheney. "According to this set of standards," Gorton hyperbolically claimed, "American democracy rests on the same moral footing as the Soviet Union's totalitarian dictatorship." In describing the *Standards* as an "ideologically driven, anti-Western monument to politically correct caricature," he contended that they were designed to "destroy our Nation's mystic chords of memory." Gorton said the *Standards* should be "recalled like a shipload of badly contaminated food," and he proposed a rider to an unfunded mandates bill that would decertify the standards. Senate Democrats let it be known that if Gorton were to scale back his proposal to a nonbinding sense-of-the-Senate vote, they would vote in favor of it. Even though most Democrats had a less apocalyptic view of the *Standards*, they voted for a resolution that denounced them because it was preferable to holding up the unfunded mandates bill. Additionally, Democrats reasoned that since a sense-of-the-Senate resolution was nonbinding, it would allow President Clinton to establish a review board that might lead to the certification of revised standards. So the United States Senate voted 99–1 in favor of a resolution recommending that no federal body should certify the *Standards* and that any future national history standards "should show a decent respect for the contributions of Western civilization." Bennett Johnson, a Republican from Louisiana, cast the only vote against the resolution because he thought a nonbinding measure too soft. But despite the fact that the nonbinding resolution left the door open to eventual federal approval, Clinton and Secretary of Education Richard Riley distanced themselves from the *Standards*. This had the net effect of allowing the Senate censure to be the final word.[35]

The *National History Standards* created such a furor in part because they challenged the racism and sexism at the heart of American history. Related to this, the *Standards*, and trends in American historiography more generally, disturbed the theological ways in which many Americans, particularly conservatives, conceptualized the nation's history. There were certain eternal truths, such that America was a beacon of freedom embodied in the great men of the American past such as George Washington. Such verities were not to be tampered with. The historical fact that Washington was a slave owner, and the historical meaning that might attach to such a fact, was irrelevant to the eternal truths about America. The goal of history was to inculcate a love of country, plain and simple. Such an objective became more paramount than ever with the loss of national purpose that accompanied the end of the Cold War—and more poignantly, the crisis of national identity that ensued alongside the decline of American power made manifest in the jungles in Vietnam.

In this way, Cold War convictions bled easily into culture war convictions, especially as the Cold War wound down. In 1993 Irving Kristol wrote: "There is no 'after the Cold War' for me. So far from having ended, my cold war has increased in intensity, as sector after sector has been ruthlessly corrupted by the liberal ethos." Kristol's lament echoed Patrick Buchanan's famous declaration of "a war for the soul of America" that was "as critical to the kind of nation we will one day be as was the Cold War itself." Kristol and Buchanan, and conservatives generally, conceptualized the "liberal ethos" as having a paralyzing effect on their various efforts to reestablish the United States as the exceptional nation among nations in the post–Cold War world. These concerns climaxed in the national controversy surrounding the Smithsonian's proposed *Enola Gay* exhibit.[36]

Although the *Enola Gay* bomber, which delivered its atomic payload to the citizens of Hiroshima on August 6, 1945, symbolized American military power better than any other war relic, it was never displayed prior to 1995. This was largely due to ambivalence about what it represented: beyond American power and the victorious end to World War II, the *Enola Gay* also stood for the onset of the nightmare-inducing nuclear age. Walter Boyne, who directed the Air and Space Museum from 1983 to 1987, refused to entertain the idea of displaying it on the grounds that most people lacked "an adequate understanding with which to view it." His successor, Cornell University astrophysicist Martin Harwit, reversed course in 1988 and created an advisory committee to take up the issue. The committee concluded that the bomber should be displayed. But, reflecting the new mood at the Smithsonian, the committee recommended that the *Enola Gay*

be presented in somber fashion. Thus, in a departure from past Air
and Space exhibits, which had extolled the uninterrupted advances of
American aviation and often fetishized military technology, curators
were tasked with creating an *Enola Gay* exhibit consistent with Harwit's curatorial philosophy: "I think we just can't afford to make war a
heroic event where people could prove their manliness and then come
home to woo the fair damsel."[37]

In July 1993 the Air and Space Museum released a planning document that outlined its objectives for the exhibit: "to encourage visitors
to undertake a thoughtful and balanced reexamination of the end of
the Second World War and the onset of the Cold War in light of the
political and military factors leading to the decision to drop the bomb,
the human suffering experienced by the people of Hiroshima and Nagasaki and the long-term implications of the events of August 6 and
9, 1945." Demonstrating the Smithsonian's newfound commitment
to aligning its content with the latest in academic research, the planning document summarized the museum's hopes that the "exhibit
can provide a public service by re-examining these issues in light of
the most recent scholarship." The original script, appropriately titled
"Crossroads," was specifically intended to engage patrons in the debate about whether dropping the atomic bombs was necessary to end
World War II, a debate that had occupied diplomatic historians since
at least 1965, when Gar Alperovitz's influential book *Atomic Diplomacy* was first published. Alperovitz made the revisionist argument
that the atomic bombs were unnecessary to end the war. Truman,
he contended, used them against Japan to better position the United
States vis-à-vis its erstwhile ally the Soviet Union.[38]

Air and Space curators gathered primary source material highlighting the fact that the bombings had always been a source of controversy, or at least unease, including Admiral William Leahy and General Dwight Eisenhower's retrospective declarations in opposition
to the bomb. "Leahy said in 1950," the script went, "that he had denounced the bombing as adopting 'ethical standards common to barbarians in the dark ages.' Eisenhower claimed in 1948, and in his later
memoirs, to have opposed the use of the bomb in conversations with
President Truman at the Potsdam Conference in July 1945." Beyond
this ongoing debate, the authors of the original script also sought to
include accounts by Japanese victims, alongside artifacts and images

of the blast zones—content intended to spur visitors to think critically about the destructive force of nuclear weaponry and, more important, about the morality of using such weapons.³⁹

When the "Crossroads" script was made public in early 1994, conservative veterans' organizations, led by the Air Force Association and the enormously powerful American Legion, coordinated a highly effective campaign to block the exhibit. John T. Correll first called attention to the issue with a heated editorial in *Air Force Magazine*, calling the script a product of "politically correct curating." A newly formed veterans' organization, the Committee for the Restoration and Proper Display of the *Enola Gay*, directed by W. Burr Bennett Jr., sent thousands of letters to members of Congress demanding that the exhibit be stopped. "It is an insult to every soldier, sailor, marine and airman who fought in the war against Japan, or who were on their way to the invasion," Bennett wrote, "to defame this famous plane by using it as the center piece of a negative exhibit on strategic bombing." Conservative pundits also chimed in. George Will charged that Smithsonian curators, much like their university brethren, "rather dislike this country." Limbaugh labeled the Air and Space Museum interpretation "blasphemous." Politicians entered the fray as well. A letter signed by twenty-four members of Congress described the script as "revisionist and offensive to many World War II veterans." A "Sense of the Senate" resolved that the Smithsonian "should avoid impugning the memory of those who gave their lives for freedom." The Smithsonian caved to the backlash. After several revised scripts failed to please the veterans groups, the museum decided to display the *Enola Gay* alone, decontextualized, aside from a few commemorative plaques.⁴⁰

In terms of specific content, opponents of "Crossroads" objected to the way the script "treats Japan and the United States," in Correll's words, "as morally equivalent." They argued that the script paid too little attention to Japanese aggression, including the Rape of Nanking and the bombing of Pearl Harbor. Critics repeatedly drew attention to an infamous passage, which they believed neatly represented the anti-American sentiments of the Smithsonian. "For most Americans," the script notoriously read, "it was a war of vengeance. For most Japanese, it was a war to defend their unique culture against Western imperialism." Although the curators arguably chose their words unwisely in that specific instance, repeated criticism of the offensive passage were made out of context. Prior to it, the script mentioned "Japanese expansionism," "marked by naked aggression and extreme brutality," with references to Nanking, Pearl Harbor, and "surprise assaults against Allied territories in the Pacific."[41]

The charge of moral equivalency was familiar. In her 1995 book *Telling the Truth*, Cheney maintained that such relativism—which encouraged compassion toward "the failings of other cultures" while fostering a censorious view "of the one in which they live"—was the driving force of the revisionism that was shaping the nation's public history. The *Standards*, for example, supposedly equivocated on the Cold War, a topic that seemed morally certain to Cheney. "The Cold War is presented as a deadly competition between two equally culpable superpowers, each bent on world domination," she lamented. "Ignored is the most salient fact: that the struggle was between the communist totalitarianism of the Soviet Union, on the one hand, and the freedom offered by the United States, on the other." In short, Cheney worried that relativism opened the back door to unflattering portrayals of the United States. She maintained that the United States is "a political and economic lodestar to people around the world," and to teach differently would be "at the cost of truth." This American exceptionalist framework proved central to the *Enola Gay* controversy. Challenges to it were not to be tolerated, particularly at the Smithsonian—the most important venue to national identity formation.[42]

In addition to philosophical disagreements about the role and identity of the American nation, more technical points informed Air and Space Museum opponents, such as disagreement over a hypothetical body count. Whereas critics insisted that five hundred thousand or more Americans would likely have suffered injury or death had an invasion of the Japanese mainland been necessary, scriptwriters based their figures on estimates made by the US government prior to Hiroshima. "It appears likely that post-war estimates of a half a million American deaths were too high," the script read, "but many tens of thousands of dead were a real possibility." The five-hundred-thousand-casualties figure, originating with an inflated after-the-fact estimate put forward by Truman in his memoirs, held steady in the collective American imagination. Such an imponderable number—more than double the combined two hundred thousand or so who died at Hiroshima and Nagasaki—might have eased lingering guilt. Indeed the figure grew during the course of the controversy, when politicians demanded that the Smithsonian give "attention to the fact that the atomic bombs prevented an invasion of Japan and an estimated one million American casualties."[43]

To those historians who studied the end of World War II, the numbers debate trivialized the issue, since some evidence suggested that prior to the atomic bombings US policy makers suspected that the Japanese might be on the verge of surrendering. Historians were thus equally interested in alternative explanations for why Truman decided to use the bomb. Was it to stave off Soviet advances in East Asia? Was it to protect the American monopoly on atomic weaponry? Was it to avoid congressional hearings about the Manhattan Project, for which an enormous price tag would have seemed gargantuan had the bomb remained idle? Was it an act of vengeance, intensely motivated by the anti-Japanese racism that permeated most layers of American society? Not surprisingly, these and other plausible questions went mostly unaddressed in the national conversation about the *Enola Gay*. Unlike in their seminar rooms or in their journals, academic historians did not set the terms of debate in the larger public arena, where a different set of rules determined what knowledge was acceptable and what was not.

Historian Martin Sherwin, as author of an influential revisionist account of the diplomatic history of the atomic bombs—*A World Destroyed*—and as a member of the Air and Space advisory committee that reviewed the original *Enola Gay* script, was at the center of the controversy, especially after he told a reporter from the *New York Times* in 1995 that he was "appalled that Congress [left] no room for informed debate." Sherwin received several angry letters from veterans who questioned his right to challenge their views. One veteran of the Pacific theater wrote that although the political history of the end of World War II was mostly unfamiliar to him, "it is still my opinion the Japanese would not have surrendered if the Atom bombs were not dropped, and this is all any of us can say on the matter." A critique of the Smithsonian from W. Burr Bennett Jr. was grounded in a similar sentiment. "It would appear," Bennett wrote to members of Congress, "that Ph.D.'s opinions were given more weight than the opinions of those who fought the war." Such anti-intellectualism also emanated from the *Washington Post*, which editorialized against historians as "narrow-minded representatives of a special-interest and revisionist point of view [who] attempted to use their inside track to appropriate and hollow out a historical event that large numbers of Americans alive at that time engaged in the war had witnessed and understood in a very different—and authentic—way." Beyond the academy, authentic feelings, not evidence, mattered more in judging winners and losers in the *Enola Gay* debate.[44]

The combined weight of the *National History Standards* and *Enola Gay* controversies placed historians at the center of political discourse to an arguably unprecedented degree. Republican presidential candidate Bob Dole warned of the threat posed by "the arbitrators of political correctness" and "government and intellectual elites who seem embarrassed by America." Texas Republican Sam Johnson, who sat on the Smithsonian Board of Regents, proclaimed that the nation wanted the museum "to reflect real America and not something that a historian dreamed up." One of the fuming letters sent to Sherwin—introduced by way of an ill-humored poem titled "Political Correctness, Yuck!"—epitomized this increasingly popular antipathy toward professional historians. "History [will go] the way of the do-do bird," the letter writer fretted, "if the present group of academicians, women's groups, Hispanic groups, African-American groups, antiwar groups, environmental groups, all belonging to the left-wing, write our history."[45]

Among those historians whose reexaminations of revered national myths had slowly but surely gained legitimacy, even hegemony, in academic venues, the attack on their work sometimes caught them by surprise. This was especially true for diplomatic historians like Sherwin, whose revisionist conclusions about the history of the atomic bomb were arrived at in epistemologically traditional ways. Unlike cultural historians, whose approaches to historical interpretation focused on ephemera, discourse, and other less tangible cultural artifacts, Sherwin and most other revisionist diplomatic historians came to their conclusions based on a straightforward empirical reading of diplomatic cables and other evidence drawn from official channels. All of this might explain why Sherwin and his colleagues seemed surprised that their interpretations created such a ruckus and why they were so slow to enter the *Enola Gay* national debate. Late in the controversy, well after the Smithsonian had scrapped the "Crossroads" script, Sherwin joined the historian Kai Bird, best known for his penetrating biographies of Cold War establishment figures, in forming the Historians' Committee for Open Debate on Hiroshima. The committee organized panels in the summer of 1995 to coincide with the

fiftieth anniversary of the Hiroshima and Nagasaki bombings, including one at the National Press Club on the eve of the grand opening of
the stripped-down version of the *Enola Gay* exhibit, or, as Bird termed
it, the "patriotically correct" iteration. But their efforts to restore academic integrity to the national debate mostly fell on deaf ears: the
public treated historians not like authorities in their field—trained
experts—but rather like just another special interest group.[46]

If the pitched rhetorical battles of the culture wars diminished the
standing of historians and other university academics who sought to
reshape the political sphere, these shouting matches decimated the
position of those who managed the Smithsonian and other public
cultural institutions. When the Smithsonian renegotiated the *Enola
Gay* exhibit script with veterans groups, the message was clear: the
Smithsonian curators had very little standing as experts and thus very
little academic independence. "Before the *Enola Gay* debacle," *New
Republic* critic Jason Zengerle wrote in his 1997 review of the controversy and its legacy, "the Smithsonian's leadership could be counted
on to resist any outside criticism that seemed to threaten the institution's intellectual integrity. These days, however, the Smithsonian
is perceived by both outside critics and some staff as more likely to
succumb to ideological pressure." Secretary of the Smithsonian I. Michael Heyman, whom historians criticized for selling out to veterans
groups, maintained, in retrospect, that "the staff of the Smithsonian
does not have the same claim to academic freedom that a university
faculty does. If a professor writes an article, he is generally not considered to be speaking for his college; by contrast, a museum exhibition is taken as a reflection of an institutional view." Zengerle thought
Heyman's logic specious, since part of the Smithsonian's charter mandate was to "increase the diffusion of knowledge," an impossible task
without intellectual independence. But in practice, Heyman's views
carried the day.[47]

Controversial interpretations of American history were more
likely to go forward on university campuses, where the traditions of
academic freedom protected heresies better than at national institutions like the Smithsonian. American University in Washington, DC,
hosted an alternative *Enola Gay* exhibit in 1995, a display intentionally pitched to counter the whitewashed Air and Space version. The
American University exhibit was composed of most of the materials
originally gathered for the Smithsonian, including artifacts from Hi-

roshima. Veterans groups sought to derail the substitute exhibit by applying the same tactics that proved so effective in censoring the Smithsonian. The president of the Jewish War Veterans sent a letter to Peter Kuznick, the historian in charge of the American University exhibit, demanding that those "whose lives were saved by the events at Hiroshima and Nagasaki" be allowed "to correct any factual inaccuracies," which would "avoid encouraging historical corruption [and] anti-American diatribe." But in this instance the tactics of intimidation failed. Kuznick and his colleagues were not compelled to alter their exhibit.[48]

The American University exhibit offered compelling evidence that the conservative attack on historical knowledge proved more effective when it was leveled against nonacademic institutions such as the Smithsonian. Of course to suggest that raw power played a decisive role in the production of historical knowledge outside the university is not to propose that academic knowledge is pure or that the ivory tower is a place where intellectuals simply investigate the truth free of bias or other human compulsions. But the norms of knowledge production on the two sides of the ivory tower differ. Outside the academy, in the so-called marketplace of ideas, positions that resonate with powerful interests, such as the idea that the United States dropped atomic bombs on Hiroshima and Nagasaki to save lives and end a just war, gain traction readily. Inside the academy, where the norms of academic freedom and peer review regulate the production of knowledge, ideas that fail to attract popular support elsewhere, such that the United States dropped the atomic bombs for reasons other than benevolence, sometimes, though not always, secure a foothold. This dichotomy proved especially true during the culture wars, when anti-intellectualism worked well alongside powerful conservative interests. When academic historical knowledge threatened powerful nonacademic interests, it was treated as just another political obstacle to be destroyed.

The frenzied national debate over the *Enola Gay* exhibit was a significant barometer of the confusion regarding the nation's role in a post–Cold War world. The history wars of the 1990s challenged the legacies of old frontiers—the West, the Cold War—precisely because new, unknown frontiers were on the horizon. When Bob Dole complained about the exhibit's message—that "the Japanese were painted not as the aggressors but as the victims of World War II"—he was expressing discontent with the lack of agreement over what he considered an exalted national purpose. Similarly, when Lynne Cheney griped about the centrality of figures like Sojourner Truth in the *National History Standards*, she was articulating her discontent with the altered landscapes of race and gender. In postmodern America, nothing was settled; everything was up for grabs, particularly history.

Conclusion

This book gives the culture wars a history—because they *are* history. The logic of the culture wars has been exhausted. The metaphor has run its course.

The culture wars of the 1980s and 1990s were poignant. Those who resisted the cultural changes set into motion during the sixties did so out of a profound sense of loss. The world they cherished was evaporating. Those who identified with the normative Americanism of the 1950s fought for its survival. But by the twenty-first century, memories of this lost world have faded. A growing majority of Americans now accept and even embrace what at the time seemed like a new nation. In this light, the late-twentieth-century culture wars should be understood as an adjustment period. The nation struggled over cultural change in order to adjust to it. The culture wars compelled Americans, even conservatives, to acknowledge transformations to American life. And although acknowledgment often came in the form of rejection, it was also the first step to resignation, if not outright acceptance.

Of course, the culture wars have left lingering residues. Many of the people who played a prominent role in the late-twentieth-century war for the soul of America are still waving the bloody flag. But insofar as the culture wars continue to be fought in the early twenty-first century, they feel less poignant and more farcical. Cultural conflict persists, but it does so in a different register, shaped by a different logic.

When Henry Louis Gates Jr., the black Harvard professor who often intervened in the culture wars, was arrested by white Cambridge police officer James Crowley for breaking into his own house in the summer of 2009, and when Obama criticized the arrest by implying that racial profiling was the source of the arresting officer's suspicions, the national media was momentarily abuzz with a controversy reminiscent of earlier cultural conflicts that pitted an elite "new class" cosmopolitanism against a white working-class provincialism. But in the wake of the financial crisis of 2008—when black households lost twice as much medium income as white households, and when black homeownership rates fell twice as far as white homeownership rates—the hullabaloo seemed absurd. Although the Black Power critique of institutional racism was as relevant as ever, the civil rights movement itself, which to a certain extent had been successful in changing American racial attitudes, was ill equipped to ameliorate the economic inequality that attached itself to the color line. Identity politics had their place in an earlier historical moment. The sixties liberation movements had won racial minorities, women, and gays and lesbians access to the nation's cultural institutions. But economic inequality persisted and, in fact, got worse.[1]

Something similar can be said about the legacy of feminism. The culture wars over women's rights live on in the twenty-first century, as was evident during the 2012 election season, when a number of Republican politicians made disturbing and inaccurate comments about the female reproductive system. In arguing that abortion was never an appropriate choice for a woman to make, Republican Senate candidate Todd Akin stated that pregnancy rarely results from what he called "legitimate rape." But despite the fact that such an alarmingly misogynistic attitude seemed of a piece with the antifeminist backlash that had been crucial to the earlier culture wars, this kerfuffle was different. At one level, the fact that Akin and other Republicans who made similar statements lost their elections demonstrated that feminism had transformed American attitudes about women. Most Americans deemed their ideas retrograde. But at another level, the debate seemed to miss the fact that class increasingly determines a woman's access to abortion and a whole lot more. Feminism, which had been so successful at making the nation less sexist, seemed incapable of reconciling this paradox. Feminism had granted women many freedoms, but it had also provided American businesses the freedom to restructure the labor market in ways that universalized economic insecurity. The happy ending of the feminist-themed 1980 film *9 to 5* anticipated this irony. American businesses were all too pleased to comply with the changes the film's female heroes made to their workplace:

an accommodating scheduling scheme, a job-share program, and an in-office daycare center. A more flexible labor force was cheaper than the older male breadwinner model that, for all its faults, guaranteed a family wage. In this way the conservative feminism of Facebook executive Sheryl Sandberg, author of the 2013 best-selling book *Lean in: Women, Work, and the Will to Lead*—which argues that women need to work harder and be more ambitious if they are to compete with men—has won out over the radical feminism of Kate Millett, Judith Butler, Susan Faludi, and even Carol Gilligan, all of whom in their various ways assumed that feminism was a vehicle to fight inequality and hierarchy.[2]

The trajectory of the gay rights movement offers another such example of historical irony. The nation's attitudes about homosexuality have become radically more tolerant. Homophobia is on the wane. A rapidly growing majority of Americans favor the legalization of same-sex unions. The courts have followed suit by upholding the legality of same-sex marriage in state after state. Even a majority of Republicans under the age of fifty now support same-sex marriage. Leaders of Focus on the Family and the Southern Baptist Convention have recently admitted defeat in the gay marriage debate. And yet the almost singular focus on marriage equality signifies a narrowing of a vision elaborated by gay liberation activists of the sixties, and later by queer theorists like Eve Kosofsky Sedgwick, who radically challenged what they saw as heterosexual norms like marriage. As cultural historian Lisa Duggan argues, the marriage agenda complements conservative economics. "In the broadest sense," Duggan writes, "'marriage promotion' in welfare policy aims to privatize social services by shifting the costs of support for the ill, young, elderly and dependent away from the social safety net and onto private households." In other words, more radical or queer notions about kinship rights—which would afford basic legal protections to those bound together in complex, often nonnuclear ways—have been forgotten in the push for gay marriage.[3]

Paradoxes are also noticeable in the popular culture, which every year moves further and further from the culture of the 1950s. Hypersexuality is de rigueur. Nothing has the ability to shock anymore. When Justin Timberlake revealed Janet Jackson's barely concealed nipple during the 2004 Super Bowl halftime show, the ensuing controversy was more than a touch strained. Could one tiny little "wardrobe malfunction" really engender outrage among viewers conditioned to endless advertising for drugs like Viagra that help alleviate male erectile dysfunction? In a world in which hard-core pornography is available to nearly anyone with access to the Internet, such faux controversies demonstrate the degree to which the culture wars have become farcical. Cultural representations that once seemed subversive—messages that once shocked normative America—have come to seem like so much crass commercialization.[4]

The culture wars over education also register in a different way. Since the 2001 passage of President George W. Bush's No Child Left Behind Act, standardized tests are increasingly tied to teacher and school evaluations, through which rewards and punishments are meted out. Obama's "Race to the Top" further codifies high-stakes testing by allocating scarce resources to those states most aggressively implementing such accountability measures. All of this has worked, in the context of economic austerity, to limit the power of teachers' unions and to make the nation's education system much less of a public good. In the desperate fight for what seems like the very survival of public education, battles over the curriculum are less fraught. When the conservative Texas board of education revised its state history curriculum in 2010 to reflect a Christian Right cosmology, many historians reacted with alarm. But in a state that had long ago committed itself to educational privatization, such curricular maneuverings seem like merely a rather cynical footnote. The progressive secular educators who had been so successful at molding the public school curriculum to better reflect a diverse, multicultural society seem helpless against a well-funded reform movement bent on reshaping American public education to fit a neoconservative agenda.[5]

A similar trajectory has altered the terms of the culture wars in higher education. In the 1980s conservatives like William Bennett criticized the academic Left on the grounds that it had destroyed the humanities with its newfangled relativistic theories. Today, in contrast, the national discussion is about whether the humanities are worth supporting at all. In 2012 Florida governor Rick Smith proposed a law making it more expensive for students enrolled at Florida's public universities to obtain degrees in the humanities. As Smith and his supporters argued, in austere times they needed "to lash higher education to the realities and opportunities of the economy," meaning that a humanities degree, unlike a business degree, was a luxury good. The terms of the debate in the 1980s—a debate over what kind of humanities would best serve a democracy—seem quaint by such standards. Today the decision is not Locke versus Fanon but Locke and Fanon versus Jack Welch, the former CEO of General Electric whose book on management coauthored with his wife Suzy Welch, *Winning*, is widely read in American business schools. The literary theorists who did so much to challenge the almighty Western canon seem feeble up against *Winning*.[6]

By concluding this book on a pessimistic note, I do not intend to render a condescending judgment born of hindsight. Marching on the metaphorical English department was a worthwhile crusade insofar as the nation's cultural gatekeepers were protecting racist, sexist, homophobic, and conservative religious norms. A more tolerant and less sadistic society was worth winning. The sixties liberation movements helped tilt the arc of the moral universe toward justice.

But, proving the historical truth of what Theodor Adorno and Max Horkheimer called the "dialectic of enlightenment," the ethos of the sixties liberation movements has merged with new constraints. American culture—American capitalism—discovered a new dynamism by incorporating the oppositional themes of the New Left. If any one ethos now represents American culture, it is that promulgated by Madison Avenue and Silicon Valley: antiauthoritarian individualism, so important to shaking up normative America, has become a commodity, no more, no less. Such are the cultural contradictions of liberation.[7]

These cultural contradictions are worth pondering. Perhaps Robert Bork was correct when he made the heretical argument that the individual freedoms enshrined in the Declaration of Independence were dangerous because they set in motion a society dedicated to permanent cultural revolution. How does one set limits on the proposition that "all men are created equal"? Against the assumptions of those who signed the Declaration, "all men" eventually came to include, in fits and starts, non–property holders, slaves and former slaves, blacks and other racial minorities, immigrants from strange lands, Catholics, Jews, and other non-Christians, atheists, women, gays, lesbians, the disabled. Viewed in this way, the sixties liberation movements made manifest an ethos that dated to the nation's founding.[8]

But as the history of the culture wars shows, such liberation, no matter how foundational its ethos, met with fierce resistance. When new peoples laid claim to the nation, when new peoples had different ideas about the nation, the national culture fractured. It could not have been otherwise.

Permanent cultural revolution makes a common culture a very difficult proposition. And without a common culture, it is extremely hard to build the solidarity necessary for social democracy. Perhaps, then, it is no coincidence that the modest American social welfare state—the New Deal state—was constructed during an era of unusual cultural stability. Perhaps it was no coincidence that the economic reforms enacted in the years between the presidencies of Franklin Roosevelt and Lyndon Johnson overlapped with a cessation in the cultural revolution. Perhaps it was no coincidence that an era of unprecedented economic equality was also an era in which cultural norms were intensely policed.

Can we have both cultural revolution and social democracy? This is a serious dilemma with no easy answers. One thing seems certain, however. The reigning American economic ideology—the belief in the goodness of capitalism—makes cultural revolution much likelier than social democracy. Even though conservatives increasingly couched their critique of liberalism in antistatist terms by the late twentieth century—such as when Christian Right leaders like Phyllis Schlafly contended that public schools and welfare agencies, in league with feminists, weakened the traditional family structure—it has become increasingly clear that capitalism has done more than the state to pitilessly destroy the values they held dear. Capitalism, more than the federal government—Mammon more than Leviathan—has rendered traditional family values passé.

Capitalism sopped up sixties liberation and in the process helped dig the grave of normative America. The next American movement for liberation—and those who resist it—will have to reckon with this historical irony.

Acknowledgments

I am excited to publish this book with the University of Chicago Press, and am deeply grateful to Robert Devens, the editor who signed me to an advance contract. Robert saw the potential for this book and was extremely helpful in giving it direction in its early stages. Timothy Mennel, who took over as my editor midway through the process, has been equally enthusiastic and has proved an insightful reader. Tim secured two fantastic readers to review my manuscript. These anonymous readers gave me confidence going forward with their praise and helped make the book that much better with their criticism. I thank them for their important service. Speaking of making the book better, Ruth Goring's deft copyediting improved the text by leaps and bounds. And last but not least, in acknowledging all of the fine people at the University of Chicago Press, I must thank Nora Devlin, who has patiently walked me through the production process with aplomb, and Timothy McGovern, who undertook the important task of creating a fine index.

Leo P. Ribuffo is a towering figure in my life as a historian. For the last thirteen years Leo has been an influential teacher, an honest critic of my work, and a good friend. He even suggested the topics for both of my books. Along with the dozens of other doctoral students advised by Leo—my fellow Ribuffoites—I owe this smart, irascible, hilarious, lovable historian an enormous debt of gratitude.

In addition to Leo, several of my friends have read the manuscript in part or in whole. David Sehat bears special mention as my most thorough and challenging reader. David has been incredibly generous with his time and intelligence in helping to make this book better. I am also grateful to Raymond Haberski, who boosted me when I needed it and helped me see the big picture when it was obscured. Two other people read the manuscript in whole: Mike O'Connor, one of the smartest and more skeptical readers of my work, and Julian Nemeth, who has preternatural editorial gifts. I owe thanks as well to Allison Perlman, Claire Potter, and Daniel Geary, who each read and offered expert criticism on chapters related to their own research. And for reading my book proposal at a much earlier stage, I appreciate the sage advice I received from George Cotkin, Timothy Lacy, and David Steigerwald.

Several people at my home institution, Illinois State University, have been wonderfully supportive of my efforts to write this book. Thanks to colleagues in the ISU College of Arts and Sciences who favorably reviewed my proposals, I received several summer research grants, which allowed me to travel to various archives, and a one-semester sabbatical, which allowed me to write a large chunk of the book. I must also thank Dean of the College of Arts and Sciences Gregory Simpson and Associate Deans Dagmar Budikova and Joseph Blaney, all of whom have been generous with their support. Of everyone at ISU, I am most grateful to my department chair, Anthony Crubaugh, a consummate professional and good friend. And I appreciate those colleagues in the history department who read and discussed my book proposal at a faculty research seminar: Richard Hughes, Lou Perez, Stewart Winger, and Amy Wood. I am thankful to Touré Reed for his guidance on the historiography of race and social policy. I also thank Alan Lessoff for introducing me to Robert Devens at the University of Chicago Press. And last but not least, I thank Issam Nassar for being such a great colleague and friend.

This book emerged from the crucible of the *U.S. Intellectual History Blog*, where I have been a regular writer since 2007. The ideas that inform this book took shape in the many conversations I have had at the *USIH Blog* with my blogmates—Benjamin Alpers, Lauren Kientz Anderson, L. D. Burnett, Robert Greene II, Ray Haberski, Tim Lacy, Elisabeth Lasch-Quinn, Rivka Maizlish, Kurt Newman, Mike O'Connor, Andy Seal, and David Sehat—and with our smart community of readers. In this way the *USIH Blog* has acted as an informal, ongoing peer-review process for the book.

Stemming from our efforts to build an online scholarly community with the blog, we formed an academic society—the Society for U.S.

Intellectual History (S-USIH)—which hosts a vibrant annual conference. The society and conference have endowed this and many other books with a community of readers, and for that I would like to thank those who have helped make it happen: Ben Alpers, Tim Lacy, Paul Murphy, Mike O'Connor, Allison Perlman, David Sehat, Lisa Szefel, and Daniel Wickberg. Nobody has done more to steward S-USIH than Ray Haberski. We all owe Ray.

Librarians and archivists are the unsung heroes of any history book. I must sing the praises of the wonderful Vanette Schwartz, history librarian at Illinois State University, who has been amazingly helpful. And I extend my gratitude to the countless librarians and archivists at the following institutions: the University of Illinois Archive Research Center, Urbana, Illinois; the Manuscript Division, Library of Congress, Washington, DC; the Hoover Institution, Palo Alto, California; Western History Collection, Denver Public Library; Special Collections Research Center, Gelman Library, George Washington University, Washington, DC; Ronald Reagan Presidential Library and Museum, Simi Valley, California; Manuscripts and Archives Division, New York Public Library; Kenneth Spencer Research Library, University of Kansas, Lawrence.

I presented several conference papers on the research I conducted for this book. I am thankful to those historians who commented on them: Beth Bailey, Martha Biondi, Casey Nelson Blake, Jonathan Holloway, Andrew Jewett, Bruce Kuklick, James Livingston, George H. Nash, Jennifer Ratner-Rosenhagen, and Martin Woessner. Their sharp commentaries have given me food for thought and have made this book much better.

In April 2011 I was invited by David Courtwright to participate in a seminar at Arizona State University on the topic "Morality, Public Policy, and Partisan Politics in Recent American History." I gave a paper on curriculum debates and received comments from an eclectic group of scholars who included Donald Critchlow, our gracious host, as well as Carolyn Acker, Beth Bailey, Ian Dowbiggin, Michael Nelson, Phillip Vandermeer, and Daniel Williams. The seminar papers were then transformed into a special issue of the *Journal of Policy History*, carefully edited by Courtwright. Reworked bits of my article— "'A Trojan Horse for Social Engineering': The Curriculum Wars in Recent American History," *Journal of Policy History* 25, no. 1 (2013): 114–36—appear in this book.

    I have given several invited talks about my research on the culture
wars. I am grateful to the following people and institutions for their
kind invitations and for providing me with smart, curious audiences:
W. Fitzhugh Brundage and the History Department at the University of North Carolina–Chapel Hill, and Christopher Waldrep and the
History Department at San Francisco State University, where I gave
job talks in February 2009, when this project was still in its infancy;
the American History Teachers' Collaborative in Urbana, Illinois; Ray
Haberski and his colleagues at Marian University, Indianapolis; Jennifer Ratner-Rosenhagen and the Harvey Goldberg Center at the University of Wisconsin–Madison; Jason Stahl and the Department of
Organizational Leadership, Policy and Development at the University
of Minnesota–Minneapolis; Keith Woodhouse, Huntington Institute
on California and the West, and the History Department at the University of Southern California; Jason Stacy and the Illinois Council
for the Social Studies, which invited me to give its keynote address in
April 2013; Christian Olaf Christiansen and ECORA at Aarhus University, Denmark; Allison Perlman and the Humanities Collective, University of California–Irvine; Clodagh Harrington and the UK-based
American Politics Group, which invited me to address its 2013 meeting at the US embassy in London; Nick Witham and the History Department at Canterbury Christ Church University, UK; Bevan Sewell
and the Department of American and Canadian Studies, Nottingham
University, UK—and Richard King, who gave smart, generous comments on my Nottingham talk; Jack Thompson and the Clinton Institute for American Studies, University College–Dublin, Ireland; Daniel Geary, Juergen Barkhoff, and the Arts and Humanities Research
Group, Trinity College, Dublin; Laurie Béreau and the Department
of English and American Studies, Université de Strasbourg, France;
and Stig Skov Mortensen and Pedagogical and Philosophical Studies,
Aarhus University–Copenhagen, Denmark. I must also thank the UK
and Irish Fulbright Commissions for funding my travel to England and
Ireland from Denmark to give several talks.
    Regarding my Fulbright experience, I am very grateful to Marie
Mønsted and the other good folks at the Danish-American Fulbright
Commission, in addition to all of my colleagues in the Center for
American Studies at the University of Southern Denmark, who, by
generously helping my transition to living and teaching in Denmark
during the 2013–14 academic year, have made it possible to finish writ-

ing this book. Special thanks in this regard to Niels Bjerre-Poulson, Thomas Bjerre, Jørn Brondol, Charlotte Granly, Mette Kobbersmed Ringsmose, Marianne Kongerslev, Anne Mørk, David Nye, and Anders Rasmussen.

I am pleased to thank three key participants in the culture wars who helped me with this project. First, my former professor and current friend Martin Sherwin, who lent me three large boxes of ephemera he had collected during his involvement in the *Enola Gay*–Smithsonian controversy. Second, Gary Nash, who walked me through the events of the *National History Standards* controversy. And third, the late Sheldon Hackney, with whom I corresponded in 2009 about his chairmanship at the National Endowment for the Humanities.

As always, I am grateful to have good friends who share my passion for history and ideas. In particular, I thank my graduate school comrades Christopher Hickman and Jason Roberts, who offered encouragement and periodically sent me sources related to the culture wars the past seven years. I am also lucky to be friends with resourceful scholars like Lisa Szefel, who has broadened my knowledge of gay and lesbian history, and David Weinfeld, who has informed my understanding of Jewish American history. My longtime friend Andres Martinez helped me grasp the importance of Chicano leaders like Corky Gonzales. And my old professor and friend Charles Angeletti started me down the path of this book and career by getting me hooked on reading Howard Zinn.

Although this is my second book, it is not far removed from my experience as a graduate student at George Washington University. Three amazing professors in particular sparked my intellectual obsessions, and thus implicitly helped shape this book: Donald Collins, Melani McAlister, and Andrew Zimmerman—thanks to you all.

I have been privileged to teach many intellectually curious students, at Illinois State University and the University of Southern Denmark, about the culture wars. They, more than anyone else, have taught me how to make complex and seemingly arcane issues relatable. I am particularly obliged to my former student Corey Cox, who compiled a bibliography on the culture wars in higher education as part of his undergraduate research project.

I spent hundreds of hours writing this book in two coffee houses. I offer my gratitude to the proprietors and baristas at the Coffeehound in Bloomington, Illinois, and at Nelle's in Odense, Denmark, for keeping me stimulated with delicious coffee and for providing the perfect ambience for writing.

Finally, I would like to thank my family. I am forever indebted to my parents Karen Hartman, who taught me how to write, and Tim Hartman, who taught me how to enjoy life. To my sister Sarah Hartman and brother Matt Hartman, who continue to inspire me each in their own ways. To my mother-in-law Jane Wilhelm, who cares for me as if I were her own son. To my father-in-law Richard Wilhelm and his wife Shelly Porges, who lovingly subsidized several research trips. And finally, to Erica, whom I will never be able to thank enough.

Over the seven years I have been working on this book—which has proved to be the biggest challenge of my academic career thus far—I saw the birth of my two boys, Asa and Eli. Although Erica is a giving partner and wonderful parent, having two young children around the house has not quite sped up the writing process. But if Asa and Eli have slowed down this book, they have also made life that much more rewarding. Many of the figures in this book fought the culture wars in a search for meaning. Asa and Eli have given more meaning to my life, and for that I dedicate this book to them. With love.

Notes

INTRODUCTION

1. Patrick Buchanan, "Republican National Convention Speech," August 17, 1992.
2. Adapted to an American context from the German word *Kulturkämpfe*—a term specific to Otto von Bismarck's 1870s crusade to limit Catholic power in Prussia— "culture wars" is a phrase of recent vintage. A *Lexus-Nexus Academic* search of all major national publications between 1960 and 1987 reveals that the first recorded instance of the "culture wars" phrase was on November 14, 1987, when Todd Gitlin and Ruth Rosen wrote a brief for liberal justices, "Give the Sixties Generation a Break," *New York Times*, 27.
3. Thomas Frank, *What's the Matter with Kansas? How Conservatives Won the Heart of America* (New York: Holt Paperbacks, 2004), 10, 8.
4. Hector St. John de Crevecoeur's famous question is from his 1782 *Letters from an American Farmer*.
5. "The sixties" is a period in US history roughly bookended by the 1963 assassination of John F. Kennedy and the 1974 Watergate scandal that ended Richard Nixon's presidency. Maurice Isserman and Michael Kazin, *America Divided: The Civil War of the 1960s* (Oxford: Oxford University Press, 1999). Van Gosse and Richard Moser, eds., *The World the 60s Made: Politics and Culture in Recent America* (Philadelphia: Temple University Press, 2003). James Davison Hunter, *Culture Wars: The Struggle to Define America* (New York: Basic Books, 1991), 42.
6. Kevin Mattson, *Intellectuals in Action: The Origins of the New Left and Radical Liberalism, 1945–1970* (University Park: Pennsylvania State University Press, 2002).
7. Gregory L. Schneider, *Cadres for Conservatism: Young Americans for Freedom and the Rise of the Contemporary Right* (New York: NYU Press, 1998). William Buckley Jr., *God and Man at Yale: The Superstition of "Academic Freedom"* (Chicago: Henry Regnery, 1951).
8. Daniel Wickberg, "Modernisms Endless: Ironies of the American Mid-Century," *Modern Intellectual History* 10, no. 1 (2013): 207-19. Paul Rabinow, ed., *The Foucault Reader* (New York: Pantheon Books, 1984), 88. Lynne Cheney, *Telling the Truth: Why Our Culture and Our Country Have Stopped Making Sense—and What We Can Do about It* (New York: Simon and Schuster, 1995), 91.

9. William James, *Pragmatism: A New Name for Some Old Ways of Thinking* (1907; repr. Indianapolis: Hackett, 1981), 76. David Hollinger, "The Accommodation of Protestant Christianity with the Enlightenment: An Old Drama Still Being Enacted," *Dædalus* 141, no. 1 (Winter 2012): 82. Alston Chase, "Harvard and the Making of the Unabomber," *Atlantic Monthly,* June 2000, 41–65. "Fracture" has become an increasingly useful metaphor for recent American political and intellectual culture thanks to the masterful book by Daniel T. Rodgers, *Age of Fracture* (Cambridge, MA: Belknap Press of Harvard University Press, 2011).

10. David Steigerwald, *The Sixties and the End of Modern America* (New York: St. Martin's, 1995).

11. Epstein is quoted in Mark Gerson, *The Neoconservative Vision: From the Cold War to the Culture Wars* (Lanhan, MD: Madison Books, 1997), 144. Gertrude Himmelfarb, *On Looking into the Abyss* (New York: Alfred A. Knopf, 1994), 6. Robert Bork, *Slouching towards Gomorrah: Modern Liberalism and American Decline* (New York: ReganBooks, 1996), vii.

12. Elaine Tyler May, *Homeward Bound: American Families in the Cold War Era* (New York: Basic Books, 1988). Frances Fitzgerald, *America Revised* (New York: Vintage Books, 1979).

13. Lary May, ed., *Recasting America: Culture and Politics in the Age of the Cold War* (Chicago: University of Chicago Press, 1989).

14. Richard Nixon, oath of office and Second Inaugural Address, January 20, 1973.

15. Newt Gingrich, *To Renew America* (New York: HarperCollins, 1996), 7.

16. Kim Phillips-Fein, "Conservatism: A State of the Field," *Journal of American History* 98, no. 3 (2011): 723–43.

17. Buchanan is quoted in "Conservative Republicans Call for 'Culture War,'" *Christian Science Monitor,* May 17, 1993.

CHAPTER ONE

1. Bob Dylan, "Subterranean Homesick Blues, " *Bringing It All Back Home,* LP (Columbia, 1965).

2. Stephen Stills, "For What It's Worth," *Buffalo Springfield,* LP (Atco, 1967).

3. George Breitman, ed., *Malcolm X Speaks: Selected Speeches and Statements* (New York: Grove, 1965), 26. Reagan is quoted in Michael Kramer, *The Republic of Rock: Music and Citizenship in the Sixties Counterculture* (London: Oxford University Press, 2013), 15.

4. The argument that the New Left reshaped American culture is the overarching theme of Van Gosse and Richard Moser, eds., *The World the 60s Made: Politics and Culture in Recent America* (Philadelphia: Temple University Press, 2003).

5. Lawrence Goodwyn, *The Populist Moment: A Short History of the Agrarian Revolt in America* (Oxford: Oxford University Press, 1978). Charles Postel, *The Populist Vision* (Oxford: Oxford University Press, 2007). Lizabeth Cohen, *Making a New Deal: Industrial Workers in Chicago, 1919–1939* (Cambridge: Cambridge University Press, 1991).

6. Tom Hayden, *The Port Huron Statement: The Visionary Call of the 1960s Revolution* (New York: Thunder's Mouth, 2005), 45.

7. Clark Kerr, *The Uses of the University* (Cambridge, MA: Harvard University Press, 1963).

8. Robert Cohen, *Freedom's Orator: Mario Savio and the Radical Legacy of the 1960s* (New York: Oxford University Press, 2009).

9. Van Gosse, *Rethinking the New Left: An Interpretative History* (New York: Palgrave Macmillan, 2005). Hayden, *Port Huron Statement,* 152.

10. Scott McKenzie, "San Francisco (Be Sure to Wear Flowers in Your Hair)," single (CBS Records, 1967). Marvin Gaye, "What's Going On," *What's Going On,* LP (1971). Michael Kazin, *American Dreamers: How the Left Changed a Nation* (New York: Alfred A. Knopf, 2011), 218.

11. Daniel Geary argues against the idea that Mills stood apart from the 1950s intellectual context: *Radical Ambition: C. Wright Mills, the Left, and American Social Thought* (Berkeley: University of California Press, 2009). Tom Hayden's master's thesis was published as *Radical Nomad: C. Wright Mills and His Times* (Boulder: Paradigm, 2006). C. Wright Mills, *White Collar: The American Middle Classes* (Oxford: Oxford University Press, 1951), and *The Power Elite* (1956; Oxford: Oxford University Press, 2000), 18.

12. Dick Flacks, "Paul Goodman and the Old New Left," *Dissent,* Fall 2010. Kevin Mattson, *Intellectuals in Action: The Origins of the New Left and Radical Liberalism, 1945–1970* (University Park: Pennsylvania State University Press, 2002).

13. Paul Goodman, *Compulsory Mis-education and the Community of Scholars* (New York: Vintage Books, 1966). Paul Goodman, *Growing Up Absurd: Problems of Youth in the Organized System* (New York: Random House, 1960). New Leftist Deborah Meier reflected on her paradoxical embrace of *Growing Up Absurd* in the Jonathan Lee film *Paul Goodman Changed My Life* (JSL Films, 2011).

14. The "forbidden to forbid" sign, sighted at the Paris May Day protests, is quoted by Eric Hobsbawm, *The Age of Extremes: A History of the World, 1914–1991* (New York: Vintage Books, 1994), 332. Theodore Roszak, "Youth and the Great Refusal," *The Nation,* 1968, quoted by Gertrude Himmelfarb, *One Nation, Two Cultures* (New York: Alfred A. Knopf, 1999), 16. Hoffman describes his experiences at Woodstock, and criticizes Townsend, in his *Woodstock Nation: A Talk-Rock Album* (New York: Random House, 1969).

15. Howard Brick, *Age of Contradiction: American Thought and Culture in the 1960s* (New York: Twayne, 1998), 114; Steigerwald, *The Sixties and the End of Modern America,* 157.

16. Abraham H. Maslow, *Religions, Values, and Peak-Experiences* (orig. 1964; New York: Arana, 1994).

17. Timothy Leary, *Flashbacks: A Personal and Cultural History of an Era* (Los Angeles: Jeremy P. Tarcher, 1983), 253. Hendrix lyrics quoted in Brick, *Age of Contradiction,* 216. Charles Reich, *The Greening of America* (New York: Random House, 1970), 219.

18. Bruce Kessler, "The Chaperone" episode, *The Monkees* (NBC, 1966). Aniko Bodroghkozy, *Groove Tube: Sixties Television and the Youth Rebellion* (Durham, NC: Duke University Press, 2001), 74.

19. Bodroghkozy, *Groove Tube*, 131.

20. Ibid., 123–63.

21. Ibid., 87–89, 163–92.

22. David Farber, *The Age of Great Dreams: America in the 1960s* (New York: Hill and Wang, 1994), 168–69. Reagan is quoted in David Courtwright, *No Right Turn: Conservative Politics in a Liberal America* (Cambridge, MA: Harvard University Press, 2010), 154.

23. Kwame Turé and Charles V. Hamilton, *Black Power: The Politics of Liberation* (orig. 1967; New York, Vintage, 1992), 9. Robin Morgan, *The Word of a Woman: Feminist Dispatches*, 2nd ed. (New York: W. W. Norton, 1994), 69. Karla Jay and Allen Young, eds., *Out of the Closets: Voices of Gay Liberation* (New York: Jove/HBJ Books, 1972), 34.

24. Johnson's speech is reprinted in Lee Rainwater and William L. Yancey, eds., *The Moynihan Report and the Politics of Controversy* (Cambridge, MA: MIT Press, 1967), 126. For a lively narrative of the Watts riot, see Rick Perlstein, *Nixonland: The Rise of a President and the Fracturing of America* (New York: Scribner, 2008), 13–17.

25. Jones quoted in Peniel E. Joseph, *Waiting 'Til the Midnight Hour: A Narrative History of Black Power in America* (New York: Henry Holt, 2006), 120. Scot Brown, *Fighting for US: Maulana Karenga, the US Organization, and Black Cultural Nationalism* (New York: NYU Press, 2003). William L. Van Deburg, *New Day in Babylon: The Black Power Movement and American Culture, 1965–1975* (Chicago: University of Chicago Press, 1992), 5, 55.

26. Eldridge Cleaver, *Soul on Ice* (San Francisco: Ramparts, 1968). Eldridge Cleaver, "On the Ideology of the Black Panther Party" (San Francisco: Black Panther Party for Self-Defense, 1970). "Ten Points: What We Want, What We Believe" (San Francisco: Black Panther Party for Self-Defense, 1967). Charles E. Jones, ed., *The Black Panther Party (Reconsidered)* (Baltimore: Black Classic, 1998).

27. Manning Marable, *Race, Reform, and Rebellion: The Second Reconstruction in Black America* (Jackson, MS: University Press of Mississippi, 1991), 110. J. Edgar Hoover, US Federal Bureaus of Investigation, Counterintelligence Program, *Top Secret Report for the President*, June 16, 1970. Huey P. Newton, *Revolutionary Suicide* (New York: Random House, 1973).

28. Timothy B. Tyson, *Radio Free Dixie: Robert F. Williams and the Roots of Black Power* (Chapel Hill: University of North Carolina Press, 2001). Ernesto Che Guevara, *The Motorcycle Diaries: A Journey around South America*, trans. Ann Wright (orig. 1953; London: Verso, 1995), 81, 96, 102.

29. Cleaver, "On the Ideology of the Black Panther Party." Immanuel Wallerstein, "Reading Fanon in the 21st Century," *New Left Review* 57 (May/June 2009). Franz Fanon, *Black Skin, White Masks* (orig. 1952; New York, Grove, 1967), 231, and *The Wretched of the Earth* (New York: Grove, 1963), 212. The quote from Richard

Wright's "The Color Curtain" is cited in Peniel E. Joseph, "Black Studies, Student Activism, and the Black Power Movement," in *The Black Power Movement: Rethinking the Civil Rights-Black Power Era*, ed. P. E. Joseph (New York: Routledge, 2006), 254.

30. Harold Cruse, *The Crisis of the Negro Intellectual* (New York: William Morrow, 1967), 7–8. Joseph, "Black Studies, Student Activism," 251–77. Carmichael and Hamilton, *Black Power*, 44.

31. Joseph, *Waiting 'Til the Midnight Hour*, 199. Carmichael and Hamilton, *Black Power*, 4, 32.

32. *El Gallo: Newsletter of Crusade for Justice*, March 1969, 3—found in Rodolfo ("Corky") Gonzales Papers, WH1971, Western History Collection, Denver Public Library (Hereon: Gonzales Papers), Box 2, File Folder 6. Rodolfo "Corky" Gonzales, *Message to Aztlán: Selected Writings*, ed. Antonio Esquibel (Houston: Arte Público, 2001), 38.

33. "I Am Joaquín," in Gonzales, *Message to Aztlán*, 16, 23, 25–26, 29. Carlos Muñoz Jr., *Youth, Identity, Power: The Chicano Movement*, rev. ed. (London: Verso, 2007), 76.

34. Gonzales Papers, Box 3, File Folder 26. Appendix 1: "El Plan de Aztlán," in Christine Marin, *A Spokesman of the Mexican American Movement: Rodolfo "Corky" Gonzales and the Fight for Chicano Liberation, 1966–1972* (San Francisco: R and E Research Associates, 1977), 36.

35. Marin, *Spokesman of the Mexican American Movement*, 9. *El Gallo*, March 1969, 3. Gonzales Papers, Box 2, File Folder 6.

36. Fabio Rojas, *From Black Power to Black Studies: How a Radical Social Movement Became an Academic Discipline* (Baltimore: Johns Hopkins University Press, 2007), 53. Martha Biondi, *The Black Revolution on Campus* (Berkeley: University of California Press, 2012).

37. Joy Ann Williamson, *Black Power on Campus: The University of Illinois, 1965–75* (Urbana: University of Illinois Press, 2003). "Curriculum Development in Black Studies," Conference Reference Documents, September 1981, Afro-American Studies and Research Program, University of Illinois Archive Research Center, Record Series 15/42/5, Box 1.

38. Muñoz, *Youth, Identity, Power*, 1, 19, 22, 76.

39. Amy Uyematsu, "The Emerge of Yellow Power," *Gidra*, October 1969, 9–13. Laura Pulido, *Black, Brown, Yellow, and Left: Radical Activism in Los Angeles* (Berkeley: University of California Press, 2006).

40. Robert Warrior and Paul Chaat Smith, *Like a Hurricane: The Indian Movement from Alcatraz to Wounded Knee* (New York: New Press, 1996). Terry H. Anderson, *The Movement and the Sixties: Protest in America from Greensboro to Wounded Knee* (Oxford: Oxford University Press, 1995), 333–36.

41. L. Ling-chi Wang, "Asian Americans in Higher Education," in *Higher Education in the United States, A-L*, ed. James J. F. Forest and Kevin Kinser (Santa Barbara, CA: ABC-CLIO, 2002), 75–80.

42. Betty Friedan, *The Feminine Mystique* (New York: W. W. Norton, 1963).

43. Alice Echols, *Daring to Be Bad: Radical Feminism in America, 1967–1975* (Min-

neapolis: University of Minnesota Press, 1989). Carol Hanisch, "The Personal Is Political," in *Notes from the Second Year: Women's Liberation; Major Writings of the Radical Feminists*, ed. Shulamith Firestone and Anne Koedt (Redstockings Pamphlet, 1970). "Redstockings Manifesto," in *Sisterhood Is Powerful: An Anthology of Writings from the Women's Liberation Movement*, ed. Robin Morgan (New York: Random House, 1970), 535.

44. C. Wright Mills, *The Sociological Imagination* (Oxford: Oxford University Press, 1959), 5, 7. Mary King, a white female member of SNCC, present when Carmichael made his infamous "prone" comment, claims that it was in the context of self-effacement and that the women present laughed as much as the men. Echols, *Daring to Be Bad*, 29.

45. Robin Morgan, *The Word of a Woman: Feminist Dispatches*, 2nd ed. (New York: W. W. Norton, 1994), 29, 62, 70.

46. Kate Millett, *Sexual Politics* (New York: Doubleday, 1970), 22, 26. Simone de Beauvoir, *Second Sex* (orig. 1949; New York: Vintage, 1989).

47. Sheila Tobias, "Beginning in the 1960s," in *The Politics of Women's Studies: Testimony from 30 Founding Mothers*, ed. Florence Howe (New York: Feminist Press at the City University of New York, 2000), 29–38. Howe quotes the Hunter College passage in her preface, xx. Roberta Salper, "San Diego State 1970: The Initial Year of the Nation's First Women's Studies Program," *Feminist Studies* 37, no. 3 (Fall 2011): 656–82.

48. Martin Duberman, *Stonewall* (New York: Plume, 1993), 203.

49. Duberman, *Stonewall*, 208.

50. John D'Emilio, *The World Turned: Essays on Gay History, Politics, and Culture* (Durham, NC: Duke University Press, 2002), 33.

51. Duberman, *Stonewall*, 221. Duberman analyzes the Stonewall Riot and, more importantly, its larger historical context by way of a close biographical study of six individuals, including Jay. Martha Shelley, "Gay Is Good," in *Out of the Closets*, ed. Jay and Young, 34.

52. D'Emilio, *The World Turned*, 25. Jefferson Cowie, *Stayin' Alive: The 1970s and the Last Days of the Working Class* (New York: New Press, 2010), 106.

53. Bruce Miroff, *The Liberals' Moment: The McGovern Insurgency and the Identity Crisis of the Democratic Party* (Lawrence: University Press of Kansas, 2007), 19, 139.

54. Beth Bailey, *Sex in the Heartland* (Cambridge, MA: Harvard University Press, 1999). "Redstockings Manifesto," 535. Elizabeth M. Schneider, *Battered Women and Feminist Lawmaking* (New Haven, CT: Yale University Press, 2000). *Memoirs v. Massachusetts* 383, U.S. 413 (1966). Raymond J. Haberski Jr., *Freedom to Offend: How New York Remade Movie Culture* (Lexington: University of Kentucky Press, 2007), 152–76.

55. Steigerwald, *The Sixties and the End of Modern America*, 172. Philip Roth, *Portnoy's Complaint* (New York: Random House, 1969). Alex Comfort, *The Joy of Sex: A Gourmet Guide to Love Making* (New York: Fireside, 1972). Norman O. Brown, *Love's Body* (New York: Random House, 1966). Haberski, *Freedom to Offend*, 152.

56. Elana Levine, *Wallowing in Sex: The New Sexual Culture of 1970s American Tele-*

vision (Durham, NC: Duke University Press, 2007), 2. Kathryn C. Montgomery, *Target: Prime Time: Advocacy Groups and the Struggle over Entertainment Television* (Oxford: Oxford University Press, 1989), 29, 35, 45.

57. James T. Patterson, *Restless Giant: The United States from Watergate to "Bush v. Gore"* (Oxford: Oxford University Press, 2005), 48–49. Stephanie Coontz, "Divorce, No-Fault Style," *New York Times*, June 16, 2010, A29.

CHAPTER TWO

1. Lionel Trilling, *Beyond Culture: Essays on Literature and Learning* (New York: Viking Adult, 1965). The best history of neoconservatism is Justin Vaïsse, *Neoconservatism: The Biography of a Movement* (Cambridge, MA: Belknap Press of Harvard University Press, 2010).

2. Corey Robin, *The Reactionary Mind: Conservatism from Edmund Burke to Sarah Palin* (Oxford: Oxford University Press, 2011), 4. George H. Nash, *The Conservative Intellectual Movement in America: Since 1945* (orig. 1976; Wilmington, DE: Intercollegiate Studies Institute, 1998), xiv. (Robin cites the Nash passage to make his point from a different evaluative perspective, 20–21.)

3. Gertrude Himmelfarb, *The De-moralization of Society: From Victorian Virtues to Modern Values* (New York: Alfred A. Knopf, 1995).

4. Jacob Heilbrunn, *They Knew They Were Right: The Rise of the Neocons* (New York: Doubleday, 2008), 6.

5. Alan Wald, *The New York Intellectuals: The Rise and Decline of the Anti-Stalinist Left* (Chapel Hill: University of North Carolina Press, 1987). Norman Podhoretz made Kempton's label famous: *Ex-Friends: Falling Out with Allen Ginsberg, Lionel and Diana Trilling, Lillian Hellman, Hannah Arendt, and Norman Mailer* (New York: Free Press 1999). Joseph Dorman, *Arguing the World*, film (First Run Features, 1998).

6. Stephen Spender, ed., *Encounters: An Anthology from the First Ten Years of "Encounter" Magazine* (New York: Basic Books, 1963).

7. Christopher Lasch, *The Agony of the American Left* (New York: Vintage Books, 1969), 172. Peter Steinfels, *The Neoconservatives: The Men Who Are Changing America's Politics* (New York: Simon and Schuster, 1979), 82.

8. Walter Lippmann, *Essays in the Public Philosophy* (orig. 1955; New York: Transaction, 1989), 42. Gerson, *Neoconservative Vision*, 94. Daniel Bell, *The End of Ideology: On the Exhaustion of Political Ideas in the Fifties* (Cambridge, MA: Harvard University Press, 1960). For the Kennedy quote, Michael Sandel, *Democracy's Discontent: America in Search of a Public Philosophy* (Cambridge, MA: Harvard University Press, 1998), 265. The likely author of the Kennedy speech was Kennedy adviser Arthur Schlesinger Jr., author of an influential pluralist book: *The Vital Center: The Politics of Freedom* (New Brunswick, NJ: Transaction, 1949).

9. Irving Kristol, "Is the Welfare State Obsolete?" *Harper's*, June 1963, 39–43; "The Best of Intentions, the Worst of Results," *Atlantic Monthly*, August 1971, reprinted in Kristol, *Neoconservatism: The Autobiography of an Idea* (New York: Free Press, 1995), 43–49. Earl Raab, "Which War and Which Poverty?" *Public Interest*, Spring 1966, 46.

10. John M. Naughton, "U.S. to Tighten Surveillance of Radicals," *New York Times*, April 12, 1970, 1—as cited in Steinfels, *Neoconservatives*, 88.

11. Display Ad 182, *New York Times*, October 15, 1972. Trilling made this claim in the Dorman film *Arguing the World*.

12. Rainwater and Yancey, *Moynihan Report and the Politics of Controversy*. For more on the Chicago school of sociology, consult Touré Reed, *Not Alms but Opportunity: The Urban League and the Politics of Racial Uplift, 1910–1950* (Chapel Hill: University of North Carolina Press, 2008).

13. Rainwater and Yancey, *Moynihan Report and the Politics of Controversy*, 43, 51, 126.

14. Letter from the Louisiana citizen is found in the Daniel Patrick Moynihan Papers, Manuscript Division, Library of Congress, Washington, DC (hereon Moynihan Papers), Box I: 184 Folder 1. The Jencks article is reprinted in Rainwater and Yancey, *Moynihan Report and the Politics of Controversy*, 217.

15. Daniel Geary, "Racial Liberalism, the Moynihan Report and the *Dædalus* Project on 'the Negro American,'" *Dædalus* 140, no. 1 (Winter 2011): 53–66.

16. William Ryan's *Nation* article "Savage Discovery: The Moynihan Report," is reprinted in Rainwater and Yancey, *Moynihan Report and the Politics of Controversy*, 457–66.

17. Godfrey Hodgson, *The Gentleman from New York: Daniel Patrick Moynihan, a Biography* (New York: Houghton Mifflin, 2000), 19, 100–101, 129.

18. Moynihan Papers, Box I: 255, Folder 1.

19. Moynihan Papers, Box I: 245, Folder 3.

20. Thomas L. Jeffers, *Norman Podhoretz: A Biography* (Cambridge: Cambridge University Press, 2010).

21. Norman Podhoretz, "My Negro Problem—and Ours," *Commentary*, February 1963, 93–101. For context, and for the Carmichael quote, see Gerson, *Neoconservative Vision*, 89.

22. Jeffers, *Norman Podhoretz*, 107, 110. "Podhoretz on Intellectuals," *Manhattan Tribune*, February 1, 1969, 4–5, found in the Norman Podhoretz Papers, Manuscript Division, Library of Congress, Washington, DC (hereafter Podhoretz Papers), Box 3.

23. Norman Podhoretz, "Laws, Kings, and Cures," *Commentary*, October 1970, 30–31.

24. Gerson, *Neoconservative Vision*, 98. Irving Kristol, "Urban Civilization and Its Discontents," *Commentary*, July 1970, 34; Kristol, *On the Democratic Idea in America* (New York: Harper and Row, 1972).

25. Steinfels, *Neoconservatives*, 52. Norman Podhoretz, "The Know-Nothing Bohemians," *Partisan Review*, Spring 1958, 305–11.

26. Norman Podhoretz, "The New Hypocrisies," *Commentary*, December 1970, 5–6. Norman Podhoretz, "Redemption through Politics," *Commentary*, January 1971, 5–6. B. Bruce Briggs, ed., *The New Class?* (New Brunswick, NJ: Transaction Books, 1979), 11. Milovan Djilas, *The New Class: An Analysis of the Communist System* (New York: Praeger, 1957).

27. Trilling, *Beyond Culture*. Moynihan Papers, Box I: 245, Folder 3.

28. Richard Hofstadter, *Anti-intellectualism in American Life* (New York: Vintage

Books, 1962). Sidney Blumenthal, *The Rise of the Counter-Establishment* (New York: Crown, 1986). William Buckley Jr., *God and Man at Yale: The Superstition of "Academic Freedom"* (Chicago: Henry Regnery, 1951).

29. Russell Kirk, "The University and the Revolution: An Insane Conjunction," *Intercollegiate Review*, Winter 1969, 18, quoted by Kevin Mattson, *Rebels All! A Short History of the Conservative Mind in Postwar America* (New Brunswick, NJ: Rutgers University Press, 2008), 62. Kirk, *Academic Freedom* (Chicago: Henry Regnery, 1955), 31.

30. Saul Bellow, *Mr. Sammler's Planet* (New York: Viking, 1969), 3, 32. Irving Stock, review of Bellow's *Mr. Sammler's Planet*, *Commentary*, May 1970, 89–94. Stephen Schryer, *Fantasies of the New Class: Ideologies of Professionalism in Post–World War II American Fiction* (New York: Columbia University Press, 2011).

31. Steinfels, *Neoconservatives*, 66, 57–58.

32. Dorothy Rabinowitz, "The Radicalized Professor: A Portrait," *Commentary*, July 1970, 62–64.

33. "An Interview with Norman Podhoretz," *Perspective* 7, no. 1 (Fall 1972): 3–18 (Podhoretz Papers, Box 3). Andrew Kopkind, "Soul Power," *New York Review of Books*, August 1967, 3–6. Dennis H. Wrong, "The Case of the 'New York Review,'" *Commentary*, November 1970, 49–63.

34. On numbers and analysis of rising student population, see James Livingston, *The World Turned Inside Out: American Thought and Culture at the End of the 20th Century* (New York: Rowman and Littlefield, 2009), 21. For Podhoretz quote, see Briggs, *New Class?*, 23.

35. Nathan Glazer, "Student Politics and the University," *Atlantic*, July 1969, 43–53; Glazer, "On Being Deradicalized," *Commentary*, October 1970, 74–80.

36. Sidney Hook, *Academic Freedom and Academic Anarchy* (Spokane, WA: Cowles Book, 1970); Seymour Martin Lipset, *Rebellion in the University* (New York: Transaction, 1971); Daniel Bell and Irving Kristol, eds., *Confrontation: The Student Rebellions and the Universities* (New York: Basic Books, 1969); "Hofstadter 1968 Commencement Speech," in CU Libraries Exhibitions, Item 5408, Columbia University Archives, Rare Book and Manuscript Library; James Q. Wilson, "Liberalism versus Liberal Education," *Commentary*, June 1972, 50–54.

37. John H. Bunzel, "Black Studies at San Francisco State," *Public Interest* 13 (Fall 1968): 22–38.

38. Maurianne Adams, ed., *Strangers and Neighbors: Relations between Blacks and Jews in the United States* (Amherst: University of Massachusetts Press, 1999). "In Search of the Real America: The War on the Intellectuals," transcript, Public Broadcasting System, June 29, 1978, found in the Podhoretz Papers, Box 3. Earl Raab, "Quotas by Any Other Name," *Commentary*, January 1972, 44. Daniel Patrick Moynihan, "The New Racialism," *Atlantic Monthly*, August 1968, 35.

39. Milton Himmelfarb, "Is American Jewry in Crisis?" *Commentary*, March 1969, 37. "An Interview with Norman Podhoretz," *Perspective*, 9. Stephen J. Whitfield, "The Longest Hatred," *Reviews in American History* 23, no. 2 (1995): 364.

40. Richard D. Kahlenberg, *Tough Liberal: Albert Shanker and the Battle over Schools, Race, and Democracy* (New York: Columbia University Press, 2007).

41. Jerald E. Podair, *The Strike That Changed New York: Blacks, Whites, and the Ocean Hill–Brownsville Crisis* (New Haven, CT: Yale University Press, 2002). Kenneth Clark, *Prejudice and Your Child* (Boston: Beacon, 1955); Kenneth Clark, *Dark Ghetto: Dilemmas of Social Power* (New York: Harper and Row, 1965), 131.

42. Diane Ravitch, *The Great School Wars: A History of the New York City Public Schools* (New York: Basic Books, 1974), 251–380.

43. Nathan Glazer and Daniel Patrick Moynihan, *Beyond the Melting Pot: The Negroes, Puerto Ricans, Jews, Italians, and Irish of New York City* (Cambridge, MA: MIT Press, 1963). Herbert Croly, *The Promise of American Life* (New York: Macmillan, 1909), 139, quoted by David Sehat, *The Myth of American Religious Freedom* (Oxford: Oxford University Press, 2011), 206.

44. The teacher's discussion question and the unsigned letter are quoted in Podair, *Strike That Changed New York*, 58, 124. The anti-Semitic poem is quoted in Gerson, *Neoconservative Vision*, 159.

45. The Carmichael quote is in Ben Carson, "Stokely Carmichael," in *African American Lives*, ed. Henry Louis Gates Jr. and Evelyn Brooks Higginbotham (Oxford: Oxford University Press, 2004); Nathan Glazer, "Blacks, Jews and Intellectuals," *Commentary*, April 1969. "Podhoretz on Intellectuals," *Manhattan Tribune*, February 1, 1969, 4. Harnett and Young are quoted in Podair, *Strike That Changed New York*, 131, 126.

46. Jonathan Rieder, *Canarsie: The Jews and Italians of Brooklyn against Blacks* (Cambridge, MA: Harvard University Press, 1985), 216–17.

47. Thomas Byrne Edsall with Mary D. Edsall, *Chain Reaction: The Impact of Race, Rights, and Taxes on America Politics* (New York: W. W. Norton, 1991), 31.

48. Nathan Glazer, "Is Busing Necessary?" *Commentary*, March 1972, 50. J. Anthony Lukas, *Common Ground: A Turbulent Decade in the Lives of Three American Families* (New York: Vintage Books, 1985). Matthew Richer, "Boston's Busing Massacre," *Policy Review*, November 1, 1998.

49. James Q. Wilson, "Crime and the Liberal Audience," *Commentary*, January 1971, 71–78.

50. Ibid., 77.

51. David Hollinger, *Postethnic America: Beyond Multiculturalism*, 10th anniversary ed. (orig. 1995; New York: Basic Books, 2005), 177; Heilbrunn, *They Knew They Were Right*, 14.

52. Historians of neoconservatism tend to ignore Midge Decter. Ronnie Grinberg serves as a useful corrective: "Jewish Intellectuals, Masculinity, and the Making of Modern American Conservatism, 1930–1980" (PhD diss., Northwestern University, 2010). Jeffers, *Norman Podhoretz*, 207. Midge Decter, *The Liberated Woman and Other Americans* (New York: Coward, McCann, and Geoghehan, 1971), and *The New Chastity and Other Arguments against Women's Liberation* (orig. 1972; New York: Capricorn Books, 1974).

53. Decter, *New Chastity*, 43.

54. Decter, *Liberated Woman and Other Americans*, 12.

55. For Bell's self-label, see his *The Cultural Contradictions of Capitalism*, 20th anniversary ed. (orig. 1976; New York: Basic Books, 1996), xi. Daniel Bell, "Sensibility

in the 60's," *Commentary*, June 1971, 63. Midge Decter, "Boys on the Beach," *Commentary*, September 1980, 38.

56. Gore Vidal, "Pink Triangle and Yellow Star," in *The Selected Essays of Gore Vidal*, ed. Jay Parini (New York: Doubleday, 2008), 343, 345, 341 (originally published in *The Nation*, November 14, 1981).

57. George Nash, *Reappraising the Right: The Past and Future of American Conservatism* (Wilmington, DE: ISI Books, 2009), 243–44.

CHAPTER THREE

1. Irving Kristol, "What Is a Neoconservative?," in *The Neoconservative Persuasion: Selected Essays, 1942–2009*, ed. Gertrude Himmelfarb (New York: Basic Books, 2011), 149.

2. Jennifer Ratner-Rosenhagen analyzes how Americans have come to grips with modernity through reading Nietzsche, who made famous the "God is dead" utterance. *American Nietzsche: A History of an Icon and His Ideas* (Chicago: University of Chicago Press, 2012).

3. George Marsden, *Fundamentalism and American Culture: The Shaping of Twentieth-Century Evangelicalism, 1870–1925* (Oxford: Oxford University Press, 1980).

4. James Davison Hunter pointed out that religious Americans gave up their sectarian prejudices in order to form political and ideological alliances in the culture wars in his now classic book *Culture Wars: The Struggle to Define America* (New York: Basic Books, 1991).

5. Leo Ribuffo, "Family Policy Past as Prologue: Jimmy Carter, the White House Conference on Families, and the Mobilization of the New Christian Right," *Review of Policy Research* 23, no. 2 (2006): 311–37. Michael Kazin, *A Godly Hero: The Life of William Jennings Bryan* (New York: Alfred A. Knopf, 2006). Marshner quote is found in William Martin, *With God on Our Side: The Rise of the Religious Right in America* (New York: Broadway Books, 1996), 182.

6. Lawrence Cremin, *The Transformation of the American School: Progressivism in American Education, 1876–1957* (New York: Vintage Books, 1961). John Dewey, *Democracy and Education: An Introduction to the Philosophy of Education* (New York: Macmillan, 1916). Adam Laats, *Fundamentalism and Education in the Scopes Era: God, Darwin, and the Roots of America's Culture Wars* (New York: Palgrave Macmillan, 2010). Mencken's quote is found in Richard T. Hughes, *Christian America and the Kingdom of God* (Urbana: University of Illinois Press, 2009), 137.

7. Jonathan Zimmerman, *Whose America? Culture Wars in the Public Schools* (Cambridge, MA: Harvard University Press, 2002), 66–78. Andrew Hartman, *Education and the Cold War: The Battle for the American School* (New York: Palgrave Macmillan, 2008).

8. Bruce J. Dierenfield, *The Battle over School Prayer: How "Engel v. Vitale" Changed America* (Lawrence: University Press of Kansas, 2007). For the conservative response to *Engel*, see Christopher Hickman, *The Most Dangerous Branch: The Supreme Court and Its Critics in the Warren Court Era* (PhD diss., George Washington University, 2010); the Buckley passage is quoted on p. 1.

9. Ronald W. Evans, *The Social Studies Wars: What Should We Teach the Children?* (New York: Teachers College Press, 2004). The NEA advocacy of inquiry learning is found in Wilcox Collection of Contemporary Political Movements, Kenneth Spencer Research Library, University of Kansas, Lawrence (hereafter Wilcox Collection), Eagle Forum, Folder 4. The Helms letter is quoted in Joanne Omang, "'New Right' Figure Sees McCarthyism in NEA's Conference on Conservatism," *Washington Post*, February 24, 1979, found in National Education Association Records, Special Collections Research Center, Gelman Library, the George Washington University, Washington, DC (hereafter NEA Papers), Box 2128, Folder 9.

10. Martin, *With God on Our Side*, 102–16. Jeffrey P. Moran, *Teaching Sex: The Shaping of Adolescence in the 20th Century* (Cambridge, MA: Harvard University Press, 2000).

11. First Hargis quote is found in Moran, *Teaching Sex*, 183. For others: Wilcox Collection, Billy James Hargis Folder 3: Letters, 1967–1969.

12. Trey Key, "The Great Textbook War," West Virginia Public Radio, October 31, 2009. The "shot heard" and Marshner quotes are from the broadcast transcript. Carol Mason, *Reading Appalachia from Left to Right: Conservatives and the 1974 Kanawha County Textbook Controversy* (Ithaca, NY: Cornell University Press, 2009); William H. Denman, "'Them Dirty, Filthy Books': The Textbook War in West Virginia," in *Free Speech Yearbook 1976*, ed. Greg Phipher (Falls Church, VA: Free Speech Association, 1976), 42–50; and Ann L. Page and Donald A. Clelland, "The Kanawha County Textbook Controversy: A Study of the Politics of Life Style Concern," *Social Forces* 57, no. 1 (September 1978).

13. Most of these quotes can be found in "The Great Textbook War" radio transcripts. The Jack Maurice quote is found in the NEA Archives, Box 2162, Folder 1. The pamphlet passage is from Martin, *With God on Our Side*, 122.

14. NEA Archives, Box 2161, Folders 4–8: "Inquiry Report: Kanawha County, West Virginia: A Textbook Study in Cultural Conflict" (NEA Teacher Rights Division, Washington DC, 1975). The national correspondent was Russell Gibbons, writing in *Commonweal*, found in Denman, "Them Dirty, Filthy Books," 44.

15. J. Brooks Flippen, *Jimmy Carter, the Politics of the Family, and the Rise of the Religious Right* (Athens: University of Georgia Press, 2011). Wilcox Collection, Mel and Norma Gabler, Folders 1 and 2. Daniel K. Williams, *God's Own Party: The Making of the Christian Right* (Oxford: Oxford University Press, 2010), 83–85. Jimmy Brown, "Textbook Reviewing Is No Small Readout," *Gladewater Mirror*, July 28, 1974, 1, 11.

16. Williams, *God's Own Party*, 134–37. Rousas John Rushdoony, *The Messianic Character of Education* (Nutley, NJ: Craig, 1963), and *Man Striving to Be God* (Fenton, MI: Mott Media, 1982).

17. Stephen L. Carter, *The Culture of Disbelief: How American Law and Politics Trivialize Religious Devotion* (New York: Basic Books, 1993).

18. Mark Chaves, "Secularization as Declining Religious Authority," *Social Forces* 72, no. 3 (1994): 749–74.

19. David Sehat shows that the separation of church and state was more abstract than

real in American life prior to the postwar era: *The Myth of American Religions Freedom* (Oxford: Oxford University Press, 2011). Charles Taylor, *A Secular Age* (Cambridge, MA: Belknap Press of Harvard University Press, 2007), 488.

20. David A. Hollinger, "The Accommodation of Protestant Christianity with the Enlightenment: An Old Drama Still Being Enacted," *Dædalus* 141, no. 1 (Winter 2012): 76–88. On the SBC convention, see Flippen, *Jimmy Carter, the Politics of the Family, and the Rise of the Religious Right*, 212. On the importance of the SBC to Christian Right political power, see Williams, *God's Own Party*, 6.

21. James Sire, foreword to Francis A. Schaeffer, *The God Who Is There* (orig. 1968; Downers Grove, IL: InterVarsity Press, 1998), 15.

22. Barry Hankins, *Francis Schaeffer and the Shaping of Evangelical America* (Grand Rapids, MI: Eerdmans, 2008).

23. See Frank Schaeffer's illuminating apostate memoir, *Crazy for God: How I Grew Up as One of the Elect, Helped Found the Religious Right, and Lived to Take All (or Almost All) of It Back* (Cambridge, MA: Da Capo, 2007), 15, 116.

24. For the reception of Nietzsche, see Ratner-Rosenhagen, *American Nietzsche*. Schaeffer, *Crazy for God*, 118. Schaeffer, *God Who Is There*, 29–30.

25. Schaeffer, *God Who Is There*, 27.

26. Ibid., 32–38.

27. Ibid., 57; Schaeffer, *Crazy for God*, 77.

28. Schaeffer, *Crazy for God*, 271–73.

29. Ibid. Williams, *God's Own Party*, 141.

30. For quotes from Falwell's "Minsters and Marches" speech, see Lee Edwards, *The Conservative Revolution: The Movement That Remade America* (New York: Free Press, 1999), 198. *Bob Jones University v. the United States* 461 U.S. 574 (1983), n. 6. Terry Sanford and David Nevin, *The Schools That Fear Built: Segregationist Academies in the South* (New York: Acropolis Books, 1976). For a recent argument that Christian day schools were mostly segregation by other means, see Joseph Crespino, *In Search of Another Country: Mississippi and the Conservative Counterrevolution* (Princeton, NJ: Princeton University Press, 2007), 248–51.

31. William J. Reese, "Soldiers for Christ in the Army of God: The Christian School Movement," in *History, Education, and the Schools* (New York: Palgrave Macmillan, 2007), 111–33. The Falwell quote, as well as the figures on Christian day school growth, is found in Williams, *God's Own Party*, 85. Tim LaHaye, *The Battle for the Public Schools: Humanism's Threat to Our Children* (Old Tappan, NJ: Fleming H. Revell, 1983). Robert J. Billings, *A Guide to the Christian School* (Hammond, IN: Hyles-Anderson, 1971), 12.

32. Falwell and Weyrich quotes are from Flippen, *Jimmy Carter, the Politics of the Family, and the Rise of the Religious Right*, 17, 199.

33. Ribuffo, "Family Policy Past as Prologue." For the first Falwell quote: Jerry Falwell, *Listen, America!* (Garden City, NY: Doubleday, 1980), 128. For the second: Flippen, *Jimmy Carter, the Politics of the Family, and the Rise of the Religious Right*, 56.

34. Robert O. Self, *All in the Family: The Realignment of American Democracy since the 1960s* (New York: Hill and Wang, 2012), 309–38. Falwell, *Listen, America!*, 128.

35. Sharon Whitney, *The Equal Rights Amendment: The History and the Movement* (New York: F. Watts, 1984).

36. Donald T. Critchlow, *Phyllis Schlafly and Grassroots Conservatism: A Woman's Crusade* (Princeton, NJ: Princeton University Press, 2005), 212–42.

37. Phyllis Schlafly, "What's Wrong with 'Equal Rights' for Women?" *Phyllis Schlafly Report*, May 1972. Critchlow, *Phyllis Schlafly and Grassroots Conservatism*, 217–18.

38. Phyllis Schlafly, *The Power of the Positive Woman* (New Rochelle, NY: Arlington House, 1977), 11–12. Monroe Flynn's quote is in Critchlow, *Phyllis Schlafly and Grassroots Conservatism*, 226.

39. Critchlow, *Phyllis Schlafly and Grassroots Conservatism*, 247, 12, 227.

40. Schlafly, *Power of the Positive Woman*, 21. Self, *All in the Family*, 313.

41. Schlafly quote is in Critchlow, *Phyllis Schlafly and Grassroots Conservatism*, 245. Robertson quote is in Flippen, *Jimmy Carter, the Politics of the Family, and the Rise of the Religious Right*, 121.

42. Marjorie J. Spruill, "Gender and America's Right Turn," in *Rightward Bound: Making America Conservative in the 1970s*, ed. Bruce J. Schulman and Julian E. Zelizer (Cambridge, MA: Harvard University Press, 2008), 71–89. "Betty Friedan," in JoAnn Meyers, *The A to Z of the Lesbian Liberation Movement: Still the Rage* (New York: Scarecrow, 2009), 122. Schlafly's first quote: Flippen, *Jimmy Carter, the Politics of the Family, and the Rise of the Religious Right*, 149; second quote: Critchlow, *Phyllis Schlafly and Grassroots Conservatism*, 247–48.

43. Ribuffo, "Family Policy Past as Prologue."

44. "The Family Protection Act," H.R. 7955, 96th Congress (1979).

45. Daniel K. Williams, "No Happy Medium: The Role of Americans' Ambivalent View of Fetal Rights in Political Conflict over Abortion Legalization," *Journal of Policy History* 25, no. 1 (2013): 42–61. The Rice passage is quoted in Williams, *God's Own Party*, 116.

46. For conservative Catholic philosophical underpinnings and how they related to abortion, see Patrick Allitt, *Catholic Intellectuals and Conservative Politics in America, 1950–1985* (Ithaca, NY: Cornell University Press, 1995).

47. Harry A. Blackmun Papers, Manuscript Division, Library of Congress, Washington, DC (hereafter: Blackmun Papers), Box 151, Folder 2.

48. Blackmun Papers, Folder 10. The *Christianity Today* editorial is quoted in Williams, *God's Own Party*, 119.

49. Williams, *God's Own Party*, 141–55. Schaeffer, *Crazy for God*, 273.

50. Falwell, *Listen, America!*, 173.

51. Flippen, *Jimmy Carter, the Politics of the Family, and the Rise of the Religious Right*, 136–38.

52. Randy Shilts, *The Mayor of Castro Street: The Life and Times of Harvey Milk* (New York: St. Martin's Griffin, 1988). Falwell is quoted in Williams, *God's Own Party*, 152.

53. Williams, *God's Own Party*, 73, 152.

54. Tim LaHaye, *The Unhappy Gays: What Everyone Should Know about Homosexuality* (Wheaton, IL: Tyndale, 1978), 41, 62.

55. Ibid., 201–2.

56. Falwell, *Listen, America!*, 16. Robertson is quoted in James Davison Hunter, *Culture Wars: The Struggle to Define America* (New York: Basic Books, 1991), 112–13. Critchlow, *Phyllis Schlafly and Grassroots Conservatism*, 8.

57. William E. Pemberton, *Exit with Honor: The Life and Presidency of Ronald Reagan* (New York: M. E. Sharp, 1998).

58. Carter supporter is quoted in Flippen, *Jimmy Carter, the Politics of the Family, and the Rise of the Religious Right*, 319.

59. Martin, *With God on Our Side*, 191–220.

60. Flippen, *Jimmy Carter, the Politics of the Family, and the Rise of the Religious Right*, 315.

61. One of the central revisions that Daniel Williams makes in *God's Own Party* is that the Christian Right did not emerge whole cloth in the 1970s, but rather that it was a movement fifty years in the making. The anecdote about Nixon and *Portnoy's Complaint* is found in Courtwright, *No Right Turn*, 76.

CHAPTER FOUR

1. W. E. B. Du Bois, *The Souls of Black Folk* (New York: New American Library, Inc, 1903), 19. Frederick Douglass, "The Color Line," *North American Review*, 1881. Ralph Ellison, "What America Would Be Like without Blacks," *Time*, April 6, 1970. The historiography of how immigrants became white is rich. Two good examples: David Roediger, *The Wages of Whiteness: Race and the Making of the American Working Class* (London: Verso, 1991); Noel Ignatiev, *How the Irish Became White* (New York: Routledge, 1995). On the "one drop" rule, see David Hollinger, *Cosmopolitanism and Solidarity: Studies in Ethnoracial, Religious, and Professional Affiliation in the United States* (Madison: University of Wisconsin Press, 2006), especially chap. 2, "The One Drop Rule and the One Hate Rule."

2. Robin J. Anderson, "Dynamics of Economic Well-Being," in *Household Economic Studies* (Washington, DC: US Census Bureau, 2011). "Home Ownership Rates by Race and Ethnicity of Householder, 1994–2010," in *Housing Vacancies and Homeownership: Annual Statistics 2010* (Washington, DC: US Census Bureau, 2011). Jonathan Kozol, *The Shame of the Nation: The Restoration of Apartheid Schooling in America* (New York: Random House, 2005). Michelle Alexander, *The New Jim Crow: Mass Incarceration in the Age of Colorblindness* (New York: New Press, 2010). Karl Marx, *The Eighteenth Brumaire of Louis Bonaparte* (orig. 1852; Moscow: Progress Publishers, 1937).

3. Terry Anderson, *The Pursuit of Fairness: A History of Affirmative Action* (Oxford: Oxford University Press, 2004), 71. K. Anthony Appiah and Amy Gutmann, *Color Conscious: The Political Morality of Race* (Princeton, NJ: Princeton University Press, 1996), 125.

4. Anderson, *Pursuit of Fairness*, 108–28. Ira Katznelson, *When Affirmative Action Was White: An Untold History of Racial Inequality in Twentieth-Century America* (New York: W. W. Norton, 2006).

5. Bunzel, "Black Studies at San Francisco State," 36. Blackmun Papers, Box 260, Folder 7: Syllabus, *University of California Regents v. Bakke*, p. II.

6. Blackmun Papers, Box 260, Folder 8.

7. The Nixon, Hatch, and Reagan quotes are found in Anderson, *Pursuit of Fairness*, 139, 166, 165. Bickel was cited in *Regents of the University of California v. Bakke*, Supreme Court of the United States, 438 U.S. 265 (June 28, 1978).

8. Clarence Thomas, *My Grandfather's Son: A Memoir* (New York: Harper's Perennial, 2008). Anderson, *Pursuit of Fairness*, 179–85.

9. Shelby Steele, *The Content of Our Character: A New Vision of Race in America* (New York: St. Martin's, 1990), 8–15.

10. Cornel West wrote the foreword to the pivotal collection of Critical Race Theory essays: Kimberlé Crenshaw, Neil Gotanda, Gary Peller, and Kendall Thomas, eds., *Critical Race Theory: The Key Writings That Formed the Movement* (New York: New Press, 1995), xi. Christopher Lasch, *The Revolt of the Elites and the Betrayal of Democracy* (New York: W. W. Norton, 1995), 74.

11. Derrick Bell, *Faces at the Bottom of the Well: The Permanence of Racism* (New York: Basic Books, 1992), 130.

12. Derrick Bell, *"Brown v. Board of Education* and the Interest Convergence Dilemma,"* republished in *Critical Race Theory*, ed. Crenshaw et al., 22. Bell, *Faces at the Bottom of the Well*, 21.

13. Historical scholarship that places the civil rights movement in a global Cold War context is catching up to Bell: Mary L. Dudziak, *Cold War Civil Rights: Race and the Image of American Democracy* (Princeton, NJ: Princeton University Press, 2000). Bell reiterates this argument in his *Silent Covenants: "Brown v. Board of Education" and the Unfulfilled Hopes for Racial Reform* (Oxford: Oxford University Press, 2004). Bell, *Faces at the Bottom of the Well*, 55. Bell, *"Brown v. Board of Education* and the Interest Convergence Dilemma,"* 23.

14. Derrick Bell, *Race, Racism, and American Law*, 6th ed. (orig. 1974; New York: Aspen, 2008). Crenshaw et al., eds., *Critical Race Theory*, xx.

15. Carmichael and Hamilton, *Black Power*, 32. Patricia J. Williams, *The Alchemy of Race and Rights* (Cambridge, MA: Harvard University Press, 1991), 48.

16. Bell, *Faces at the Bottom of the Well*, x, 6. W. E. B. Du Bois, *Black Reconstruction in America, 1860–1880* (New York, Russell and Russell, 1935).

17. Lani Guinier, "Keeping The Faith: Black Voters in the Post Reagan Era," *Harvard Civil Rights–Civil Liberties Law Review* 24 (1989): 393–435. Clint Bolick, "Clinton's Quota Queen," *Wall Street Journal*, April 30, 1993. Clinton letter to Moynihan, June 7, 1993; Thomas L. Jipping, "Beyond Quotas: An Analysis of President Bill Clinton's Nomination of Lani Guinier to be Assistant Attorney General for Civil Rights," Judicial Selection Monitoring Project, May 24, 1993: Moynihan Papers, Box II: 591 Folders 8–9 (Lani Guinier).

18. William Buckley Jr., "Why the South Must Prevail," *National Review*, August 24, 1957.

19. Charles Murray, *Losing Ground: American Social Policy, 1950–1980* (New York: Basic Books, 1984), 9, 156–60. Michael Katz, ed., *The "Underclass" Debate: Views from History* (Princeton, NJ: Princeton University Press, 1993).

20. Robin D. G. Kelley, *Yo' Mama's Disfunktional! Fighting the Culture Wars in Urban America* (Boston: Beacon, 1997), 3.

21. Murray, *Losing Ground*, 146.

22. Richard J. Herrnstein and Charles Murray, *The Bell Curve: Intelligence and Class Structure in American Life* (New York: Free Press, 1994), xxii.

23. *New Republic*, October 31, 1994. All of the related *New Republic* essays are reprinted in Fraser Steven Fraser, ed., *The Bell Curve Wars: Race, Intelligence, and the Future of America* (New York: Basic Books, 1995). *National Review*, December 5, 1994. All of the related *National Review* essays and the Herbert op-ed are reprinted in Russell Jacoby and Naomi Glauberman, eds., *The Bell Curve Debate: History, Documents, Opinion* (New York: Times Books, 1995).

24. Gates in Fraser, *Bell Curve Wars*, 95. For a history of the concept of "social disorganization," see Touré Reed, *Not Alms but Opportunity: The Urban League and the Politics of Racial Uplift, 1910–1950* (Chapel Hill: University of North Carolina Press, 2008). Oscar Lewis, *Five Families: Mexican Case Studies in the Culture of Poverty* (New York: Basic Books, 1959). Alice O'Connor, *Poverty Knowledge: Social Science, Social Policy, and the Poor in Twentieth-Century U.S. History* (Princeton, NJ: Princeton University Press, 2001).

25. Arthur Jensen, "How Much Can We Boost IQ and Scholastic Achievement?," *Harvard Educational Review* 39, no. 1 (Winter 1969): 8–9. For mutually sympathetic correspondence between Moynihan and Jensen, see the "Robert Jensen" folder in the Moynihan Papers, Box I: 286 Folder 5. *New York Times*, May 20, 1969. Herrnstein, "IQ," *Atlantic Monthly* 228, no. 3 (September 1971): 43. N. J. Block and Gerald Dworkin, eds., *The IQ Controversy: Critical Readings* (New York: Pantheon Books, 1976).

26. William Julius Wilson, *The Truly Disadvantaged: The Inner City, the Underclass, and Public Policy* (Chicago: University of Chicago Press, 1987), 56–61.

27. Adolph Reed Jr., "The Liberal Technocrat," *The Nation*, February 6, 1988, 169. Wilson, *Truly Disadvantaged*, viii. Henry Louis Gates Jr., "Why Now?" in *Bell Curve Wars*, ed. Fraser, 95.

28. Stephen Jay Gould, *The Mismeasure of Man* (New York: W. W. Norton, 1981). Stephen Jay Gould, "The Curveball," originally in the *New Yorker*, reprinted in *Bell Curve Wars*, ed. Fraser, 12–13.

29. Stephen Jay Gould, "The Curveball," in *Bell Curve Wars*, ed. Fraser, 12–13. Christopher Winship, a nominally liberal Harvard sociologist, argued that *The Bell Curve* should be taken seriously on the grounds that it addressed black illegitimacy: "Lessons of *The Bell Curve*," originally published in the *New York Times*, reprinted in *Bell Curve Debate*, ed. Jacoby and Glauberman, 301.

30. Pat Shipman, "Legacy of Racism," originally published in *National Review*, reprinted in *Bell Curve Debate*, ed. Jacoby and Glauberman, 328. For Murray and Herrnstein's analysis of the relation between IQ and welfare dependency, see *Bell Curve*, 191–202.

31. Dan T. Carter, *From George Wallace to Newt Gingrich: Race in the Conservative*

Counterrevolution, 1963–1994 (Baton Rouge: Louisiana State University Press, 1994), 76 (for first Atwater quote). Second Atwater quote, his infamous "southern strategy" statement, is found here: "Exclusive: Lee Atwater's Infamous 1981 Interview on the Southern Strategy," *The Nation* online, November 13, 2012.

32. David Mills, "Sister Souljah's Call to Arms," *Washington Post*, May 13, 1992, B1. Anthony Lewis, "Abroad at Home: Black and White," *New York Times*, June 18, 1992.

33. Kevin Baker, "A Fate Worse than Bush: Rudolph Giuliani and the Politics of Personality," *Harper's* (August 2007): 35.

34. Spike Lee, *Do the Right Thing*, film (Forty Acres and a Mule Filmworks, 1989). Jason Bailey, "When Spike Lee Became Scary," *Atlantic*, August 22, 2012.

35. Roger Ebert, "Review: *Do the Right Thing*," *Chicago Sun-Times*, June 30, 1989. Bailey ("When Spike Lee Became Scary") brought my attention to how Ebert differed from other white critics. Gates is quoted in "*Do the Right Thing*: Issues and Images," *New York Times*, June 9, 1989.

36. The Kroll, Denby, and Klein quotes are found in Bailey, "When Spike Lee Became Scary." Michael Marriott, "Raw Reactions to Film on Racial Tensions," *New York Times*, July 3, 1989.

37. Baker, "Fate Worse than Bush," 35.

38. George Kelling and James Q. Wilson, "Broken Windows: The Police and Neighborhood Safety," *Atlantic*, March 1982, 29–38.

39. Ibid.

40. Gertrude Himmelfarb, *The De-moralization of Society: From Victorian Virtues to Modern Values* (New York: Alfred A. Knopf, 1995), 68. Daniel Patrick Moynihan, "Defining Deviancy Down," *American Scholar* 62, no. 1 (Winter 1993): 17–30.

41. Molefi Kete Asante, *The Afrocentric Idea*, rev. and exp. ed. (orig. 1987; Philadelphia: Temple University Press, 1998), 1–2.

42. Amy J. Binder, *Contentious Curricula: Afrocentrism and Creationism in American Public Schools* (Princeton, NJ: Princeton University Press, 2002). Massimo Calabresi, "Dispatches Skin Deep 101," *Time*, February 14, 1994. Leonard Jeffries, interview by T. L. Stanclu and Nisha Mohammed, *Rutherford Magazine*, May 1995, 13.

43. "Linguistic Confusion," *New York Times*, December 24, 1996. For the other quotes, see Laura Lane, "Bootstraps Literacy and Racist Schooling in the U.S.," *Z Magazine*, January 1998.

44. Martin Bernal, *Black Athena: The Afroasiatic Roots of Classical Civilization*, vol. 1 (New Brunswick, NJ: Rutgers University Press, 1987).

45. Molly Myerowitz Levine, "The Use and Abuse of *Black Athena*," *American Historical Review* 97, no. 2 (April 1992): 449, 456. Irving Kristol, "The Tragedy of Multiculturalism," *Wall Street Journal*, July 31, 1991.

46. Gerard Delanty, ed., *Routledge Handbook of Cosmopolitan Studies* (New York: Routledge, 2012).

47. Charles Taylor, *Multiculturalism: Examining the Politics of Recognition* (Princeton, NJ: Princeton University Press, 1994), 73. Franz Fanon, *The Wretched of the Earth* (New York: Grove, 1961). For the Bellow quote, see John Blades, "Bellow's Latest Chapter," *Chicago Tribune*, June 19, 1994.

48. Kwame Anthony Appiah, "Race, Culture, Identity: Misunderstood Connections," in Appiah and Gutmann, *Color Conscious*, 82–83, 94, 104.

49. David Hollinger, *Postethnic America: Beyond Multiculturalism*, 10th anniversary ed. (orig. 1995; New York: Basic Books, 2005), 201. Hollinger, *Cosmopolitanism and Solidarity*, xvi–xvii.

50. Henry Louis Gates Jr., *Loose Canons: Notes on the Culture Wars* (London: Oxford University Press, 1992), xvii, 38. Linda Chavez is quoted in Daniel T. Rodgers, *Age of Fracture* (Cambridge, MA: Belknap Press of Harvard University Press, 2011), 141. Toni Morrison is quoted in Michael Bérubé, *Public Access: Literary Theory and American Cultural Politics* (London: Verso, 1994), 57.

51. Hollinger, *Postethnic America*, 167–68.

CHAPTER FIVE

1. Elisabeth Bumiller, "Schlafly's Gala Goodbye to ERA," *Washington Post*, July 1, 1982, C1. Brian T. Kaylor, *Presidential Campaign Rhetoric in an Age of Confessional Politics* (New York: Lexington Books, 2010), 55.

2. Susan Faludi, *Backlash: The Undeclared War against American Women* (New York: Crown, 1991).

3. Joan W. Scott, "Gender: A Useful Category of Historical Analysis," *American Historical Review* 91, no. 5 (December 1986): 1053–75.

4. The anti-ERA flyer is quoted in Daniel T. Rodgers, *Age of Fracture* (Cambridge, MA: Belknap Press of Harvard University Press, 2011), 171.

5. George Gilder, *Sexual Suicide* (New York: Quadrangle, 1973).

6. Ibid., 21.

7. George Gilder, *Wealth and Poverty* (New York: Basic Books, 1981).

8. Christopher Lasch, *Haven in a Heartless World: The Family Besieged* (New York: W. W. Norton, 1977). Andrew Hartman, "Christopher Lasch: Critic of Liberalism, Historian of Its Discontents," *Rethinking History* 13, no. 4 (2009): 499–519. Eric Miller, *Hope in a Scattering Time: A Life of Christopher Lasch* (Grand Rapids, MI: Eerdmans, 2010).

9. Bernard Murchland, "On the Moral Vision of Democracy: A Conversation with Christopher Lasch," *Civil Arts Review* 4 (1991): 4–9. Lasch, *Haven in a Heartless World*, xvi, xi, 18.

10. R. Emerson Dobash and Russell P. Dobash, *Women, Violence, and Social Change* (New York: Routledge, 1992).

11. Paul Glick, the Census Bureau demographer, is quoted in John D'Emilio and Estelle B. Freedman, *Intimate Matters: A History of Sexuality in America* (Chicago: University of Chicago Press, 1988), 332.

12. Colin Higgins, dir., *9 to 5* (Twentieth Century Fox, 1980).

13. Himmelfarb, *One Nation, Two Cultures*, 18. Faludi, *Backlash*, 97, 112. Adrian Lyne, dir., *Fatal Attraction* (Paramount Pictures, 1987).

14. Mari Jo Buhle, *Feminism and Its Discontents: A Century of Struggle with Psychoanalysis* (Cambridge, MA: Harvard University Press, 1998), 14.

15. Nancy Chodorow, *The Reproduction of Mothering: Psychoanalysis and the Sociol-*

ogy of Gender (orig. 1978; Berkeley: University of California Press, 1999), and *Feminism and Psychoanalytic Theory* (New Haven, CT: Yale University Press, 1989), 2. On the historical importance of Chodorow, see Buhle, *Feminism and Its Discontents*, chap. 7, "Feminine Self-in-Relation." Buhle quotes Freud on p. 3.

16. Chodorow, *Feminism and Psychoanalytic Theory*, 101.

17. Carol Gilligan, *In a Different Voice: Psychological Theory and Women's Development* (Cambridge, MA: Harvard University Press, 1982), 17.

18. *Equal Employment Opportunity Commission v. Sears, Roebuck & Company*, United States Court of Appeals for the Seventh Circuit, January 14, 1988. Ruth Milkman, "Women's History and the Sears Case," *Feminist Studies* 12, no. 2 (Summer 1986): 376.

19. Milkman, "Women's History and the Sears Case," 376.

20. Faludi, *Backlash*, 327.

21. Whitney Strub, *Perversion for Profit: The Politics of Pornography and the Rise of the New Right* (New York: Columbia University Press, 2011). Carole S. Vance, ed., *Pleasure and Danger: Exploring Female Sexuality* (Boston: Routledge and Kegan Paul, 1984). Elizabeth Wilson, "The Context of 'Between Pleasure and Danger': The Barnard Conference on Sexuality," *Feminist Review* 13 (Spring 1983): 35–41. Andrea Dworkin, *Pornography: Men Possessing Women* (orig. 1979; New York: Putnam, 1981), 69.

22. Catharine MacKinnon, *Feminism Unmodified: Discourses on Life and Law* (Cambridge, MA: Harvard University Press, 1987), 23, 7.

23. Strub, *Perversion for Profit*, 248–49. D'Emilio and Freedman, *Intimate Matters*, 351.

24. "Women against Pornography," *Firing Line*, Firing Line Collection, Box 179 (transcripts of show taped on February 25, 1985, later aired on PBS), Hoover Institution, Palo Alto, CA.

25. The Southern Baptist leader is N. Larry Baker of the Religious Alliance Against Pornography: OA 19224, Box 6 Folder 1: "Pornography," Ronald Reagan Presidential Library and Museum, Simi Valley, CA (hereafter Reagan Papers).

26. Meese quotes from Box 20: "Press Conference: Attorney General's Porno Commission Final Report"; Box 109: "Pornography Commission," Edwin Meese Papers, Hoover Institution, Palo, Alto, CA.

27. Attorney General's Commission on Pornography, "Final Report" (Washington, DC: US Department of Justice, 1986).

28. D'Emilio and Freedman, *Intimate Matters*, 350. Carol Tavris, "A Commission Struggles to Define Victims of Pornography," *Hartford Courant*, July 9, 1986.

29. Martha Duffy, "The Bête Noire of Feminism: Camille Paglia," *Time Magazine,* January 13, 1992. Naomi Wolf, "Feminist Fatale," *New Republic*, March 16, 1992, 23–25.

30. Camille Paglia, interview by Daniel Nester, bookslut.com, April 2005. Camille Paglia, *Sexual Personae: Art and Decadence from Nefertiti to Emily Dickinson* (New Haven, CT: Yale University Press, 1990).

31. Camille Paglia, *Vamps and Tramps: New Essays* (New York: Vintage Books, 1994), x, 23.

32. Paglia, *Vamps and Tramps*, 26–27. Randy Thornhill and Craig T. Palmer, *A Natural History of Rape: Biological Bases of Sexual Coercion* (Cambridge, MA: MIT Press, 2000).

33. Christina Hoff Sommers, *Who Stole Feminism? How Women Have Betrayed Women* (New York: Simon and Schuster, 1994), 27, 21, 75.

34. As one example of many: Avik Roy, "LSU's War against Men," *Heterodoxy* 1, no. 3 (June 1992).

35. Daphne Patai and Noretta Koertge, *Professing Feminism: Education and Indoctrination in Women's Studies* (orig. 1994; Lanhan, MD: Lexington Books, 2003), xiv, 3.

36. Kristen Luker, *Abortion and the Politics of Motherhood* (Berkeley: University of California Press, 1984). N. E. H. Hull and Peter Charles Hoffer, *Roe v. Wade: The Abortion Rights Controversy in American History*, 2nd ed. (Lawrence: University Press of Kansas, 2010).

37. Hull and Hoffer, *Roe v. Wade*, 210–13. Robert M. Collins, *Transforming America: Politics and Culture during the Reagan Years* (New York: Columbia University Press, 2007), 192.

38. Hull and Hoffer, *Roe v. Wade*, 183–84.

39. Robert Bork, "The Supreme Court Needs a New Philosophy," *Fortune*, December 1968, and "Original Intent and the Constitution," *Humanities*, February 1986, 22. Both articles found in the Carla A. Hills Collection, Hoover Institution, Palo Alto, CA (hereafter Hills Papers), Box 331.

40. Ronald Dworkin, "Reagan's Justice," *New York Review of Books*, November 8, 1984. For the Reagan administration lawyer (Lee Casey) quote, see Hills Papers, Box 331.

41. David Courtwright, *No Right Turn: Conservative Politics in a Liberal America* (Cambridge, MA: Harvard University Press, 2010), 181–85. John Fund, "The Borking Begins," *Wall Street Journal*, January 8, 2001.

42. Courtwright, *No Right Turn*, 187. Bork, *Slouching towards Gomorrah*, 173.

43. Bork, *Slouching towards Gomorrah*, vii, 4, 50, 183, 177, 192.

44. Wilcox Collection, "Gay and Lesbian Advocates and Their Defenders (GLAD)," Folder 1. Michael Swift, "Gay Revolutionary," *Gay Community News*, February 15–21, 1987, found in the Wilcox Collection, "America for Family Values," Folder 1.

45. Buchanan is quoted in Collins, *Transforming America*, 135. Falwell is quoted in Allen White, "Reagan's AIDS Legacy: Silence Equals Death," *SFGate*, June 8, 2004. *Moral Majority Report*, July 1983. Materials on Cameron are found in the Reagan Papers, Morton Blackwell Files, Box 7, "Homosexuals" (3 of 5); "Family Protection Act" (3 of 5).

46. "AIDS: The Rights of the Patient, the Rights of the Public," *Firing Line*, Firing Line Collection, Box 181 (December 2, 1985), Hoover Institution, Palo Alto, CA.

47. Jennifer Brier, *Infectious Ideas: U.S. Political Responses to the AIDS Crisis* (Chapel Hill: University of North Carolina Press, 2009). William Bennett, "AIDS: Education and Public Policy," speech at Georgetown University, April 30, 1987, transcript found in the Reagan Papers, Gary Bauer Files, Box 1, Folder: "William Bennett." Dannemeyer quote found in the C. Everett Koop Papers, National Library

of Medicine, online archive, Section "AIDS, the Surgeon General, and the Politics of Public Health" (hereafter Koop Papers), "Letter from William E. Dannemeyer, United States House of Representatives to Edwin Meese, United States Department of Justice," October 28, 1986.

48. Kramer is quoted in Collins, *Transforming America*, 2. Waxman is quoted in a March 27, 1987, memo written by Gary Bauer, Reagan Papers, Bauer Files, Box 3, Folder: Abortion / Family Planning. James Davison Hunter, *Culture Wars: The Struggle to Define America* (New York: Basic Books, 1991), 152. James Dobson detailed the ACT-UP prank on Helms in an October 1991 letter to Focus on the Family members, Wilcox Collection: "Focus on the Family," Folder 1. Helms quote is found in Wilcox Collection: "Human Rights Campaign Fund," Folder 1.

49. C. Everett Koop, "Understanding AIDS—A Message from the Surgeon General" (1986), found in the Koop Papers.

50. "Flying the Koop," *Washington Times*, October 27, 1986. Bennett is quoted in Brier, *Infectious Ideas*, 94. D'Emilio and Freedman, *Intimate Matters*, 367. "Koop Urges Early Sex Education to Fight AIDS," *Washington Times*, October 23, 1986. AIDS figures are from White, "Reagan's AIDS Legacy."

51. Dan Gilgoff, *The Jesus Machine: How James Dobson, Focus on the Family, and Evangelical America Are Winning the Culture War* (New York: St. Martin's, 2007). Also Wilcox Collection, "America for Family Values," Folder 1.

52. For Bork and Scalia quotes, see Bork, *Slouching towards Gomorrah*, 113–14.

53. For the Amendment 2 architect (Tony Marco) quote, see Wilcox Collection, "America for Family Values," Folder 1.

54. Judith Butler, *Gender Trouble: Feminism and the Subversion of Identity* (New York: Routledge, 1990), 34, 7, 46.

55. Eve Kosofsky Sedgwick, *Epistemologies of the Closet* (Berkeley: University of California Press, 1991), 85. The links to DeGeneres and Vidal, and the quote from the latter, were made by Richard Kim: "Eve Kosofsky Sedgwick: 1950–2009," *The Nation*, April 13, 2009. Bruce Handy, "Yep, I'm Gay! Roll Over Ward Cleaver," *Time Magazine*, April 14, 1997.

56. Michel Foucault, *The History of Sexuality*, vol. 1, *An Introduction*, 5th ed. (orig. 1976; New York: Vintage, 1990). Sedgwick, *Epistemologies of the Closet*, 3, 13.

57. Nancy Fraser, *Unruly Practices: Power, Discourse and Gender in Contemporary Social Theory* (Minneapolis: University of Minnesota Press, 1989), 19–27.

58. Barbara Ehrenreich, *Hearts of Men: American Dreams and the Flight from Commitment* (Norwell, MA: Anchor, 1987), 152.

59. Susan Faludi, *Stiffed: The Betrayal of the American Man* (New York: William Morrow, 1999), 9.

60. Bethany Moreton, *To Serve God and Wal-Mart: The Making of Christian Free Enterprise* (Cambridge, MA: Harvard University Press, 2009).

61. Faludi, *Stiffed*, 227–40.

62. Gilgoff, *Jesus Machine*, 21–24.

63. James Dobson, *Love Must Be Tough: New Hope for Families in Crisis* (Waco, TX: Word Books, 1983), 25.

64. James Dobson, *Love for a Lifetime* (Sisters, OR: Multnomah, 1987), 20, 29, 38, 41–44.

65. William Bennett, *The Death of Outrage: Bill Clinton and the Assault on American Ideals* (New York: Touchstone, 1998), 14, 8, 9.

CHAPTER SIX

1. Pat Buchanan, "The Cultural War for the Soul of America," speech, September 14, 1992. Cooper is quoted in Thomas R. Lindlof, *Hollywood under Siege: Martin Scorsese, the Religious Right, and the Culture Wars* (Lexington: University Press of Kentucky, 2008), 309.

2. I do not mean to paint liberals with too wide of a brush. Charles Lyons, *The New Censors: Movies and the Culture Wars* (Philadelphia: Temple University Press, 1997), shows that plenty of left-leaning media activists persisted in thinking that culture mattered and that Hollywood portrayed minorities, women, and homosexuals unfairly.

3. For an analysis of conservative media activism, see Allison Perlman, *Conflicting Signals*, unpublished manuscript, particularly chap. 4, "The Politics of 'Television's Redemption': The PTC, the Family Hour, and Gay Visibility in the 1990s." Sidney Blumenthal, "Reaganism and the Neokitsch Aesthetic," in *The Reagan Legacy*, ed. Sidney Blumenthal and Thomas Byrne Edsall (New York: Pantheon Books, 1988), 285. Michael Medved, *Hollywood versus America: Popular Culture and the War on Traditional Values* (New York: HarperCollins, 1992), 129.

4. Benjamin Alpers, "*American Graffiti* and the Sixties in the Seventies," *U.S. Intellectual History Blog*, s-usih.org, November 11, 2013. George Lucas, dir., *American Graffiti*, film (Los Angeles: Universal Pictures, 1973). Randall Kleiser, dir., *Grease*, film (Los Angeles: Paramount Pictures, 1973). Garry Marshall, *Happy Days*, TV series (Paramount Domestic, 1974–84). Jill Lepore, *The Whites of Their Eyes: The Tea Party's Revolution and the Battle over American History* (Princeton, NJ: Princeton University Press, 2010), 97.

5. Ronald Reagan, "Farewell Address to the Nation," January 11, 1989. Patrick Buchanan, "Losing the War for America's Culture?," *Washington Times*, May 22, 1989.

6. Elana Levine, *Wallowing in Sex: The New Sexual Culture of 1970s American Television* (Durham, NC: Duke University Press, 2007). Medved, *Hollywood versus America*, 129.

7. Medved, *Hollywood versus America*, 20. Peter Biskind, *Easy Riders, Raging Bulls: How the Sex-Drugs-and-Rock ''n' Roll Generation Saved Hollywood* (New York: Simon and Schuster, 1999). Kevin S. Sandler, *The Naked Truth: Why Hollywood Doesn't Make X-Rated Movies* (New Brunswick, NJ: Rutgers University Press, 2007.) Medved, *Hollywood versus America*, 20. Although television and film grew more liberal, especially in their embrace of the sexual revolution, there continued to be plenty of conservative representations of the US role in the world, such as in the Rambo films.

8. Gene Simmons, interview by Terry Gross, *Fresh Air* (National Public Radio), February 4, 2002. Ian Christe, *Sound of the Beast: The Complete Headbanging History*

of Heavy Metal (New York: Harper Paperbacks, 2004), 117. "Heavy Metal," *20/20* (ABC), May 21, 1987.

9. Robert Segal, "Tipper Gore and Family Values," National Public Radio, January 11, 2005. Tipper Gore, *Raising PG Kids in an X-Rated Society* (Nashville: Abingdon, 1987). "Record Labeling," Hearing before the Committee on Commerce, Science, and Transportation, US Senate, 99th Congress, September 19, 1985.

10. "Record Labeling," Senate Hearings, 1985. Dee Snider, "We're Not Gonna Take It," *Stay Hungry and Still Hungry,* music video dir. Marty Callner (Atlantic, 1984).

11. "Record Labeling," Senate Hearings, 1985. Patrick Goldstein, "Parents Warn: Take the Sex and Shock Out of Rock," *Los Angeles Times,* August 25, 1985.

12. Glen Danzig, "Mother," *Danzig* (Def American, 1988). Ice-T, "Freedom of Speech," *The Iceberg / Freedom of Speech . . . Just Watch What You Say!* (Sire / Warner Bros. Records, 1989).

13. George Will, "No One Blushed Anymore," *Washington Post,* September 15, 1985.

14. "Dirty Rock Lyrics," *Firing Line,* Firing Line Collection, Box 182 (June 8, 1988), Hoover Institution, Palo Alto, CA. The Jello Biafra quote comes from his appearance alongside Tipper Gore and Ice-T on "Rap Music," *The Oprah Winfrey Show,* March 7, 1990.

15. Alex Ogg and David Upshal, *The Hip Hop Years: A History of Rap* (Mt. Prospect, IL: Fromm International, 2001). Jeffrey O. G. Ogbar, *Hip Hop Revolution: The Culture and Politics of Rap* (Lawrence: University Press of Kansas, 2007). Grandmaster Flash, "The Message," *The Message* (Sugar Hill, 1982). Public Enemy, "911 Is a Joke," *Fear of a Black Planet* (Def Jam, 1990). Arthur Kempton is quoted in Jack Nachbar and Kevin Lause, *Popular Culture: An Introductory Text* (New York: Popular, 1992), 354. The Ice-T and Nelson George quotes are from their appearance on "Rap Music," *The Oprah Winfrey Show,* March 7, 1990. The Chuck D quote about rap and CNN is found in "Crime," in *Encyclopedia of African American Popular Culture,* ed. Jesse Karney Smith (Westport, CT: Greenwood, 2010), 384. Richard Wright, *Native Son* (New York: Harper and Brothers, 1940).

16. David Samuels, "The Rap on Rap," *New Republic,* November 11, 1991, 24–29. The Ice-T quote about N.W.A. is from "Rap Music," *The Oprah Winfrey Show,* March 7, 1990. N.W.A., "Fuck tha Police," *Straight Outta Compton* (Priority/ Ruthless, 1988). "How Ronald Reagan Invented Gangsta Rap," *Village Voice,* October 8, 1996.

17. 2 Live Crew, "We Want Some Pussy," *The 2 Live Crew Is What We Are* (Luke /Atlantic Records, 1986). 2 Live Crew, "Me So Horny," *As Nasty as They Wanna Be* (Life Records, 1989).

18. James LeMoyne, "Recording Ruled Obscene Brings Arrest," *New York Times,* June 9, 1990. Chuck Phillips, "The 'Batman' Who Took On Rap," *Los Angeles Times,* June 18, 1990. Chuck Phillips, "Appeals Court Voids Obscenity Ruling on 2 Live Crew Album," *Los Angeles Times,* May 8, 1992.

19. George Will, "America's Slide into the Sewer," *Newsweek,* June 30, 1990: 64. Phil Donahue, "Indecency and Obscenity," *The Phil Donahue Show,* 1990.

20. Phil Donahue, "Indecency and Obscenity," *The Phil Donahue Show,* 1990. Rob-

ert Bork, *Slouching towards Gomorrah: Modern Liberalism and American Decline* (New York: ReganBooks, 1996), 124.

21. Henry Louis Gates Jr., "2 Live Crew, Decoded," *New York Times*, June 19, 1990.

22. Ben Bagdikian, "The Public Must Reject 2 Live Crew's Message," letter to the editor, *New York Times*, July 3, 1990. Gates, "2 Live Crew, Decoded." For an ambivalent black feminist critique of 2 Live Crew and the Gates defense, see Kimberle Williams Crenshaw, "Beyond Racism and Misogyny: Black Feminism and 2 Live Crew," in *Words That Wound: Critical Race Theory, Assaultive Speech, and the First Amendment*, ed. Mari J. Matsuda, Charles R. Lawrence III, Richard Delgado, and Kimberle Williams Crenshaw (Boulder: Westview, 1993).

23. Madonna, "Like a Prayer," *Like a Prayer*, music video dir. Mary Lambert (Sire, 1989). Mark Bego, *Madonna: Blind Ambition* (New York: Cooper Square, 1992). Camille Paglia, *Sex, Art, and American Culture: Essays* (New York: Viking, 1992), 12. Bork, *Slouching towards Gomorrah*, 152, 143.

24. Camille Paglia, "Madonna: Finally a Real Feminist," *New York Times*, December 14, 1990.

25. Nikos Kazantzakis, *The Last Temptation*, English translation (New York: Simon and Schuster, 1960). Salman Rushdie, *Satanic Verses* (New York: Viking, 1988). My analysis of the controversy over *The Last Temptation of Christ* is heavily reliant upon Thomas R. Lindlof's thoroughly researched *Hollywood under Siege*. The Rushdie quote comes from Lindlof, 16.

26. Lindlof, *Hollywood under Siege*, 40–56.

27. Ibid., 45–80, 9.

28. Christopher M. Finan and Anne F. Castro, "The Rev. Donald E. Wildmon's Crusade for Censorship, 1977–1992" (New York: Media Coalition, 1994).

29. Lindlof, *Hollywood under Siege*, 130–59.

30. For more on the People for the American Way, see James C. Carper and Thomas C. Hunt, eds., *The Praeger Handbook of Religion and Education in the United States* (Westport, CT: Praeger, 2009), 340–42.

31. Lindlof, *Hollywood under Siege*, 163–67.

32. Martin Scorsese, dir., *The Last Temptation of Christ*, film (Studio City, CA: Universal Pictures, 1988). Lindlof, *Hollywood under Siege*, 195–96.

33. Lindlof, *Hollywood under Siege*, 56. Medved, *Hollywood versus America*, 46–47. See also Carole Iannone, "The Last Temptation Reconsidered," *First Things* 60 (February 1996).

34. Lindlof, *Hollywood under Siege*, 2–3, 250–63.

35. Ibid., 302–4.

36. Gregory D. Black, *Hollywood Censored: Morality Codes, Catholics, and the Movies* (London: Cambridge University Press, 1994). Medved, *Hollywood versus America*, 40–41.

37. Medved, *Hollywood versus America*, 3, 7.

38. Ibid., 21, 23.

39. Ibid., 33.

40. Joseph Wesley Zeigler, *Arts in Crisis: The National Endowment for the Arts versus*

America (Chicago: A Cappella Books, 1994), 69. "Rev. Donald Wildmon, Letter concerning Serrano's *Piss Christ*, April 5, 1989," in *Culture Wars: Documents from the Recent Controversies in the Arts*, ed. Richard Bolton (New York: New Press, 1992), 27.

41. Andres Serrano, *Andres Serrano: Body and Soul* (New York: Takarajima Books, 1995). Paul Monaco, *Understanding Society, Culture, and Television* (Westport, CT: Praeger, 2000), 100. Grant H. Kester, *Art, Activism, and Oppositionality: Essays from Afterimage* (Durham, NC: Duke University Press, 1998), 126. Peter Simek, "A Nun Defends *Piss Christ*, Which Was Attacked on Sunday," *Front Row*, April 20, 2011.

42. The Kennedy and Serrano quotes are found in the Moynihan Papers, Box II: 759, Folder 3, and 757, Folder 3. The Helms and D'Amato quotes are found in Bolton, *Culture Wars*, 10, 3.

43. Todd Gitlin, *The Twilight of Common Dreams: Why America Is Wracked by Culture Wars* (New York: Metropolitan Books, 1995), 2. Richard Marshall, Richard Howard, and Ingrid Sischy, *Robert Mapplethorpe* (New York: Whitney Museum of American Art and New York Graphic Society Books, 1988). Patricia Morrisroe, *Mapplethorpe: A Biography* (New York: Random House, 1995). Patti Smith, *Just Kids* (New York: Ecco, 2010).

44. Zeigler, *Arts in Crisis*, 74–76.

45. Zeigler, *Arts in Crisis*, 74–76. Bolton, *Culture Wars*, xvii. Deborah Levinson, "Robert Mapplethorpe's Extraordinary Vision," *The Tech*, August 6, 1989. Peggy Phelan, "Serrano, Mapplethorpe, the NEA, and You: 'Money Talks,'" *TDR*, October 1989.

46. Isabel Wilkerson, "Trouble Right Here in Cincinnati: Furor over Mapplethorpe Exhibit," *The New York Times*, March 29, 1990; "Cincinnati Jury Acquits Museum in Mapplethorpe Obscenity Case," *New York Times*, October 6, 1990. Steven Litt, "Dennis Barrie Looks Back on His Cincinnati Obscenity Trial 20 Years after His Acquittal," *Cleveland Plain Dealer*, October 5, 2010.

47. George Will, "The Helms Bludgeon," *Washington Post*, August 3, 1987, A27.

48. Irving Kristol, "It's Obscene, but Is It Art?" *Wall Street Journal*, August 1, 1990, A16. Cooper is quoted in Buchanan, "Cultural War for the Soul of America."

49. Camille Paglia, "The Beautiful Decadence of Robert Mapplethorpe: A Response to Rochelle Gurstein," in *Sex, Art, and American Culture*, 40–44.

50. Armey is quoted in James Davison Hunter, *Culture Wars: The Struggle to Define America* (New York: Basic Books, 1991), 231. The quote from the Armey-authored letter sent to the NEA is found in Zeigler, *Arts in Crisis*, 75. Richard Meyer, "The Jesse Helms Theory of Art," *October* 104 (Spring 2003): 131–48.

51. Rohrbacher is quoted in Bolton, *Culture Wars*, 4.

52. John Frohnmayer, *Leaving Town Alive: Confessions of an Arts Warrior* (New York: Houghton Mifflin, 1993). Stephen Salisbury, "NEA Chief Says He Won't Be Decency Czar," *Philadelphia Inquirer*, December 15, 1990. On the NEA Four, see Zeigler, *Arts in Crisis*, 105–15. *National Endowment for the Arts v. Finley*, 524 U.S. 569 (1998).

53. Michael Oreskes, "Bush's Decision on Art Evokes Protest on Right," *New York Times*, March 23, 1990.

54. Zeigler, *Arts in Crisis*, 134–35, 140. Patrick Buchanan, "Pursued by Baying Yahoos," *Washington Times*, August 3, 1989. For more on Buchanan's southern television campaign ad, see Dan T. Carter, *From George Wallace to Newt Gingrich: Race in the Conservative Counterrevolution, 1963–1994* (Baton Rouge: Louisiana State University Press, 1994), 94.

55. Charen is quoted in Medved, *Hollywood versus America*, 143–46. "Dan Quayle versus Murphy Brown," *Time*, June 1, 1992. Stephanie Coontz, "For Better, For Worse," *Washington Post*, May 1, 2005.

56. Buchanan, "Cultural War for the Soul of America."

CHAPTER SEVEN

1. The Simonds quote is found in James Davison Hunter, *Culture Wars: The Struggle to Define America* (New York: Basic Books, 1991), 201.

2. For the Lippmann quote, see Jonathan Zimmerman, *Whose America? Culture Wars in the Public Schools* (Cambridge, MA: Harvard University Press, 2002), 9.

3. "Historical Summary of Public Elementary and Secondary School Statistics," table 36, in National Center for Education Statistics, *Digest of Education Statistics 2004* (Washington, DC: U.S. Department of Education, 2004). Carol Belt, the Christian Right pamphleteer, is quoted in Fritz Detwiler, *Standing on the Premises of God: The Christian Right's Fight to Redefine America's Public Schools* (New York: New York University Press, 1999), 218.

4. Stephen L. Carter, *The Culture of Disbelief: How American Law and Politics Trivialize Religious Devotion* (New York: Basic Books, 1993), 4, 8.

5. NEA Archives, Box 2128, Folder 3: "Affirmative Action Notebook" by Dr. Shirley McCune. Files from the 1971 HCR conference are held in Box 2129, Folder 3.

6. Paolo Freire, *Pedagogy of the Oppressed* (New York: Herder and Herder, 1970). Proceedings of the 1979 NEA Conference on Human and Civil Rights in Education, "Rise of the New Right: Human and Civil Rights in Jeopardy," NEA Archives, Box 2128, Folder 9.

7. "Celebrate People: A Manual to Help State and Local Education Associations Recognize the Achievements and Contributions of America's Diverse People" (NEA pamphlets, 1983), NEA Archives, Box 2183, Folder 2. Books authored by influential multicultural theorist James Banks were assigned in teachers' colleges nationwide: *Teaching Strategies for Ethnic Studies* (New York: Simon and Schuster, 1975); *Multiethnic Education: Theory and Practice* (Boston: Allyn and Bacon, 1981).

8. "Directive on Religion in Public Schools." *Historic Documents of 1995*, 546–52 (Washington, DC: CQ, 1996).

9. Robertson and Swaggart are quoted in Hunter, *Culture Wars*, 202–3.

10. Tim LaHaye, *The Battle for the Public Schools: Humanism's Threat to Our Children* (Old Tappan, NJ: Fleming H. Revell, 1983), 38, 29, 71. David Bollier, *The Witch Hunt against "Secular Humanism"* (Washington, DC: People for the American Way, 1983), 4—found in the Moynihan Papers, Box II: 1112, Folder 8.

11. Duggan is quoted in Hunter, *Culture Wars*, 24. Richard John Neuhaus, introduction to Brevard Hand, *American Education on Trial: Is Secular Humanism a Reli-*

gion? (Washington, DC: Center for Judicial Studies, 1987). John J. Dunphy, "A Religion for a New Age," *The Humanist*, January/February 1983, 26. NEA Archives, Box 2161, Folders 4–8: "Inquiry Report: Kanawha County, West Virginia: A Textbook Study in Cultural Conflict" (NEA Teacher Rights Division, Washington, DC, 1975).

12. Bell is quoted in Zimmerman, *Whose America?*, 181. Phyllis Schlafly, ed., *Child Abuse in the Classroom* (excerpts from official transcript of proceedings before the US Department of Education in the matter of proposed regulations to implement the Protection of Pupil Rights Amendment—the Hatch Amendment) (Alton, IL: Pere Marquette, 1984), 12, 13, 29–30, 60.

13. US Supreme Court, *Torcaso v. Watkins* 367 U.S. 488 (1961). The secular humanist reference is found in footnote 11.

14. US Supreme Court, *United States v. Seeger* 380 U.S. 163 (1965).

15. US Supreme Court, *Wallace v. Jaffree* 472 U.S. 38 (1985).

16. For a discussion of the Tennessee case and of Judge Hand's ruling, consult the preface to "Curriculum Group on Religion in Schools," in *Historic Documents of 1987* (Washington, DC: CQ, 1988).

17. Bill Bright is quoted in Marjorie Hunter, "Evangelist Calls for Restoration of Prayer in U.S. Public Schools," *New York Times*, July 31, 1980, A14.

18. Gary Bauer, "The Reagan Record on the Family and Traditional Values," Reagan Papers, Gary Bauer Files, Box 1: OA 16706, Chronological File (July 1988), Folder 3. Reagan quotes are found in Catherine A. Lugg, *For God and Country: Conservatism and American School Policy* (New York: Peter Lang, 1996), 71, 91. A transcript of the Reagan school prayer speech is in the Reagan Papers, Gary Bauer Files, Box 1: OA 16706, Chronological File (July 1988), Folder 3.

19. John Rudolph, *Scientists in the Classroom: The Cold War Reconstruction of American Science Education* (New York: Palgrave Macmillan, 2002).

20. "Federal District Court on 'Creation Science,'" in *Historic Documents of 1982*, 3–16 (Washington, DC: CQ, 1983). Roger Lewin, "A Tale with Many Connections," in *Science and Creationism*, ed. Ashley Montagu (Oxford: Oxford University Press, 1984).

21. George Marsden, "Understanding Fundamentalist Views of Science," in *Science and Creationism*, 98.

22. Stephen Jay Gould, "Evolution as Fact and Theory," in *Science and Creationism*, ed. Montagu, 118–25.

23. Ibid., 125.

24. Amy J. Binder, *Contentious Curricula: Afrocentrism and Creationism in American Public Schools* (Princeton, NJ: Princeton University Press, 2002). For details on *Edwards v. Aguillard*, see the preface to "Federal District Court on Intelligent Design," in *Historic Documents of 2005* (Washington, DC: CQ, 2006).

25. The Gallup polls are cited in Carter, *Culture of Disbelief*, 161. *Teaching about Evolution and the Nature of Science* (Washington, DC: National Academy Press, 1998), viii, 4, 8; *Science and Creationism: A View from the National Academy of Sciences*, 2nd ed. (Washington, DC: National Academies Press, 1999).

26. James Fraser, *Between Church and State: Religion and Public Education in a Multicultural America* (New York: St. Martin's, 1999). Hand, *American Education on Trial*, 7.

27. Reed is cited in Detwiller, *Standing on the Premises of God*, 220. Binder, *Contentious Curricula*, 161–69.

28. Paul D. Ackerman and Bob Williams, *Kansas Tornado: 1999 Science Curriculum Standards Battle* (El Cajon, CA: Institute for Creation Research, 1999), 11, 24. The Easterbrook quote is cited in Frank, *What's the Matter with Kansas?*, 211.

29. Detwiller, *Standing on the Premises of God*.

30. Timothy Keesee and Mark Sidwell, *U.S. History for Christian Schools* (Greenville, SC: Bob Jones University Press, 1991).

31. Adam Laats, "Forging a Fundamentalist 'One Best System': Struggles over Curriculum and Educational Philosophy for Christian Day Schools, 1970–1989," *History of Education Quarterly* 49, no. 1 (January 2010): 55–83. John Dewey, *Democracy and Education: An Introduction to the Philosophy of Education* (New York: Macmillan, 1916), 206. Hartman, *Education and the Cold War*. Rouhas John Rushdoony, *Philosophy of the Christian Curriculum* (Portland, OR: Ross House Books, 1985).

32. Milton Gaither, *Homeschool: An American History* (New York: Palgrave Macmillan, 2008), 181, 183.

33. US Department of Health, Education, and Welfare, *Equality of Educational Opportunity* (Washington, DC: Government Printing Office, 1966). Christopher Jencks, *Inequality: A Reassessment of the Effect of Family and Schooling in America* (New York: Basic Books, 1972). Chester Finn, "The Schools," in *What to Do About . . . : A Collection of Essays from "Commentary" Magazine*, ed. Neal Kozodoy (New York: ReganBooks, 1995), 118.

34. Chester Finn, *Troublemaker: A Personal History of School Reform since Sputnik* (Princeton, NJ: Princeton University Press, 2008), x, 150. Bennett is quoted in Peter Schrag, "The New School Wars: How Outcome-Based Education Blew Up," *American Prospect*, December 1, 1994.

35. William J. Bennett, *The De-valuing of America: The Fight for Our Culture and Our Children* (New York: Summit Books, 1992), 18–22.

36. Bennett, *De-valuing of America*, 22, 52. The Gallup Poll and the study on moral values are found in the Reagan Papers, Gary Bauer Files, Box 1: OA 16706, Chronological File (July 1988).

37. David Wagner, "Bill Bennett's Dilemma," *National Review*, June 19, 1987, 28–31, 60.

38. Stephen Tonsor, "Why I Too Am Not a Neoconservative," *National Review*, June 20, 1986, 55. Wagner, "Bill Bennett's Dilemma," 60.

39. Hannah Arendt, "The Crisis in Education," *Partisan Review* 25 (Fall 1958): 494.

40. Lugg, *For God and Country*. Milton Friedman first outlined his plan for education in the following essay: "The Role of Government in Education," in *Economics and the Public Interest*, ed. Robert A. Solo (New Brunswick, NJ: Rutgers University Press, 1955). The Chester Finn quote is from Thomas Toch, *In the Name of Excellence: The Struggle to Reform the Nation's Schools, Why It's Failing, and What Should Be Done* (Oxford: Oxford University Press, 1991), 24.

41. National Commission on Excellence in Education, *A Nation at Risk: The Imperative for Education Reform* (Washington, DC: Department of Education, 1983). Ernest L. Boyer, *High School: A Report on Secondary Education in America* (New York: Harper and Row, 1983). Theodore Sizer, *Horace's Compromise* (New York: Houghton Mifflin, 1984). John I. Goodlad, *A Place Called School: Prospects for the Future* (New York: McGraw-Hill, 1984).

42. For more on the reform response to *A Nation at Risk* in general, see Toch, *In the Name of Excellence.*

CHAPTER EIGHT

1. George Will, "Literary Politics," *Newsweek*, April 21, 1991.

2. Allan Bloom, *The Closing of the American Mind* (New York: Simon and Schuster, 1987); E. D. Hirsch, *Cultural Literacy: What Every American Needs to Know* (New York: Houghton Mifflin, 1987); Dinesh D'Souza, *Illiberal Education: The Politics of Race and Sex on Campus* (New York: Free Press, 1991); Roger Kimball, *Tenured Radicals: How Politics Has Corrupted Our Higher Education*, 3rd ed. (1990; Chicago: Ivan R. Dee, 2008); Lynne Cheney, *Telling the Truth: Why Our Culture and Our Country Have Stopped Making Sense—and What We Can Do about It* (New York: Simon and Schuster, 1995).

3. On the Locke-Fanon debate, see Kimball, *Tenured Radicals*, 58–60. "Marching on the English Department While the Right Took the White House" is the title of a chapter in Todd Gitlin, *The Twilight of Common Dreams: Why America Is Wracked by Culture Wars* (New York: Metropolitan Books, 1995). The "prominent literature scholar" is noted deconstructionist J. Hillis Miller, "An Open Letter to Professor Jon Wiener," in *Responses: On Paul de Man's Wartime Journalism*, ed. Werner Hamacher, Neil Hertz, and Thomas Keenan (Lincoln: University of Nebraska Press, 1989), 339.

4. The Paglia quote is found in Francois Cusset, *French Theory: How Foucault, Derrida, Deleuze, & Co. Transformed the Intellectual Life of the United States* (Minneapolis: University of Minnesota Press, 2008), 106. William James, *Pragmatism: A New Name for Some Old Ways of Thinking* (orig. 1907; Indianapolis: Hackett, 1981), 76.

5. "Always historicize!" is the opening slogan of Fredric Jameson, *The Political Unconscious: Narrative as a Socially Symbolic Act* (Ithaca, NY: Cornell University Press, 1981). For the Fish quote and a contemporary journalistic account of the role of the Duke English Department, see James Atlas, "On Campus: The Battle of the Books," *New York Times Magazine*, June 5, 1988.

6. Stanley Fish, *Is There a Text in This Class? The Authority of Interpretive Communities* (Cambridge, MA: Harvard University Press, 1980), vii. E. D. Hirsch Jr., "Culture and Literacy," *Journal of Basic Writing*, Fall/Winter 1980, 27–47. Hirsch, *Cultural Literacy.*

7. Fish, *Is There a Text in This Class?*, 10. The Baker and Fish quotes are from Atlas, "On Campus."

8. Michel Foucault, *The Archaeology of Knowledge* (1969; New York: Routledge,

2002). The Tompkins quote is from Atlas, "On Campus." Cusset, *French Theory*, 131.

9. William J. Bennett, *To Reclaim a Legacy: A Report on the Humanities in Higher Education* (Washington, DC: National Endowment for the Humanities, 1984), 3, 9, 19, 20.

10. Ibid., 16, 30.

11. Herbert Lindenberger, *The History in Literature: On Value, Genre, Institutions* (New York: Columbia University Press, 1990), chap. 7, "On the Sacrality of Reading Lists: The Western Culture Debate at Stanford University." Donald Lazere, "The Well Stocked Brain ... and the Open Mind," *New York Times*, December 17, 1989.

12. "Bennett Draws Fire in Stanford Talk Assailing Course Change," *Los Angeles Times*, April 19, 1988, I3; Robert Marquand, "Stanford's CIV Course Sparks Controversy," *Christian Science Monitor*, January 25, 1989, 13. The Bloom letter is quoted in Lindenberger, *History in Literature*, 160.

13. W. B. Carnochan, *The Battleground of the Curriculum: Liberal Education and American Experience* (Stanford, CA: Stanford University Press, 1993), 100. For the Hayes passage and a good history of the Western Civilization course, see Lawrence Levine, *The Opening of the American Mind: Canons, Culture, and History* (Boston: Beacon, 1996), 63.

14. Rebecca Lowen, *Creating the Cold War University: The Transformation of Stanford* (Berkeley: University of California Press, 1997). Paul Seaver was the director of the Stanford Western Civilization program in 1969 and is quoted in Levine, *Opening of the American Mind*, 65.

15. Lindenberger, *History in Literature*.

16. Donald Lazare, "*The Closing of the American Mind*, 20 Years Later," *Inside Higher Ed*, September 18, 2007. William Goldstein, "The Story behind the Bestseller: Allan Bloom's *The Closing of the American Mind*," *Publisher's Weekly*, July 3, 1987, repr. in *Essays on the Closing of the American Mind*, ed. Robert L. Stone (Chicago: Chicago Review Press, 1989).

17. Bloom, *Closing of the American Mind*, 336, 25, 26, 30.

18. Ibid., 19, 320, 159–60. Jennifer Ratner-Rosenhagen, *American Nietzsche: A History of an Icon and His Ideas* (Chicago: University of Chicago Press, 2012).

19. Bloom, *Closing of the American Mind*, 379, 147, 42.

20. Ibid., 313–14, 94.

21. George Lowery, "A Campus Takeover That Symbolized an Era of Change," *Cornell University Chronicle Online*, April 16, 2009. Christopher Hitchens, "The Egg-Head's Egger On," *London Review of Books*, April 2000, 21–23. The "snob" quote is from a Richard Heffner interview of Bloom on *The Open Mind*, digital archive (http://www.theopenmind.tv/). I owe my understanding of Bloom as a Straussian to Benjamin Alpers.

22. Benjamin Barber, "The Philosopher Despot: Allan Bloom's Elitist Agenda," *Harper's Magazine*, January 1988, 61, as reprinted in Stone, *Essays on the Closing of the American Mind*, 81. William Kristol, "Troubled Souls: Where We Went Wrong,"

Wall Street Journal, 1987, as reprinted in Stone, *Essays on the Closing of the American Mind*, 41.

23. Bloom, *Closing of the American Mind*, 79. "How Dumb Are We?," *The Oprah Winfrey Show*, January 3, 1988.

24. Gerald Graff reflects on his appearance on Oprah in his book *Beyond the Culture Wars: How Teaching the Conflicts Can Revitalize American Education* (New York: W. W. Norton, 1993), 93–94. Richard Hofstadter, *Anti-intellectualism in American Life* (New York: Vintage Books, 1962).

25. Saul Bellow, *Ravelstein* (New York: Viking, 2000). Bellow, foreword to Bloom, *Closing of the American Mind*, 11. The Wolff quote, from a review in *Academe*, is quoted in full by Hitchens, "Egg-Head's Egger On." The Bloom quote about *Closing*'s lack of partisan attachment is from Werner J. Dannhauser, "Allan Bloom and the Critics," *American Spectator*, 1987, as reprinted in Stone, *Essays on the Closing of the American Mind*, 35.

26. Levine, *Opening of the American Mind*, xviii, 19.

27. Richard Rorty, "Straussianism, Democracy, and Allan Bloom I: That Old Time Philosophy," *New Republic*, April 4, 1988, as reprinted in Stone, *Essays on the Closing of the American Mind*, 102. Richard Rorty, "Trotsky and the Wild Orchids," reprinted in *Philosophy and Social Hope* (New York: Penguin Books, 1999). Rorty, *Achieving Our Country: Leftist Thought in Twentieth-Century America* (Cambridge, MA: Harvard University Press, 1998).

28. Gitlin, *Twilight of Common Dreams*. Here my analysis lends support to James Livingston's otherwise overstated claim that the culture wars were largely an "intramural sport on the left." *The World Turned Inside Out: American Thought and Culture at the End of the 20th Century* (New York: Rowman and Littlefield, 2009), 53.

29. Paul de Man, *Allegories of Reading: Figural Language in Rousseau, Nietzsche, Rilke, and Proust* (New Haven, CT: Yale University Press, 1979), 293. David Lehman, *Sign of the Times: Deconstruction and the Fall of Paul de Man* (New York: Simon and Schuster, 1991).

30. Lehman, *Sign of the Times*, 22. Jacques Derrida, *Of Grammatology*, trans. Gayatri Chakravorty Spivak (1967; Baltimore: Johns Hopkins University Press, 1998). Jacques Derrida, *Positions* (Chicago: University of Chicago Press, 1981), 42. Paul de Man, *Blindness and Insight: Essays in the Rhetoric of Contemporary Criticism* (Minneapolis: University of Minnesota Press, 1971), 17. De Man, *The Rhetoric of Romanticism* (New York: Columbia University Press, 1984), 81.

31. Krauthammer is quoted in Levine, *Opening of the American Mind*, 11. Lehman, *Sign of the Times*, 35.

32. Jon Wiener, "Deconstructing de Man," *The Nation*, January 9, 1988, 22–24.

33. Wiener, "Deconstructing de Man," 23. J. Hillis Miller, "An Open Letter to Professor Jon Wiener," and Jacques Derrida, "Like the Sound of the Sea Deep within a Shell: Paul de Man's War," both appearing in *Responses: On Paul de Man's Wartime Journalism*, ed. Hamacher, Hertz, and Keenan, 337, 148.

34. Paul Berman, ed., *Debating P.C.: The Controversy over Political Correctness on College Campuses* (New York: Dell, 1992), 6–7.

35. Gitlin, *Twilight of Common Dreams*, 146, 126.

36. George H. W. Bush's commencement address (May 4, 1991) was published in the *Michigan Daily*, February 11, 2010; courtesy of the George Bush Presidential Library and Museum.

37. Gerald Uelmen, "The Price of Free Speech: Campus Hate Speech Codes," *Issues in Ethics* 5, no. 2 (Summer 1992).

38. Gitlin is quoted by Berman, *Debating P.C.*, 22. Phyllis Franklin letter to Senator Edward Kennedy, March 4, 1991; Cheney responded directly to Franklin in another widely circulated letter (March 15, 1991). Both are found in the Moynihan Papers, Box II: 761 (Folder 9).

39. Carole Iannone, "Literature by Quota," *Commentary*, March 1991, 12–13. The transcript of the Moynihan speech (July 19, 1991) is found in the Moynihan Papers, Box II: 761 (Folder 9).

40. The Himmelfarb letter to Kennedy (April 6, 1991) is in the Moynihan Papers, Box II: 761 (Folder 9). Hatch is quoted in Carol Innerst, "Panel Rejects Non-PC Iannone," *Washington Times*, July 18, 1991, A4.

41. Bruce Jackson, "Right Turn at NEH," *Artvoice*, June 7, 2001. Mary Jacoby, "Madame Cheney's Cultural Revolution," *Salon*, August 26, 2004. Donald J. Cosentino, ed., *Sacred Arts of Haitian Vodou* (Los Angeles: University of California–Los Angeles / Fowler, 1995).

42. Sheldon Hackney, *The Politics of Presidential Appointment: A Memoir of the Culture War* (Montgomery, AL: New South, 2002).

43. For an alternative account to Hackney's, see Alan Charles Kors and Harvey Silverglate, *Shadow University: The Betrayal of Liberty on America's Campuses* (New York: Free Press, 1998).

44. Hackney, *Politics of Presidential Appointment*; Hors and Silverglate, *Shadow University*. "Buffaloed at Penn," *Wall Street Journal*, April 26, 1993.

45. Sheldon Hackney Nomination Hearings, Committee on Human and Labor Resources, 103rd Congress (June 25, 1993).

46. D' Souza, *Illiberal Education*. Michael Bérubé, *Public Access: Literary Theory and American Cultural Politics* (London: Verso, 1994). Jason Stahl, "Selling the New Right: Think Tanks and the Revolt against New Deal Liberalism, 1945–Present" (PhD diss., University of Minnesota, 2009).

47. D'Souza, *Illiberal Education*, 13, 5, 50, 229, 157.

48. Kimball, *Tenured Radicals*, xxxvi, 5, 3, 81.

49. Cheney, *Telling the Truth*, 15, 16, 14, 91–92, 179.

50. Gertrude Himmelfarb, *On Looking into the Abyss* (New York: Alfred A. Knopf, 1994), 6.

51. Alan Sokal and Jean Bricmont, *Fashionable Nonsense: Postmodern Intellectuals' Abuse of Science* (New York: Picador USA, 1998), 2, 269–73.

52. Fredric Jameson, "Postmodernism, or The Cultural Logic of Late Capitalism," *New Left Review* 1, no. 146 (July-August 1984): 53–94; the article was later expanded into a book by the same title, *Postmodernism, or The Cultural Logic of Late Capitalism* (Durham, NC: Duke University Press, 1991). For more on how fracture

is a symptom of political reaction, see Corey Robin's review of Daniel Rodgers, *Age of Fracture*, *London Review of Books*, October 25, 2012, 23–25.

CHAPTER NINE

1. Mike Wallace, *Mickey Mouse History and Other Essays on American Memory* (Philadelphia: Temple University Press, 1996), x–xi, 159–76.

2. Norman Podhoretz, *Why We Were in Vietnam* (New York: Simon and Schuster, 1982). "Why We Were in Vietnam: Norman Podhoretz interviewed by Richard Heffner," *Open Mind*, March 6, 1982. Ronald Reagan, "Peace: Restoring the Margin of Safety," speech at VFW convention, Chicago, August 18, 1980.

3. Howard Zinn, *A People's History of the United States* (New York: Harper and Row, 1980), and *The Politics of History* (Boston: Beacon, 1970), 24. Martin Duberman, *Howard Zinn: A Life on the Left* (New York: New Press, 2012).

4. Gary B. Nash, *Red, White, and Black: The Peoples of Early America* (Englewood Cliffs, NJ: Prentice-Hall, 1974), 3.

5. Peter Novick, *That Noble Dream: The "Objectivity Question" and the American Historical Profession* (Cambridge: Cambridge University Press, 1988), 424. Lemisch is quoted in Duberman, *Howard Zinn*, 166. Jesse Lemisch, "Jack Tar in the Streets: Merchant Seamen in the Politics of Revolutionary America," *William and Mary Quarterly* 25, no. 3 (July 1968): 371–407.

6. Nash, *Red, White, and Black*, 16. Howard Zinn, *You Can't Be Neutral on a Moving Train: A Personal History of Our Times* (Boston: Beacon, 1994). Joyce Appleby, Lynn Hunt, and Margaret Jacob, *Telling the Truth about History* (New York: W. W. Norton, 1994), 200.

7. Lynn Hunt, ed., *The New Cultural History* (Berkeley: University of California Press, 1989). Daniel Wickberg, "Heterosexual White Male: Some Recent Inversions in American Cultural History," *Journal of American History* 92, no. 1 (June 2005): 136–57.

8. Gertrude Himmelfarb, "Some Reflections on the New History," *American Historical Review* 94, no. 3 (June 1989): 667–69. Himmelfarb, *The New History and the Old: Critical Essays and Reappraisals* (1987; Cambridge, MA: Belknap Press of Harvard University Press, 2004). Joan Wallach Scott, *Gender and the Politics of History*, rev. ed. (orig. 1988; New York: Columbia University Press, 1999).

9. Joan Wallach Scott, "History in Crisis? The Other Side of the Story," *American Historical Review* 94, no. 3 (June 1989): 686. Lawrence Levine, "The Unpredictable Past: Reflections on Recent American Historiography," *American Historical Review* 94, no. 3 (June 1989): 675.

10. Hayden White, *Metahistory: The Historical Imagination in 19th-Century Europe* (Baltimore: Johns Hopkins University Press, 1973), 3. Appleby, Hunt, and Jacob, *Telling the Truth about History*, 11, 2, 229.

11. Wallace, *Mickey Mouse History*, 3–32.

12. William H. Truettner, ed., *The West As America: Reinterpreting Images of the Frontier, 1820–1920* (Washington, DC: Smithsonian, 1991), vii, 35.

13. Michael Kimmelman, "Old West, New Twist at the Smithsonian," *New York Times*,

May 26, 1991. Boorstin, Krauthammer, and the *Wall Street Journal* are quoted in Andrew Gulliford's review of the exhibit, *Journal of American History* 79, no. 1 (June 1992): 199.

14. "New York Report on Multicultural Textbooks," in *Historic Documents of 1991* (Washington, DC: CQ, 1992).

15. Arthur Schlesinger Jr., *The Disuniting of America: Reflections on a Multicultural Society* (New York: W. W. Norton, 1991), 16–17, and *The Vital Center: The Politics of Freedom* (New Brunswick, NJ: Transaction, 1949). Raymond Carr, "Best Books of the Year," *The Spectator*, November 21, 1992, 42, found in the Arthur Schlesinger Jr. Papers, Manuscripts and Archives Division, New York Public Library, New York City, NY (hereon Schlesinger Papers), Box 283: "*Disuniting of America.*"

16. Schlesinger, *The Disuniting of America*, 71, 55.

17. Baker and Schlesinger correspondence is found in the Schlesinger Papers, Box 388: "*Disuniting.*"

18. Schlesinger, *Disuniting of America*, 124. Robin D. J. Kelley, *Yo' Mama's Disfunktional! Fighting the Culture Wars in Urban America* (Boston: Beacon, 1997), 108. Kelley's point, of course, is backed up by a great deal of recent scholarship on how Enlightenment thought was embedded in racial, gendered, and imperialist discourses. See Barbara Taylor and Sarah Knott, eds., *Women, Gender, and Enlightenment* (New York: Palgrave Macmillan, 2007). Also Emmanuel Chukwudi Ezi, ed., *Race and Enlightenment: A Reader* (Oxford: Blackwell, 1997).

19. Donald Collins makes this argument about the conflation of multiculturalism and Afrocentrism in his *Fear of a "Black" America: Multiculturalism and the African American Experience* (New York: IUniverse, 2004).

20. Chester Finn and Diane Ravitch, *What Do Our 17-Year-Olds Know? A Report on the First National Assessment of History and Literature* (New York: HarperCollins, 1988). Chester Finn, *Troublemaker: A Personal History of School Reform since Sputnik* (Princeton, NJ: Princeton University Press, 2008), 141. Lynne Cheney, *American Memory: A Report on the Humanities in the Nation's Public Schools* (Washington, DC: National Endowment for the Humanities, 1987), 7.

21. Charlotte Crabtree and Diane Ravitch, *The History-Social Science Framework for California Public Schools* (Sacramento: California Department of Education, 1988). Robert Orrill and Linn Shapiro, "From Bold Beginnings to an Uncertain Future: The Discipline of History and History Education," *American Historical Review*, June 2005, 727–51.

22. Crabtree and Ravitch, *History-Social Science Framework for California Public Schools*. Schlesinger, "Multiculturalism in the Curriculum" (November 27, 1989), Schlesinger Papers, Box 388: "*Disuniting.*"

23. Crabtree and Ravitch, *History-Social Science Framework for California Public Schools*. Ross E. Dunn, "The Two World Histories," *Social Education* 72, no. 5 (2008): 257–63.

24. Gary Nash's involvement in the creation of the *National History Standards* is outlined in a special edition of the *History Teacher*: "A Life in Public Education: Honoring Gary B. Nash," 42 (January 2009).

25. Gary B. Nash, Charlotte Crabtree, and Ross E. Dunn, *History on Trial: Culture Wars and the Teaching of the Past* (1997; New York: Vintage Books, 2000). Lisa Symcox, *Whose History? The Struggle for National Standards in American Classrooms* (New York: Teachers College Press, 2002). Ronald W. Evans, *The Social Studies Wars: What Should We Teach the Children?* (New York: Teachers College Press, 2004).

26. *National Standards for United States History: Exploring the American Experience* (Los Angeles: National Center for History in the Schools, 1994). *National Standards for History* (Los Angeles: National Center for History in the Schools, 1994). Nash, Crabtree, and Dunn, *History on Trial*, 162–64.

27. Nash, Crabtree, and Dunn, *History on Trial*, 165–70.

28. Todd Gitlin, *The Twilight of Common Dreams: Why America Is Wracked by Culture Wars* (New York: Metropolitan Books, 1995), 8–33.

29. Finn is quoted in Symcox, *Whose History?*, 121.

30. Lynne Cheney, "The End of History," *Wall Street Journal*, October 20, 1994, A22, A26–A27. Frank Rich, "Eating Her Offspring," *New York Times*, January 26, 1995. When Cheney's piece first appeared the Gingrich-led Republican victory was still a few weeks away. But surely she had been reading polls.

31. Nash, Crabtree, and Dunn, *History on Trial*, 189. *The Rush Limbaugh Show* transcript. WMAL-AM Radio, October 24, 1994. Ravitch is quoted in Symcox, *Whose History?*, 134.

32. John Patrick Diggins, *The Rise and Fall of the American Left* (New York: W. W. Norton, 1992), 291, 298. Letter from Jack Diggins to Schlesinger, February 27, 1995, Schlesinger Papers, Box 388: "*Disuniting.*"

33. Nash, Crabtree, and Dunn, *History on Trial*, 192–98.

34. Nash, Crabtree, and Dunn, *History on Trial*, 196, 227.

35. Gorton is quoted in Symcox, *Whose History?*, 1. Also see Nash, Crabtree, and Dunn, *History on Trial*, 228–35.

36. Irving Kristol, "My Cold War," *National Interest*, Spring 1993, 144.

37. Edward T. Linenthal, "Anatomy of a Controversy," in *History Wars: The "Enola Gay" and Other Battles for the American Past*, ed. E. T. Linenthal and Tom Engelhardt (New York: Metropolitan Books, 1996), 14.

38. Uday Mohan, "History and the News Media: The Smithsonian Controversy," in *Cultural Difference, Media Memories: Anglo-American Images of Japan*, ed. Phil Hammond (London: Cassell, 1997), 180. Gar Alperovitz, *Atomic Diplomacy: Hiroshima and Potsdam* (New York: Simon and Schuster, 1965).

39. "Crossroads" transcript (January 1994), found in Martin Sherwin's private collection of documents on *Enola Gay* exhibit and controversy (hereafter referred to as Sherwin / *Enola Gay* papers).

40. John T. Correll, "War Stories at Air and Space," *Air Force Magazine*, April 1994, 24. W. Burr Bennett Jr., letter dated January 13, 1994, Box II: 348, Folder 9, Moynihan Papers. The George Will quote is from *This Week with David Brinkley* transcript, ABC-TV, August 28, 1994. *The Rush Limbaugh Show* transcript, WMAL-AM Radio, August 19, 1994. Letter from the office of Peter Blute (R-MA), August 10, 1994.

"Sense of the Senate," Resolution 257 (September 22, 1994). All of these materials are found in Sherwin / *Enola Gay* papers.

41. Correll, "War Stories at Air and Space," 25. "Crossroads transcript," found in Sherwin / *Enola Gay* papers. The shorter out-of-context passage is quoted in literally thousands of articles, the full passage only rarely.

42. Cheney, *Telling the Truth*, 26, 29, 30.

43. In 1959 Truman rationalized his decision to drop the bomb thus: "I wanted to save half a million boys on our side." Quoted in Barton J. Bernstein, "A Postwar Myth: 500,000 U.S. Lives Saved," *Bulletin of Atomic Scientists*, June 1986, 38. Blute letter, Sherwin / *Enola Gay* papers.

44. Martin Sherwin, *A World Destroyed: The Atomic Bomb and the Grand Alliance* (New York: Alfred A. Knopf, 1975). Letter to Sherwin, August 14, 1995, Sherwin / *Enola Gay* papers. Bennett letter to Congress, Moynihan Papers, Box II: 348, Folder 9. "The Smithsonian Changes Course," *Washington Post*, February 1, 1995, A18.

45. Bob Dole's speech was given before the American Legion in Indianapolis on September 4, 1995 (Washington, DC: Federal Document Clearing House, 1995), 5. Johnson quoted in Linenthal and Engelhardt, ed., *History Wars*, 59. Letter to Martin Sherwin, February 6, 1995, Sherwin / *Enola Gay* papers.

46. Kai Bird, *The Chairman: John J. McCloy and the Making of the American Establishment* (New York: Random House, 1992). Kai Bird and Martin Sherwin, *American Prometheus: The Triumph and Tragedy of J. Robert Oppenheimer* (New York: Alfred A. Knopf, 2005). Kai Bird, "*Enola Gay*: 'Patriotically Correct,'" *Washington Post*, July 7, 1995, A21.

47. Sherwin was interviewed by Uday Mohan, "History and the News Media: The Smithsonian Controversy." Jason Zengerle, "Exhibiting Bias," *New Republic*, October 20, 1997, 18–19.

48. Letter to Peter Kuznick from the director of the Jewish War Veterans of the U.S.A., dated April 11, 1995, Sherwin / *Enola Gay* papers.

CONCLUSION

1. Abby Goodnough, "Harvard Professor Jailed; Officer Is Accused of Bias," *New York Times*, July 20, 2009. Rakesh Kochhar, Richard Fry, and Paul Taylor, "Wealth Gaps Rise to Record Highs between Whites, Blacks, Hispanics," Pew Research Social and Demographic Trends, July 26, 2011.

2. Josh Eligon and Michael Schwirtz, "Senate Candidate Provokes Ire with 'Legitimate Rape' Comment," *New York Times*, August 19, 2012. Nancy Fraser, *Fortunes of Feminism: From State-Managed Capitalism to Neoliberal Crisis* (London: Verso, 2013). Sheryl Sandberg, *Lean in: Women, Work, and the Will to Lead* (New York: Alfred A. Knopf, 2013).

3. Samuel G. Freedman, "Focus on Family Works to Change Its Message," *New York Times*, March 8, 2013. Lisa Duggan, "Beyond Marriage: Democracy, Equality, and Kinship for a New Century," *Scholar and Feminist Online* 10, nos. 1–2 (Fall 2011 / Spring 2012). Lisa Duggan, *The Twilight of Equality? Neoliberalism, Cultural Politics, and the Attack on Democracy* (Boston: Beacon, 2003).

4. Daniel Kreps, "Nipple Ripples: 10 Years of Fallout from Janet Jackson's Halftime Show," *Rolling Stone*, January 30, 2014.

5. Diane Ravitch, *Reign of Error: The Hoax of the Privatization Movement and the Danger to America's Public Schools* (New York: Alfred A. Knopf, 2013). On the Texas curriculum battle, see Sam Tanenhaus, "Identity Politics Leans Right," *New York Times*, March 21, 2010, and Keith A. Erekson, ed., *Politics and the History Curriculum: The Struggle over Standards in Texas and the Nation* (New York: Palgrave Macmillan, 2012).

6. Commission on the Humanities and Social Sciences, *The Heart of the Matter: The Humanities and Social Sciences for a Vibrant, Competitive, and Secure Nation* (Cambridge, MA: American Academy of Arts and Sciences, 2013). Lizette Alvarez, "Florida May Reduce Tuition for Select Majors," *New York Times*, December 9, 2012. Jack Welch and Suzy Welch, *Winning* (New York: HarperCollins, 2005).

7. Theodor Adorno and Max Horkheimer, *The Dialectic of Enlightenment* (1944; New York: Herder and Herder, 1972). Luc Boltanski and Eve Chiapello, *The New Spirit of Capitalism* (London: Verso, 2005). Also Slavoj Žižek, "Multiculturalism, or The Cultural Logic of Multinational Capitalism," *New Left Review* 1, no. 225 (September/October 1997): 28–51.

8. Robert Bork, *Slouching towards Gomorrah: Modern Liberalism and American Decline* (New York: ReganBooks, 1996), 67.

Index

Made in the USA
Columbia, SC
16 August 2018